FIELD GUIDE

to
Academic
Leadership

FIELD GUIDE
to
Academic
Leadership

ROBERT M. DIAMOND, editor

BRONWYN ADAM, assistant editor

JOSSEY-BASS
A Wiley Imprint
www.josseybass.com

Published by Jossey-Bass
A Wiley Imprint
989 Market Street, San Francisco, CA 94103-1741 www.josseybass.com

Jossey-Bass books and products are available through most bookstores. To contact Jossey-Bass directly, call (888) 378-2537, fax to (800) 605-2665, or visit our website at www.josseybass.com.

Substantial discounts on bulk quantities of Jossey-Bass books are available to corporations, professional associations, and other organizations. For details and discount information, contact the special sales department at Jossey-Bass.

We at Jossey-Bass strive to use the most environmentally sensitive paper stocks available to us. Our publications are printed on acid-free recycled stock whenever possible, and our paper always meets or exceeds minimum GPO and EPA requirements.

Jossey-Bass also publishes its books in a variety of electronic formats. Some content that appears in print may not be available in electronic books.

Library of Congress Cataloging-in-Publication Data
Field guide to academic leadership / Robert M. Diamond, editor ; Bronwyn Adam, assistant editor.— 1st ed.
      p. cm. — (The Jossey-Bass higher and adult education series)
Includes bibliographical references and index.
    ISBN 0-7879-6059-4 (alk. paper)
  1. Universities and colleges—United States—Administration—Handbooks, manuals, etc. 2. Educational leadership—United States—Handbooks, manuals, etc. I. Diamond, Robert M. II. Adam, Bronwyn E. III. Series.
  LB2341 .F43 2002
  371.2—dc21
                                                  2002004711

first edition
HB Printing   10 9 8 7 6 5 4 3 2

CONTENTS

PART FOUR **Assessment**

PART FIVE **Other Issues**

This book is dedicated to my grandson

Joshua Dean Rozental

and all his generation who may benefit from the efforts of
committed, caring, and talented faculty, staff, and administrators.

A publication of the National Academy for Academic Leadership

The National Academy for Academic Leadership is sponsored by Syracuse University. It has received support from the W.K. Kellogg Foundation, The John S. and James L. Knight Foundation, The Park Foundation, Syracuse University, Eckerd College, and the National Education Association.

For further information on the Academy, visit our website at http://thenationalacademy.org.

LOUIS S. ALBERT is vice chancellor for educational services, San Jose/Evergreen Community College District. He came to the district from the American Association for Higher Education (AAHE), where he served as interim president and vice president and director of professional service. He has been academic dean at Villa Julie College and Essex Community College, where he also held a variety of administrative and faculty positions. Albert was responsible for designing and implementing one of the nation's first community college–based physician's assistant programs. Serving on a number of national boards, he presently chairs the board of trustees of the International Partnership for Service-Learning. He has taught at a number of other institutions, including the University of Maryland, Johns Hopkins University, Iowa State University, and the University of Denver. He is active in a number of national initiatives to improve learning.

SUSAN STETSON CLARKE is a principal in Unconventional Wisdom, a consulting firm that specializes in creative approaches for educational and cultural institutions. Clarke's current projects include serving as administrative coordinator for the National Consortium for Continuous Improvement in Higher Education. She has authored a chapter on institutional planning in *College and University Business Administration* and several articles in the *Business Officer.* She was associate vice president for operations at New York Medical College and previously vice president for administration at Rensselaer Polytechnic Institute. She served as director of administration at the National Center for Atmospheric Research in Boulder, Colorado, and held various administrative posts at the National Academies of Sciences and Engineering/National Research Council in Washington, D.C.

ROBERT M. DIAMOND is research professor at Syracuse University and president of the National Academy for Academic Leadership. Diamond has held faculty and administrative positions at Syracuse, the State University of New York at Fredonia, the University of Miami, and San Jose State University. He directed the National Project on Institutional Priorities and Faculty Rewards and was coauthor of *A National*

Study of Research Universities on the Balance Between Research and Undergraduate Teaching and *A National Study on the Relative Importance of Research and Undergraduate Teaching at Colleges and Universities.* His published work includes *Designing and Assessing Courses and Curricula; Preparing for Tenure and Promotion Review; Serving on Promotion, Tenure, and Faculty Review Committees;* and *Aligning Faculty Rewards with Institutional Mission: Statements, Policies, and Guidelines.* He is coeditor of the two-volume series *The Disciplines Speak.*

STEPHEN C. EHRMANN is a cofounder of the Teaching, Learning, and Technology Group, an affiliate of the American Association for Higher Education. He serves as its vice president and is director of the Flashlight Program, a national initiative to help educators design and evaluate their own uses of technology. He has served as a program officer with the Annenberg–CPB Project and the Fund for the Improvement of Postsecondary Education and was director of education and research and assistance at Evergreen State College. A member of the National Academy of Sciences–National Research Council Committee on Information Technology, Ehrmann's publications include "Improving the Outcome of Higher Education: Learning from Past Mistakes," "Technology and Revolution in Education: Ending the Cycle of Failure," and "When Outcomes Assessment Misses."

JAMES EISON is director of the Center for Teaching Enhancement at the University of South Florida. He directed the Center for Teaching and Learning at Southeast Missouri State and has held faculty positions at the University of Tennessee and Roane State Community College. Winner of numerous teaching awards, Eison has coauthored *Active Learning: Creating Excitement in the Classroom, Making Sense of College Grades,* and *Textbook Tests: Guidelines for Item Writing.* Among his articles and book chapters are "Teaching Improvement Practices: Successful Strategies for Higher Education," "Challenging Student Passivity," and "Revising General Education Programs." He is a consultant to colleges and universities throughout the United States and overseas.

LION F. GARDINER is associate professor of zoology at Rutgers University, founding principal of the National Academy for Academic Leadership, coeditor of *Learning Through Assessment: A Resource Guide for Higher Education,* and author of *Redesigning Higher Education: Producing Dramatic Gains in Student Learning* and *Planning for Assessment: Mission Statements, Goals, and Objectives.* He is a consultant to colleges and universities on general-liberal education, learning and student cognitive development, defining intended outcomes, and assessment.

STEVEN W. GILBERT is cofounder and president of the Teaching, Learning, and Technology Group, an independent nonprofit organization affiliated with the American Association for Higher Education. Formerly vice president of EDUCOM, Gilbert directed AAHE's technology projects. A frequent speaker and consultant, his publications include "Making the Most of a Slow Revolution" and "Information Technology, Intellectual Property, and Education." He coauthored "Great Expectations: Content, Communications, Productivity, and the Role of Technology in Higher Education." He is also the author of the "Technology Information" column that appears in *Syllabus* magazine.

ALAN E. GUSKIN is codirector and senior scholar, Project on the Future of Higher Education, and Distinguished University Professor and President Emeritus, Antioch University. From 1985 to 1997, he was president and then chancellor of the five-campus Antioch University. Before Antioch, his leadership positions included chancellor, University of Wisconsin-Parkside (1975 to 1985), and acting president (1973 to 1974) and provost (1971 to 1973) at Clark University in Worcester, Massachusetts. He has held faculty positions at the University of Michigan as well as Clark, the University of Wisconsin-Parkside, and Antioch. Guskin recently received the 2001 Morris T. Keeton Award from the Council on Adult and Experiential Learning for his contributions to higher education as administrator, teacher, writer, consultant, and speaker and his demonstrated commitment to student learning and innovation and change in higher education.

WALLACE HANNUM is associate professor, School of Education, University of North Carolina at Chapel Hill. Formerly a senior research director in the department of cell biology in the School of Medicine at Duke University, Hannum has held faculty positions at Florida State and Florida A&M. He is coauthor of *Task Analysis Methods for Instructional Design, Instructional Systems Development in Large Organizations,* and *Computers in Effective Instruction: Computers and Software in the Classroom* and author of "Job Task Analysis," "Reconsidering Computer Literacy," "Push Technology for the World Wide Web," "Desktop Video Conferencing," and "Transforming Teaching with Technology." A consultant on applications for educational technology to corporations, national and state governments, colleges, universities, and public schools, his present research focus is developing an on-line learning infrastructure for delivering interactive learning materials over the World Wide Web.

SARA E. HINKLE is assistant director, Office of Summer Freshman Programs, at Indiana University, where she also serves as judicial officer in the Office of Student Ethics. In the process of completing her Ph.D. in higher education, Hinkle has held student affairs positions at Brenau University, Oglethorpe University, Delaware Valley College, and Kennesaw State University. In spring 2000, she served as resident director of the Semester at Sea, sponsored by the Institute for Shipboard Education.

EUGENE HOTCHKISS is president emeritus at Lake Forest College and former interim president at Eckerd College. He has held administrative appointments at Chatham College, Harvey Mudd College, Dartmouth College, and Cornell University. He has served as chairman of the Associated Colleges of the Midwest and the Associated College of Illinois and as a director of the Lake Forest Graduate School of Management. Hotchkiss was appointed by the Illinois Supreme Court to two blue ribbon committees concerned with attorney discipline and the appointment of judges. More recently, he has held positions as Senior Fellow of the Foundation for Independent Higher Education and Senior Fellow to the Foundation of Governing Boards. He is author of "Prescription for Small Liberal Arts Colleges."

GEORGE D. KUH is chancellor's professor, director of the National Survey of Student Engagement, and director of the College Student Experience Questionnaire Program at Indiana University, where he has held numerous faculty and administrative positions. Kuh's many publications include *Indices of Quality in the Undergraduate Experience, Involving Colleges, The Invisible Tapestry, Culture in American Colleges and Universities,* and *Improving the Undergraduate Experience: National Benchmarks of Effective Educational Practices* (as principal author on the latter). In 2001 he received the Tracy Sonneborn Award for Distinguished Teaching and Research from Indiana University and the Albert B. Hood Distinguished Alumni Award from the University of Iowa. He is a past president of the Association for the Study of Higher Education.

LEO M. LAMBERT is president, Elon University, and former provost and vice chancellor for academic affairs at the University of Wisconsin-La Crosse. He has held faculty and administrative positions at the University of Wisconsin-La Crosse, Syracuse University, and the University of Vermont. He is coauthor of *Linking America's Schools and Colleges: Guide to Partnerships and National Directory, University Teaching: A Guide for Graduate Students,* and *A Guide to Evaluating Teaching for Tenure and Promotion.* On the board of directors of the American Council on Education and formerly a board member of the American Association for Higher Education, he was recognized by *Change* magazine as a "young leader of the academy."

DERYL R. LEAMING is former dean of the College of Mass Communication, Middle Tennessee State University, and of the College of Liberal Arts, Marshall University, and has held administrative posts at Georgia State University, the University of Tulsa, and Kansas State University. Leaming is the author of *Academic Leadership: Practical Guide to Chairing a Department, History of American Journalism: An Outline Approach,* and *Managing People: A Guide for Department Chairs and Deans.* He is also editor and publisher of the *Online Journal of Academic Leadership.*

DALE W. LICK is former president of Georgia Southern University, the University of Maine, and Florida State University. He is presently university professor in the Learning Systems Institute and Department of Educational Leadership at Florida State University, where he has been focusing on leadership and managing change, transformational leadership, learning organizations, new learning systems, strategic planning, and visioning. A mathematician by training, he has held administrative and faculty positions at a number of state and private institutions. Lick's many publications include *New Directions in Monitoring: Creating a Culture of Synergy,* "Transforming Higher Education: A New Vision for Learning and Change Management," "Megalevel Strategic Planning: Beyond Conventional Wisdom," and "Change Creation."

MARY B. MARCY has been codirector and senior administrator of the Project on the Future of Higher Education, Antioch University, since fall 2000. Marcy was a Rotary Foundation scholar at Trinity College, Oxford, where she received her Master of Philosophy and Doctor of Philosophy in Politics. She then served as the director of government relations at Central Washington University and executive assistant to the president at Western Washington University. In 1997 she moved to Antioch University-Seattle as the first dean of university relations. Marcy has taught courses on American women and politics and Washington State politics. She has recently written articles on the new philanthropy, and with Alan Guskin, on leadership and change in higher education.

JUDITH A. RAMALEY is assistant director of the Education and Human Resources Directorate at the National Science Foundation. She was president of the University of Vermont from 1997 to 2001 and of Portland State University from 1990 to 1997. At Portland she also held the position of professor of biology. She served as executive vice president for academic affairs at SUNY-Albany and has held administrative appointments at the University of Nebraska and the University of Nebraska Medical Center, where she was an American Council on Education Fellow. Ramaley is active on numerous boards and is chair of the subcommittee on College Drinking of the Advisory

Council of the National Institute on Alcohol Abuse and Alcoholism (NIH). Editor of *Covert Discrimination: Women in the Sciences,* her publications include "New Role for the Academic Department in an Era of Reform," "Preparing the Way for Reform in Higher Education: Drawing Upon Resources of the Community at Large," and "Large-Scale Institutional Change to Implement an Urban University Mission."

KENNETH A. SHAW is chancellor and president of Syracuse University. He was formerly president of the University of Wisconsin system, chancellor of the Southern Illinois University system, president of Southern Illinois University-Edwardsville, and vice president and dean at Towson State University. Active in the NCAA, he received that organization's Silver Anniversary Award in 1986. He has served on the boards of numerous associations, including the American Council on Education, the National Association of Colleges and Universities, and the National Association of Independent Colleges and Universities. He is the author of *The Successful President.*

JOSEPH H. SILVER, SR., is vice president for academic affairs and professor of political science at Savannah State University. His prior appointments include assistant vice chancellor for academic affairs, University System of Georgia, State Board of Regents, and faculty member at Kennesaw State University. Winner of a number of awards for teaching and service, Silver directed projects designed to improve and evaluate educational programs, address the needs of at-risk students, and improve the dialogue between students, faculty, staff, and the community. He serves on a number of boards of nonprofit agencies and was president of the National Conference of Black Political Scientists. His publications are in the areas of urban politics and policies, civil rights, and higher education.

CHARLES M. SPUCHES is associate dean for educational outreach, instructional quality improvement, and instructional technology at the State University of New York, College of Environmental Science and Forestry, and adjunct associate professor at Syracuse University's graduate program in instructional design, development, and evaluation. He was also a faculty member in the College of Arts and Sciences, Idaho State University. He is coauthor of "Focusing on Process to Improve Learning," "Instructional Improvement Revisited: Lessons in Strategic Design," "Sensitizing Industrial Designers to Gerontology: Instructional Modules That Bridge the Gap," and author of "The Application of Instructional Development in Continuing Professional Education." From 1998 to 2000 he was a founding principal of Syracuse University's National Academy for Academic Leadership.

MARILLA SVINICKI is director, Center for Teaching Effectiveness, and associate professor in the department of educational psychology at the University of Texas at Austin. She is editor-in-chief of the New Directions for Teaching and Learning series and has been a leader in the faculty development movement in the United States. She is a consulting editor to *Innovative Higher Education* and has served in this role for the *Journal of Excellence in College Teaching*. Her publications include "University Teaching in the Twenty-First Century: New Skills for a New Millennium," "Creating a Foundation for Instructional Decisions," and "When Teachers Become Learners." She has won awards from the Professional Organizational Development Network, the Southwestern Sociological Association, and the state of Texas for her leadership and publications.

MICHAEL THEALL is associate professor of educational leadership and director of the Center for Teaching and Learning at the University of Illinois at Springfield. Theall has extensive teaching, curriculum design, and evaluation experience at both the public school and university levels. He has written and managed funded projects, produced instructional media, and consulted internationally on college teaching and learning, faculty evaluation, and student ratings of instruction. He is coauthor of a computer-managed evaluation and improvement system for college teaching. He was co-winner of the 2001 W. J. McKeachie Career Achievement Award of the American Education Research Association. Author of numerous articles on teaching and learning and evaluation, he has edited a number of New Directions issues, including *The Student Rating Debate: Are They Valid? How Can We Best Use Them?; Motivation from Within: Approaches for Encouraging Faculty and Students to Excel;* and *Effective Practices for Teaching Improvement,* with J. Franklin.

WILLIAM G. TIERNEY is the Wilber-Kieffer Professor of Higher Education and director, Center for Higher Education Policy Analysis, Rossier School of Education, University of Southern California. Tierney was named by *Change* magazine as one of the forty "young leaders of the academy." He received the 1997 Distinguished Research Award from the Association for the Study of Higher Education. His many publications include *Building the Responsive Campus: Creating High Performance Colleges and Universities; Faculty Productivity: Facts, Fictions, and Issues;* and *Building Communities of Difference: Higher Education in the Twenty-First Century.* President of the USC Academic Senate in 1999 to 2000, he is currently president of the Association for the Study of Higher Education.

JON F. WERGIN is professor of education, Virginia Commonwealth University. A senior scholar at the American Association for Higher Education, he was founding director of AAHE's Forum on Faculty Roles and Rewards and has directed projects for the Pew Charitable Trusts on quality assurance in academic departments, and the assessment of student learning outcomes in institutional accreditation. He has directed educational planning at Virginia Commonwealth and on its Medical College of Virginia campus. Wergin is coauthor of *Understanding and Evaluating Educational Research* and the award-winning *Educating Professionals: Responding to New Demands for Competence and Accountability* and author of *The Collaborative Department: How Five Campuses Are Inching Toward Cultures of Collective Responsibility* and *Consulting in Higher Education: Principles for Consultants and Colleges.* He also edited *New Directions for Institutional Research: Analyzing Faculty Workload* and *New Directions for Higher Education: Using Consultants Successfully.*

DANIEL W. WHEELER is professor and coordinator of professional and organizational development at the University of Nebraska, and founding principal of the National Academy for Academic Leadership. He is coauthor of *The Department Chair: New Roles, Responsibilities and Challenges; Enhancing Faculty Careers: Strategies and Development and Renewal; Academic Leadership in Community Colleges;* and *The Academic Chairperson's Handbook.* He serves as a consultant to colleges and universities on academic career development and the role of the chairperson in facilitating faculty growth and development.

FRANKLIN P. WILBUR is associate vice president and executive director of the Center for Support of Teaching and Learning at Syracuse University. At Syracuse, Wilbur has directed the institution's nationally known and award-winning school-college partnership Project Advance and is an adjunct associate professor in the graduate school of education. As part of his responsibility, he directed Syracuse University's initiative to improve advising, which won the National Academic Advising Association's highest national award for quality. Wilbur is coauthor of *Linking America's Schools and Colleges* (second edition) and author of *School-College Partnerships: Building Effective Models for Collaboration.* He is a Senior Research Fellow in the American Association for Higher Education.

When one considers the forces for change, the present state of teaching and learning in most of our classrooms, and the complex needs of society, one reaches the inescapable conclusion that the future of our nation and the survival of higher education as we know it rests on the willingness of those in academic leadership roles to work together to rethink what they do and how they do it. This means fundamental changes in the process of education and the structure of institutions. Business as usual is no longer an option.

We are talking about a fundamental restructuring of colleges and universities, a willingness to take risks, and significant changes in the roles of administration and faculty.

As an academic leader, you are in a position to make a difference—a difference in the quality of your institution, the lives of your faculty and staff, the community your institution serves, and the lives of your students. As part of your responsibility, you will need to make many decisions in a staggering array of areas, from budget and facilities to programs and personnel issues. You will often find yourself the buffer between opposing viewpoints, between your institution and the surrounding community and between students, faculty, alumni, and donors. In addition, change is constant, and so the amount of knowledge and information you need to be an effective leader is always increasing.

If your institution is to be responsive to the needs of a changing world, it will rest on you and your colleagues in leadership positions. Deciding to act is the first essential step, but it is meaningless if you and others do not have a clear vision and commitment and the knowledge and skills to lead a successful change process. Your role in bringing about significant and long-lasting institutional change is the focus of the *Field Guide to Academic Leadership*. It is designed to provide you with information and suggestions for action and administrative practice around a range of issues.

Whether you came to your present position from outside of higher education, as a growing number of chief executives do, or rose up through the academic ranks, it is unlikely that you feel fully prepared for the challenges you face, the decisions you must make, and the leadership you are called on to provide. This book has been specifically designed to assist you by blending what research tells us about leadership, change, and teaching and learning with the practical expertise and insights of academic leaders and researchers from around the country.

In addition, a number of chapters address the need for cooperation and collaboration among the leaders and units in your institution to avoid the silo mentality that is so common on many campuses. Whenever units work in isolation, when cooperation becomes difficult and trust evaporates, the institution suffers. The primary goal of this guide is to facilitate improvement of colleges and universities by strengthening the quality of academic programs and services provided.

FINDING WHAT YOU NEED

Although the *Field Guide to Academic Leadership* can serve as a primer on leadership and change in higher education, it has been organized so that you can find the information you need on a specific topic as easily as possible. The emphasis is on practical information and suggestions. Much of the material is research-based, but our goal is to get to the important points as quickly as possible. If you are interested in an in-depth review of the literature, a list of resources is included at the end of most chapters. For practical purposes, the guide is divided into several broad topical areas.

Part One: Basics

The two chapters in this section provide the foundation for the book. Chapter One reviews the many forces for change now affecting higher education, and Chapter Two introduces what we believe are the essential elements for significant and long-lasting changes at colleges and universities.

Part Two: Leadership

The chapters in this section focus on leadership, the need for clear mission and vision statements, and common challenges and problems you can anticipate in your role as an institutional leader. Also included in this section is a chapter that focuses on interactional styles and preferences. Knowing about your own personal style and understanding others' preferences can enhance your effectiveness in dealings with them.

Part Three: Academics

In this, the longest section of the guide, the focus shifts to the primary function of a college or university: teaching and learning. The authors provide you with a solid base on educational research and its implications for teaching, student learning and development, and evaluation and assessment. Also included are practical chapters on curriculum and course design, educational technology, new instructional methodologies, developing a strong advising system, and how faculty development can support ongoing institutional improvement.

Part Four: Assessment

Good long-term decision making requires the collection and use of solid information. In this section of the book, you will find chapters on assessment at the department, unit, or program level, leadership in faculty evaluation, and the faculty reward system as a lever for change. These discussions follow an introductory chapter that places evaluation and assessment in a broader institutional context.

Part Five: Other Issues

As an academic leader, you are required to deal with a wide variety of difficult issues. This section highlights several of the more complex but fairly common organizational issues. Chapters discuss improving cooperation between academic and fiscal affairs, collaboration between academic and student affairs, administrative issues relating to the use and investment in technology, and the important issue of campus diversity.

Part Six: Position-Specific Issues for Academic Leaders

Those in different positions have different responsibilities in the change process, and roles and responsibilities vary in different types of institutions. Consequently, the chapters in Part Six were written specifically for trustees and regents, new presidents, presidents of smaller institutions, leaders at community colleges, chief academic officers, deans, and department chairs. Although a specific chapter may address your present position, you will also find relevant information in chapters addressed to others. For example, a self-inventory described in the chapter for deans could be used by anyone in a leadership role.

Part Seven: In Conclusion

It was impossible to cover all of the important issues facing academic leaders in the chapter structure. In this section, we take up a number of these topics. We also take this opportunity to tie together a number of themes that seem to loom large in the future of higher education.

Glossary of Academic Terms

All too often we find ourselves trying to understand ill-defined terms and surrounded by subject matter specialists who assume that everyone shares their working vocabulary. Furthermore, in recent years a new jargon has evolved from the change literature and from the assessment movement. Some of these terms have been defined in the body of the book, but we thought a glossary might be helpful as well. To assist us in this work, each author recommended specific terms for inclusion. You will find the glossary at the back of the book.

RECURRING THEMES

As you read the various chapters, you will note a number of recurring themes. In many ways these fundamental points serve as a foundation on which this *Field Guide* stands.

- Each institution needs clearly articulated vision and mission statements that address the needs of students and society and are supported by everyone at the institution.
- Each unit of the institution must have its own statement of priorities that specifically supports the vision and mission.
- Students' learning and development are the primary function of colleges and universities.

- Research on change, leadership, learning and teaching, and knowledge of your institutional culture must be at the foundation of decision making.
- Academic leaders must have a vision for their institution and a clear understanding of the process needed to get there.
- Institutional change does not happen by chance; it requires effective and integrated leadership throughout the institution.
- Successful leaders need a wide array of knowledge and skills and an understanding of their own strengths and weaknesses.
- Good decision making requires continuous monitoring of quality and the collection and use of data.
- The need for professional development of faculty and staff at all levels is important and ongoing.

FROM RESEARCH TO PRACTICE

Almost twenty years ago (1984), Peter Ewell made the following observation about American higher education: "Given that we have constructed a culture in higher education that appears so publicly to value information, it is surprising how little of it we tend to have about ourselves. And more surprising is the fact that what works and what does not in particular colleges and universities has had but little effect on actual teaching and administration" (p. 5).

Although the last two decades have seen an increase in what we know about how students learn, leadership and change, and how institutions work, there has been little change in how this information is used. It has been a goal of this *Field Guide* to help close this gap between research and practice. We hope to help you to be an effective agent of change by providing you with the best information possible, in a way that is practical and direct. I hope we have succeeded.

We wish you well in your efforts to enhance the quality of your institution and the experience of your students.

ACKNOWLEDGMENTS

The *Field Guide* would not have been possible without the hard work and dedication of a number of talented individuals. I would like to express my thanks to the academic leaders who participated in the two Minnowbrook conferences; to the authors of the individual chapters who took far more time on this project than they originally intended; to the Knight, Kellogg, and Park Foundations who made it all possible; and to "Buzz" Shaw, whose early support in the establishment of the National Academy for Academic Leadership was an essential element in its founding. To Stephanie Waterman and Samantha Puckett for their outstanding clerical support and to Bronwyn Adam who provided invaluable editorial assistance.

Reference

Ewell, P. (1984). *The self-regarding institution: Information for excellence.* Boulder, CO: National Center for Higher Education Management Systems.

June 2002   *Robert M. Diamond*
                                                               St. Petersburg, Florida

PART ONE

Basics

I have no doubt that the forces buffeting higher education today are powerful and will change it considerably. My fear is that America's colleges will ignore them and the important questions that they demand we confront—or that, simply through complacency or the glacial speed of our decision-making process, we will fail to respond in time to help shape tomorrow.

—Arthur E. Levine, *Chronicle of Higher Education,* October 27, 2000

CHAPTER 1

Pressures for Fundamental Reform
Creating a Viable Academic Future

ALAN E. GUSKIN, MARY B. MARCY

For almost a decade, there has been a great deal of discussion about the need for the fundamental reform of colleges and universities in order to meet future financial and societal pressures. In the mid-1990s, there were a number of major foundation-funded projects developed around this theme of restructuring. Most significant among them were the Pew Roundtable, the ACE-Kellogg Project on Leadership and Institutional Transformation, and the Irvine Foundation's Futures Project. Together they involved over one hundred institutions.

Yet for all the good work done and changes made, little of it has led to fundamental reform. Indeed, accomplishing such significant change is a very difficult venture and it is only when the pressures for change are great that it is likely to happen. It is not by chance that the most often cited examples of significant institutional reform have occurred in institutions that were in considerable crisis—for example, Portland State University and Olivet College in the mid-1990s.

Although the discussion of institutional restructuring during the last decade sensitized people in many colleges and universities to the need for institutional change, the pressures necessary to initiate fundamental changes did not reach a critical stage. In many ways, the increases in financial resources at most institutions in the last few years of the 1990s may have dulled some of the momentum of the early and mid-1990s. But

---

Note: This chapter is a revised excerpt from the more extensive paper "Facing the Future: Faculty Work, Student Learning, and Fundamental Reform," which is copyrighted as part of the Working Paper Series of the Project on the Future of Higher Education published by Antioch University.

the underlying pressures remained and are now intensifying. Higher education in this new century faces the paradox of being more critical than ever to society's future while at the same time being under great pressure to prove its worth in educating students and justify its use of financial resources. Expectations of and pressures on colleges and universities are high.

In the next decade or so, increasingly severe financial and accountability pressures may well disrupt the educational and administrative practices of our nation's colleges and universities, and undermine the quality of faculty work life and student learning. The key to overcoming these potential problems will be fundamental reform in how colleges and universities educate students, especially undergraduates. Leverage for such change will require joining together the professional interests of faculty with institutional needs to respond to pressures for significant reform. To accomplish this, faculty and administrators will need to challenge their basic assumptions about teaching and learning.

PRESSURES FOR CHANGE

In the last few years, the pressure for significant institutional change in higher education has reached a crescendo, culminating in demands for major reform. The focus is on three primary issues: the costs of higher education for students and the state, what students are learning and assessment of student learning outcomes, and the use of new information and computer technologies in the core of the educational process.

Costs of Higher Education

It is generally accepted in higher education that the expenses involved in educating undergraduate students will continually increase. Faculty salaries, the costs to educate increasing numbers of students by hiring new faculty and staff members, increasing costs of materials and facilities, and more recently, the huge and continually increasing investment in new information and computer technologies all contribute to escalating costs. As a result, even with the considerable savings from painful cuts made over the last decade or so, maintaining the present academic structures requires fiscal resources that surpass the ability or the willingness of societal institutions and individuals to provide them.

The severity of this problem is summarized in a 1997 report by the Council on Aid to Education (Benjamin, 1998) entitled *Breaking the Social Contract: The Fiscal Crisis in Higher Education:*

> The Higher Education Price Index (HEPI) rose more than sixfold between 1961 and 1995, much faster than inflation as measured by the Consumer Price Index (CPI). Between 1980 and 1995, the annual average rate of growth in the costs of providing higher education exceeded the CPI by a full percentage point. A sector whose costs grow faster than inflation for an extended period ultimately reaches the limits of available resources, as has been demonstrated in the health care industry. . . . [p. 8]
>
> [Although] public support per student has just kept pace with inflation, . . . real costs per student have grown by about 40 percent. . . . Until now, institutions have been paying for [these] rising costs by sharp tuition increases; however, such increases will shortly begin to keep Americans from pursuing higher education. . . . [p. 11]
>
> In 1995 dollars, higher education will have to spend about $151 billion in 2015 to serve future students if costs continue to grow at current rates. Assuming that public appropriations to higher education continue to follow current trends, government funding will be about $47 billion in that year. Tuition, grants, and endowment income will account for another $66 billion. In other words, the higher education sector will face a funding shortfall of about $38 billion—almost a quarter of what it will need. [p. 11]

Most institutions have tried to face these challenges with greater fundraising efforts as well as tuition increases and cuts in nonacademic areas. But although these initiatives add some important resources, they cannot address the fundamental present and future operating costs of institutions except in a very small percentage of upper-echelon institutions that already have huge endowments.

Student Learning Outcomes

Colleges and universities need to focus on student learning: this has become a rallying cry for many who are demanding the reform of undergraduate education. Concurrently, demands for colleges and universities to demonstrate the outcomes of student learning have also been growing for some time. Over the last decade, the six regional higher education accreditation associations have increasingly pressured colleges and universities to assess the outcomes of student learning as part of their accreditation reviews.

There has also been a growing emphasis among governors and state legislatures to tie part of the annual state allocations for higher education to institutional performance, as measured in one way or another by the outcomes of student learning. Because of the lack of well-developed student learning outcome measures, institutional performance tends to be viewed in terms of crude measures of learning, such as attrition, graduation rates, and the like. As learning outcome measures become available, it is likely that the funding of institutional performance will focus more on actual demonstrations of learning rather than on these gross measures. An indication of the movement in this direction may be seen in the conclusion of a national survey of the nation's governors carried out by the Education Commission of the States and reported in the *Chronicle of Higher Education*: "Although governors throughout the country see postsecondary education as a top spending priority, they believe that taxpayer support for public colleges should be tied to fundamental changes in the institution's policies and practices" (Schmidt, 1998, p. A38).

New Information and Computer Technologies

There have been significant improvements in information and computer technologies over the last few years, and innovations are likely to continue at an increasing pace over the years ahead, especially when it comes to sophisticated software. These advances will enable colleges and universities to integrate technology further into the core of the educational process. This point is emphasized by Newman and Scurry in a recent article (2001): "As the inexorable improvement in digital technology continues, and we gain a better understanding of how to use it, we will experience further improvements in the capacity, reliability, cost-effectiveness, and ease of use. Soon it will be impossible, even with great effort, to achieve the same learning results without the use of technology that we can achieve with it" (p. B7).

As a result, pressures will mount from both outside and inside the traditional higher education sector—including competing institutions, funding agencies, policymakers, governing boards, and students themselves—to use technology as a key part of the learning process, not only as important components of courses and a means for students to learn on their own but also as alternatives to courses. Like many revolutionary innovations, new technologies cannot be adequately accommodated through traditional means. As Carol Twigg (1996) argues: "As you design mediated programs, you will find that the more you replicate the traditional campus model, the more your operating costs will resemble or exceed traditional campus costs. . . . You will save money only if you substitute one function for another function at less cost. This isn't a matter of research; it's a matter of logic and common sense." Technology does offer tremendous promise for higher education. But it is a promise that can only be realized through innovation and significant change.

These three major pressures—costs, student learning outcomes, and new technologies—are beginning to be reflected in the increasingly common calls for significant reform in higher education from key sectors of society. For example, the National Commission on the Cost of Higher Education concluded: "The commission believes significant gains in productivity and efficiency can be made through [alternative approaches to] the basic way institutions deliver most instruction, i.e., faculty members meeting with groups of students at regularly scheduled times and places. . . . [We] should consider ways to focus on the results of student learning regardless of time spent in the traditional classroom setting" (American Council on Education, 1998, p. 28).

In effect, the commission—like the nation's governors, the Council on Aid to Education, and many others—recognizes that there must be fundamental change in the delivery of education at our colleges and universities. Ignoring the future fiscal realities and the need to focus on student learning can, and probably will, have a devastating impact on colleges and universities.

These are not just abstract policy issues; there will be concrete effects on people's lives. Simply stated, maintaining the present structures and processes of higher education institutions without fundamental reform will eventually undermine the two things on which higher education has found its past success and must base its future: the quality of faculty work life and student learning.

HOW THE EDUCATIONAL DELIVERY SYSTEM UNDERMINES THE QUALITY OF FACULTY WORK LIFE

In facing this challenge for fundamental reform, we should note that over the last half-century colleges and universities have made adjustments and changes in the face of difficult educational problems. There have been many evolving undergraduate academic reforms as colleges and universities have struggled with student attrition, the arrival of new generations of academically and demographically diverse students, and the explosive growth of new information technologies, among others. But the changes made have not been fundamental; rather, the reforms have, with a few exceptions, maintained the traditional academic and financial structures.

The present educational delivery system—composed of courses, quarter or semester calendars, and faculty teaching classes—is likewise assumed to be unchangeable, and this situation has contributed to continuing increases in institutional costs. Further, because these academic structures have been maintained while costly new computer technologies and the necessary support infrastructure have been introduced, the escalation of expenses has been enormous.

The task for faculty and administrators at almost all colleges and universities is to deal with these pressures by reviewing and challenging the educational assumptions of their institutions. But challenging basic assumptions about teaching and learning is simply not part of the intellectual training and interests of most faculty members or administrators. Teaching is about substance, not process; what students need, it is thought, is an understanding of the specific disciplinary knowledge area of the course being taught. Although the substance of almost all courses taught has evolved with powerful advances in knowledge, the basic process by which they are delivered has, with some exceptions, remained unchanged for many, many decades.

Higher education now faces a critical choice about this process: present forces in higher education will either lead to significant reform in the undergraduate educational environment or to a significant diminution in the quality of faculty work life because of sharp increases in faculty teaching loads and related work. For, as the fiscal and political pressures increase, academic administrators will reach deeper and deeper into faculty positions to continue to enhance the financial flexibility and viability of their institutions. In the past, they responded to such pressures by increasing tuition beyond the growth of inflation, deferring maintenance, and cutting administrative and support staff and expense budgets. But each of these solutions has been or is being exhausted.

The present educational delivery system limits our ability to reduce the per student costs of education without major diminution in the work lives of faculty. The educational delivery system is based on two interlocking assumptions: in order for students to learn they have to be grouped together in courses taught by faculty members, and therefore, in order for a college or university to increase academic productivity (that is, reduce per-student costs) faculty members need to teach more courses or teach more students in their classes.

In a time of continuous growth in institutional resources and number of faculty positions, institutions can add teaching faculty to address the issue, although there still will be serious questions about student learning outcomes. But if the per-student resources available to an institution remain flat or decrease, then the main response in the current educational delivery system will be to increase faculty productivity, and also make major institutional cuts.

The Growing Number of Nontenure Track Faculty

Many colleges and universities have faced financial stress in the last decade or so, and as a result have developed short-term coping strategies. Because little thought is given to a fundamental reform of the process by which education is delivered and students learn, and there is significant pressure to maintain the present arrangements for existing faculty, the short-term strategies for dealing with the need to increase academic productivity tend to focus on hiring inexpensive faculty in order to serve the same (or an increasing) number of students with reduced resources. Rather than filling open positions with tenure track faculty, the strategy is to hire full-time nontenure track faculty, who are expected to teach more classes per year, often at lower annual pay, and part-time faculty, who teach individual classes at very low cost.

The use of these two alternatives is reflected in data developed by the National Center for Educational Statistics in 1987, 1992, and 1998 from research, doctoral, and comprehensive and liberal arts institutions for the *National Study of Postsecondary Faculty* (Kirchstein, Matheson, & Zimbler, 1997; Zimbler, 2001). According to our analysis of these data, from 1987 to 1998 the number of full-time nontenure track faculty more than doubled—from about thirty-six thousand to ninety thousand. During this same eleven-year period there was a substantial decrease in tenure track faculty members (about 12 percent). If we look at these data by institutional type (research, doctoral, and comprehensive universities and liberal arts colleges), this reduction in tenure track faculty and increase in full-time nontenure track faculty holds for all institution types, with the largest decreases in tenure track faculty and increases in full-time nontenure track faculty occurring in the research and doctoral institutions.

Also from 1987 to 1992 there was a substantial overall increase in the use of part-time faculty. In addition, from 1992 to 1998 three of the four institution types showed an increase in the use of part-time faculty: research universities decreased their use of part-time faculty, but comprehensive universities showed modest increases and doctoral institutions and liberal arts colleges showed substantial increases in the use of part-time faculty.

Considering present trends, it is likely that the number of tenure track faculty will continue to fall. Roger Baldwin and Jay Chronister (2001) report that 37 percent of eighty-eight institutions they sampled expect to increase hiring of full-time nontenure track faculty members, another 51 percent project their hiring to stay the same, and only about 10 percent expect it to decrease. In their book *Teaching Without Tenure,* the authors write: "A host of external and internal forces is encouraging colleges and universities to rethink their staffing policies and patterns. . . . As institutions try to cope with demands for greater accountability and responsiveness, new technologies and competitors, and strident criticism of the tenure system, faculty appointments off the tenure track have become increasingly attractive" (p. 30).

What seems apparent is that given the present financial strains and uncertainty about future fiscal resources, university leaders have considerable anxiety about the future of higher education. Because all thoughtful academic administrators know that laying off tenured faculty is not good for their professional health or that of their institution, the hiring on limited-term (two- to three-year) contracts of inexpensive full-time nontenure track faculty who have good academic credentials remains a desirable option. Although this is not a happy solution for most institutions, or for many of these individuals hired, it does appear to solve immediate problems in a time of slow deterioration of the fiscal health of a college or university. These faculty members have lower salaries, and especially at research and doctoral universities, teach more classes than those on tenure track.

It should be noted that not all hiring of part-time and full-time nontenure track faculty comes in response to the need for financial flexibility. In some cases (the health fields, the arts, for example), such practitioner-faculty members fill a program's educational needs in selected areas where full-time employment or a tenured position would not. There is little doubt that such practitioner-faculty are important for educational reasons, and some of the increases in their numbers since 1987 may be attributed to that. But the scale of the increases in the hiring of full-time nontenure track faculty from 1987 to 1998 as well as the observations of Baldwin and Chronister indicate strong fiscal reasons as well.

The Impact of Hiring Strategies on Tenured and Tenure Track Faculty

The assumption behind the short-term faculty hiring strategy is that higher education's present fiscal conditions will not get worse and will likely get better. Therefore, at a minimum, the present balance between financial resources and costs must be maintained over time. But maintaining this balance will be very difficult. As for costs, there is every indication that without fundamental changes college and university costs will continue to increase beyond inflation—as they have done for many decades. As for financial resources, in order to maintain the present balance colleges and universities will have to continue to increase their tuition above the level of annual inflation and receive increased funding above inflation levels from state and federal governments. But neither seems likely. First, the pressure to reduce the rate of tuition increases has been growing for some time and is not likely to abate, nor will it be possible for many people to afford higher education if tuition continues to rise at too high a rate. Second, government support for higher education is not likely to exceed inflation given the available resources and the intense competition among all public programs. Hence, the combination of tax cuts and rebates, the predicted continuing economic slowdown, state spending priorities, and the inability of students to afford substantial increases in tuition will limit the financial resources available to private and public colleges and universities alike.

Given the cost structure of higher education and the unavailability of adequate public and private funds, the short-term strategy already described—protecting the work of tenured and tenure track faculty and the status quo in educational practice by hiring inexpensive faculty—is not a viable long-term solution. For in the context of static or decreasing fiscal resources and growing institutional expenses, the long-term tendency will be for universities to reduce faculty costs by not rehiring part-time and full-time nontenure track faculty members. These actions will be consistent with the basic rationale for hiring these inexpensive faculty on limited-term contracts in the first place. For the most part, the policy was created *both* to decrease faculty costs immediately and to allow for dealing with future decreases in financial resources by terminating these contract faculty members, something that could not easily be done with tenured and tenure-track faculty.

Paradoxically, these decisions—which were made to protect tenured and tenure track faculty—will put enormous pressure on those remaining members to increase their workload and thus will significantly undermine the quality of their professional lives. As one faculty member at a doctoral institution stated: "These arrangements support the privileges of tenure-line faculty. But are we really signing our own death warrants here?" (Wilson, 1998, p. A12).

The message is clear: we must look carefully at how the education delivery system can be transformed to enable both faculty work life and student learning to be enhanced. Except for the relatively small number of extremely wealthy, heavily endowed colleges and universities, higher education institutions and the faculty themselves face, at best, a very difficult future. And in particular, young faculty members looking out over the next thirty years must wonder if higher education is a viable career. After spending so many years preparing for their careers, will faculty members be able to have a meaningful professional life, teaching and exploring issues of interest to them, and have a decent private life as well?

CONCLUSION

The pressure to transform our colleges and universities fundamentally continues to intensify and may well put at risk the quality of the educational environment. Accountability demands for student learning outcomes and for justifying the use of fiscal resources combined with continually increasing per-student costs and static or reduced per-student available resources over the next decade will put enormous pressure on colleges and universities to make fundamental reforms in how students learn and faculty teach. Although making such significant institutional change is difficult, the alternative is worse: undermining the quality of faculty work life and diminishing student learning.

Decreasing per student costs and bringing them into balance with future per student resources requires fundamentally reforming the present educational delivery system. This means there will be significant changes in the academic structure and processes—involving, for example, the academic calendar, the assessment of student learning, the counting processes for student learning (credits), and faculty workload (courses taught). Technology will be used in the core of the educational process and will reduce the use of faculty time. This will also mean that courses will be only one means for student learning and faculty teaching, and they will not necessarily be spread over the length of a quarter or semester.

In the past, most faculty questioned the legitimacy of significant change because they feared undermining the quality of education students receive as well as their own professional lives. In the future, faculty may be the main proponents of fundamental change in the educational delivery system, because maintaining the present system is contrary both to their professional interests and to the quality of their students' educational experience. Probably the most important stumbling block for fundamentally reforming the educational delivery system is the lack of viable models of transformed institutions. There is a need for the development of such models.

Another critical impediment to fundamental reform is higher education leaders' lack of understanding of how to create such systemic change. Clearly, there is a need for the leadership skills that make such change possible. At the same time, institutions need to choose leaders who have these capabilities, provide resources for the education of leaders who do not, and provide support to those leading fundamental reform. Finally, institutions need to encourage successful leaders to remain in their positions long enough to achieve fundamental reform.

The opportunity to make a fundamental transformation in colleges and universities may be aided and abetted because it is a special moment in the modern history of higher education: over 50 percent of the faculty presently teaching are fifty years old or older, and most are likely to retire in the next decade or so. With the likelihood of huge numbers of faculty retirements over a ten- to fifteen-year period, we can meet financial and other accountability pressures by making fundamental changes in how faculty work and students learn while also minimizing layoffs and human pain. We have a special opportunity to face this future head-on; avoiding doing so could be disastrous.

References

American Council on Education. (1998). *Straight talk about college costs and prices: Final report and supplemental material from the National Commission on the Cost of Higher Education.* Washington, DC: American Council on Education–Oryx Press.

Baldwin, R., & Chronister, J. (2001). *Teaching without tenure.* Baltimore, MD: Johns Hopkins Press.

Benjamin, Roger W. (1998). *Breaking the social contract: The fiscal crisis in California higher education.* Santa Monica, CA: Rand Corporation.

Kirchstein, R. J., Matheson, N., & Zimbler, L. J. (1997). *Statistical analysis report. 1993 national study of postsecondary faculty: Instructional faculty and staff in higher education institutions, fall 1997 and fall 1992.* Washington, DC: National Center for Educational Statistics, U.S. Department of Education.

Newman, F., & Scurry, J. (2001, July 13). Online technology pushes pedagogy to the forefront. *Chronicle Review,* p. B7.

Schmidt, P. (1998, June 19). "Governors want fundamental changes in colleges, question place of tenure." *Chronicle of Higher Education,* p. A38.

Twigg, C. (1996, March-April). Is technology a silver bullet? *EduCom Review.* [http://www.educause.edu/pub/er/review/reviewArticles/31228.html].

Wilson, R. (1998, June 12). "Contracts replace the tenure track for a growing number of professors." *Chronicle of Higher Education,* p. A12.

Zimbler, L. J. (2001). *1999 national study of postsecondary faculty: Background characteristics, work activities, and compensation of faculty and instructional staff in postsecondary institutions, fall 1998.* Washington, DC: National Center for Educational Statistics, U.S. Department of Education.

CHAPTER 2

Requisites for Sustainable Institutional Change

ROBERT M. DIAMOND, LION F. GARDINER,
DANIEL W. WHEELER

Implementing major, long-lasting change at colleges and universities is a complex and challenging process. It has been observed that changing higher education is like changing a religion in which tradition abounds, the status quo is honored, and any innovation is met with both resistance and high emotion. Reform in higher education is further complicated by leadership turnover, a reward system focused more on priorities external to the institution than inside it, and search committees that often apply criteria that have little to do with the institution's needs or the position's actual demands.

Despite the difficulties involved and the many barriers to overcome, most colleges and universities today must address the reform agenda. They have no choice. The need to serve a growing and more diverse student body combines with decreasing financial support per student and revised accreditation standards to make major academic reform a necessity. In addition, there are pressures from employers and taxpayers and increased competition from for-profit educational service providers. With the advent of new technologies and the information age, we have entered a new era of continuous and ongoing institutional change.

The long-treasured isolation of the ivory tower of decades past is simply no longer possible. Priorities are changing, our understanding of the teaching and learning process is rapidly evolving, technology is having an increasing impact on both how students learn and how institutions operate, and as a result the roles of campus governing boards, leaders, faculty, staff, and students must undergo major transformation.

CHANGE AND INSTITUTIONAL TRANSFORMATION

Many change models exist, and new theories about change continue to provide interesting perspectives. Successful change initiatives share a number of characteristics. Although change occurs all the time, whether we intend for it to happen or not, change *initiatives* are intentional, planned, and directed, and ideally, are viewed as important to constituents across the institution. They are not isolated activities but involve faculty and staff, and in many cases, the entire campus community. Successful change is sustainable. It is not a fad. It is institutionalized, and the results of the initiative are expected to last. The type of change we envision affects the institution by changing practices, structures, roles, and procedures. In 1972, Gregory Bateson coined the term *second-order change* for this type of transformation. Such change

- Represents a new way of seeing things
- Requires a shift of gears
- Is irreversible; after it is implemented, things cannot go back to the way they were
- Is a transformation to something quite different from what existed previously
- Requires new learning on the part of administrators, faculty, and staff
- Results in a new story being told about the institution by faculty, students, staff, and the community served

REQUISITES FOR SUSTAINABLE CHANGE

Most of us in higher education have not been prepared to serve as change agents. In fact, we may find ourselves in leadership roles based on successes we have had meeting very different challenges. The key to success in leading change is identifying the knowledge and skills you will need in this period of transformation.

In the summers of 1998 and 1999, with support from the W.K. Kellogg Foundation, the Park Foundation, the Knight Foundation, and Syracuse University, two working conferences were held at the university's Minnowbrook Conference Center in Blue Mountain Lake, New York. The purpose of the gatherings was to establish the National Academy for Academic Leadership. (See the Appendix at the end of this book for a list of the participants.) One of the goals of the conferences was to address core questions about the skills, knowledge, and conditions necessary to create intentional, significant, and sustainable institutional change. The term *requisites* was used because participants considered the understandings gained and characteristics identified as not just desirable but essential for everyone in a leadership role.

Different leadership roles require different levels of specificity in requisites dealing with knowledge and skills. For example, whereas presidents should know the characteristics of a quality tenure and promotion system so that they can ask the right questions, the chief academic officer, the deans, and the department chairs need to have a detailed understanding of what should be included in the institutional, school, college, and departmental procedural statements and of the faculty evaluation process itself. The closer the individuals are to where the action takes place, the more detailed knowledge they require. Although no leader will have or need to have deep knowledge in every area, all leaders need to be conversant with these topics in order to perform the roles associated with their positions.

As an academic leader, you need to keep in mind that although change can be planned, it is extremely difficult to predict exactly how a change initiative will proceed. Organizational and cultural change are complicated processes. Flexibility and openness, therefore, are key ingredients for successful change initiatives. Although you may know what you want to happen *and* have a vision of the steps you will take, your path may change along the way and your destination may end up being quite different, and often far better, than you imagined. Fortunately, certain principles, ideas, and skills can guide you through this difficult process. The following requisites for sustainable institutional change were identified at the Minnowbrook sessions. It is your responsibility as an academic leader to encourage these conditions so important to lasting change. Each will be dealt with in more detail in succeeding chapters.

Institutional Mission Statement

The institution must have an institutional mission statement that is consistent with stated institutional values and that guides work throughout the college or university as it addresses the needs of a changing society.

An institution's public statements of mission and vision should reflect its particular history, context, and realities. Each institution has its own unique culture, strengths, and priorities. What is crucial is that the mission statement be supported by decisions made at all levels of the institution. If learning is the institution's primary mission—and in most cases it is—then this should be the emphasis in how resources are allocated and decisions are made, and in the reward and recognition systems for individuals, programs, and support units. Colleges and universities have different strengths and serve different publics. To express the uniqueness of an institution, many academic leaders find it useful to have a clearly articulated mission statement that is further developed in detail by other documents that operationalize the mission.

Leaders Who Recognize and Address Inconsistencies

Campus leaders must be able to recognize gaps between the mission statement and institutional practices and be willing to address inconsistencies.

The priorities expressed in an institutional mission statement are not always supported by administrative policies and practices, the faculty reward system, or the criteria used in resource allocation decisions. Institutional mission and vision statements must be the foundation on which priorities are established and decisions are made. Campus leaders must know how decisions are made outside their direct purview and be vigilant in insisting that the mission drive institutional decisions and priorities. It is not enough for leaders to recognize inconsistencies; they must also be willing to correct them.

Leaders Who Articulate a Vision

Institutional leaders must articulate a vision for the future, including the need for change, have the ability to communicate this vision to faculty, students, staff, and the general public, and be willing to take the risks necessary for this vision to become a reality.

Significant change requires risk taking and a leadership that accepts responsibility for failure and recognizes the contributions of others to success. Successful institutions have clearly articulated goals for the future and a total commitment to reaching those goals. Leaders at all levels of the institution must recognize the need for change to ensure the long-term health and future of their institution. People do not leave the comfort of the status quo without a compelling reason for doing so. Leaders must work hard to bring others along with them by sharing information about the reasons for their plans and decisions. Leaders must also be willing to act and take the risks associated with leading important change initiatives—including sometimes "taking the heat" for unpopular positions or decisions. They cannot be risk-averse with respect to their vision for the future.

Leaders Who Encourage Collaborative Leadership

Academic leaders must encourage the collaborative leadership of committed faculty, students, and staff and maintain mutual respect among all members of the campus community.

A challenge facing anyone in a leadership role is to shape and share a vision and commitment. Leadership must be successfully developed and rewarded at all levels of the institution. Faculty and staff members, as well as union and student leaders, must feel they are an integral part of any significant initiative. When groups or individuals feel marginalized as members of the campus community or do not believe they have a voice in important decision making, it will be difficult to get them to participate in the initiative. Collaboration cannot be contrived. Constituents need to have tangible means of influencing decision making if they are to feel committed to a course of action—especially one that involves significant change. The key to successful initiatives is *ownership,* and it is your job to build and maintain it.

Leaders Who Are Committed to Leadership

Academic leaders must have a commitment to both formal and informal leadership in effecting change.

Leadership potential comes not only from one's formal organizational position but also from the roles one assumes in any initiative. Successful leaders recognize their role in the change process and are able to identify, encourage, and involve those without formal administrative appointments who are potential institutional leaders. Informal leaders exist in every group, large and small, from committees to departments to task forces. Learning to recognize and support them is crucial to formal leadership success.

Research, Technology, and Best Practice

Research, technology, and best practice must be at the foundation of all institutional change.

Considerable research and practical experience are available on learning and student development, teaching, curriculum design and instruction, assessment, and organizational change. This research must inform policy and decision making. Technology can be an ally in the change agenda as well. The research literature can guide technological applications for enhanced learning, efficiency, and increased profitability. Too many administrators and faculty members are unaware of the rich research literature available and fall back on anecdotal information or historical precedent to solve problems and make decisions. Professional research findings in combination with institutional research and the knowledge gained from your own successes and failures, as well as those of others, provide an invaluable foundation for institutional thinking and decision making.

Collection and Use of Data

Leaders at all levels of the institution must be committed to systematic and continuous collection and use of data on academic processes and outcomes.

Assessment and evaluation are integral components in improving programs, teaching, and learning outcomes. Although assessment provides the information necessary for improving programs and procedures, it is often perceived as a threat rather than an essential element in the education process. Establishing policies that foster trust in assessment as a means to improvement should be an important goal.

Integration of Financial and Academic Planning

There must be close integration of financial and academic planning at all institutional levels.

The fiscal and academic sides of the house must work together toward achieving learning goals. Policies and priorities for all institutional operations should support stated missions. Financial operations, the fundraising priorities of the development office, and budgeting practices should be integrated with the academic goals of the institution. You must forge alliances with staff members across campus to ensure that policies and practices do not work against important learning goals.

Reward Structures That Support the Mission

The reward structures for faculty and staff members and departments must support the mission, vision, and priorities of the institution.

The criteria used to determine compensation, promotion, recognition, discretionary funds for travel and research, and space allocation must support the priorities articulated in the mission and vision statements. All too often, what we say is important is not what is recognized in practice or celebrated in formal reward structures. This inconsistency sends a powerful, counterproductive message to campus constituents that certain statements have only rhetorical value. Sending honest messages and seeing them through in consistent policies is an important leadership challenge.

Leaders Who Are Self-Aware and Communicative

Academic leaders must be aware of their own strengths and weaknesses and have excellent interpersonal and communicative skills.

Our effectiveness as leaders is frequently determined by how well we work and communicate with others. Having a vision and technical knowledge is one thing, but having the ability to persuade others to pursue a particular course of action is another. An effective leader is able to recognize his or her own interpersonal style, and its strengths and weaknesses, as well as the strengths and weaknesses of others' styles. As you move up the administrative ladder, you may also need to adjust your style to remain successful. Self-knowledge, adaptability, and a concern for others are key elements of successful leadership.

Leaders Who Understand the Value of Development

Institutional leaders must recognize the need for ongoing professional development for themselves and for their faculty and staff.

Business and industry learned long ago the importance of providing substantial resources for professional and leadership development; higher education has not. Perhaps this is one reason why business and industry are so much more adaptable when addressing challenges. Although faculty have funds for travel to professional conferences, institutions are only now beginning to support travel for faculty and staff that focuses on and supports institutional priorities and initiatives. If you want the participation and support of an informed faculty and staff, you must commit to ongoing professional development at all institutional levels. Leadership too needs to be revitalized and developed in an ongoing fashion. Remember, the change we are experiencing is not an event—it is a continuous process and a condition of life in a new age.

AN INTEGRATED MODEL OF ACADEMIC LEADERSHIP

Our colleague, Paula P. Brownlee, President Emerita of the Association of American Colleges and Universities and consultant to numerous institutions, has made the following observation about institutional change and leadership (Paula P. Brownlee, letter to the authors, June 15, 2001):

> Successful planning and implementation of "megaplans" for a campus or system require a new kind of thinking about all the components that go into a multidimensional, moving activity like transformational change. Most often, leaders analyze some of the issues-structures and identify the skills and knowledge needed by different parts of the planning and implementation without seeing the vision in its entirety. It is not a fixed, static whole we are talking about—for it is understood differently by various colleagues, and does in fact change as circumstances change (a constant factor these days). Thus, the key leader (president, chancellor, system head, chair of the board, whomever) can no longer *only* analyze all the components and pick away at getting these going separately as circumstances permit, but needs help in holding, in his or her head and actions, a vastly complicated moving, multidimensional set of issues—and all in an intensely political context.

This view of the complex nature of institutional change suggests several important points.

- Initiatives cannot be undertaken piece by piece. Actions must be planned and integrated.
- Learning across the entire community is an integral part of the change process.
- As any initiative moves ahead, conditions change and responsibilities shift.
- As an initiative moves ahead, needs and goals also may change, along with the criteria used to measure success.
- The president or chief academic officer is responsible for ensuring that people share the vision articulated by the leadership and work collaboratively toward its goals.

What makes change so difficult, as Paula Brownlee suggested, is that leaders are dealing with a complex system with many diverse, moving parts. Roles and responsibilities vary, and as projects evolve, new learning will be required for almost everyone.

Once that learning has been applied, needs will change and new changes will be called for in response to those needs. Another variable has to do with changing personnel. As key people leave the institution or their particular roles and are redefined, it is important that leaders pay attention to the need for continuity. The following example of integrated leadership may help clarify some of the ideas we have presented in this chapter.

When the leadership of a college or university decides to change the promotion and tenure systems to reflect more directly the institution's mission and priorities, a number of specific actions are required at every level of academic affairs. The trustees and the president must have a clear understanding of the goals of the initiative. They need to know what a system that will support the learning mission will look like and how they can be sure that the system is supporting learning. The chief academic officer (CAO) is responsible for communicating this plan to the academic community and must understand his or her role in implementing the many actions required and approving the procedures that are developed. The CAO is also responsible for ensuring that campuswide policies support this new initiative. The deans and department chairs are responsible for communicating with faculty and establishing revised guidelines at the school, college, and departmental levels. They must develop procedures for orienting faculty serving on promotion and tenure committees and faculty who will be reviewed under the new guidelines. Once the new procedures are in place, it is the role of every academic leader to ensure that the guidelines are followed, that the needed support programs are implemented, and that, when necessary, appropriate modifications are made.

This example shows how leadership for change is needed across an institution. Because institutions are complex systems, change has to be accommodated and reinforced at a number of levels. This integrated notion of change is an important aspect of change in dynamic systems like colleges and universities. Everyone has a role to play in the change process.

CONCLUSION

In this chapter we proposed eleven requisites for significant, sustainable change. For some people in leadership roles, new skills and an expanded knowledge base will be needed; for others, a change in perspective on their roles and the future of the institution may be in order. The requisites for change and the need for integrated leadership make up the foundation on which this *Field Guide to Academic Leadership* is based. The importance of institutional mission is a theme across the chapters, as is a focus on shared leadership. Some chapters address specific requisites; others focus on specific roles, relationships, and types of institutions. We firmly believe that effective academic leaders in the years ahead will need a far wider range of skills, expanded knowledge base, and clearer understanding of the change process than ever before. Higher education is changing and so must every one of us who has leadership responsibilities.

Reference

Bateson, G. (1972). *Steps to an ecology of mind.* New York: Ballantine.

Resources

Collins, J. C., & Porras, J. (1994). *Built to last: Successful habits of visionary companies.* New York: HarperCollins.
Case studies of successes and failures in American business. The insights about effective leadership and the process of stimulating change are as useful in higher education as they are in the for-profit sector. An enjoyable read.

Eckel, P., Hall, B., Green, M., & Mellon, B. (1999). *On change: Reports from the road: Insights on institutional change.* Washington, DC: American Council on Education.
What has worked and what has not. A report on successful strategies for change and leadership at colleges and universities. Practical and to the point.

Kotter, J. P. (1995, March-April). Why transformation efforts fail. *Harvard Business Review, 61,* 59–67.
If you do not have a great deal of time to read the literature on change and need a solid introduction to the steps involved in sweeping change initiatives, get this article—solid and direct.

PART TWO

Leadership

Leaders are learners . . . They find out what they need to know in order to pursue their goals. The leader gives himself or herself entirely to the task when it is necessary. This may be the one attribute that is the most difficult to cultivate. It conveys maturity, respect for your followers, compassion, a fine sense of humor and a love of humanity. The result is that leaders have the capability to motivate people to excel.

—Ray Findlay, "Develop a Passion for Leadership," *The Institute*, Vol. 25, No. 9, September 2001, p. 11

CHAPTER 3

Leadership and Change

DALE W. LICK

Our environment is changing at a dramatic, ever-accelerating pace. Globalization now means that competition is worldwide, aggressive, and touches all of our lives and virtually everything we do. The knowledge, communications, and technology explosions are almost uncontrollable, driving change in every sector of society. Earlier strategic planning efforts are no longer adequate to deal with today's dynamic circumstances. Educational cultures and subcultures are among the most rigid and inhibiting, yet major educational transformations are now the order of the day. With all of this, is it any wonder that visionary leadership and change creation have become so important to the future of education?

This description of our environment helps us appreciate why higher education today must have visionary leadership that will effectively lead it into a progressive future. In this chapter, we discuss the forces driving this changing environment and why change is so critical for higher education. We also look at how our institutions can lead and manage today's dramatic and dynamic events, discovering their vision and reaching their goals for the future. We are at an important turning point. A good place for us to begin is with the recognition of where we are and what is happening to us. Dee Hock, founder of VISA, says, "We are at the very point in time when a four-hundred-year-old is dying and another is struggling to be born, a shift of culture, science, society, and institutions enormously greater than the world has ever experienced" (Waldrop, 1996, p. 75).

Has higher education positioned itself to respond? Unfortunately, an honest answer to this question tells us what we may not want to hear. Dolence and Norris (1995) suggest that although it has changed a great deal, American higher education has not transformed itself. The reason is clear. We have not yet formulated a compelling vision for learning in the information age. Absent this vision, we have not reshaped structures, roles, functions, and services to address those changing needs. Consequently, this is the time to discover and create new, innovative pathways of transformation to the future and act on them.

This chapter discusses a sequence of topics concerning leadership and change that can help you create a map for a pathway to the future for you and your institution of higher education. The chapter begins by asking you to broaden your thinking about your institution so you can see its place in a learning society. It then expands on the concept of the information age, or the age of knowledge, by introducing the six key characteristics of this period, which may more rightly be called the *age of transformation.* The chapter goes on to discuss how we deal with change, its impact on higher education, our failed change efforts, and the number one issue facing higher education today: *change creation.*

The central focus of the chapter is on leadership, how it compares with management, and its role as an instrument in the meaningful transformation of higher education. Learning is seen as a vehicle for change that is fundamental to both effective leadership and the application of the overarching change facilitator: the *universal change principle,* which will be described later in the chapter. The elements and roles of change and academic and institutional cultures are discussed to help you understand the higher education environment and what must be done to accomplish and sustain significant change. One of the most critical paradigm shifts is then illustrated through a detailed comparison of tomorrow's learning paradigm with today's lingering teaching paradigm. The chapter closes with a comprehensive eleven-step change creation process, as well as a reference to several other notable change models.

HIGHER EDUCATION AND THE LEARNING SOCIETY

This section introduces the modern-day *learning society* big-picture approach as the proper framework in which an institution of higher education can create its vision, do its strategic planning, and set its main priorities for the future.

A *learning society* is one in which everyone understands, accepts, and functions on the basis of the following four premises: (1) people, organizations, society, the world, and all of their desires and requirements, are ever-changing; (2) learning can be a creative and transformational vehicle for dealing with the desires and requirements of a dynamically changing environment; (3) learning opportunities and information are readily available to everyone (for example, through schools, colleges, and other societal institutions); and (4) there is a true learning culture, where learning is valued and designed to bring all members of society to the fullest development of their powers.

In a learning society, human capital is essential for strong productivity and competitiveness. Consequently, organizations and entities functioning with a learning society mindset enhance the society's long-term potential, especially as it competes nationally and globally. Higher education institutions will play an especially important role in the development of a genuine learning society. The better our colleges and universities, along with other sectors, fulfill their roles in enhancing society's human capital and in helping to develop a true learning society, the more effective and successful will be the society and its citizens.

Characteristics of the Age of Transformation

The period in which we now find ourselves has often been called the *information age* or the *age of knowledge*. This designation is not wrong but it is incomplete for an adequate understanding of what we must deal with in the future. A more insightful title is the *age of transformation*. Transformation means a fundamental change in condition, nature, or function. The six characteristics of the age of transformation provide a framework for tomorrow's thinking and functioning:

Information Grows

The information available is doubling every five years or less.

Communications Are Global

Modern communications have become worldwide, relatively inexpensive, and almost instantaneous, making the entire world a network, affecting the lives of almost everyone on the planet, and changing how and where we function.

Technology Explodes

The number of new technical inventions is doubling every fifteen years or less, with more and more technology being created and change and innovation occurring at unprecedented rates.

Relationships Are Critical

People remain one of the constants in all that is happening. Relationships are critical to success, including relationships between people and groups; between people and technology devices (Naisbitt, 1982); between outsiders and groups, such as when outsiders try to force their wishes on the operation of an entity; and in new partnerships and alliances, such as when similar or very different entities collaborate.

Paradigms Shift

Major change continues to happen faster and faster, causing dynamic and dramatic paradigm shifts in virtually every sector of society. This transformational change requires a new breed of leader—a paradigm pioneer (Barker, 1992, 1993)—one who, as a paradigm shifts, is able to lead the new paradigm from rough concept to practical application, such as when people move from the teaching paradigm to the learning paradigm. (This is discussed more fully later in the chapter.)

Organizational Cultures Change

The culture of an organization is its collective essence (that is, its fundamental nature and inherent characteristics), and in a sense, its personality. It is how-we-think-about-and-do-things-around-here. From a change perspective, the culture reflects the interrelationship of shared assumptions, beliefs and values, and behaviors that are acquired over time by its members (Conner, 1993). Significant problems in times of rapid change relate to the rigidity of the institutional culture, "culture paralysis" (being locked into the status quo), and difficulties in modifying the culture to create a new one (that is, developing new assumptions, beliefs and values, and behaviors), allow transformations, and sustain them. Culture change is very difficult. However, most significant change will not be successful and sustained in an institution unless there is at least some appropriate cultural change.

Change Creation: The Main Issue for Higher Education

The difference between the kind of change we experienced yesterday and that of today is intensity: speed, magnitude, and momentum. The nature of our times and the technology explosion are driving change virtually everywhere. Change expert Daryl Conner (1993) puts it well: "Never before has so much changed so fast and with such dramatic implications for the entire world" (p. 3). Change may be called a *silent juggernaut*—a persistent, irresistible force. It permeates everything, with no respect for persons, professions, or organizations, for faculty, academics, parents, communities, or higher education. A recent statement by the American Association of University Professors provides an overview for those of us in higher education ("AAUP Special Report," 1999): "The world of higher education is in the midst of accelerating and sometimes turbulent change. New modes of communication are profoundly affecting the work of faculty members: they are reshaping the processes of teaching and learning, redefining the role and authority of faculty members in organizing and overseeing the curriculum, and altering the bases for evaluating student—and faculty—performance. The implications of this change extend [to] major facets of higher education, deeply influencing its organization, governance, and finances" (p. 41). How have we in higher education responded to this dynamic, ubiquitous change? We and our institutions typically have chosen, consciously or by default, to resist, ignore, or sidestep the realities and impact of change, all potentially self-defeating responses. Instead, we must join change, embrace it as a partner, and use it creatively for the advancement of our goals, institutions, and society.

Thus, growing societal expectations and pressures are literally forcing a revolution in colleges and universities. As the revolution gains momentum, it will raise basic questions of survival. Higher education's best hope for success is to re-create itself appropriately for the new, transformed environment. Accordingly, the number one issue facing higher education today is this: effectively initiating, implementing, and managing intentional, meaningful, planned change. In other words, the urgent need is for *change creation.*

Change creation (Lick & Kaufman, 2000) is the process by which an institution and its people accept and welcome change as a vital component in achieving future success, define the future they want to design and deliver, develop and implement a comprehensive transition plan to create the designed future, and continuously improve and move ever closer to the desired future.

Change creation is responsive. As the world around colleges and universities changes in dynamic ways, higher education must become more adaptable and transform itself accordingly in order to serve effectively and acceptably in the future. Higher education and its people must become more effective leaders and practitioners of change creation. This means that they must take genuine responsibility for leading change, effectively define and plan for the desired change, comprehensively prepare the organization for the planned change, and develop and implement a change approach that transforms people, processes, and circumstances from existing paradigms to the new, desired, and required ones (Lick & Kaufman, 2000). The process for change creation is discussed in a later section of this chapter.

Why Change Efforts Fail

Why do at least two-thirds of our significant change efforts fail? Usually, change fails because of leaders' actions—or lack of them—as follows (Lick & Kaufman, 2000; Kaufman & Lick, 2000; Conner, 1993):

- Leaders have not fundamentally reframed their own thinking and that of their institution relative to major change. Effective leaders reframe their own thinking and that of those whom they guide, enabling them to see that transformational changes are imperative and achievable.
- Leaders have implemented a strategic planning approach that is incomplete and inadequate for the massive, holistic, systemic change required.
- Leaders have not provided or implemented a detailed, structured, disciplined transition plan for identifying and implementing the change, a plan that would transform people, processes, and most importantly, the culture from the old paradigms to the new ones.

Leadership Versus Management

Leadership and management in higher education are quite different but complementary functions, and both are critical. The key is to have the proper balance between effective management and visionary leadership. Unfortunately, in higher education we often have an imbalance, with too much emphasis on management and not enough on transforming leadership. In simple terms, management is about "doing things right"— that is, working in a given paradigm to make things better. In contrast, leadership is about "doing the right thing"—that is, shifting a paradigm from "what is" to "what should be." As Stephen Covey (1990) writes: "The leader is the one who climbs the tallest tree, surveys the situation, and yells, 'Wrong jungle!' But how do busy, efficient faculty, administrators, and staff often respond? 'Shut up! We're making progress!'" Kotter (1998), in the *Harvard Business Review on Leadership,* gives us an excellent overview of leadership and management. Management deals with *coping with complexity;* leadership deals with *coping with change:*

Management	*Leadership*
Planning and budgeting	Setting a direction
Organizing and staffing	Aligning people
Controlling and problem solving	Motivating and inspiring

Kouzes and Posner (1995) refine these concepts further in *The Leadership Challenge:* "The leadership challenge is about how leaders get extraordinary things done in organizations. The domain of leaders is the future. The most significant contributions leaders make are not to today's bottom line but to the long-term development of people and institutions who adapt, prosper, and grow" (pp. 37–38). Consequently, as higher educational leaders, we must do three important things: accept change as a vital partner and resource and intentionally spend a significant portion of our time and effort on understanding and coping with transformational change and the future; continually keep questioning the answers, especially those of our culture and subcultures, in search of fundamental changes that will alter the nature, productivity, and effectiveness of important aspects of our institution (for example, move from the teaching to the learning paradigm described later); and create a shared and inspiring vision that provides direction, motivation, and commitment of others to our institution's desired long-range future. In change efforts, vision is the essential direction-setter, people-aligner, and emotion-grabber! And for those of us in higher education who are truly committed to the long-term transformation of our colleges and universities, the *Harvard Business Review on Leadership* (Kotter, 1998) describes the ultimate act of leadership: institutionalizing a leadership-centered culture.

Transformational Learning

Learning is fundamental to effective leadership. The learning that this chapter focuses on may be called *capacity* or *action learning,* as follows:

- Learning *(verb):* gaining capacity (willingness and ability) for effective action
- Learning *(noun):* capacity (willingness and ability) for effective action

Effective action is to be interpreted in relation to the totality of change being considered, and *ability* would include information, knowledge, skill, experience, and understanding, as well as such characteristics as nuances and qualities that would enhance effective action. Also, *capacity* in this discussion means both willingness and ability, for if either is missing, the capacity is not there.

This kind of learning involves a "fundamental shift or movement of the mind," as learning organization expert Peter Senge (1990) put it. "Through learning we re-create ourselves. Through learning we become able to do something we never were able to do before. Through learning we perceive the world and our relationship to it differently. Through learning we extend our capacity to create, to be part of the generative process of life. There is within each of us a deep hunger for this type of learning" (pp. 13–14). This kind of learning is essential to human transformation and effective leadership.

The Universal Change Principle and Examples

Appropriate learning helps people understand change and more effectively deal with their fears and anxiety about it. Such learning can give people a sense of control over change and a greater ability to anticipate change, increasing their feelings of comfort and security and lessening their resistance (Conner, 1993). The seemingly simple but overarching principle for dealing with change, the *universal change principle,* is this: learning must precede change.

Here is an illustration. Instead of just buying computers for faculty members who are participating in a change project, a university responded to their technology concerns with a summer training program on how, when, and why to use computers and computer support. The additional learning paid off; in the fall semester, faculty became positively involved, things were running efficiently, and learner performance had improved.

Putting this principle to use does not guarantee that resistance to change will be eliminated or that a desired change will be accomplished, but its proper application does significantly improve a change effort's chances for success. People will react more favorably to change and assist with it if you take the time to provide them with a basis of learning and understanding about the change project.

Large higher education initiatives often require significant learning, such as several well-planned, multidimensional, multilevel iterations of appropriate learning across many sectors and over a substantial time period. As a practical matter, it is usually beneficial to develop, in advance of the announcement of the change initiative, a plan based on the universal change principle that details a series of appropriate and necessary learning dimensions, opportunities, and repeated applications required to implement the desired change.

Here is another illustration. Suppose the chair of the English department wants her faculty to implement a new technology-driven approach to composition instruction. If the chair simply announced that the faculty would be using this new approach the next semester, most of the faculty would probably feel uncomfortable with the proposed change and resist rather than help facilitate the process. If, in contrast, she employed the universal change principle, she would, before making any announcement, ask the question: "What learning must take place before this change effort can be successfully implemented?" For instance, discussions with the faculty about the new instructional approach might cover why the new approach is critical to improving student learning; what the implications are for students, faculty, and the department; when and how the approach will be implemented; and what will be the support and rewards for effectively implementing it. The universal change principle will probably be your most effective change tool, and it is applicable, directly or indirectly, to essentially all change initiatives.

Roles in the Change Process

Understanding the four roles in the change process—*change sponsorship, change agent, change target,* and *change advocate*—assists with the meaningful use of the dynamics of change and in building required levels of commitment to bring about and sustain major change. These roles are as follows (Conner, 1993):

- A *change sponsor* is a person or group with the authority to legitimate a change, such as a system or institutional board; a system chancellor; an institutional president; a dean, division director, department chair, or a combination of these individuals; the faculty senate; or the faculty itself.
- A *change agent* is a person or group responsible for implementing the desired change, such as institutional administrators, administrative and faculty groups, and faculty members.
- A *change target* is an individual or group that must change as a result of the change effort, such as administrators, faculty members, and students.
- A *change advocate* is a person or group supporting a change but with no authority to sanction the change effort, such as administrators, faculty members, students, and noninstitutional people, such as parents or alumni.

Depending on the situation, an individual might perform more than one of these roles at different times in the change effort.

Here is an illustration. If a university were to consider a new initiative to expand technology applications, the board and president who authorized the initiative might be the initial sponsors for this change effort; the provost, deans, and department chairs who are responsible for implementing the initiative might be the change agents; and the faculty and students who actually have to change to apply the technology might be the targets. Advocates might include other individuals and groups who encourage the initiative but have no authority to sanction it, such as business and industry representatives, alumni, and parents.

Initial (beginning) and sustaining (continuing) sponsorship is particularly critical to the implementation and completion of major change. For change efforts to be successful, sponsors must demonstrate strong commitment and support. In other words, if strong, relevant sponsorship is not available or cannot be obtained for a change project, the effort should not be undertaken. The difference between success and failure in higher education change initiatives often comes down to the effectiveness of the sponsorship. Furthermore, when the initiating sponsor and the target have a substantial difference in commitment to a change effort, the change is likely to fail. To overcome this problem, the initiating sponsor must generate the support of sustaining sponsors down the hierarchy in the organization to the one who has the target in his or her arena of influence. In particular, sustaining sponsors must set an agenda of importance and consequences down the chain of command to the target so that intermediate sustaining sponsors and the target will commit to the change effort. This process is called *cascading sponsorship*.

Here is an illustration. In a university, the president usually sets the agenda of importance and provides the appropriate transitional learning for the provost, the provost provides it for the deans, the deans provide it for department chairs, and the chairs provide it for the faculty.

ACADEMIC AND INSTITUTIONAL CULTURES

Higher education and its institutions have cultures that have evolved over generations and provide stability and powerfully protect the status quo. These cultures are among the strongest and most rigid in our society. Thus, for a large change effort to be successful and sustainable in higher education, we must understand academic and disciplinary cultures and how to modify them accordingly. As we have already discussed, an institution's culture is its collective essence, its fundamental nature and inherent characteristics, a common bond that holds together its various aspects and creates its central features, structures, and approaches. It is a powerful force that is always present, setting and rewarding given values and establishing ground rules for what people assume to be right and wrong, true and false, appropriate and inappropriate—that is, for how they think and behave.

Culture reflects the interrelationship of shared assumptions, beliefs, and behaviors that are acquired over time by members of the institution (Conner, 1993). *Assumptions* are usually unconscious and unquestioned perceptions concerning what is important and how people and processes function in the institution. For example, Guskin notes that faculty members assume that lecturing to students provides a good form of learning, whereas educational research indicates that it is one of the least effective strategies for student learning (Barr & Tagg, 1995). *Beliefs* are values and expectations that people hold to be true about themselves, others, and their profession, and institution (for example, what is right or wrong, good or bad, or relevant or irrelevant in their institution and its operation). *Behaviors* are ways people conduct themselves on a day-to-day basis (how they teach, evaluate students, introduce technology, and so on).

Cultural change is extremely difficult to accomplish in higher education, but required. An institution of higher education must alter some of its cultural building blocks—its assumptions, beliefs, and behaviors—for meaningful change to occur. Simply put, for colleges and universities to be fully effective in tomorrow's world, they must learn how to create new cultures—cultural shifts that best suit their needs and desires.

For example, distance learning was ignored as a fad and therefore seen as inconsequential for many years even though such initiatives as the British Open University were achieving quiet acceptance. Today, distance learning is competing for larger numbers of learners by shifting the mindsets (assumptions and beliefs) and behaviors of administrators, faculty, students, and employers from focusing on traditional on-campus, teacher-oriented experiences to off-campus, learner-oriented opportunities. Conner (1993) provides a practical principle for understanding and dealing with the juxtaposition of culture and change: whenever a discrepancy exists between the current culture and the objectives of a change effort, all other things being equal, the culture always wins. So when facing an organizational culture that may hinder a desired change effort, your options are to modify the change effort to be more in line with the existing culture; modify the assumptions, beliefs, or behaviors of the current culture to be more supportive of the change effort; or prepare for the change effort to fail.

THE LEARNING PARADIGM

Among the most important paradigm shifts in higher education today requiring significant culture shifts are continuous professional development (for administrators, faculty and staff), the shift from the teaching paradigm to the learning paradigm (see the following paragraphs), megalevel strategic planning (see Kaufman & Lick, 2000), transformational leadership (see Northhouse, 1997; Conner, 1998), change creation (see Lick & Kaufman, 2000–01), learning organizations (see Garratt, 1987; Senge, 1990), and the learning society (see Hutchins, 1968; National Association of State Universities and Land-Grant Colleges, 2000).

The importance of leadership and change initiatives in higher education can be seen from an exploration of one of the central paradigm shifts, the *learning paradigm*. Any discussion of the learning paradigm must include a shift in our mindset to a deeper focus on learning. As Ted Marchese (1997) noted: "Indeed, the absence of ideas about learning itself is the hollow core of today's efforts to improve teaching, curricula, assessment, and resource allocation. A clearer focus on learning would bring higher education the sense of purpose and alignment it needs for a different order of outcome" (p. 4). Two of the most insightful discussions on the learning paradigm in today's literature can be found in *Transforming Higher Education* (Dolence & Norris, 1995) and the article in *Change* (Barr & Tagg, 1995) titled "From Teaching to Learning."

Dolence and Norris discuss the learner-driven educational processes. The *teaching franchise* will be joined by an emerging *learning franchise.* Both are important in the information age. What do we mean by the teaching franchise? It is the current system by which teaching and the awarding of course credits and degrees are bundled together seamlessly in accredited institutions of higher education. In contrast, the learning franchise provides access to powerful learning systems, information, knowledge bases, scholarly exchange networks, and other mechanisms for delivery of learning.

Barr and Tagg add importantly to this discussion, emphasizing the necessary mindset shift from teaching, a means, to learning, an end. A paradigm shift is occurring in American higher education. Briefly, the paradigm that has governed is that a college is an institution *to provide instruction.* Subtly but profoundly, we are shifting to a new paradigm: a college is an institution *to produce learning.* This changes everything. Now, however, we are beginning to recognize that our dominant paradigm mistakes a means for an end. It takes the means or method—called *instruction* or *teaching*—and makes it the college's end or purpose. To say that the purpose of colleges is to provide instruction is like saying that the business of General Motors is to operate assembly lines or that the purpose of medical care is to fill hospital beds. We now see that our mission is not instruction but rather to produce *learning* with every student by whatever means work best. Author and colleague Roger Kaufman summarizes the learning paradigm as follows: learners will select, with learning facilitators, the objectives they want to commit to and master, based on what they want to accomplish in school and life, and will interact with valid and useful learning systems and materials at times and places convenient to them to achieve competence. A clear comparison of the teaching and learning paradigms is provided in Exhibit 3.1.

EXHIBIT 3.1. **The Teaching Versus the Learning Paradigm.**

Teaching Paradigm	*Learning Paradigm*
Faculty focus	Student focus
Faculty as teacher	Faculty as synthesizer, navigator, coordinator of learning
Talking head, sage on stage	Multiple delivery systems
Faculty as conveyor of information	Information from many sources (the Internet, electronic libraries, and so on)
Input orientation (resources and library, classrooms, faculty)	Output orientation (learning and institutional effectiveness)
Classroom- or site-based	Not necessarily classroom- or site-based
Group or class delivery	Individualized delivery and collaborative learning with group communications
Massive infrastructure	Distributed infrastructure
Campus-based learning	Ready learning (appropriate learning, anytime, anyplace)
Rigidity	Flexibility
Mostly a continuation of the past	Innovative, creative
Transactional approach (fixes)	Transformational approach and processes (shifts); technology push and learning vision pull (see Dolence & Norris, 1995)

Source: Adapted from Lick, 1999, p. 77.

What this comparison suggests about teaching and learning is that the question is *not* "What must we do to be effective teachers?" but rather, "What must we do to promote effective learning?" Frankly, each of us must change our whole frame of reference and mindset from teaching to learning.

THE CHANGE CREATION PROCESS

Change creation, as defined earlier, is the primary challenge for higher education. The process of change creation is extensive, complex, and multifaceted. A recommended *change creation process*—a change model—is outlined in the following paragraphs (for additional details see Lick & Kaufman, 2000; for related model sources, see ODR, 1993; Addison & Lloyd, 1999; Bridges, 1991; Norris & Morrison, 1997).

Lick-Kaufman Change Creation Process

The Lick-Kaufman process includes eleven steps.

Step 1: Prepare Your Leadership Team for Planning and Change

In other words, prepare your leaders for defining the world and the organization you would create for tomorrow and for change. Before proceeding, leaders (a broadly representative leadership-sponsoring team that includes faculty and staff) must reasonably understand the substance, complexities, and ramifications of the planning and change efforts.

Step 2: Prepare Your Institution for Major Planning

Your leadership team is responsible for the planning effort (which represents potential change to others), so you must provide your stakeholders with sufficient learning for them to gain a sense of the anticipated planning effort, its long-term importance to the organization, and its implications to them and to others.

Step 3: Complete Megalevel Strategic Planning

Megalevel planning sees society as the primary client and beneficiary of everything an organization uses, does, produces, and delivers. It provides an ideal vision, a mission, and objectives, and the framework and direction for the balance of the change creation effort. (See Kaufman & Lick, 2000; Kaufman, 1998, 2000, for more on this.)

Step 4: Write Down a Description of Your Desired Change Project

It is important that your project be described in sufficient detail and in writing so that all stakeholders have the same understanding of the project, its parameters, and its expectations. Multiple change efforts require coordination.

Step 5: Clarify Scope and Commitment

Clarify the scope of your change project and the level of commitment necessary for its success. Before you announce a major change project, your leadership team must understand the scope and basic commitments necessary for its success, including project expectations, transition process, markers for success, sponsorship commitment, consistency with the culture, past history, and other restraints and barriers.

Step 6: Communicate

Communicate about your change project and its importance and implications to your stakeholders (trustees, administrators, faculty, staff, students, alumni, parents, and key community leaders). Communications must be well planned and executed; the process should identify the stakeholder groups, analyze their initial learning requirements, and execute a communication plan for each group.

Step 7: Diagnose

Diagnose your institution's present status and capacity to accomplish the change goals. If you reduce the risks and meaningfully use the institution's existing capacity, it will significantly increase the probability of successful change. Critical elements include the organization's change history, its readiness for change, change assimilation resources, change sponsorship strength, cultural issues, change agents' preparation, and targets' resistance and commitment.

Step 8: Create a Transition Plan

Create a detailed transition plan for the implementation and long-term success of your change project. This plan must not only lead to the transition of processes and circumstances from the old paradigm to the new but must, most importantly, effectively provide for the transition of a critical mass of the people from the old to the desired paradigm. The universal change principle (that is, learning must precede change) becomes the key tool for the design of the plan. In a comprehensive manner, each facet (structure, process, people, and culture) of the organization involved must be identified and a specific subplan developed for it. For each facet identified, this question must be asked: "What learning (that is, capacity for effective action) must be provided and to whom?"

Step 9: Execute, Monitor, and Refine the Transition Plan

For a major change project, the transition plan will be a comprehensive approach to change that contains a multilevel, multidimensional, iterative process for helping people, processes, and circumstances make the transition from the old paradigm to the new. The implementation (change agent) team, together with the leadership team, will execute the plan, monitor its processes and developments, and coordinate its unfolding to project completion.

Step 10: Assess and Report

Assess and report regularly the progress and status of your change project to stakeholders, seek their input, and celebrate success milestones. Because people have a reasonable comfort level with change when they feel a sense of control or at least can anticipate what is going to happen, it is critical that the progress and status of the unfolding change process be regularly and effectively communicated to stakeholders and that they be given opportunity for additional input.

Step 11: Evaluate

Evaluate the final results of your change project—what worked and what did not work. Every change project should have a final evaluation of its results so that they are known and so that the lessons learned may be appropriately applied in the future as you prepare for your institution's next major change effort.

Other Change Models

In addition to the preceding comprehensive change model there are many other models worth serious consideration. The book *Surviving Change: A Survey of Educational*

Change Models (Ellsworth, 2000; reviewed in Lick, 2000) discusses seven change models and approaches. There are discussions of diffusion of innovation (Rogers, 1995), conditions of change (Ely, 1990), educational change (Fullan & Stiegelbauer, 1991), a change agent's guide (Havelock & Zlotolow, 1995), concerns-based adoption (Hall, Wallace, & Dorsett, 1973), strategies for planned change (Zaltman & Duncan, 1977), and systemic change (Reigeluth & Garfinkle, 1994). Two other change models are especially notable.

Bolman and Deal Model

This model uses a comprehensive multiframe approach that emphasizes the four dimensions of organizational change: human resources, structural, political, and symbolic (Bolman & Deal, 1997).

Kotter Model

This model encompasses an eight-stage process for creating major change, including establishing a sense of urgency, creating the guiding coalition, developing a vision and strategy, communicating the change vision, empowering broad-based action, generating short-term wins, consolidating gains and producing more change, and anchoring new approaches in the culture (Kotter, 1996).

CONCLUSION

The mindset in higher education today remains at the level of incremental change. But required for the future is a new kind of leadership, transformational leadership, and transforming change—change creation. This chapter provided a set of concepts and approaches for higher education that can help us understand and meet these requirements. It introduced the big-picture mindset for a learning society, characterized our time as the age of transformation, described the change environment and its impact on our institutions, showed why large change efforts fail, and discussed change creation as the number one issue facing higher education for the future.

The chapter focused on leadership—transforming leadership—and highlighted learning as the foundation for leadership and change, the powerful universal change principle, the key roles and elements of change, and the critical academic and institutional cultures of higher education. The learning paradigm was illustrated and compared with the teaching paradigm. Finally, an eleven-step change creation process was outlined, and reference was made to several other commonly used change models.

For many, the future is exciting but seems daunting. It offers us new, expanding opportunities but requires a new mindset and new leadership. As we work and struggle to reach that new and exciting future, we owe it to ourselves to realize that we have the ability to do all that is necessary if we are willing. Biologist and philosopher Norman Cousins (1981) reminds us of our human potential and capacity: "The human species is unique because it alone can create, recognize, and exercise options. This means that it can do things for the first time. We can reasonably argue, therefore, that human beings are equal to their needs, that a problem can be solved if it can be perceived, that progress is what is left after the seemingly impossible has been retired, and that the crisis today in human affairs is represented not by the absence of human capacity, but by the failure to recognize that the capacity exists" (p. 8).

References

AAUP. (1999, May–June). Distance education and intellectual property issues. *Academe,* pp. 41–45. [www.aaup.org/govrel/distlern/DistncED.htm].

Addison, R., & Lloyd, C. (1999). Implementation: The glue of organizational change. *Professional Improvement, 39*(6), 8–11.

Barker, J. A. (1992). *Future edge: Discovering the new paradigms of success.* New York: Morrow.

Barker, J. A. (1993). Paradigm pioneers. *Discovering the future series* [Videotape]. Burnsville, MN: ChartHouse International Learning Corporation.

Barr, R., & Tagg, J. (1995, November-December). From teaching to learning: A new paradigm for higher education. *Change,* pp. 13–25.

Bolman, L., & Deal, T. (1997). *Reframing organizations: Artistry, choice, and leadership* (2nd ed.). San Francisco: Jossey-Bass.

Bridges, W. (1991). *Managing transitions: Making the most of change.* Reading, MA: Addison-Wesley.

Conner, D. (1993). *Managing at the speed of change.* New York: Villard Books.

Conner, D. (1998). *Leading at the edge of chaos: How to create the nimble organization.* New York: Wiley.

Cousins, N. (1981). *Human options.* New York: Norton.

Covey, S. (1990). *The seven habits of highly effective people.* New York: Simon & Schuster.

Dolence, M., & Norris, D. (1995). *Transforming higher education.* Ann Arbor, MI: Society for College and University Planning

Ellsworth, J. (2000). *Surviving change: A survey of educational change models.* Syracuse, NY: Syracuse University.

Ely, D. (1990). Conditions that facilitate the implementation of educational technology innovations. *Journal of Research on Computing in Education, 23*(2), 298–305.

Fullan, M., & Stiegelbauer, S. (1991). *The new meaning of educational change.* New York: Teachers College Press.

Garratt, B. (1987). *The learning organization.* New York: HarperCollins.

Hall, G., Wallace, R., & Dorsett, W. (1973). *A developmental conception of the adoption process within educational institutions* (Report No. 3006). Austin: University of Texas, Research and Development Center for Teacher Education.

Havelock, R., & Zlotolow, S. (1995). *The change agent's guide* (2nd ed.). Englewood Cliffs, NJ: Educational Technology Publications.

Hutchins, R. (1968). *The learning society.* New York: Praeger.

Kaufman, R. (1998). *Strategic thinking: A guide to identifying and solving problems* (rev. ed.). Arlington, VA, & Washington, DC: American Society for Training and Development and International Society for Performance Improvement.

Kaufman, R. (2000). *Mega planning: Practical tools for organizational success.* Thousand Oaks, CA: Sage.

Kaufman, R., & Lick, D. (2000). Megalevel strategic planning: Beyond conventional wisdom. In J. Boettcher, M. Doyle, & R. Jensen (Eds.), *Technology-driven planning: Principles to practice* (Chapter One). Ann Arbor, MI: Society for College and University Planning.

Kotter, J. (1996). *Leading change.* Boston: Harvard Business School Press.

Kotter, J. (1998). *Harvard Business Review on leadership.* Boston: Harvard Business School Press.

Kouzes, J., & Posner, B. (1995). *The leadership challenge: How to keep getting extraordinary things done in organizations.* San Francisco: Jossey-Bass.

Lick, D. (1999, Fall). Transforming higher education: A new vision, learning paradigm, and change management. *International Journal of Innovative Higher Education, 12,* 75–78.

Lick, D. (2000, November). A road map to the literature of change. *Administrator,* p. 8.

Lick, D., & Kaufman, R. (2000). Change creation: The rest of the planning story. In J. Boettcher, M. Doyle, & R. Jensen (Eds.), *Technology-driven planning: Principles to practice* (Chapter Two). Ann Arbor, MI: Society for College and University Planning.

Lick, D., & Kaufman, R. (2000–01, Winter). Change creation: The rest of the planning story. *Planning for Higher Education, 29*(2), 24–36.

Marchese, T. (1997, March-April). Editorial. *Change,* p. 4.

Naisbitt, J. (1982). *Megatrends: Ten new directions transforming our lives.* New York: Warner Books.

National Association of State Universities and Land-Grant Colleges. (2000). *Returning to our roots: A learning society* (Fourth Kellogg Commission Report). Washington, DC: National Association of State Universities and Land-Grant Colleges.

Norris, D., & Morrison, J. (1997). *Mobilizing for transformation: How campuses are preparing for the knowledge age.* San Francisco: Jossey-Bass.

Northhouse, R. (1997). *Leadership: Theory and practice.* Thousand Oaks, CA: Sage.

ODR. (1993). *Comprehensive applications of implementation architecture.* Atlanta: ODR.

Reigeluth, C., & Garfinkle, R. (Eds.). (1994). *Systemic change in education.* Englewood Cliffs, NJ: Educational Technology Publications.

Rogers, E. (1995). *Diffusion of innovations* (4th ed.). New York: Free Press.

Senge, P. (1990). *The fifth discipline: The art and practice of the learning organization.* New York: Doubleday.

Waldrop, M. (1996, October-November). The trillion-dollar vision of Dee Hock. *Fast Company,* *5,* 75–81. [www.fastcompany.com/learning].

Zaltman, G., & Duncan, R. (1977). *Strategies for planned change.* New York: Wiley.

Resources

Barker, J. A. (1993). Paradigm pioneers. *Discovering the future series* [Videotape]. Burnsville, MN: ChartHouse International Learning Corporation.
This Joel Barker video on paradigm pioneers and transforming leadership is one of the best educational and leadership videos available. Leaders at every level should see it.

Barr, R., & Tagg, J. (1995, November-December). From teaching to learning: A new paradigm for higher education. *Change,* pp. 13–25.
This is the most helpful piece of literature on teaching and learning paradigms and implementing the latter. This article in *Change* is the magazine's most referenced ever.

Conner, D. (1993). *Managing at the speed of change.* New York: Villard.
This is the best book on change available today. It gives excellent coverage of the fundamentals of change (for example, nature, process, and roles of change) and includes key discussions of synergy, cultures, and resilience.

Conner, D. (1998). *Leading at the edge of chaos: How to create the nimble organization.* New York: Wiley.
This award-winning book on change and organizations includes leading edge and in-depth discussions of leadership and leadership styles.

Dolence, M., & Norris, D. (1995). *Transforming higher education.* Ann Arbor, MI: Society for College and University Planning.
This is one of the most insightful books available for those seeking to understand the transformation of higher education and what is required to accomplish it.

Ely, D. (1990). Conditions that facilitate the implementation of educational technology innovations. *Journal of Research on Computing in Education, 23*(2), 298–305.
The eight-condition change model discussed in this article is effective, validated, and easy to use. It provides a powerful and basic understanding of change and the conditions for change.

Hutchins, R. (1968). *The learning society.* New York: Praeger.
Over the years this has remained the signal book on the learning society. Its insights into the learning society provide the best basic foundation on the subject, going well beyond in creativeness and meaningfulness what higher education is actually doing (but should be doing!).

Kaufman, R., & Lick, D. (2000). Megalevel strategic planning: Beyond conventional wisdom. In J. Boettcher, M. Doyle, & R. Jensen (Eds.), *Technology-driven planning: Principles to practice* (Chapter One). Ann Arbor, MI: Society for College and University Planning.

Chapter One of this book discusses the new approach to strategic planning in higher education that will be required for the future. It goes beyond the traditional approaches to strategic planning that have been used in higher education over the last several decades.

Kouzes, J., & Posner, B. (1995). *The leadership challenge: How to keep getting extraordinary things done in organizations.* San Francisco: Jossey-Bass.
This book, which has become a classic, continues to be one of the best leadership books available. It is a book that every leader should have and appreciate.

Lick, D., & Kaufman, R. (2000). Change creation: The rest of the planning story. In J. Boettcher, M. Doyle, & R. Jensen (Eds.), *Technology-driven planning: Principles to practice* (Chapter Two). Ann Arbor, MI: Society for the College and University Planning.
Chapter Two introduces and develops the important new concept of change creation. It also discusses and provides the step-by-step process of the most comprehensive change model in the literature today.

Northhouse, R. (1997). *Leadership: Theory and practice.* Thousand Oaks, CA: Sage.
This is one of the better leadership books available. It provides an excellent overview of leadership theory, including an impressive discussion of transformational leadership.

Senge, P. (1990). *The fifth discipline: The art and practice of the learning organization.* New York: Doubleday.
This now-classic book introduced learning organizations to this country. (Bob Garratt did it a decade earlier in the United Kingdom.) It is a relatively difficult book to read, but is filled with wonderful material on learning, systems, mental models, personal mastery, shared vision, and team learning. See also the companion *Fifth Discipline Fieldbook* by P. Senge, A. Kleiner, C. Roberts, R. Ross, and B. Smith (New York: Doubleday, 1994) for a wealth of illustrations and valuable ideas about learning organizations.

CHAPTER 4

Mission and Vision Statements

An Essential First Step

WILLIAM G. TIERNEY

A mission statement is the double-edged sword of academic life: we cannot do without it, but we usually cannot do much with it, either. Far too often we waste precious time and resources debating a mission statement's words and phrases that ultimately have no practical implications for the health of our institutions. A new president arrives and decides that as one of her first acts she will create a committee to redraft a mission and vision statement for the university. Because the topic is universal, the committee is a Noah's ark of administrators, faculty, staff, students, board members, and local citizens. They spend the better part of a year drafting a twenty-page document that begins, "Wavering State University is committed to academic excellence and the ability of each student to pursue his or her dreams."

During that year, there is considerable discussion about whether to use the word "dreams" in the vision statement. A member of the board of trustees and a professor from business argue that "dreams" has no place in the mission of Wavering State; two professors from humanities, the assistant vice president for student affairs, and the president of the student government finally wear down the committee by filibuster, and the word is accepted. As a compromise, the English professor relents about her concern over the use of the awkward but necessary construction—"his or her." And so it goes. The president is simply relieved when the committee finally produces the mission statement, and gratefully accepts it, disseminates it, and forgets about it.

Ultimately, of course, such discussions amount to little more than dreary academic arguments about nothing. The meetings consume time, and as with my hypothetical Wavering State, they ultimately reach their goal—a mission statement is drafted—but no sooner is the statement disseminated to everyone on campus than everyone moves on to the humdrum tasks of campus life.

Institutional leaders who claim that they are going to redefine the university's mission do so at their own risk. But those who do not look at the mission also do so at their peril. Productive staff and faculty will run from a committee assignment where the discussion revolves around what the university's vision should be. I entirely understand the reluctance to begin a conversation that is filled with pitfalls and seems to lead nowhere. The temptation will always be to forget the mission. Just start planning the plan! Get in there and create time lines, objectives, and PERT charts. Make decisions! Start doing!

And yet there is that nagging voice in the back of our heads that reminds us that somewhere in the Bible the prophets wrote that without a vision the people will perish. In the here and now, we recognize that there are so many choices to be made we do not know how to make them if we do not have some overarching focus. Should not all major academic decisions flow from, and relate to, the institution's mission and vision? If there is not some unifying idea that binds us together, then do we not run the risk of implementing fads rather than lasting changes? Do not newfangled words like "branding" relate to product definition, which is just another way of saying that a mission is needed? Do not the most successful businesses actually have a mission and vision statement?

Mission and vision statements are important first steps on the road to creating improved, more responsive organizations for the twenty-first century. Creating and sustaining change involves an overarching framework for principles and practices. A mission statement is the blueprint that will energize faculty, staff, and external constituents and enable us to get started and remain on track. Such a statement helps establish priorities for programs, budgeting, reward structures, and a host of institutional activities. So maybe we should think about a mission statement after all. But how? In what follows, I offer five main points:

- Define the central themes of your institution.
- Create a mission and vision statement that specifically refers to the curriculum, to key constituencies, and to the external environment.
- Develop core activities that have explicit links to the mission and vision statement.
- Communicate the mission repeatedly.
- Rethink and revisit the mission from time to time.

DEFINING WHAT MATTERS: MISSION AND VISION

The best examples of mission statements are from colleges and universities that Burton Clark (1980) called *distinctive*. A mission statement helps people make sense of the institution, where it has been, and where it wants to go. A good mission statement not only helps set the direction for where the institution wants to go but also helps define where it will not go. At a time when we all suffer from information overload and the choices we face seem endless, a mission statement helps define the parameters of possibility.

A mission is not simply formulaic goals and objectives. The first route to failure is to let a group quarrel over the definition of a mission. *Is a mission a goal? How does mission differ from vision? Is a core value part of the mission or the vision?* Although such discussions might be useful in a logic class, they do little to help the institution define what it wants to be and where it wants to go. As institutional leaders, we are well advised to set the definitional parameters of what we mean by mission and vision before we call a committee together.

- *Rule no. 1:* A mission statement contains two parts. The vision is a preamble to a mission statement. It is short and to the point. It speaks in generalities about the hopes and aspirations for the institution. The mission sets the context for goal setting. It is less broad, a bit longer, and paints a picture of how the hopes and aspirations of the institution will be put into place.

I am suggesting that we need to expand what a mission and vision statement is so that people do not just see it as a formulaic list of goals and objectives. *A mission and vision statement should inspire.* The mission hooks up the history of the organization with its present and moves the institution into the future. It is a rallying point and helps insiders and outsiders see how your college or university is different from the rest.

Consider two presidents who talk about their mission in the following manner:

President no. 1 says, "We are for educational excellence so that you can be all you can be. We have a new library and gym, the student dorms have been wired for the Internet, and service learning is a component of our curriculum. Our mission is to prepare you for the twenty-first century."

President no. 2 says, "Our mission is to create leaders. We believe in the concept of servant leadership and in the concepts of cooperation and respect for diversity. Every student, faculty, and staff member is expected to perform community service in town and at the college. All of our classes are co-taught and diversity across the curriculum is a requirement. A team project is required in most coursework, and a senior thesis is an interactive project with a student, a community member, a professor, and younger students."

Some of us may reject president no. 2's definition of leadership or the activities of the institution, but we at least have a clear picture of what is a core value of the institution. The college of president no. 1 does not stake out any special territory. It is committed to a vague notion of excellence and preparation for the new century. Big deal.

The second example helps people understand how the college is unique. It sets itself off from the rest by outlining core values. As a leader, you continually need to ask, "What is unique about my institution?" The mission serves as a reference point for change so that those who work in the organization are able to see how their work relates to the work of the institution. *To avoid talking about the mission or to overlook it as irrelevant and a waste of time denies faculty, staff, and administrators a sense of institutional meaning.*

CREATING THE MISSION STATEMENT

Do not think of the mission statement as a marketing document. (For simplicity sake, I will often refer here to the vision and mission statement simply as the mission statement.) Think of it as an internally generated document that expresses to the world what the institution's hopes and dreams are (Tierney, 1999). Statements such as, "We intend to be the best public state university in the region," or "We are committed to providing a curriculum that gets good jobs for our graduates" are developed for external audiences, rather than internal ones. *Do not create a mission statement with an eye toward what others will say about you; create a mission statement about what the institution's participants want to say about themselves.* As Peter Block comments, "The vision statement expresses the contribution we want to make to the organization, not what the external world is going to bestow on us" (1987, p. 115). The focus is on who we are to ourselves, and this focus will make it clearer to others what we are about. Once we know who we are, then we will be able to convey to others what we are about through words and deeds.

- *Rule no. 2:* Think about your mission statement as an internally generated document that expresses to the world the core values at work in the institution.

In a college or university, a mission statement also focuses on two related points: people and ideas (Tierney, 1998). Who is your audience and how do you serve them? What are the ideas of the organization that tie it together?

Most organizations need to think of their clientele, so a concern for audience is not very different for a university or for a company. A restaurant develops its menu based on the consumers it serves. It hires employees based in part on the people who buy its services. The menu at McDonald's and at the Ritz will differ because of a different clientele. A waiter at the Ritz is unlikely to move on to a job at McDonald's. Similarly, in a competitive age, colleges and universities need to advance in their mission and vision statements a commitment to their core clientele. If you do not know who your core clientele is, then you are in as much trouble as a restaurant that is unsure if its diners favor Big Macs or foie gras.

- *Rule no. 3:* Define your clientele and track how they have changed and if they will change. Determine how well you serve them and what the mission says about them.

One difference between postsecondary institutions and traditional businesses is a concern for ideas. A business gauges success in large part by how much profit it makes. Although we need to balance the books, colleges and universities are different. Insofar as most educational organizations focus on learning and the intellect rather than profit, ideas that will get embedded into the curriculum need to be outlined in the mission. What are the guiding ideas or concepts of the institution? In the preceding example, president no. 2 mentioned cooperative learning and servant leadership. Such ideas help focus organizational action.

One clear example of how mission statements emphasize a concern for people and ideas comes from Christian universities. Such institutions inevitably discuss in their mission statements their commitment to one or another aspect of the Bible and how they translate the teachings of Jesus Christ into the daily activities and curriculum of the institution. The mission defines the core constituency of the institution: Christian students. True, non-Christian students may be welcome, but the mission has carved out a niche and defined who the institution sees as its primary clientele and how the curriculum and out-of-class activities are linked to its ideas.

- *Rule no. 4:* Define the central organizing idea of the institution. Determine how well it is being employed.

PUTTING THE MISSION STATEMENT INTO PLAY

Although I have cautioned against creating a mission statement that is a laundry list of do's and don'ts, a mission is not merely a grand statement. True, it needs to inspire people and create a sense of organizational excitement. It also needs to be specific enough so that all people know where to focus their energies. As Peter Drucker observed, "A mission statement has to be operational, otherwise it's just good intentions" (1990, p. 4). In effect, a mission statement should contain a finite list of core values. A core value of a liberal arts college might be that interdisciplinary work and teaching are central to how the institution defines and articulates knowledge. Perhaps not everyone, but a sizable majority of the institution must believe the value is true—that it is a central aspect of what the college is about—and individuals need to be able to put the value into action.

The implications of a core value in a mission and vision statement are quite clear. If an individual produces quality research in an interdisciplinary area, then we expect that individual will receive tenure. The curriculum will be interdisciplinary, as will teaching. Core means core, not "nice if we have the time and money."

When I visit a college or university I am troubled, then, when I ask individuals about the driving theme of the institution and am met with a shrug of the shoulders or laughter. I recall one senior professor saying to me after I asked what the mission of the place was: "You know: truth, motherhood, apple pie. We're an apple pie kind of institution." An apple pie college is a recipe for disaster in a consumer-oriented competitive environment where individuals need a sense of what the institution stands for and how it articulates what it values. What I hope to hear from someone on the faculty or staff when I ask what is the mission of the institution is something like, "We serve working-class students in the region and we believe in community involvement; you'll see that in our curriculum and how academic affairs and student affairs work together," or "We see our relationship to the business community as essential and we believe that everyone should be involved with issues pertaining to the Pacific Rim, so the faculty take an interest in sending kids abroad, and student affairs has a very heavy concentration of study abroad programs." The point with these comments is that they are finite, summative, and concise.

COMMUNICATING THE MISSION STATEMENT

Mission statements need to have pictures attached to them so that listeners can see what you mean when you say that you want educational excellence. It cannot be a laundry list because people cannot remember more than about four points. If you have ten tasks that you want to accomplish, that is fine—but do not cram them into a mission statement. And once you have completed writing the mission and vision statement remember that it is necessary to talk about it every chance you have. One mistake that institutional leaders often make is that they think of the mission statement as a document somewhat akin to the Bible. The document gets printed, disseminated, and the president gives a stirring speech at the start of the school year about the mission of the university. On historic occasions—Founder's Day, commencement, and the like—the president dusts the document off and talks about the mission. That is a fatal mistake.

Mission statements mean nothing and consume vast amounts of time and energy if the people in the college or university are not able to articulate what such ideas mean. As Louis Pondy has noted, "The real power of Martin Luther King, Jr. was not only that he had a dream but that he could describe it, that it became public and therefore accessible to millions of people" (1978, p. 20). A leader's job is to follow in King's communicative footsteps. Print the mission on a one-page sheet of paper and memorize it. Speak about it at every talk you give. "Thank you for asking me to speak at the alumni luncheon," you may say. "As you all know, the three values we hold dearly in our mission statement. . . . " Or perhaps, "I am honored to speak about the role of athletics in college life. At my university our mission holds that we value. . . . "

The president is the institution's main communicator. In part, the understanding of the mission will succeed or fail based on a president's ability to communicate it—clearly, constantly, and consistently. However, we often overlook the central importance of all of the institution's leaders' ability to articulate the institutional mission. The president is not ubiquitous; he cannot be everywhere. Faculty see and hear much more from their dean over the course of a year then they do from the president. Faculty often listen to the president of the academic senate in a different way than they do other individuals. Student affairs personnel pay attention to what the dean of students has to say. What we need to hear is a consistent message about what the institution stands for and how it is tied to clearly articulated goals. Those goals usually get played out on local levels, such as in student affairs or in a college.

- *Rule no. 5:* Develop a mission that has no more than four main points and communicate those points at every opportunity.

CHANGING THE MISSION

One concern that some individuals have with the creation of a mission in the manner that I am speaking about is that it might appear to be an institutional straitjacket. How often have we all heard someone kill an idea by saying, "That's not the way we do it around here. That's just not us." Although we need to hold onto the core values that get embedded in the mission statement, as times change, so should the manner in which we articulate the mission.

During a time of significant structural change there is a need for a sense of who we are, what people believe, and what we hope to accomplish. Sometimes that means we need to shed assumptions about the past. Think of a religion. Certainly there are religions that hold onto their values and traditions so tightly that they go out of business, but most religions constantly think about what it means to be Catholic, Jewish, Methodist, and the like, and how they are to keep pace with the times. If anything, a mission is not an encumbrance but an anchoring ideology that serves as a focal point for discussion and reformulation. The art of administration is always one of balance. Although an institution that dramatically reformulates its mission every year is one that I assume has no identity, we also ought not fool ourselves into thinking that a mission is so rigid that in a decade's time there will not be reconsideration and renewal.

In effect, I am suggesting that a mission statement is an organic document that needs to be nurtured, supported, and every now and then, fine-tuned. A company will be in danger of going out of business if consumers do not know what it offers because it changes its product every season. But that same company will also go out of business if it blindly follows "what works" without thinking about how to change its core values from time to time.

- *Rule no. 6:* After agreement about the mission statement has been reached, set a time three to five years down the road when you will want the statement brought back for reconsideration. Such a time frame communicates that there will not be any further changes until that time, but the document is also a living one that benefits from periodic reflection.

CONCLUSION

If we seek lasting changes, rather than helter-skelter, flash-in-the-pan kinds of changes, then a focus on the vision and mission of the institution is imperative. A mission and vision statement needs to be owned by the entire university—it cannot rest in the domain of one or another group. If student affairs defines the mission and the faculty avoid thinking about it, or the board of trustees sees its prerogative to be the creation of the mission to the exclusion of everyone else, then the institution will fall short on living up to its potential. A college or university's mission needs to be owned and nurtured at all levels of the institution. People need to work collaboratively and supportively toward a clearly articulated and agreed on mission and vision statement. Once we have reached agreement, the hard work of communicating it and enacting it begins. The mission and vision statement is the living testimony of the institution, and because it defines the institution we need to see traces of it in the curriculum, in student affairs, and in how we work with one another. When we do this, a properly executed mission and vision statement is not so much a double-edged sword as the Holy Grail that propels us toward institutional excellence.

HOW CLEAR IS THE MISSION OF MY INSTITUTION?

1. Define the mission in sixty seconds. If you cannot do it, then the mission is too complicated and cannot be communicated.
2. Describe two examples of when an outsider would see the mission at work.
3. Ask new faculty to the institution what they see as the mission.
4. Ask longtime faculty what they see as the mission. If the faculty's response differs radically from yours, you have a problem.
5. What are the three central projects that took place over the last twelve months and how do they relate to the mission? If they do not relate to it, then the mission needs to be realigned.
6. How does your mission differ from a similar institution's? If there is no difference, then get to work.

References and Resources

Block, P. (1987). *The empowered manager: Positive political skills at work.* San Francisco: Jossey-Bass.
A book about how to create change in organizations. The author outlines the problems that exist in organizations and works from the assumption that politics pervades them. Successful managers are able to see organizational life through a political lens.

Clark, B. (1980). The organizational saga in higher education. In H. Leavitt (Ed.), *Readings in managerial psychology.* Chicago: Chicago University Press.
The seminal piece on what a distinctive mission is about. The author outlines the pieces of a saga and provides examples of colleges that are distinctive based on his research.

Drucker, P. F. (1990). *Managing the nonprofit organization: Principles and practices.* New York: HarperBusiness.
Practical, hands-on guide about management from the guru of organizational change. He first outlines the current dilemmas faced by nonprofits, then suggests how to use organizational principles and what might be done.

Pondy, L. (1978). Leadership is a language game. In M. McCall & M. Lombardo (Eds.), *Leadership: Where else can we go?* Durham, NC: Duke University Press.
A thoughtful article about the importance of communication in leadership. The author makes the compelling case that leadership is not a simple list of do's and don'ts. Instead, leadership depends on effective communications.

Tierney, W. G. (Ed.). (1998). *The responsive university: Restructuring for high performance.* Baltimore, MD: Johns Hopkins University Press.
A group of scholar-practitioners discuss how to create change in academe. In each chapter the contributors diagnose a specific problem and show how reorienting basic work strategies and designing more creative organizations can lead to solutions.

Tierney, W. G. (1999). *Building the responsive campus: Creating high-performance colleges and universities.* Thousand Oaks, CA: Sage.
A guide for reform based on the ideas of reengineering. The book offers a critique of modern colleges and universities and suggests how better to meet the needs of clients and customers.

CHAPTER 5

Moving Mountains
Institutional Culture and Transformational Change

JUDITH A. RAMALEY

Our institutions are changing all the time but for the most part these changes do not make a big difference, either because the results are confined to an isolated segment of the organization or because the environment is not responsive. To be considered truly transformational, the initiative must alter the culture of the institutions by changing select underlying assumptions and institutional behaviors, processes, and products; it must be deep and pervasive, affecting the whole institution; it must be intentional; and it must occur consistently over time (Eckel, Hill, & Green, 1998).

QUESTIONS FOR LEADERS UNDERTAKING TRANSFORMATIONAL CHANGE

For those of you who are seeking to introduce transformational change, here are five questions to ask yourself. If you consider them carefully, your answers can improve your chances of leading a successful change effort.

- Do you have a mandate for change? If so, from whom?
- Do you understand the factors in the institutional culture and history as well as in the external environment that can support or resist change?
- Is the campus ready to change? If not, what might you do to create a more receptive climate for change?
- Have you thought through a strategy to manage institutional response as the change process unfolds?
- Can you undertake and lead change?

Do You Have a Mandate?

Do you have a mandate? If so, from whom? When new leaders are hired, those who hire them usually have intentions for what these new leaders must accomplish as well as a model, often somewhat deeply buried in their thinking, about what the problems or opportunities are and the right ways to go about addressing them. Most of us are attracted to places that are seeking to accomplish goals that we cherish. We often assume that because we were chosen, the board or the person to whom we report must have given us a mandate to move forward. But this is often not the case. It is important to know clearly *what* you are expected to accomplish and whether there are any expectations about *how* you will do so.

It is also helpful to recognize that gender biases still exist and that governing boards and campus community members may expect leadership to be exercised according to the models they know best—often behaviors developed by the majority culture. If you are a woman or a person of color, you may encounter difficulties simply because you do not look or act "like a leader." You may also open up questions if you happen to ascribe to some of the more contemporary ideas about connective leadership (Lipman-Blumen, 1996) or women's ways of knowing (Belenky, Clinchy, Goldberger, & Tarule, 1997), which place the leader in a collaborative working relationship rather than a directive relationship with the members of the community.

At one institution that I served, the mandate from the governing board was to repair relationships with the state legislature and citizens, develop a clear vision for the institution, and put the budget on a healthy footing. Although these challenges were articulated by the governing board, they were not endorsed as strongly by the campus community, which was fairly evenly divided between people who wanted to introduce some new ideas and people who thought things were just fine as they were. For this latter group, there was no clear mandate except to respect the traditions of the place.

It is important to take time to explore both what you are expected to accomplish and how you are expected to go about doing it. In the case of a budget, for instance, you may be planning to balance it by generating new sources of revenue and redesigning critical campus operations. Your board may want you to eliminate duplication and cut programs. Both are avenues to balancing the budget, but they differ dramatically in approach, implementation time, involvement of the campus community, and consequences.

This example illustrates a growing tension between the academic model of shared governance and the dictates of either a political or a corporate leadership model. In a recent essay, Roger Bowen (2001) describes the battle he has experienced between two cultures—the academic and the political—which offer very different views of the academy that are "contradictory and inhospitable to each other"(p. 14B). According to Bowen, underlying the growing gulf between the experiences and expectations of governing boards and campus leaders is a "suspicion of academe and its arcane traditions; its inefficient, labor-intensive ways of educating students; its practice of lifetime employment through tenure; and its procedures of shared governance" (p. 14B). Members of governing boards may be impatient and suspicious whether they come from the political sector or the corporate sector. This changing set of expectations among those choosing to become members of a governing board and the satisfaction they hope to derive from the experience have made it harder to define a mandate for change. This situation helps explain why leaders must check to be sure that they are in accord with the governing board about not only *what* needs to be accomplished but also *how* it is to be done.

Do You Understand Factors That Support or Resist Change?

Do you understand the factors in the institutional culture and history as well as in the external environment that can support or resist change? It is difficult to capture everything that a newcomer needs to know about the culture of an institution. However, at the very least, a new leader must explore a few issues.

First, what does your new institution expect from its leaders? If you are the founding president or the first provost or dean this is not likely to be an issue, because you are going to set the example that will teach the institution what to expect. But if you are succeeding someone else or a whole line of other people, this first question matters a great deal. At some institutions, leaders are expected to be aloof and somewhat mysterious, and no one remarks if they are off-campus a lot. At other institutions, leaders are expected to be accessible, approachable, and always available. On such campuses, every trip is looked at with suspicion, and rumors may soon fly that you are already looking for another job. Why else would you need to be off-campus so often? Similarly, some institutions want their leaders to be hands-on and involved in everyday campus decision making. Elsewhere, such behavior would be labeled micromanagement and viewed with disfavor.

Second, it is important to know the basic model on which your campus operates. I have found Birnbaum's classification to be especially helpful. As Birnbaum says,

"Culture provides the 'central tendencies' that make it possible to generalize about the character of " the systems that make up a campus. Culture establishes "an 'envelope' or range of possible behaviors within which an organization usually functions (1988, p. 73). He goes on to define four models of institutional behavior to help us think about the range of normal behaviors of the organization we are seeking to change: the *collegial institution,* where power and values are shared throughout the campus community; the *bureaucratic institution* that is based on a rational structure and decision making that follows standard pathways of influence, usually top-down; the *political organization,* where different constituencies vie for power and influence and resources; and the *anarchical organization,* where each component is an island unto itself and the institution as a whole has problematic goals and decision-making channels that are unclear and shifting. Leaders must develop their influence very differently in these distinctive cultures. It is unlikely that your own institution is a pure example of any one kind of organization and decision making, but these models offer a way to size up your environment.

Third, it is important to understand that culture actually has several layers: surface, unspoken, and deep. The *surface* layer is discernable by observation. Do students address the president as President So-and-So or do they use his or her first name? Do students of all backgrounds sit together in the student commons or do groups stay pretty much to themselves? How do men and women interact? Are there symbols and places that hold special meaning for the campus?

Underneath this surface there is a set of *unspoken* rules about conduct and expectations that determine whether new people will be accepted. Often, special expectations apply to the new leader. It is this level that we seek to address when we set up mentoring programs for new faculty or support programs for new students. If only there were such programs for new presidents! Some unspoken rules hold sway on most campuses, but some rules may be unique to your particular institution. It is sometimes possible to discern some of the outlines of this level of culture by noticing carefully how people answer such questions as, "Why do we do things this way?" The explanations that people use to account for things can offer valuable clues to the mental models and the boundaries of the culture.

Most *deeply* buried in a culture, and only brought to the surface when open challenges to leadership occur, is the sense of identity, belonging, and citizenship in a community of like-minded people. Unfortunately, transformational change efforts may disturb this cultural layer. When this happens, the resulting emotional response may be either anger or cynicism. The predominant emotion depends on the primary outcome of change. If the results mostly show that the "new way" has some problems or faults, the result is likely to be cynicism on the part of people who were willing to go out on a limb and try it. If the outcome seems to suggest that there were some genuine advantages to the old way, senior members of the campus community may become outraged at the efforts of others to meddle with perfectly good programs and processes that did not, in their opinion, need to be meddled with in the first place. Cynicism slows down the change process and may derail it because its proponents abandon the effort. Campus anger may unseat the leader instead, thus also derailing the change process. As Lipman-Blumen (1996) has observed, we often have unrealistic expectations of our leaders, and when they fail to perform miracles, even if what we expect is impossible, we often drive them out rather than acknowledge that we too have some responsibility for a good outcome.

Is the Campus Ready to Change?

A final aspect of institutional culture worth examining before you undertake transformational change is the question of the receptivity of the campus. This topic is covered in detail in a series of occasional papers based on the experience of the institutions that participated in the American Council on Education (ACE) project on Leadership and Institutional Transformation (see the ACE Web site at www.acenet.edu for PDF versions of these documents). One of these monographs, called *On Change III: Taking Charge of Change* (Eckel, Green, Hill, & Mallon, 1999), offers extensive advice for creating the context of change and analyzing institutional culture and readiness for change. According to Eckel et al., a good exercise for a leadership team to use to analyze campus culture at the start of a change process and during the transitions that accompany it is to ask each of its members to answer the following questions. The resultant pattern of observations and agreements and disagreements can be very helpful.

- List ten adjectives that describe the campus culture.
- Describe primary subcultures in the institution. To what extent could the same adjectives used for the campus culture be used to describe the subcultures? What other adjectives might be more appropriate for particular subcultures?
- What are the implications of these answers for the change agenda and for the process to accomplish it?

It is helpful to carry out this exercise with careful attention to what the ACE project calls *artifacts*—namely, the language people use, the myths and stories that they often repeat again and again to newcomers, observable rituals, the published mission, and what people say when asked to talk about the institution. If the surface and the underlying layers of culture are congruent, significant change may be possible. If there is more of a covert subculture that diverges significantly from the formal values and goals of the organization, then trouble may lie ahead. It is important to know if there is a "firm cultural and attitudinal base for action" (Eckel et al., 1999, p. 22).

Do You Have a Strategy to Manage Institutional Response?

Have you thought through a strategy to manage institutional responses as the change process unfolds? It is helpful when undertaking transformative change to adopt strategies that can lead to the creation of a special form of institutional democracy, where the individual members of a campus community develop a shared sense of purpose, learn to communicate effectively with each other, and acquire the capacity to participate in collaborative work. To accomplish the goals of an institutional democracy in which learning is predominant, a university must become a true learning organization (Senge, 1990). According to David Garvin, "A learning organization is skilled at creating, acquiring, interpreting, and transferring knowledge, and at modifying its behavior to reflect new knowledge and insights" (1995, p. 78). In a learning organization, change is intentional, based on a valid body of knowledge, and rigorously assessed. That is, change is a *scholarly act* (Ramaley, 2000). To develop the capacities of a learning organization, support collaborative behavior, and establish a scholarly basis for action, a university community must accomplish six tasks (Martin, Manning, & Ramaley, 2001):

- Instill a discipline of reflection and a culture of evidence, insisting that everyone support their perspectives with real information (qualitatively and quantitatively derived), not just opinions.
- Create new patterns of conversation and interaction that encourage and support; everyone is to be involved in defining the essential issues in a learning organization and transformative institution.
- Engage in genuine conversation about difficult and controversial subjects as one way to disperse power and leadership throughout the organization. These conversations promote discipline and clarity of purpose rather than confu-

sion about goals and actions. Informed, respectful, thoughtful dialogue is the greatest learning tool of any organization today, and few of us know how to do it. We lack skill in managing contentious issues—when there are strong feelings about rights or entitlements, or when two worthwhile principles come in conflict with each other. We often resort to defensive or blaming behavior rather than real conversation, or we go into debate mode and seek to defeat our critics rather than understand them.

- Adopt a philosophy of experimentation, assessment, and management of reasonable risks.
- Create new ways to access information and a common base of acceptable knowledge about the institution and its performance and condition. This activity encourages everyone to make informed choices among the many options.
- Create legitimacy for planning and assessment by documenting the research and practice from which the approaches are derived. In the process of creating a research-based foundation for action, the different norms and standards of knowledge espoused by the disciplines making up the academic community must be understood, subcultures must be defined and recognized, and common and agreed-upon standards developed to guide good decision making.

In a learning organization, the role of the leader is to build a shared vision, surface and challenge prevailing mental models, foster systemic patterns of thinking, and model intellectual virtues. These virtues include "the willingness to explore widely, the ability to test one's ideas against those of others, the capacity to listen thoughtfully, and the strength to adduce reasons for one's assertions" (Payne, 1996, p. 19). Furthermore, this capacity cannot be exercised just at the top of an organization but must be widely distributed throughout. Therefore, leaders must also foster and develop the leadership skills of people in their organization.

A learning organization that values shared governance is likely to be psychologically much safer than an organization that is led autocratically. People in a more democratic setting believe they are wanted and belong; that they are valued, so ideas and thoughts are listened to and used; and that they are respected and free from harassment and discriminatory behavior (Manning & Coleman-Boatwright, 1991). They also feel empowered to share responsibility for achieving institutional goals and purposes, are comfortable and knowledgeable enough to make decisions in areas of responsibility, and share in a vision for the future. They also respect each other's expertise.

Can You Undertake and Lead Change?

The exercise of leadership, like every other experience in a group or organization, is shaped in several ways: on the personal level through a leader's personal qualities and values and beliefs; through interactions between the leader and others and how these communications interpret the experience of others in the organization and thereby create meaning and direction; and by the climate created in an organization based on the permission and expectations of the leadership. By now, most of us have learned that leadership's influence cannot be felt only at the top levels of an organization. It must be widely distributed throughout the organization.

Critical Organizational Qualities

William O'Brien, former CEO of the Hanover Insurance Company, recently said that a new wave is forming, one that we cannot yet describe or name. O'Brien suggested that if an organization or community has several abilities they will help it cope with rapid, as yet poorly defined, change. First, in this period of dimly discernible trends and patterns, organizations must learn how to disperse power in an orderly way. It is important to remember that empowerment without discipline and clarity is dangerous. Organizations must also learn how to disperse power so that self-discipline replaces the control they have traditionally exercised in this century through bureaucracy.

Organizations must also become adept at systemic thinking. Most of us in academia are good at dealing with problems stated with clear questions and a clear, research-based answer. We have very little experience managing unclear problems with unclear answers that require us to understand systems and interrelationships. In *Educating the Reflective Practitioner,* Donald Schön (1988) says, "In the varied topography of professional practice, there is a high, hard ground overlooking a swamp. On the hard ground, manageable problems lend themselves to solution through the application of research-based theory and techniques. In the *swampy lowlands,* messy, confusing problems defy technical solutions" (p. 3). As a president, I have spent most of my time in the swampy lowlands where problems have many dimensions and clear answers are few. The only way out of a swamp is to invent as you go (see Ramaley, 2000).

Finally, organizations must accept the fact that leadership can no longer be exercised by mandate. Increasingly, all employees, not just faculty, may be better thought of as volunteers. Command-and-control strategies must give way to collaboration, competence, and creativity.

Remaining Accessible

So how can a president set significant changes in motion and model the appropriate behaviors to deal with them? Consider ways to maintain accessibility and direct contact with members of the campus community through e-mail, open forums, coffees with a cross section of campus community—students, faculty. Next, spend time identifying the change agents on campus, the people with a "can-do" or "make-something-good-happen" attitude. Invite these people to participate in a campus leadership series where they can work with each other, learn about the larger context of the campus and its environment, develop trustworthy communication networks, and acquire a genuine commitment to a shared purpose. If you do not already have them, consider introducing individual development plans that encourage faculty and staff to identify their changing interests and skills and then make sure there are avenues for such interests to be fostered and new opportunities offered. Ask your leadership colleagues to identify projects that involve teamwork. This will encourage networking and practicing the habits of a learning organization.

Becoming a Storyteller

Encourage members of the campus community to tell you about good things that are happening and that they think are especially contributing to the enhancement of the institution in quiet ways. With this material you can become a storyteller, as you acquire new knowledge of the institution through all of these means. Your stories will help create meaning and direction for the institution. Howard Gardner in *Leading Minds: An Anatomy of Leadership* (1995) argues that "leaders achieve their effectiveness chiefly through the stories they relate" (p. 9). He uses the verb *relate* rather than *tell* because a story can be conveyed in many ways—through words, artistic expression, or scholarly work. In each case, the leader embodies the stories.

To relate a compelling story, a leader must characterize and resolve important life issues for himself or herself and then successfully influence the views of various audiences to effect desired changes. Gardner sees leadership as a process that occurs in the minds of individuals who live in a culture—a process that entails the capacity to create stories, understand and evaluate them, and appreciate and manage the struggle among competing stories. The extent to which a story takes hold and shapes how people see the world depends on both their developmental stage and how effectively the leader adapts the story to their minds; the leader does this by being attuned to their basic questions and search for identity.

Dealing with the Campus Reaction

It is also helpful to know how people react to and interpret changes that are beginning to take place around them. Change can generate serious and unsettling questions that can unbalance established routines. This will usually cause anxiety. If properly channeled, these questions can be thought-provoking and encourage organizational members to think more deeply about what is happening (Isabella, 1992). This can, in turn, contribute to the development of the better communication, clarity, and agreement that will be so essential for guiding institutional progress toward excellence.

The campus reaction to a significant change or *trigger event* unfolds in four predictable stages, each requiring a different leadership response.

- As rumors fly about change, members adopt an "assembly" or detective mindset, assembling rumors and tidbits of information and drawing often sweeping inferences and conclusions from them. The management task at this stage is to promote open and honest discussion of fears and concerns and to provide accurate information to dispel rumors.
- When the change begins, members draw on traditional explanations and familiar patterns of the organization to explain what is happening and to resist the change. At this point, the management task is to offer new and more constructive interpretations of what the changes mean.
- Once the change is in place, people move to an "amended" mindset as they search for the symbolic meaning of what has happened and what it portends for them personally. As they do so, they are "trying to actively reconstruct their environment: deciding what to retain and what to alter" (Isabella, 1992, p. 23).
- As the change progresses, managers and others review the consequences of what has taken place and reinterpret what it all means. People are doing their best to put the change in perspective. Unless this stage is actively managed, all will draw their own individual conclusions, which may vary significantly with the institution's mission and strategies.

Achieving Direction

Achieving clarity and direction in a loosely coupled institution—with connections between people and units that are often fragmentary or nonexistent—requires either a major environmental change or mandate, a fiscal crisis that is honestly and openly addressed, or the deliberate introduction of a significant internal imbalance. Whatever the cause of the destabilization of the loosely coupled internal systems of a campus community, a successful outcome depends on consistent and open communication and leadership accessibility at each stage of the planning or change process. Leaders must consistently help people understand what is happening and what it means as well as uncover and deal with rumors and misperceptions through open and honest dialogue. Good storytelling helps, especially when the material comes right from real conversations with campus constituents.

As long as we understand that academic institutions are distinctive cultures unto themselves—both as a sector of society and as individual institutions with their own senses of place and tradition—it becomes clear that change constitutes a cultural change, and leadership is the process of telling compelling stories about a different kind of reality or identity. In such a culture, according to William G. Tierney (1999), leadership means doing several things: putting people first; studying the unique culture of the campus; connecting people together; defining and embodying the values and beliefs that will support needed change; being attentive to the diversity of experience of the people who make up the campus and the need to create conditions where everyone can be fully themselves; practicing change strategies that are based on an acknowledgment of the campus culture; promoting courageous participation by enhancing trustworthiness and reducing the risks associated with experimentation; fostering leadership in others; being accessible; and supporting and rewarding collective responsibilities and efforts as well as individual excellence. In other words, *to lead is first to learn and then to teach* through the example of one's own conduct and through compelling stories.

Having a Good Theory of Change

Finally, it is important to have a well-grounded theory of change. My own preference is for a model that lays out several components that must be attended to in order to introduce and sustain meaningful change. To move an institution intentionally in a desired direction, four conditions must exist, or be put in place if they do not already exist. They will be summarized here, but those interested in exploring this issue further may wish to consult the case study of Portland State University, which is one of the few institutions in recent years to undergo truly transformational change (Ramaley, 1996).

- A *compelling case* for systemic or transformational change must be made. Most people are unwilling to embark on major change without both a compelling reason and the confidence that their efforts will be supported and recognized.

- There must be *clarity of purpose.* Even when the reasons are clear, the goals must also be clear. Otherwise, there will be no way to judge the value of the efforts made or to convince honest skeptics of the value and legitimacy of the work.
- There must be *significance of scale.* Most change is too small and piecemeal to make a real difference in an organization. The choice of the first project is critical.
- A *conducive campus environment* is essential. There are many barriers to change at most institutions. Some time must be spent identifying factors that will impede change.

Observers and practitioners of change continue to argue about whether large-scale change can occur in the absence of some serious and ongoing crisis. Given the traditional strengths of higher education and the slowly growing pressures on our enterprise, it is a good idea to anticipate changing social and economic conditions in society and respond to them—before they are imposed on us.

QUESTIONS FOR INSTITUTIONS UNDERGOING TRANSFORMATIONAL CHANGE

Here are the kinds of questions that should be asked about an institution in order to establish clarity of purpose when embarking on intentional or transformative change without a precipitating crisis to generate the need for change (modeled on Hamel & Prahalad, 1994). These questions should be asked not just once, but continuously.

- What are our core values and what is our mission?
- What lessons can we draw from our own history and tradition?
- What new core competencies will we need in the future?
- What core competencies must we retain and enhance?
- What organizational values and principles will guide our decision making?
- What new educational models must we build?
- What new alliances must we form?
- What promising programs must we nurture?
- What long-term regulatory initiatives must we pursue to reshape the marketplace in which we operate regionally, statewide, or nationally?

- What new learners must we serve?
- How will we generate the resources to invest in new competencies?

An important step in the process of change is to have a firm grasp on the institution's actual condition before you begin and then measure your progress along the way. A useful way to assess the extent to which a particular change has truly become transformational is to use the matrix developed by Holland (1997), a scale of low, medium, high, and full integration of service into an institutional mission. The matrix can be used just as well to examine any other kind of meaningful change, such as curricular reform. The scan is comprehensive and includes the wording of the mission itself; promotion, tenure, and hiring policies; organizational structure; student involvement; faculty involvement; community involvement; and the content, perspective, and intended audiences of campus publications and communications.

Finally, it is wise to keep an eye on the conditions on the campus that can either support change or impede it. A redefinition of faculty roles and rewards is often required, and a conscious link must be made between faculty work and the tasks necessary to achieve the institutional mission. This generally means reworking the standards and documentation required for promotion and tenure.

Most of the procedures and policies of an institution have accumulated over time and often are overly complex and unintentionally fail to facilitate or reward the behaviors and working relationships necessary to achieve desirable changes. In addition, the introduction of new technologies as well as new working relationships with other organizations changes the kind of support structure needed and the competencies of support staff. Old systems of work classification and traditional forms of employee development often cannot keep pace with these changes.

Many institutions fail to take into account the importance of students in shaping the institution—as student employees, participants in outreach and public service, members of research teams, and citizens of the community that the institution serves.

In many institutions, individual departments act as self-contained entities and reward department-centered activity but not participation in cross-disciplinary work or campus activities that benefit the institution but not the department directly. To bring the work of departments into alignment with the needs of the institution as a whole, it is helpful to create a direct relationship between the setting of goals and priorities at the department level and the articulation of institutional goals and to reward departments and programs that contribute to the campus goals. For a strategic resource cycle to work and be sustainable, an institution must have three elements in place (Ramaley, 1998): a clarity of vision and purpose translated into goals and objectives; a clear understanding of how resources are generated and consumed by activities; and a culture of evidence that provides good measures of the results obtained by various programs and activities and a model whereby the future setting of goals and the distribution of resources is guided by outcomes.

CONCLUSION

A leader who wishes to foster transformational change must work in a complex three-dimensional mental space. Such leaders must learn about the culture of the organization and work in ways that respect it, must embody the qualities that are associated with a true democratically guided learning community, and must have a clear and compelling model for change that guides the actions they take. In the beginning, this can be a demanding exercise, but over time, practiced leaders begin to work naturally in this space and can effectively bring out the best in their institution.

References

Belenky, M. F., Clinchy, B., Goldberger, N. R., & Tarule, J. M. (1997). *Women's ways of knowing. Tenth anniversary edition.* New York: Basic Books.

Birnbaum, R. (1988). *How colleges work.* San Francisco: Jossey-Bass.

Bowen, R. W. (2001, June 22). The new battle between political and academic cultures. *Chronicle of Higher Education,* pp. B14–15.

Eckel, P., Green, M., Hill, B., & Mallon, W. (1999). *On change III: Taking charge of change: A primer for colleges and universities.* Washington, DC: American Council on Education.

Eckel, P., Hill, B., & Green, M. (1998). *On change: En route to transformation.* Washington, DC: American Council on Education.

Gardner, H. (1995). *Leading minds: An anatomy of leadership.* New York: Basic Books.

Garvin, D. A. (1995). Barriers and gateways to learning. In C. R. Christensen, D. A. Garvin, & A. Sweet (Eds.), *Education for judgment. The artistry of discussion leadership* (pp. 3–12). Boston: Harvard Business School Press.

Hamel, G., & Prahalad, C. K. (1994). *Competing for the future.* Boston: Harvard Business School Press.

Holland, B. (1997, Fall). Analyzing institutional commitment to service. *Michigan Journal of Community Service Learning, 4,* 30–41.

Isabella, L. A. (1992). Managing the challenges of trigger events: The mindsets governing adaptation to change. *Business Horizons, 35,* 59–66.

Lipman-Blumen, J. (1996). *Connective leadership: Managing in a changing world.* New York: Oxford University Press.

Manning, K., & Coleman-Boatwright, P. (1991). Student affairs initiatives toward a multicultural university. *Journal of College Student Development, 32*(4), 367–374.

Martin, R., Manning, K., & Ramaley, J. (2001). The self-study as a chariot for strategic change. In J. Ratcliff, E. Lubiescu, & M. Gaffney (Eds.), *How accreditation influences assessment.* New Directions for Higher Education, no. 113. San Francisco: Jossey-Bass.

Payne, H. C. (1996, Fall). Can or should a college teach virtue? *Liberal Education,* pp. 18–25.

Ramaley, J. A. (1996). Large-scale institutional change to implement an urban university mission: Portland State University. *Journal of Urban Affairs, 18*(2), 139–151.

Ramaley, J. A. (1998). The making of a budget: Strategic thinking at a public research university. *Vermont Connections, 19,* 8–15.

Ramaley, J. A. (2000). Change as a scholarly act: Higher education research transfer to practice. In Kezar, A., & Eckel, P. (Eds.), *Moving beyond the gap between research and practice in higher education.* New Directions for Higher Education, No. 110. San Francisco: Jossey-Bass.

Schön, D. A. (1988). *Educating the reflective practitioner.* San Francisco: Jossey-Bass.

Senge, P. M. (1990). *The fifth discipline: The art and practice of the learning organization.* New York: Doubleday.

Tierney, W. G. (1999). *Building the responsive campus: Creating high-performance colleges and universities.* Thousand Oaks, CA: Sage.

CHAPTER 6

Building on Style for More Effective Relationships and Results

ROBERT M. DIAMOND, CHARLES M. SPUCHES

Since earliest times people have tried to figure out why people behave as they do. Medieval scholars believed that an individual's predilections and actions were based on four general humors. These humors, thought to be body fluids, were responsible for a person's health, disposition, and temperament. By the 1700s, these same fluids were believed to be responsible for a person's character, style, sentiment, and spirit. Our understanding of human behavior has become more complicated with the advent of modern psychology, theories of social construction, and notions of human activity as influenced by many variables. Despite this understanding, attempts to categorize disposition and personal style have continued, and it is interesting to note that even the most recent approaches tend to divide behavior into four general categories reminiscent of the humors; although the labels in these different models may differ, the approaches have much in common.

Although we no longer look to such models to explain the complexity of our health or "spirit," there is no question that knowing about ourselves—our preferred interactional or working style as well as the styles of our colleagues and associates—can assist us as leaders. Using this knowledge can make us more productive in our relationships with others, thereby making our lives and the lives of those around us far more satisfying.

The age-old wisdom of Delphi, "Know thyself," is perhaps even more relevant today in our fast-paced, high-stress, high-tech world. The challenges that colleges and universities face are more complex than ever before. Our institutions are becoming more diverse, with more women in leadership roles; more diversity in ethnicity, cultural identity, and age; and more diverse capabilities among faculty, staff, and students. These changes pose real challenges to our ability to communicate, relate to one another, and create meaningful and productive shared experiences.

Few of us would disagree with the notion that we work in a world best characterized as "permanent white-water change." To be successful in this world it is most important that we be as effective as possible in our dealings with others—how we communicate and how we work one-on-one and in group settings. One result of the increasing complexity of our world is that those in leadership roles need a wide array of subject matter and technical knowledge and skills, and they must also be adept at a range of process skills—interpersonal and communications, problem solving, creative and critical thinking, conflict resolution, active listening. Moreover, leaders need to be able to do these things in coordination with others in increasingly team- and project-based organizations. Our ability to do these things well directly relates to both our productivity and our satisfaction in our work.

In this chapter we will focus on several approaches to help you identify style and will discuss how you can use this information to improve your relationships and effectiveness. We will describe different models, or inventories, for collecting and using this information, and we will discuss the limitations of these techniques. As noted earlier, it is important to keep in mind that although categories and labels used and the focus of the various approaches may vary, the models themselves have much in common.

WHY PAY ATTENTION TO STYLE?

We propose three reasons why you will want to consider style—your own and that of your colleagues—as an important component in your interpersonal and communications skill set.

- *Knowing yourself.* Awareness of style begins with you. Step one is knowing and understanding your own strengths and what you require in a work situation to be successful. It will also help you select those whose strengths and perspectives are different from your own to serve on your leadership team.
- *Relating to others.* You will be more sensitive to the needs of others, and as a result, will be able to work with them and benefit from their strengths.
- *Assigning responsibility.* The more you know about another person's strengths and preferences, the more effectively you will be able to make assignments and put together effective working teams.

Before we look at a selection of style inventories you might consider, there are several important points to keep in mind.

Several Factors Affect Performance

Although most of us have a style preference, it is not the only factor that influences how we behave in a given situation. Our behavior is affected by a number of factors:

- *How important the topic or activity is to us.* The more we care, the greater the involvement.
- *How deep our knowledge or skills are in the topic or activity.* The more we know, the more likely we are to participate actively.
- *How we feel.* If we are tired, overcommitted, or not feeling well, our energy level will be lower and so will our interest in the activity.

We Are Adaptable

You cannot change others' styles, but you can adapt your style to be more effective in working with them.

If you know that certain approaches tend not to be successful in interactions with an associate or colleague, you can modify your approach to increase their comfort level. If, for example, you are working with a person who rarely moves quickly and always wants more information before taking action, you can reduce the time required by having the anticipated information available when the topic is introduced. Knowing how your style and the style of others interact can be helpful as you introduce new initiatives and change.

Preferred Styles May Change Under Stress

Although some individuals are quite consistent in their preferred style, others shift significantly under stress. An individual who functions as a team player under most conditions can become far more independent under pressure, whereas an individual who is viewed as an effective leader may become much more passive when faced with difficult decisions.

Stress May Make Us Ineffective

Under stress, every individual reaches a point at which his or her style becomes ineffective and counterproductive. As Gilmore and Fraleigh have pointed out (1992), *leading* can become *dominating,* which can become *oppressing.* A reserved person can become guarded, and then, under tremendous stress, totally unresponsive. As a leader, it is important for you to be able to recognize when you or others with whom you work are moving toward this counterproductive behavior.

Not Everyone Has Only One Style

Although most of us have one preferred style, this is not true of everyone. It has been estimated that as many as 25 percent of us have two or more styles with which we are equally comfortable. These individuals can, at any given time, perform in the style of any one of a number of categories.

No One Style Makes a More Effective Leader

In their study of American business, Collins and Porras (1994) found, much to their surprise, that strong leaders had many different styles. The key, they claimed, was how well these individuals recognized their strengths and weaknesses and how carefully they surrounded themselves with individuals with different strengths.

A Preferred Working Style May Need to Change

As your professional role changes and you take on new responsibilities, you may need to change your preferred style of working with others. A successful leader needs to delegate responsibilities and provide others with the opportunity to grow. Leaders often must shift styles so that others can develop ownership. As Morley and Eadie (2001) have observed (for a more in-depth discussion of this phenomenon, see Chapter Four of their book):

> One of the ironies in the business of leadership is that styles that might have helped you through the ranks can turn out to be liabilities—at least

if not kept under stern control—in the realm of leadership. In this regard, perhaps the most sensible course of action is for you to take a detailed style inventory, asking yourself if there are any aspects of your management style that appear potentially—or perhaps have proved in practice—to be counterproductive. This may require some serious thinking and probing on your part, since the way we do things can become so ingrained that it seems natural and inevitable. [p. 22]

Gender Differences

Studies have shown that the styles of women and men in leadership positions do tend to differ. These reports show that women place greater emphasis on team and community whereas men, as a rule, place greater emphasis on the outcomes or results of change.

Cultural Differences

Cultural background can also play an important role in determining how individuals will perform in a given situation. Different groups have been socialized to respond to stress in different ways. There are also differences in how people of different cultural backgrounds have learned to deal with others and in the behaviors they consider acceptable under certain circumstances. With increasing cultural diversity on most campuses, it is critical that those in leadership roles be sensitive to these differences. Keep in mind that initial visual and oral responses may not always represent an individual's actual thoughts and feelings.

Information Should Be Shared

Although some style inventories can be used independently and may prove helpful when used this way, the maximum benefit comes when individuals working together to complete the inventory then share the results. Although this sharing is most effective when facilitated by someone trained in the use of the instrument and in group process skills, it requires that all participants (with the exception of the 360-degree instruments) agree ahead of time to do this sharing. This sharing makes the process more enjoyable for participants, and it can play an important role in helping to develop an effective team with mutual respect among members.

Most importantly, *the more you know about yourself and those with whom you work the more effective you can be as a contributor to significant institutional change.* As you learn about your style, keep in mind that nothing is absolute. Other factors will always be at play. What this knowledge will do is help you to make a "best guess" about how you and others will address issues and accept challenges. Knowing about style preferences will also help you to prepare for others' reactions and to maintain control over yourself and the situation.

LEARNING ABOUT STYLE: SELECTED INSTRUMENTS AND INVENTORIES

You will find the following instruments and inventories useful for your individual use and for use in group settings. Each instrument has its own unique perspective but also much in common with other approaches. For one, all of these instruments are intended to allow you to become more self-aware and reflective about your own work and leadership style. Ultimately, these instruments, if used appropriately, can empower you to contribute your best, and as a leader, bring out the best in teams and other work groups.

Myers-Briggs Type Indicator (MBTI)

The MBTI is the most frequently used personality (or style) instrument in the world. Based on the work of psychologist Carl Jung, the MBTI was developed by Katherine Briggs and her daughter, Isabel Myers. The MBTI is applied in settings that range from career counseling to marriage counseling and corporate team building. The MBTI uses four pairs of self-reported preferences to identify a matrix of sixteen type or style categories based on four core processes (Hirsh & Kummerow, 1998):

- *Energizing (introversion versus extroversion):* How we are energized, either by focusing our attention outwardly or inwardly
- *Perceiving (sensing versus intuition):* Where we focus our attention and how we gather information
- *Deciding (thinking versus feeling):* How we process information and make decisions

- *Living (judging versus perceiving):* How we relate to others and events and organize our lives

The MBTI has been studied and used widely. This has advantages and drawbacks; in any group, a number of individuals may have already used it. It is recommended for use with a trained and qualified facilitator. The MBTI is available from Consulting Psychologists Press, 3803 East Bayshore Road, Palo Alto, California 94303; (800) 624-1765 or http://www.mbti.com.

Style Profile for Communication at Work (SP)

Developed by Susan K. Gilmore and Patrick W. Fraleigh, this twenty-item instrument is designed to help you understand your work style. Style is defined as your "characteristic way of perceiving and thinking about yourself, others, and things" (p. 7). Gilmore and Fraleigh argue that the best reason to learn about style is to have better self-control, particularly in times of conflict or stress. They contend that using style information to manage yourself more effectively tends to bring out the best in others, whereas attempting to use such information to control others usually does just the opposite! The inventory's four categories are *accommodating-harmonizing, analyzing-preserving, achieving-directing,* and *affiliating-perfecting.*

The SP provides information about how you are likely to respond in a variety of circumstances, what Gilmore and Fraleigh characterize as "calm and storm conditions" (p. 19). One of the less expensive instruments to use, it includes a well-designed users' guide. The SP inventory is easy to use independent of a facilitator. It is available from Friendly Press, 5120 Franklin Boulevard, Suite 3, Eugene, Oregon 97403-2700; (541) 686-0336.

Thomas-Kilmann Conflict Mode Instrument (TKI)

The Thomas-Kilmann Conflict Mode Instrument is based on the notion that conflict is a natural part of our interactions with others. TKI is a self-scoring thirty-item exercise that takes about fifteen minutes to complete. Interpretation and feedback materials help you to learn about the most appropriate uses for each mode of handling conflict. The materials also provide suggestions for increasing your familiarity and comfort level with less frequently used styles. The TKI is a very useful tool for group formation and development purposes. It is available from Consulting Psychologists Press (see MBTI section for contact information).

Strength Deployment Inventory

The SDI was developed by Elias H. Porter, a student of Carl Rogers. The SDI is based on Porter's relationship awareness theory, the focus of which is relationships and how they affect individuals, teams, organizations, and "the bottom line." Porter argues that relationship awareness is nonjudgmental and emphasizes "a person's strengths in relating to others, and suggests how those strengths may be used to improve relationships" (http://www.personalstrengths.com/rl overview.ra.theory.htm).

The SDI is described as a "whole-life profile that helps people identify their personal strengths under two conditions: when everything is going well and when they are faced with opposition or conflict. It explores motivational values—the basis for how people feel and act in different situations." This instrument can be used independently. The SDI is available from Personal Strengths Publishing, P.O. Box 2605, Carlsbad, California 92018-2605; (800) 624-7347 or http://www.personalstrengths.com/index.html.

360-Degree Instruments

Understanding how you are perceived by others is important to your ability to lead and manage change. Over the last decade or so, business and industry have begun to use instruments that are designed to help you learn about yourself by surveying how you are perceived by those around you (thus the notion of 360 degrees). These instruments and processes have proven effective. Although they are time consuming, they can provide you with invaluable information.

Initially designed for use in the for-profit sector, this strategy is readily applicable to colleges and universities. The most thorough 360-degree feedback processes involve performance evaluations collected from many sources in addition to yourself—those you supervise, your peers, your supervisors, and others with whom you work both inside and outside the organization.

At its best, 360-degree feedback provides you with valuable information on how others perceive your skills, abilities, and performance. Its power lies in the nature of the comprehensive information it gathers from several sources representing multiple perspectives. Good 360-degree protocols include a professional development feedback system. Research on the use and value of 360-degree feedback is increasing. However, keep in mind that if not used well or overused, this approach has the potential of interfering with teamwork, producing stress, and if the information is not used, being viewed as counterproductive and a complete waste of time.

One of the better 360-degree instruments is the Conflict Dynamics Profile (CDP). Rather than addressing preferred *styles,* this unique instrument focuses instead on the *behaviors* that people usually display when facing conflict. Illustrative of a 360-degree approach, the result of the CDP process is a conflict profile that provides information on the "hot buttons" that provoke an individual; the individual's perceptions of how he or she usually responds to conflict; others' view of how that individual responds to conflict; how the individual behaves before, during, and after a conflict situation; and the responses to conflict that may be constructive or destructive to the individual and his or her place in the organization.

Based on psychometrically sound approaches, the CDP reflects evidence of validity and reliability, and, as CDP documentation points out, has been normed against a variety of organizations. Moreover, the CDP may be used in "the context of an existing training program, as a stand-alone assessment for an individual or group, or as part of a coaching intervention" (J. Anderson, personal communication with the authors, March 12, 2001). The CDP has a thorough development guide. The CDP is available from Eckerd College, Management Development Institute, 4200 54 Avenue South, St. Petersburg, Florida 33711; (800) 753-0444 or www.conflictdynamics.org.

CONCLUSION

Knowing and understanding your own style and the styles of those around you will improve your individual effectiveness and your group relationships. Through an awareness of style, you can ensure that you include people with a variety of styles and interests in your groups and on your teams. This kind of synergy can happen by chance, but it rarely does. Moreover, sharing this information with your team can improve the members' awareness of the way style contributes to more effective relationships.

Awareness of style will also point out differing preferences. Although some of us are comfortable and eager to be out in front of groups speaking and facilitating, others prefer and thrive in situations requiring intense concentration and isolation. Style diversity in groups will enable you to make assignments appropriate to the life cycle of a project and the styles and strengths of group members. As you discuss styles, keep several things in mind.

- There is strength in diversity. Each style can make important contributions.
- Every style can carry out every demand—some more effectively than others.
- Many of us draw from different styles for the different roles that we play; roles change and so do our styles.
- What constitutes "storm" conditions varies across styles. What causes difficulty for one style may not for another.
- We *do not* choose our style. A complex interaction of forces shapes most human behavior.
- We can, however, develop the skills to manage others' styles.

In the end, recognition and appreciation for the value of diverse styles will allow you to take maximum advantage of the unique and important contributions of everyone on your team. Such knowledge can make an important contribution to effective leadership and successful change initiatives.

References

Collins, J. C., & Porras, J. I. (1994). *Built to last: Successful habits of visionary companies.* New York: HarperBusiness.

Gilmore, S. K., & Fraleigh, P. W. (1992). *Communication at work.* Eugene, OR: Friendly Press.

Hirsh, S. K., & Kummerow, J. M. (1998). *Introduction to type in organizations.* Palo Alto, CA: Consulting Psychologists Press.

Morley, J., & Eadie, D. (2001). *The EXTRAordinary higher education leader.* Washington, DC: National Association of College and University Business Officers.

Resources

Capobianco, S., Davis, M. H., & Kraus, L. A. (2001). *Managing conflict dynamics: A practical approach.* St. Petersburg, FL: Eckerd College.
This book provides background information on dealing with conflict and guidance for using the results of the Conflict Dynamics Profile. It includes worksheets to aid your professional development, strategies for dealing with conflict, reflection questions, approaches to soliciting feedback, and abundant references and resources.

Collins, J. C., & Porras, J. I. (1994). *Built to last: Successful habits of visionary companies.* New York: HarperBusiness.

A report on a benchmark study in which eighteen visionary companies were compared with their less successful competitors. It focuses on why some companies did better than others over a long period of time. A key part of the answer is leadership processes and team building. Has much to say to higher education leaders. An enjoyable read.

Felder, R. (1996, December). Matters of style. *PRISM,* pp. 18-23.
Published in the American Society of Engineering Education magazine PRISM, this article argues for the value of professionals and scientists being able to work well in all learning style modes. Felder provides a pithy outline of the Myers-Briggs Type Indicator (MBTI), Kolb's Learning Style Model, and Hermann Brain Dominance Instrument (HBDI) and discusses their applications.

Gilmore, S. K., & Fraleigh, P. W. (1992). *Communication at work.* Eugene, OR: Friendly Press.
Practical and down-to-earth, this volume includes an easy-to-use instrument and a comprehensive workbook on interpreting and using the information collected.

Hammer, A. L. (1993). *Introduction to type and careers.* Palo Alto, CA: Consulting Psychologists Press.
Provides a thorough discussion of how to use the MBTI to select a new job or career, change jobs or careers, and increase your satisfaction with your present job and career.

Hirsh, S. K, & Kummerow, J. M. (1998). *Introduction to type in organizations.* Palo Alto, CA: Consulting Psychologist Press.
Provides a thorough outline of the MBTI and its application in organizations.

Lepsinger, R., & Lucia, A. D. (1997). *The art and science of 360-degree feedback.* San Francisco: Jossey-Bass.
A thorough treatment of 360-degree processes, including commitment, methodologies, use, feedback, and follow-up.

McCauley, C. D., Moxley, R., & Velsor, E. (Eds.). (1998). *The Center for Creative Leadership handbook of leadership development.* San Francisco: Jossey-Bass.
One of the more widely used leadership references in business and industry, this handbook contains an outstanding section on 360-degree feedback: its benefits, how best to use this approach, and the most common barriers to expect. Also contains extremely useful advice on a number of topics relevant to those of us in higher education, including race, gender, and cross-cultural issues.

Morley, J., & Eadie, D. (2001). *The EXTRAordinary higher education leader.* Washington, DC: National Association of College and University Business Officers.
Focuses on moving from a managerial role to that of leader or career development. Nice section on why changing your style may be key to your success as you move up to leadership responsibility but not a strong emphasis on interpersonal relationships.

Schroeder, C. G. (1993, September-October). New students, new learning styles. *Change, 25*(4), 21–26.

> This issue of this magazine, published by the American Association for Higher Education, reports on a study in which the MBTI was administered to approximately four thousand entering students to explore the role of individual differences in the learning process.

Tannen, D. (1995, September-October). The power of talk: Who gets heard and why. *Harvard Business Review,* pp. 138–148.

> Tannen explores linguistic style as a way to understand communication, power, and authority. She concludes that there is no one best way to communicate and that "the results of a given way of speaking will vary depending on the situation, the culture of the company, the relative rank of speakers, their linguistic styles, and how those styles interact with one another" (p. 147).

Tieger, P. D., & Barron-Tieger, B. (1992). *Do what you are.* New York: Little, Brown.

> Coauthored by the founder of the New England Type Institute, this book focuses on career choice and the job search process. It begins with the process of discovering your own personality type based on the MBTI.

PART THREE

Academics

The framework of higher education policy should encourage each institution to strive for high quality in all of its chosen tasks. We need policies that encourage the institutional reality to match the institutional rhetoric in every aspect—teaching, scholarship, and service. In the current setting, we have too often settled for the rhetoric rather than the hard work of ensuring the reality.

—The Futures Project: Vision for Higher Education, 2001
(www.futuresproject.org)

CHAPTER 7

Research on Learning and Student Development and Its Implications

LION F. GARDINER

Whatever other purposes there may be among the thousands of American institutions of higher education, all of them share the core mission of learning. The very concepts school, college, and university imply fostering learning and student development. Most institutional mission statements specifically articulate this purpose. And this human development raison d'être derives its justification from society's need for well-educated citizens and workers who can skillfully and wisely contribute to democratic decision making, social harmony, and economic progress.

Accomplishing this essential but difficult mission—to engender learning and human development on the scale characteristic of most colleges and universities and at the level needed by society—requires skilled, finely tuned management of an institution's educational processes. These activities need to adhere closely to research-based principles of learning so that each student's learning can be maximized. Administrators, faculty and staff members, trustees, and others holding fiduciary responsibility for learning must have knowledge and skills of various sorts to accomplish their learning mission.

This chapter provides an overview of key issues related to your core learning mission so that you might recognize a need for change where it exists in your institution and know where to get additional information to help you. The chapter reviews the literature on the present state of student learning in American colleges and universities and identifies important conditions necessary for student learning and development in the early adult years. It concludes with a checklist of questions for you to ask about your institution and provides a number of resources to help you continue with your own professional development.

CONDITIONS THAT FOSTER STUDENT SUCCESS

Higher education researchers, employers, government officials, and educated citizens have identified higher-order cognitive skills, such as critical thinking, principled ethical reasoning, and ability to solve real-world problems, along with creativity, adaptability, acceptance of human difference, and effective teamwork skills, as some of the most important competencies for college and university graduates. A number of conditions nurture the development of these abilities. As an administrator or faculty or board member who provides leadership, you are responsible for ensuring that these conditions are present in the learning environment.

It should be noted that studies whose specific findings are mentioned in this chapter are identified. For studies whose results are aggregated, and for more extensive reviews of research on learning, student development, and college effects on students, see Astin (1993), Bransford, Brown, and Cocking (1999), Gardiner (1996), and Pascarella and Terenzini (1991).

Learning and Student Development

The research substantiates that virtually all of our students have the potential to learn at a high level so long as they have essential prerequisite knowledge, proceed at a reasonable pace, and are offered both intellectual challenge and intellectual and emotional support. Intelligence can be thought of as the ability to learn and solve complex problems. Rather than seeing it as a genetically determined trait, however, today researchers believe intelligence is substantially influenced and constructed by experience. Your work as an educator can, therefore, be thought of as a process of increasing intelligence. All students, regardless of their starting point, can increase their intelligence with the right kinds of college experiences.

Based on empirical research, particularly in the fields of cognitive and developmental psychology and neuroscience, we know much about how learning occurs. This knowledge is relevant to learning at both the undergraduate and graduate levels. The goal of learning is development of knowledge, skills, attitudes, values, and other cognitive, affective, and motor qualities that are needed to deal effectively with life. What is learned must be durable rather than evanescent; it must be retained in long-term memory if it is to be transferred to new situations where it can be applied when needed. This type of meaningful learning cannot occur with surface learning methods such as memorization of isolated facts. Knowledge transfer requires extended practice using knowledge in contexts other than where it was learned, and understanding the principles for using it appropriately in diverse life situations—that is, deep learning (Bransford et al., 1999). Deep learning requires application and practice.

Learning Must Be Active

Knowledge is actively constructed by a learner through deep processing—practice seeking personal meaning and integrating new knowledge with knowledge already available in the brain's cognitive structure. During active learning, physical changes occur in the brain. Synapses—connections among neurons—are differentially established—synaptic remapping—and new patterns or relationships among neurons are set up, depending on what is being learned. The synapses are modified and the new knowledge is integrated with old knowledge into coherent and meaningful, and therefore useful, structures or wholes.

When we use our knowledge of learning and student development together with research-based practice to design curricula and courses, as well as other educational processes, carefully, we are managing learning specifically to produce particular desired brain reorganizations or transformations. These cognitive changes are ultimately justified by the learning mission and guided by close assessment of students' particular knowledge and developmental stages and needs.

Learning turns novices into experts. Expert cognition is characterized by the ability to perceive meaningful patterns in the world. It is possession of significant knowledge in various areas, the mental organization of which stems from deep understanding in contexts where that knowledge can be applied effectively and in the service of which use it can be relatively easily retrieved when needed (Bransford et al., 1999). Our task as educators is to help novice students move toward expertise: as learners, as broadly developed—liberally educated—human beings, and as professionals in specialized fields. To ensure that student learning is broad and deep and available for transfer, students must be actively involved in the learning process.

Learners Must Be Self-Aware

A learner's self-awareness—that is, his or her *metacognition*—aids learning. Metacognitive learners are aware of, understand, and evaluate their thinking and learning behaviors, know when they do or do not understand something, and are able to regulate their learning and cognitive behavior to improve their effectiveness; in other words, they self-regulate (Bransford et al., 1999; Weinstein, 1994). Metacognitive skill is essential for independent and lifelong learning. Students need to be specifically taught how to develop the awareness and complex skills of self-regulation—how to learn.

Learners Must Be Motivated

High learner motivation and effort are essential to high-level learning. Given appropriate conditions, students will work hard to become competent and solve problems (Bransford et al., 1999). Maintaining high motivation depends on learning tasks being at an appropriate level of challenge. Boredom and frustration are the result if tasks are too easy or too hard, respectively. If students perceive learning as interesting and personally useful, and believe that they are capable of the task, their motivation to learn is increased.

Learning Leads to Development

As people learn, they become more cognitively complex. Development can be thought of as a series of mental changes that accumulate, leading to a new, relatively stable and durable equilibrium that progressively allows a more mature, useful understanding of self and environment (Blasi, 1976). This increased conceptual, or brain, complexity permits a person to develop hypotheses about various aspects of the world—for example, how knowledge and value are derived and what moral behavior is. Thus, the person is able to respond more effectively to complex and difficult-to-understand personal, societal, and professional issues, situations, and problems.

Two dimensions of development essential to becoming an educated person that have been well researched with college students—epistemology and moral judgment—illustrate the concept. Epistemological development is the gradual modification of assumptions a person makes about the source of knowledge and value. A dualistic, authority-based, rigid, black-white perception of reality seeks the right answers from authorities such as parents, religious figures, politicians, and teachers. Under effective educational conditions, a student develops the more complex and nuanced understanding that she must construct knowledge by herself, that she can gain the raw materials for this by seeking evidence and critically evaluating competing claims. When a person develops moral judgment, his reasoning about right action when faced with a moral dilemma gradually evolves from a strictly self-oriented focus on force and obedience to superior power, through several stages to concern for communal social relations and the well-being of others as valued persons. In both types of development, progress is gradual, requires consistent reinforcement and practice in realistic situations, is often substantially aided by social interaction, such as with cooperative learning teams, and leads to increased cognitive complexity and capacity to manipulate difficult abstractions. Like other types of higher-order learning, neither of these capacities is well served by lectures where learners are passive.

Critical Thinking

Perhaps the most culturally and personally valuable abilities we can foster are the cognitive skills and affective dispositions of critical thinking. Critical thinking is a powerful type of higher-order thinking that attempts to understand the world in an accurate, fair, and unbiased fashion. It requires both the skill and the will to engage in rigorous thinking that examines one's own behavior as well as that of others. Critical thinking uses clear intellectual criteria and standards and requires metacognitive awareness and self-regulation (Facione, 1990; Paul, 1995). Its development requires specific efforts and continued practice with guidance; again, listening to lectures alone is ineffective.

Critical thinking is integrally related to both of the developmental dimensions discussed earlier. A mature epistemology makes its development possible, and principled, ethical reasoning may be seen as critical thinking skillfully applied to the moral domain. These difficult-to-develop skills and dispositions are poorly represented in the populace as a whole and among college students. Their development would have a dramatic and salutary impact on every aspect of society.

ENSURING EDUCATIONAL EFFECTIVENESS

The quality of the experiences we provide for our students powerfully affects our contribution to their learning and development and thus the quality of their lives and capacity to contribute positively to society. Skilled management and leadership are crucial to ensuring high-quality experiences for each student. Colleges and universities are enormously complex organizations. Among the variables contributing to this institutional complexity are our students' diverse knowledge and skill levels, motivation, goals, age, and ethnic and sexual identities; a faculty and staff diversity similar to that of the students; the variety of disciplines our faculty represent; and the range of outcomes we hope to achieve. Together, these variables clearly necessitate significant knowledge and skill for all members of the faculty, staff, and administration and close management of the diverse organizational processes supporting learning.

Effective management ensures that institutional and unit missions are each translated into practice through carefully specified learning outcomes, that all educational programs use research-based learning activities, and that all important aspects of the organization are carefully monitored through ongoing assessment research. We should be regularly collecting data about our actual learning outcomes, educational processes, and student input characteristics so that we can continuously monitor and improve learning (see Chapter Eight of this volume for more on this). There is considerable evidence in higher education research and literature to help us understand and improve the effectiveness of our educational processes. This section will summarize some representative research findings related to four key components that affect learning: curriculum, instruction, campus climate, and academic advising.

Curriculum

The purpose of the curriculum is to provide a set of experiences that will ensure that each student's development occurs in an orderly, balanced, and thorough fashion. The curriculum should provide both appropriate challenge and support to produce diverse types of cognitive, affective, and motor development and professional abilities appropriate to each person. According to the research, however, the actuality is different. Although modern curricular design depends on carefully specifying the curriculum's intended outcomes in terms of goals and objectives as appropriate to the institution's mission, relatively few curricula have this essential foundation of a clear desired result to guide their design, implementation, assessment, and improvement. Curricula should be continuously monitored by careful assessment research to track the success of every student in achieving each of the intended outcomes as well as the performance of the curriculum itself (again, see Chapter Eight). In actuality, few curricula are closely examined, and many are not examined at all. More often than not, these complex learning systems are virtually unmanaged. Learning, and thus student development, may or may not be happening; no one understands either the intended or the actual outcomes in any detail.

Distributional general education curricula—where students pick their courses from menus of options—are used by as many as 97 percent of U.S. institutions (Hutchings, Marchese, & Wright, 1991). Most of these curricula are very similar. Yet despite their popularity, they perform relatively poorly when it comes to reliably producing learning. They usually allow considerable flexibility of choice among courses. Naive and often underprepared students must therefore rely on high-quality academic advising to ensure that they are electing the best courses for their developmental needs. But academic advising, as practiced today, is generally not high quality.

An important study of general education curricula revealed that the specific structure of the curriculum, types and breadth of courses, requirements, and amount of choice all lack significant impact on student development (Astin, 1993). In contrast, interdisciplinary core curricula, offered by a handful of colleges and taken by all of their students, have a positive impact on many learning outcomes and on overall satisfaction with college. Astin suggests that the ways in which an institution presents its curriculum and the students approach it are much more important for producing learning than the curriculum's content and structure. Because students frequently do not understand the importance of general education courses and thus devalue them, they may attempt to get such courses "out of the way" as quickly as possible, thus defeating the institutional intent and foreclosing essential developmental opportunities. A study of a large sample of students from fifty-six diverse colleges and universities discovered that 95 to 98 percent of the students' overall college learning from first year through senior year occurred during their first two years (Flowers, Osterlind, Pascarella, & Pierson, 2001). What was happening during the rest of their time on campus?

A study of seventy-three graduating university seniors and four thousand courses revealed "general learned abilities" failed to show substantial gains from the curriculum among students scoring both high and low on entry (Jones & Ratcliff, 1990). Even required courses are not necessarily correlated with outcomes produced, although other courses may be (Ratcliff & Associates, 1990). A curricular design that ignores modern practice by failing to define and monitor its intended outcomes is likely to be ineffectual in promoting learning for many students. *Overall, research does not support the value of distributional curricula in fostering student development.* Clearly, graduating students on the basis of "seat time," and having the right courses listed on their transcripts, ensures very little learning and development. In contrast, assessing competencies prespecified as intended outcomes would.

Instruction

The curriculum affects learning and development through a variety of means, courses chief among them. There are well-established models for designing courses so that intended learning outcomes are clear and consistent with those of the curriculum, instructional methods are appropriate for the desired outcomes, and valid, reliable assessment mechanisms are in place to provide credible evidence of learning and development. But research suggests that most teachers do not use modern instructional design practices. For example, their actual goals in instruction tend to focus on learning concepts, rather than developing thinking skills—their avowed goal—and few teachers focus on developing values (Stark et al., 1990). Only a third of the teachers in one study concerned themselves with the goals of the curriculum; a mere 8 percent used the ideas of instructional experts (Stark, Lowther, Ryan, & Genthon, 1988). How effective are our courses in accomplishing the learning and development mission?

The Lecture

Various studies reveal that as many as 70 to 90 percent of faculty members use the traditional lecture as their preferred teaching strategy, although the lecture is one of the weakest methods of facilitating higher-order cognitive skills. Traditional lectures do not usually actively involve students in sustained higher-order thinking or interaction with either the teacher or their peers. What level of intellectual stimulation and thus opportunity for high-level cognitive development do students experience here? Numerous studies consistently show that, no matter the discipline or institutional type and size, the emphasis in college courses is overwhelmingly on transmission of facts. Class time spent questioning students is often minimal, and only a small amount of it involves problem solving; most exchanges are focused on recalling facts or taking care of housekeeping details. Research tells us that in lectures, students' attention typically drifts after twenty minutes. During only about half the time in class are they doing what their teachers want them to do. Not surprisingly, relatively little content tends to be recalled from these lectures, even immediately afterward.

Studying

No matter the course quality, most of what students learn is learned outside of formal class sessions. Studies suggest, however, that relatively few college students have ever been taught to learn in high school or college. Many routinely take an ineffective surface approach to learning, striving to memorize isolated facts, rather than a deep approach, which is an attempt to understand and make meaning from what they are studying that would result in learning, retention, and transfer. Furthermore, their effort is not sustained, with students studying on average only about 0.3 to 1.0 hour per classroom hour, far from the minimum 2.0 hours that their teachers ordinarily believe is necessary for successful learning.

Seven Principles for Good Practice

One widely published summary of principles derived from research is the *Seven Principles for Good Practice in Undergraduate Education* (Chickering & Gamson, 1987). The principles urge teachers to use methods that encourage the following: student-faculty contact, both in and outside of class; cooperation among students; active learning; prompt feedback on performance; emphasis of time on task; communication of high expectations; and respect for different learning styles and talents. (See Chapter Ten.)

The findings summarized thus far in this chapter suggest that, in the main, college and university faculty are not adhering closely to the seven principles.

Classroom Tests

What, then, are college students' actual learning outcomes? Various studies have produced these representative results: less than half of college seniors know what the Koran is or when the American Civil War was fought (Heller, 1989), only half of an Ivy League student sample could name their own state's U.S. senators, and almost a quarter did not know the number of U.S. Supreme Court justices (Big Gaps, 1993; New Poll, 1993). Moreover, studies suggest that many students may not understand the key concepts of their own major fields. Other studies tell us that about half of four-year college graduates are unable to state an argument presented by a newspaper editorial, use a bus schedule effectively, or calculate the cost per ounce of peanut butter from a shelf label in a supermarket (Barton & Lapointe, 1995). Perhaps most important, graduates have a poorly developed capacity for critical thinking, which as we have seen is often the college outcome most strongly desired by faculty and needed by society.

Classroom assessment practices have a marked impact on student learning behavior and should provide essential evidence about learning and teaching effectiveness. Faculty can learn a lot about their instructional and evaluation practices by paying attention to the results of their efforts, listening to student feedback, and consulting the research literature. Many studies show that teacher-made classroom tests require little writing, even in small colleges, and although faculty may believe otherwise, they overwhelmingly require only the recognition or recall of facts and conceptual knowledge. Relatively few test items require the problem-solving skills of analysis, evaluation, and synthesis. Even in technical fields, where student examinations contain many problems, research shows these generally only involve straightforward tasks such as "plug and play" exercises solving familiar equations. Thus, research suggests that most classroom tests have serious deficiencies as mental measuring devices, such as lacking validity—not measuring what the teacher thinks they measure—and having unknown reliability, thus being unable to provide useful evidence of learning or form a sound foundation for grades. (For a discussion and critique of grades as indicators of learning see Chapter Eight.)

Campus Climate

Climate refers to the emotional tone of a campus, including its classrooms, offices, and residence halls. Is the campus a welcoming, supportive environment or indifferent and alienating? *Research shows a clear correlation between campus climate and student learning and development, retention, and satisfaction with college.* This association results from a sense of academic and social integration into a community of learners and is mediated through relationships among students and between students and faculty members. If faculty and staff care about students, it leads to a sense of being valued and part of a community. Today, over 80 percent of students commute to campus. Providing a supportive environment for these students is a special challenge. Great care must be taken to ensure that each person feels integrated into the campus community.

The relationships among climate, feeling of integration, and important learning outcomes, and the faculty and staff impact on the climate are clear. Studies suggest, however, that many institutions lack a supportive climate for all students' learning. Many campuses have serious, even pervasive problems with underage drinking and student alcoholism, which can interfere with all students' learning. Women students and faculty are often treated poorly, and on many campuses people may be harassed as a matter of course on the basis of their ethnic or sexual status. As many as half of all students on campuses express a sense of alienation. Large impersonal classes, lack of out-of-class contact with faculty and other students, and impersonal treatment in campus offices all work to degrade campus climate.

In addition, accumulating research suggests that men and women have very different college experiences. Transcript analysis shows that men and women enroll in significantly different sets of courses: "a men's curriculum and women's curriculum" (Adelman, 1990, p. 242). One large study of college outcomes found that, on average, women's cognitive development benefited only about two-thirds as much as men's in all subject areas tested from their first through senior years (Flowers et al., 2001). Whatever the specific causative variables, Astin (1993) concludes his huge study by pointing out that, overall "it seems clear that colleges do not serve to eliminate or even reduce many of the stereotypic differences between the sexes. . .[but]. . .preserve and strengthen. . .[them with respect to] behavior, personality, aspirations, and achievement" (pp. 405–406). This situation remained unchanged over the decade-and-a-half since Astin's previous study (Astin, 1977). Clearly, the campus climate at a sizable number of institutions is not being managed effectively to support rather than undermine the learning mission.

Academic Advising

For most of our students, higher education is a very new experience. The academic culture may be very different from any they previously knew in its demands or customs, and the types of people they encounter. College can be a scary place. Planning a personal curriculum that can meet their needs for diverse cognitive, emotional, social, and other types of development is a daunting task, especially when they are confronted with a distributional curriculum. Many are the first in their families to attend college, and thus they can find little useful guidance at home. The wider culture communicates various insistent anti-intellectual, materialistic, and take-the-easy-way-out messages. Their peers offer a chorus of contradictory information, opinions, and values. High-quality academic advising is essential to ensure effective decisions about these complex issues.

Modern developmental academic advising, as it is usually known, is a form of teaching that can address all of a student's needs for developmental guidance very directly and can allow an institution to provide personal out-of-class faculty-student contact for every person. Developmental academic advising focuses on human learning and development. It begins with the student's own values and goals and helps him or her design a curriculum and array of other experiences to answer specific developmental needs. Developmental academic advising is central to students' college experience: it enables them to integrate diverse courses, involvement in student organizations, psychological and career counseling, off-campus learning, employment, and other activities into a holistic educational experience.

To what extent do we provide high-quality academic advising to our students? *The research suggests that, despite three decades of national experience with developmental advising, few institutions have such programs in place.* In fact, academic advising generally seems to be held in low esteem as a faculty activity. Studies suggest that most students experience academic advising as a means of getting information such as rules, deadlines, and procedures for registration and graduation, not personalized guidance for effective learning and development. It is primarily a clerical endeavor more likely to meet the bureaucratic needs of the institution for course enrollment projections than to support students' developmental needs. Perhaps this, together with the sometimes voluntary nature of academic advising, is why students seek advising as infrequently as research suggests. Rather than spending the three hours per year minimum that the literature indicates students need, fully one-third of students in a study of fifty-five institutions spent as little as fifteen minutes during each of two or fewer meetings each year (Noble, 1988). Institutional support for advisers that could ensure high-quality advising—that is, training, evaluation, and rewards—is "at best unsystematic and at worst nonexistent" (Habley, 2001, p. 42).

PRACTICES THAT WILL FOSTER LEARNING

The following paragraphs enumerate some of the important conditions and features of educational programs that support student learning and development, according to decades of research and practice.

- *Have a clear, well-crafted mission statement for the institution and each unit that articulates the learning mission.* Also ensure that unit mission statements are all consistent with and support accomplishment of the institutional mission.
- *Be sure that each mission statement is carefully translated into practice by means of a set of well-written goals and objectives that describe the intended outcomes for each program.* These statements, together with the missions from which they are derived, are instrumental at every point for designing, implementing, and monitoring curricula and instruction and other relevant educational activities. These statements of intended outcomes should set very high expectations for both students and staff.

- *Have a high-quality program of assessment.* The program should provide for each student, faculty, and staff member, and other institutional stakeholder, the accurate information he or she needs about learning and institutional functioning in a timely manner and understandable form.
- *Be sure that every curriculum is carefully balanced.* Each should provide the right distribution of types of learning and be integrated so that it is not just a series of fragments corresponding to the current teachers' disciplinary specialties. Having a set of intended outcome goals and objectives provides the foundation for a balanced and effective curriculum. Modern learning and student development theory are essential planning components when structuring these intended outcomes, and when designing and implementing courses.
- *Integrate general education and disciplinary major field curricula.* They should reinforce each other so that together they can produce higher-order cognitive development. Furthermore, curricula should be integrated with other components of the educational program, such as academic advising, co-curricular activities, career and psychological counseling, and employment.
- *Have a high-quality developmental academic advising program.* Every student should have a positive and productive relationship, and spend adequate time with, a fully trained and skilled faculty adviser.
- *Be sure that students are actively involved in each of the components of their educational programs from first contact before admission through graduation.* The importance of active involvement in learning cannot be overstated. The committee of experts responsible for the report *Involvement in Learning* stated, "The amount of student learning and personal development associated with any educational program is directly proportional to the quality and quantity of student involvement in that program," and "The effectiveness of any educational policy or practice is directly related to the capacity of that policy or practice to increase student involvement in learning" (Study Group, 1984, p. 19).
- *Create an engaged and supportive campus climate.* Furthermore, regularly monitor its quality throughout the institution by assessment research.
- *Support faculty and staff.* Provide for each faculty and staff member high-quality training, support, and rewards for competent work as an educator.
- *Exercise leadership.* Increase and maintain the level of urgency for change so everyone is motivated to learn and function in new and effective ways to produce learning and student development at a high level.

KEY QUESTIONS TO ASK ABOUT YOUR INSTITUTION

Professional methods and a large literature are available to aid you in studying and improving your organization. You must take responsibility to ensure your own level of professional knowledge and skill is always at a high level.

This section presents some key questions to ask about your institution or unit to begin to explore its current capacity to support learning and development for all of your students. These questions can stimulate your own thinking and also serve as a means of exploring learning and institutional performance with colleagues. You will think of many other questions as well. Ask them too. (For additional specific questions to ask about educational conditions in your organization, see again Chapter Eight on assessing learning.)

- How great an impact do your courses have on your students' learning, and what are your institution's actual learning outcomes? How much of what they have learned do your graduates retain, and how much of that can they apply—transfer—when needed? How do you know these things?
- Do your institution and unit prepare incoming students from first contact through admission and orientation so that each one understands how college can contribute to his or her development and has the knowledge, skills, and disposition required for deep learning?
- Do you have a high-quality developmental academic advising program that provides all students with regular, productive contact with a *trained and skilled* faculty adviser throughout their time on campus?
- Does each curriculum have a mission statement conceptually linked to the institutional mission statement? Is each of these curricular mission statements accompanied by a set of well-written intended learning outcome goals and objectives that translate the mission statement into action? Do all of these intended outcomes set a high standard for students and teachers? Are these documents *used* on a regular basis?
- Is each course designed so that its instructional goals and objectives derive from and specifically contribute to the accomplishment of its curricular goals and objectives in a planned and systematic way?
- Does each course use appropriate research-based educational methods that can support learning at a high level as specified by its statements of intended outcomes?

- Does each course employ appropriate, valid, and reliable assessment methods that can provide accurate and useful information about actual learning outcomes for each student and concerning course performance?
- Does the institution and its units have effective, appropriate assessment programs that monitor all aspects of student and program performance—for example, admission, orientation, advising, curriculum and course design and implementation, assessment, and professional development for faculty and staff?
- Are the examples of student knowledge described earlier in the section on learning and student development representative of students in your institution or unit? How do you know? If they are representative, specifically why?
- Is each person—faculty, staff member, or administrator—aware of changes that must be made in his or her area of responsibility to improve learning, and does he or she have the knowledge, skills, and support from administrators required to make these changes and a plan of action?
- Do administrators and faculty and other staff members in your institution or unit apply research-based best professional practice to each aspect of their work as educators? How do you know?
- Do you, yourself, apply this knowledge to your own work as a manager, teacher, or in other professional roles you may have?
- Do you make sure you keep current with the knowledge and skills essential to your roles in the institution?
- Does your institution have a professional development program that provides appropriate state-of-the-art, research-based training regarding students and learning for all faculty and staff with managerial and teaching responsibility on an ongoing basis? Is participation in and active use of learning acquired in the program voluntary, and is it an expected component for promotion, tenure, and salary increases?
- How high is the level of urgency for educational change in your institution? Are you providing vigorous leadership for educational change and the improvement of learning quality on your campus and in your unit? Are your efforts informed by the professional literature as well as by careful on-campus assessment research in your areas of responsibility?
- Do all people who report to you understand that you expect them to be leaders for change? Do all your faculty and staff feel a high level of urgency for change? Do they all feel empowered to lead? Is each one well trained to lead?

CONCLUSION

Some students learn at a high level while they are in college and regard their experiences positively, and some teachers are very effective in assisting their students' development. But the accumulated research findings clearly indicate pervasive problems in the quality of the college experiences of most students.

We often blame high schools for failing to educate their students and for sending them to us underprepared. But research shows that high school teachers often model their teaching practice on former college professors in their disciplines. Teachers and principals are trained in *our* institutions and usually educated in colleges of arts and sciences. One sad outcome of our failure to use modern research-based methods that work has been a vicious cycle of mediocrity, wherein graduates who teach in the schools continue to send us students they are unable to prepare adequately for college-level learning because of their own limited educational experiences in college.

In their policies and the public information they produce, many institutions make much of their wealth and research prowess and suggest a general and substantial benefit of faculty research and scholarly activity for undergraduate student learning. Concluding their authoritative synthesis of research on college effects on students, Pascarella and Terenzini (1991) state, "There is little consistent evidence to indicate that college selectivity, prestige, or educational resources have any important net impact on students in such areas as learning, cognitive and intellectual development, other psychosocial changes, the development of principled moral reasoning, or shifts in other attitudes and values" (p. 592). In sharp contrast with much academic myth, these researchers suggest that characteristics of individual students and the conditions they experience in institutions are far more influential in their learning and cognitive development than an institution's selectivity, prestige, or wealth.

A meta-analysis of many studies exploring a relationship between research quality and teaching quality found a less than 2 percent positive impact of faculty research on teaching (Feldman, 1987). Astin (1993) found a strong negative correlation ($r = -.69$) between his faculty variables Student Orientation—one of the most powerful influences on student outcomes in his large study—and Research Orientation. He also found a similar negative correlation ($r = -.72$) between faculty Research Orientation and "commitment to student development" (p. 411).

Overall, the research reviewed in this chapter suggests that among the reasons institutions are as generally ineffectual as they are in fostering learning, one of the most important is the failure to use modern, research-based educational practices. Perhaps chief among the reasons for this failure is our traditional lack of professional training for our work as educators. Despite clear evidence from studies of the importance of teacher competence for student learning, and even twenty-five years after the inception of professional faculty development methodologies, faculty and staff remain unfamiliar with research on learning and student development and best professional practice for curricular and instructional design, teaching strategies, developmental academic advising, and assessment. Yet, ironically, studies also show that college faculty rate the quality of their teaching very highly.

In addition to their lack of professional preparation for their work, faculty are usually isolated from one another, student affairs professionals, and administrators. The teamwork among these professionals essential to fulfill the learning mission is not strong on many campuses. Administrators are equally untrained and unprepared for their complex professional responsibilities as managers of learning and leaders of educational change, and they ordinarily have only the most general understanding of the conditions required for learning. Thus, their capacity to manage learning effectively and lead change is severely constrained.

Your own systematic professional development should be one of your highest priorities. You, yourself, must take responsibility for your own training. The potential effect on learning and student development in your institution—not to mention your own sense of accomplishment and fulfillment—stands as an exciting, ongoing challenge.

References

Adelman, C. (1990). *A college course map. Taxonomy and transcript data: Based on the postsecondary records, 1972–1984, of the high school class of 1972.* Washington, DC: U.S. Department of Education. (ERIC Document Reproduction Service No. ED 326 153)

Astin, A. W. (1977). *Four critical years.* San Francisco: Jossey-Bass.

Astin, A. W. (1993). *What matters in college? Four critical years revisited.* San Francisco: Jossey-Bass.

Barton, P. E., & Lapointe, A. (1995). *Learning by degrees: Indicators of performance in higher education.* Princeton, NJ: Educational Testing Service, Policy Information Center.

Big gaps found in college students' grasp of current affairs. (1993, 18 April). *The New York Times,* p. 36.

Blasi, A. (1976). Concept of development in personality theory. In J. Loevinger (Ed.), *Ego development* (pp. 29–53). San Francisco: Jossey-Bass.

Bransford, J. D., Brown, A. L., & Cocking, R. R. (Eds.). (1999). *How people learn: Brain, mind, experience, and school.* Washington, DC: National Academy Press.

Chickering, A. W., & Gamson, Z. F. (1987). Seven principles for good practice in undergraduate education. *Wingspread Journal, 9,* 1–4.

Facione, P. A. (1990). *Critical thinking: A statement of expert consensus for purposes of educational assessment and instruction* (Research Findings and Recommendations Prepared for the Committee on Pre-College Philosophy of the American Philosophical Association). Fullerton: California State University. (ERIC Document Reproduction Service No. ED 315 423)

Feldman, K. A. (1987). Research productivity and scholarly accomplishment of college teachers as related to their instructional effectiveness: A review and exploration. *Research in Higher Education, 26*(3), 227–298.

Flowers, L., Osterlind, S. J., Pascarella, E. T., & Pierson, C. T. (2001, September-October). How much do students learn in college? Cross-sectional estimates using the College BASE. *Journal of Higher Education, 72*(5), 564–583.

Gardiner, L. F. (1996). *Redesigning higher education: Producing dramatic gains in student learning.* Washington, DC: George Washington University, Graduate School of Education and Human Development. (ERIC Document Reproduction Service No. ED 394 442)

Habley, W. R. (2001). Current practices in academic advising. In V. N. Gordon, W. R. Habley, & Associates (Eds.), *Academic advising: A comprehensive handbook* (pp. 35–43). San Francisco: Jossey-Bass.

Heller, S. (1989, October 11). More than half of students in survey flunk history and literature test. *Chronicle of Higher Education,* p. A15.

Hutchings, P., Marchese, T., & Wright, B. (1991). *Using assessment to strengthen general education.* Washington, DC: American Association for Higher Education.

Jones, E. A., & Ratcliff, J. R. (1990, April). *Is a core curriculum best for everybody? The effect of different patterns of coursework on the general education of high- and low-ability students.* Paper presented at the annual meeting of the American Educational Research Association, Boston.

New poll: Ivy League students fail current affairs test. (1993, April 4). Washington, DC: Luntz-Weber.

Noble, J. (1988). What students think of academic advising. In W. R. Habley (Ed.), *The status and future of academic advising: Problems and promise.* Iowa City: ACT National Center for the Advancement of Educational Priorities.

Pascarella, E., & Terenzini, P. (1991). *How colleges affect students: Findings and insights from twenty years of research.* San Francisco: Jossey-Bass.

Paul, R. W. (1995). *Critical thinking: How to prepare students for a rapidly changing world.* Santa Rosa, CA: Foundation for Critical Thinking.

Ratcliff, J. L., & Associates. (1990). *Determining the effect of different coursework patterns on the general learned abilities of college students* (Working Paper OR 90–524). Washington, DC: U.S. Department of Education.

Stark, J. S., Lowther, M. A., Bentley, R. J., Ryan, M. P., Martens, G. G., Genthon, M. L., Wren, P. A., & Shaw, K. M. (1990). *Planning introductory college courses: Influences on faculty.* Ann Arbor: University of Michigan, National Center for Research to Improve Postsecondary Teaching and Learning. (ERIC Document Reproduction Service No. ED 330 277)

Stark, J. S., Lowther, M. A., Ryan, M. P., & Genthon, M. (1988). Faculty reflect on course planning. *Research in Higher Education, 29*(3), 219–240.

Study Group on the Conditions of Excellence in American Higher Education. (1984). *Involvement in learning: Realizing the potential of American higher education.* Washington, DC: National Institute of Education. (ERIC Document Reproduction Service No. ED 246 853)

Weinstein, C. E. (1994). Students at risk for academic failure: Learning to learn classes. In K. W. Prichard & R. M. Sawyer (Eds.), *Handbook of college teaching: Theory and applications* (pp. 375–385). Westport, CT: Greenwood Press.

Resources

The following books contain a rich store of up-to-date information about research on student learning and development and best practice for producing these outcomes in supporting the learning mission.

Reviews of Research on Learning, Student Development, and College Effects on Students

Astin, A. W. (1993). *What matters in college? Four critical years revisited.* San Francisco: Jossey-Bass.
This volume describes findings of a large study of college effects on students that followed up a similar, notable earlier study (Astin, 1977). The new study involved the interaction of 420 input, environmental, and outcome variables for many thousands of students and hundreds of faculty members and institutions. It leads to many valuable insights into how students develop in colleges and universities and looks at trends since the author's earlier study done fifteen years before.

Bransford, J. D., Brown, A. L., & Cocking, R. R. (Eds.). (1999). *How people learn: Brain, mind, experience, and school.* Washington, DC: National Academy Press.
This synthesis of research on learning results from the work of a National Research Council committee. The book provides an overview of what is known about learning and how to employ this new knowledge to improve learning in schools and colleges.

Evans, N. J., Forney, D. S., & Guido-DiBrito, F. (1998.) *Student development in college: Theory, research, and practice.* San Francisco: Jossey-Bass.
The authors review student development as an area of research and a source of practical guidance in higher education. They examine numerous theories on the development of various aspects of students' identity, cognitive capacities, ways of learning, careers, and personalities. Descriptions of each theory or group of theories includes historical overview, research support, applications, available assessment methods, and critique and future directions. The book concludes with suggestions for the future of development theory and recommended readings.

Gardiner, L. F. (1996). *Redesigning higher education: Producing dramatic gains in student learning.* Washington, DC: George Washington University, Graduate School of Education and Human Development. (ERIC Document Reproduction Service No. ED 394 442)
This monograph is a quickly readable review and synthesis of research on student development and the effectiveness of colleges and universities in facilitating it. It is designed to stimulate critical thinking and raise the level of urgency for change among administrators, faculty members,

and others concerned with learning. The Introduction describes key competencies society needs and several dimensions that underpin these abilities and their development in students. The book looks at research findings on whether common practices support or undermine learning and development, the degree to which today's students can learn at a high level, and the role of effective leadership in improving learning. It offers the recommendations of researchers for improving learning.

Pascarella, E. T., & Terenzini, P. T. (1991). *How college affects students: Findings and insights from twenty years of research.* San Francisco: Jossey-Bass.
Based on a review of almost three thousand studies—conducted between 1968 and 1991—of college effects on all aspects of students' learning and development, this encyclopedic volume synthesizes what is known about student learning and development and how colleges influence them. Two important chapters—"How College Makes a Difference" and "Implications of the Research for Policy and Practice"—conclude the volume by summarizing the research reviewed. An appendix discusses technical research issues for assessing the impact of colleges on students.

Curriculum

Gaff, J. G., Ratcliff, J. L., & Associates. (1997). *Handbook of the undergraduate curriculum: A comprehensive guide to purposes, structures, practices, and change.* San Francisco: Jossey-Bass.
Fifty-seven authors contributed to this comprehensive practical compendium of ideas about the undergraduate college curriculum. Intended to be selectively read by anyone with an interest in or responsibility for curriculum—from faculty members to presidents and trustees and others, such as legislative education committee members—the volume attempts to present an overarching review of curricular issues. It is based on the thesis that the long-sustained and increasing specialization of the undergraduate curriculum has resulted in its fragmentation and the diminution of student learning and that it must therefore change. Thirty-four topical chapters organized into six sections review the purposes and aims of the curriculum, its historical development, the outcomes a curriculum should produce, specific academic disciplines that make up the curriculum, innovations that can improve learning, how to manage the curriculum for effective and efficient learning (including assessing and evaluating the curriculum), and finally, how to facilitate curricular change. Each chapter provides references to the most useful literature in the field.

Stark, J. S., & Lattuca, L. R. (1997). *Shaping the college curriculum: Academic plans in action.* Needham Heights, MA: Allyn & Bacon.
Based on an extensive and meticulous review of a variety of literatures as well as their own research, the authors make suggestions for faculty and administrators to improve "academic plans" and thus learning. Topics discussed include defining curriculum, curricular debates and efforts at curricular reform, designing curricula, the role of learning and learners in curricular and course design, selecting methods of instruction, managing academic plans and leading change, and curricular research. An appendix includes a time line of U.S. curricular trends from 1636 through 1994.

Instruction

Diamond, R. M. (1998). *Designing and assessing courses and curricula: A practical guide.* San Francisco: Jossey-Bass.

This is a practical manual. Using a systematic approach, the author guides readers through each stage of design. Detailed graphical representations of design processes, numerous examples at both the undergraduate and graduate levels, an emphasis on grounding design in research-based practice, and nine appendixes with further examples and tools increase the usefulness of this book.

Millis, B. J., & Cottell, Jr., P. G. (1998). *Cooperative learning for higher education faculty.* Phoenix: American Council on Education–Oryx Press.

Cooperative learning is a highly researched and flexible array of methods for involving learners actively in their learning and with other learners. This is a handbook for anyone desiring to understand the rationale for active involvement in learning and for a major change in the way instruction is designed and implemented in higher education. Other topics include classroom management, structuring cooperative courses, assessment, and strategies for leaders who desire to support faculty use of cooperative learning.

Academic Advising

Gordon, V. N., Habley, W. R., & Associates. (2000). *Academic advising: A comprehensive handbook.* San Francisco: Jossey-Bass.

This practical handbook for developing and managing a modern developmental academic advising program is sponsored by the National Academic Advising Association (NACADA). Thirty-four experts discuss the theoretical basis for academic advising; student diversity as it relates to advising; managing a program; training, evaluation, and recognition and rewards for advisers; and change and the future of advising. Three appendixes present NACADA core values, professional standards for advising, and resources.

CHAPTER 8

Student Development
Monitoring the Quality of Learning and Development

LION F. GARDINER

Good decision making requires good information. To make effective decisions that allow your institution, agency, or unit to accomplish its learning mission reliably, you must have accurate and timely information that will enable you to understand your student clients as they enter your institution, as they change, and after they leave. You also need to understand your organization's educational processes, such as its curricula and courses, and its academic advising, assessment, and faculty development programs. You need to comprehend the campus climate as it is experienced by students, faculty, and staff, and the attitudes of these people toward the institution and their work. With accurate information you can compare your educational processes and climate against best practice and improve your institution's contribution to learning. But if you lack relevant, current, and accurate evidence on any one of the key learning-related components of your institution, you compromise your ability to manage and lead for mission accomplishment and for continuous improvement of institutional quality. In a time of rapid environmental change and growing competition, your institution's health may be at risk.

A system's complexity conceals variables and relationships among them. If you do not perceive and understand these relationships that can lead to poor decision making. In academe's new competitive environment, not having high-quality information about the organization is courting disaster. If you look only at surface appearances and listen to people who give you "happy talk" about the institution, or rely on the speculations and ratings of your institution's quality in popular magazines, you may be taking unacceptable risks. Lack of good information is a main reason for complacency in organizations (Kotter, 1996). You must have information about your graduates' abilities and to what extent these abilities are attributable to your institution's influence—that is, the value you have added to your students' lives. Today, information is key to success.

This chapter provides an overview of essential issues to consider if you are to manage learning effectively on the large scale that is characteristic of colleges and universities. The first part describes the foundation for all institutional action—identification of intended outcomes—and the following parts examine the process of monitoring actual outcomes. For other aspects of assessment and evaluation see Chapter Nine ("Curricula and Courses: Administrative Issues"), Chapter Fourteen ("Evaluation and Assessment: An Institutional Context"), and Chapter Sixteen ("Leadership in Faculty Evaluation").

BEING CLEAR ABOUT RESULTS: DEFINING INTENDED OUTCOMES

The saying goes: "If you don't have any goals, any road will take you where you're going." Being clear about what graduates should know and be able to do is a sine qua non of effective education planning. Then all institutional activity can be directed toward producing a carefully defined result. A clear description of graduates' desired characteristics is an essential foundation for all curriculum planning and implementation, instruction, assessment design, academic advising, and faculty and staff development. Yet despite experts' advice on this point dating back at least seven decades (Tyler, 1934), relatively few colleges and universities have heeded it and developed descriptions of their intended results. This deficiency in planning has contributed to the questionable quality of learning in much of higher education as well as enormous waste. Everyone is busy with "activity," but this activity does not necessarily focus on predetermined, agreed-on aims—nor does it necessarily use research findings to reach these often-obscure ends (see Chapter Seven). They all "do their own thing" without the necessary focus and coordination required to produce a high-quality result.

Effective monitoring of learning requires a clear understanding of the institution's or unit's educational purpose—its learning mission—as presented in its mission statement, and a clear description of what its graduates should look like—a set of carefully constructed statements of intended learning outcomes. Indeed, these documents form a necessary foundation for managing all aspects of learning in the institution, not just assessment research. Statements of intended outcomes serve a similar function in an institution as the standards now commonplace in K–12 education. They are vehicles for determining the types of disciplinary content, dispositions, and values that should be learned, and for setting high expectations for students.

Characteristics of Effective Statements of Intended Outcomes

Outcomes should be identified based on an institution's or unit's mission statement. The mission statement articulates the learning purpose and forms a foundation for all action. However, mission statements are necessarily written in broad language. They require interpretation if they are to guide specific action. Interpretation is the role of the institution's or unit's statements of intended outcomes. Intended outcomes are stated in terms of outcome goals and objectives. An *outcome goal* describes a relatively broad result that is more fully described by two or more associated outcome objectives. The goal is what one cares most about, and it provides justification for each of the objectives. The *outcome objectives* fully describe the goal in the detail needed to design and implement programs and to design valid assessments of goal achievement. If the assessable objectives are achieved, one assumes the goal has been reached. Goals and objectives should be developed and used at every institutional level.

A goal that is part of the natural science component of an undergraduate general education curriculum might be stated as follows: *Use science reasoning to solve problems.* By itself, this goal is a broad, general statement of the overall outcome desired for all students, not nearly specific enough to serve as a basis for curriculum or assessment design. What aspects of science reasoning are intended? Here are more specific objectives that could accompany this goal and more fully describe its meaning:

- *Objective 1: Given laboratory or field observations, construct one or more hypotheses that can plausibly explain the observations.*
- *Objective 2: Design experiments that can test hypotheses.*
- *Objective 3: Interpret experimental tests of hypotheses, including identifying all assumptions and inferences made.*

A goal's objectives should completely describe it. These are the particular parts of the goal content that will be taught and assessed. In the preceding case, additional objectives might be needed to describe the goal fully.

Accurate Goals and Objectives

Goals and objectives must accurately communicate the institution's desired results. Therefore, they must be carefully articulated. Language matters. To ensure consistent interpretation by all users, an intended outcome statement must have three characteristics: it must be put into language that describes an outcome, it must be behavioral, and it must be as specific as appropriate and as possible. For example, the statement "Develop an understanding of science" is not useful for purposes of planning or assessment. First, this goal states a learning *process,* not an outcome. Are the faculty to develop the understanding in students or are the students to develop their own understanding? The intended meaning is unclear. Furthermore, both of these activities are processes. Outcomes constitute knowledge, abilities, or values that exist in a learner when learning (a process) in a class, course, or curriculum has been completed. They are the result of learning.

A second problem with this statement is the word *understanding,* a classic "weasel" word. No one reading the statement can be sure what behaviors are intended. The words *know* and *think* and the phrase *be aware of* present similar problems. Substituting action verbs such as *use, solve, apply, construct,* or *write* clarifies the meaning. The desired behavior is observable and therefore assessable.

A third problem with this statement is its vagueness; one cannot determine which aspect of science is important. Rewording the statement can transform it into a useful outcome. One possible revised version is this: *Use experiments to answer questions about natural phenomena.* The statement now describes an outcome, what students should be able to do after learning is complete; it is behavioral, including the action verb *use;* and it refers to a specific aspect of science, experimentation.

There are several additional issues to be alert to with intended outcomes.

Mission Statements and Goals and Objectives

Mission statements, goals, and objectives form a logical hierarchy. An institution's various mission statements and sets of outcome goals and objectives should be internally consistent. Each unit's goals and objectives should be consistent with its own mission statement. Each unit's mission statement should also be consistent with the successively higher units' mission statements and that of the institution as a whole. The outcome goals and objectives for a course should derive from, be consistent with, and contribute to accomplishing the course's curriculum's goals and objectives, rather than be left to the idiosyncratic choices of the individual faculty member who is teaching the course.

Intended Outcomes and Institutional Values

Your statements of intended outcomes reflect your values. Are they consistent with your institutional value statement?

General Education and Major Field Outcomes

Some of the most important outcomes for society, such as critical thinking and principled ethical reasoning, are complex and depend for their development on fundamental changes that must occur in students' cognitive frameworks (see Chapter Seven for more on this). They are difficult to develop. These profound developmental changes take time; ordinarily they cannot occur during a single course or semester. Therefore, cognitive abilities specified in general education goals must be carried over into courses in your major field curricula and spelled out in their intended outcomes as well.

Socially and Personally Significant Outcomes

An institution's statements of intended outcomes should articulate knowledge, skills, and values that are important to society. Student time is limited; you cannot accomplish everything. When you are defining intended results, eliminate much of the low-level learning that we now usually emphasize and that distracts students from culturally and personally useful learning (again, see Chapter Seven).

Make sure that the writers of your outcome statements use a professional tool, such as the Bloom Taxonomy for cognitive learning, as a guide for thinking and writing (Anderson & Krathwohl, 2001; Bloom, 1956). Be sure you include important affective learning outcomes (interests, attitudes, values). Taxonomies have also been developed for the two types of learning other than cognitive: affective learning (Krathwohl, Bloom, & Masia, 1964) and psychomotor (movement) skills (Harrow, 1972).

A key point when defining intended cognitive outcomes is the level of learning desired. For example, listing the names of chemical elements is a low-level task that requires only memorization of names, the lowest level of the Bloom Taxonomy, but no understanding of characteristics. When a student is able to describe in his own words the properties of different elements and how these affect their behavior it shows that he has acquired these concepts and is functioning at the second level. If you want your graduates to be able to use this conceptual knowledge to solve problems in chemistry, however—analyzing, evaluating, and synthesizing—more complex problem-solving skills are required. The wording of outcome goals and objectives must reflect these differences in cognitive level. An important reason why most college courses emphasize facts in classroom activities and in assessment is that, even today, faculty members generally are unaware of the Bloom Taxonomy and other tools that could help them reliably control intellectual level as they design curricula, courses, and assessments. Your faculty and staff will require training to use such tools skillfully.

Prioritized Outcomes

Part of the process of developing goals and objectives is prioritizing your intended outcomes. Again, because your students do not have time to learn everything, you must decide what is most important. Focus on what society and students need most. Ensure that essential higher-order cognitive abilities are well developed. Chop away low-level factual and conceptual underbrush that so often and unproductively dominates curricula and student time.

The Process of Developing Effective Outcome Statements

Pay close attention to the *process* of developing these important outcome statements because much depends on their results.

The Process Takes Time

Developing a set of high-quality intended outcome statements is difficult intellectual work. You are dealing with all aspects of human development in the case of general education, or the full range of learning in a discipline or professional field in the case of a major field of specialization. Most faculty members ordinarily deal with more limited aspects of their fields, and many have never thought in as much detail about the field as they must do now. Colleagues view the field differently and put a different value on various kinds of knowledge, skills, or values. It takes time to talk and think these things through to come to consensus.

The Process Takes Skill

It requires considerable practice to be able to think clearly about intended outcomes and write effective goals and objectives. Most academicians have difficulty doing this at first. They need training and adequate supervised practice with corrective feedback to become skilled.

When beginning to work with outcomes and develop a set of goals and objectives for an institution or unit, an external consultant's assistance can be a wise—even essential—investment. However, you should ensure that high-level expertise is eventually developed internally. Today, the knowledge and skills required for working with goals and objectives, and the educational methods required to actualize and assess them, should be standard components of the academician's professional toolbox.

The Process Takes Involvement

An administrator or single faculty member should not draft your outcome statements. The people who will have to implement them should be involved—as involved as they possibly can be. Benefits of this approach include increased available knowledge and creativity and thus a better product, a distributed workload, and a commitment to use the product and take responsibility for revising the goals as needed.

Although a general education committee or departmental faculty acting as a committee-of-the-whole may supervise the development of a set of outcome goals and objectives, a writing committee of two or three—not one—will be more efficient than the entire large group. The larger group identifies outcomes it desires and then directs the work of the writing committee, which in turn translates these general ideas into sharp, well-formed goals and objectives. Drafts of these statements are periodically sent to the committee for review, comment, and eventual approval. A cyclical expert review process can similarly help the writing team develop a polished product. The team develops a draft that is periodically reviewed and critiqued by someone with excellent goal development skills and sent back for polishing.

Goals Should Be Considered First

Experience suggests that you complete work on your intended outcome goals and objectives before considering ways to assess them. Premature thinking about assessment will quickly reveal that some outcomes will be easier to assess than others, and there may be a tendency to eliminate some important outcomes because the writers do not now know how to assess them. This can corrupt the curriculum and is certainly a species of "teaching to the test," a test you know how to make right now. Leave assessment design until later, and then get expert assistance where needed.

The Process Should Be Used to Build Community

The process of defining outcomes can be a powerful community-building device. Faculty members, who are usually isolated from colleagues, have the opportunity, some for the first time, to work with one another on issues they care about. People have to listen carefully to each other as they articulate their values concerning their disciplines, learning, and human development. Through this process they can get to know and respect each other more than ever before.

Goals and Objectives Should Be Used and Reviewed

Once developed, a set of outcome goals and objectives should not be cavalierly changed. However, goals should be reviewed periodically to ensure that they are still relevant to the institution's needs. Five-year programmatic evaluations provide opportunities for careful goal review and modification.

Furthermore, goals and objectives must be used. As in the case of mission statements, stated outcome goals and objectives are useful in managing learning only if they are actively used. A beautifully written set of outcome statements filed away on a shelf is only a shelf document. It is of no practical use except perhaps for purposes of public relations or to impress a visiting accreditation team. The time, energy, and goodwill invested in developing it have been wasted.

LEARNING AND DEVELOPMENT: MONITORING EFFECTIVENESS

As the statisticians put it: "In God we trust; all others must bring data."

Colleges and universities have long assessed their students' learning. Since about 1985, however, assessment of learning in the United States has become a major concern of state governments, regional and disciplinary accrediting agencies, and others who have a stake in the quality of college graduates. The technology of assessment has benefited from this increased interest, and today numerous methodologies are available to help you.

Institutions have responded to new assessment mandates and regulations with a spate of committees, initiatives, and plans. According to many observers, however, the result of all this activity is often less than meets the eye. Motivated more by external pressures or by a desire to maintain a good public image than by a concern to understand and improve themselves, some institutions seem to go through the motions of assessment but show little enthusiasm for the process. As a result, after a decade or more of "assessment" work, they may still have little understanding of their graduates' knowledge, skills, and values, or how their programs function.

Levels of Assessment

Assessment must occur at all levels: institution, program (curriculum), course, and individual student. The questions that interest you determine the appropriate unit of analysis and therefore the assessment design.

Course-level assessment is the most common type in colleges and universities. All faculty members assess; however, relatively few have studied the theory and methodology of modern assessment and developed the knowledge and skills required for effective measurement. Most have been trained in their discipline, not in human development. This lack of professional development reveals itself in many ways, and the inadequacy of much—or even most—classroom assessment, discussed in Chapter Seven, is one of them. As already noted, most course-level assessment currently focuses on the recall or recognition of isolated facts and low-level conceptual knowledge. Such assessment is often not well aligned with intended outcomes of either curriculum or course. If not incorporated in meaningful ways into students' cognitive structures, this type of low-level learning will soon be forgotten. Because the nature of student assessments strongly influences the way they study, this low-level cognitive focus wastes their time and reinforces unproductive learning patterns that can limit their futures.

Furthermore, assessment of curricula is essential. Although course-level assessment is pervasive and necessary, it is inadequate as a measure of program effectiveness. First, have the courses that make up the general education or disciplinary major programs worked together to produce curricular intended outcomes? Second, one cannot be sure in all cases—or perhaps even many—of what is being measured in courses. The tendency to assess low cognitive-level learning, certainly not what the institution desires for its curricula, invalidates these assessments as the sole measure of learning. Third, as already noted, some developmental outcomes such as critical thinking, epistemology, and principled ethical reasoning require taking many courses. Determining how much change has occurred in students by the end of the first and second years or by graduation requires assessment across courses in a program. Overall institutional effectiveness requires institutionwide assessment across programs. (See also Chapter Fourteen on institutional assessment.)

Aligning Assessment Efforts

Many institutions center their assessment efforts on undergraduate students alone. All students' learning progress should be assessed—undergraduates and graduates alike—as well as students in all other programs, such as continuing and adult education.

Consider an institution, unit, curriculum, or course as a system whose components are functionally interrelated. Assessment can examine the *inputs* (resources that can influence learning, such as entering students' knowledge, skills, and values), *processes* (activities such as curricula and academic advising, or study abroad programs) and other environmental factors such as campus climate, and *outcomes* (results of learning—what graduates know and are able to do and values they hold). You must understand the outcomes that your institution and units produce to monitor its success in effecting learning, but knowing outcomes is not enough. You must also have detailed information about the functioning of your educational processes and environment to improve them and thus close the quality gap between current and best practice. *Process assessment* compares the behavior of, for example, your instructional or academic advising programs with characteristics of these programs shown in the professional literature to be important for learning. You need both baseline data and measurements of progress in learning and development for each of your programs, as well as data on the behavior of the programs themselves.

Input assessment can give you the detailed information you need about your entering students individually and in the aggregate. You and your colleagues cannot respond effectively to students' developmental needs without this information. Important entry characteristic data would include their levels of epistemological and moral judgment development, skill in critical and creative thinking, ability to learn (study skills), values, and attitudes toward learning and hard work. Only by knowing such things can you develop educational processes appropriate to your students' needs.

Combining outcome and process assessment permits you to examine the alignment of your educational processes with curricular goals and objectives. Is the curriculum being implemented in ways consistent with research-based best practice? This question should be your primary focus for improving learning.

Finally, your assessments must be appropriate for your intended learning outcomes, as must be your educational processes. All three components of your educational system must be carefully aligned—and, of course, aligned with your mission statement. All planning and monitoring decisions flow from your stated outcome goals and objectives.

Understanding the Needs of All Stakeholders

An institution may be satisfied with its 70 percent first- to senior-year graduation rate, but this rate shows that the institution loses almost one-third of its students before graduation. A for-profit company that lost one-third of it customers, and thus income, would sit up and take notice. To reduce attrition by improving institutional quality requires detailed information about students' backgrounds and needs and their experiences on campus. How many feel alienated from the institution, defeated and uncared for, bored to death by their courses? How many do not understand the personal development and educational processes they are involved in? How many do not know how to learn effectively? These common problems are eminently addressable by modifying educational processes, and thus students' experiences, with good effect on learning and retention.

Of course, graduation alone does not guarantee highly developed, culturally useful abilities. Of your students who persist to graduation, what percentage show a high level of critical-thinking skills and capacity for principled ethical reasoning, hold socially productive values, and have deep knowledge and extensive skills in their major fields? Most colleges and universities today cannot answer these questions. Assessment research can provide you with answers.

Furthermore, various institutional constituents require different types of accurate and timely information for high-quality decision making: parents, prospective and current students, faculty and staff members, board members, governors and legislators, the media. You must take into consideration the needs of all your stakeholders when you develop an assessment plan. Assessment *data* produced must be transformed into *information* that is *understandable* and thus useful to various stakeholders.

Assessing Value Added

Outcome assessment at the end of a student's curriculum cannot by itself reveal how much the institution has contributed to his or her development. Students arrive on campus already having achieved diverse levels and types of knowledge and skills and holding very different values. Moreover, once they are there, factors other than the institution's efforts, such as maturation and learning in outside contexts, contribute to their development. Entry assessment is needed to develop baseline data so that later you can determine the institutional *value added.*

Continuing Assessment

Assessment should be continuous because every institution needs a steady stream of information about its behavior; quality improvement can never end. Assessment should provide campus constituents with the information they need when they need it so they can perform their roles in accomplishing the mission at the highest level. Some assessment is needed at relatively frequent intervals. For example, students in courses require very frequent assessment of their learning, together with corrective feedback. Other kinds of information are appropriately collected less frequently. Cognitive development proceeds at a relatively slow pace. Ability for critical thinking or principled ethical judgment might be collected at entry and annually thereafter, or even less often, depending on the purpose of the study. More frequent assessment may provide no additional useful information and thus waste resources.

Assessment and Institutional Transformation

Assessment research can play an important role in efforts to lead institutional transformation. Without accurate information, people can grow complacent; urgency for quality improvement and change remains low. Thought-through, prespecified outcomes can provide high standards, and evidence about results in learning provided by outcome assessment can permit honest discussion of the institutional realities (Kotter, 1996).

SOME TECHNICAL CONSIDERATIONS IN ASSESSMENT AND EVALUATION

There are a number of issues related to assessment and evaluation that are necessary to understand.

Assessment Versus Evaluation

Assessment and evaluation are commonly conceived as two different processes that go hand in hand. *Assessment* research is a process of discovery: determining what is. *Evaluation* is a process of judgment based on evidence produced by assessment. Evaluation determines whether conditions revealed by assessment are acceptable when compared with predetermined standards articulated by goals and objectives.

Assessment provides the information on which to base two different types of evaluation. *Formative evaluation* is based on evidence of quality collected during an educational process, such as midway through a course or curriculum. It is used for program improvement—formation. *Summative evaluation* occurs at the completion of a process; it is a summing up of how much students know at the end of a course (the assessment phase) and whether this level of knowledge is adequate (the evaluation). Both of these types of evaluation of quality are essential. Depending only on summative five-year program evaluations to examine the quality of learning in a curriculum, or end-of-course grades in a course, is sometimes known as quality by inspection. But after the product has been made, it is too late to improve it. Formative information supports quality improvement by allowing adjustment of the educational process along the way.

Technical Qualities of Assessments

Among an assessment's most important qualities are its validity and reliability. A *valid* assessment measures what it is alleged to measure. Its design aligns it with the prespecified intended outcomes about which information is sought. It can thus produce evidence for valid decisions. A *reliable* assessment functions similarly from one use to the next. Its behavior is stable. It will give similar results reliably time after time.

The Assessment Blueprint

All assessments, even common classroom quizzes, are devices for making mental measurements. Their validity and reliability depend on careful design. An assessment blueprint, or table of specifications, lays out the design for an assessment like an architect's plan for a building or a musician's score for a symphony.

An effective assessment design may involve a similar level of complexity as a symphony. Various types of disciplinary content and levels of cognitive skill as represented by the Bloom Taxonomy are spelled out in the goals and objectives. Some assessments also involve affective and psychomotor outcomes. In addition, a host of assessment strategies must be considered and specified.

The formats of assessment blueprints are diverse. One uses a matrix with types of disciplinary content arranged along one axis and levels of the Bloom Taxonomy along the other. Using this type of blueprint, the assessment designer can control both the content and cognitive demand of various components of the assessment. Be sure your institution is designing its assessments professionally.

Using Appropriate Assessment Methods

Today there are a variety of assessment methodologies. Whatever aspect of the institution you want to learn about probably can be assessed. The method you use must be appropriate for the research questions you are asking if the data produced are to be useful for making valid inferences.

If you want to learn what your students know and can do and what values they hold, you must assess these properties directly. Surveys of student opinions about their learning may be important, and sometimes easier and cheaper to conduct than direct measures, but they do not assess learning itself.

Tests Versus Assessments

We often associate assessment with paper-and-pencil tests. However, tests are only one form of assessment. Often they are appropriate, sometimes not. Alternatives to testing include portfolios, juried performances, interviews, focus groups, and ethnographic observations. *Assessment methodology must align with intended outcomes.*

Designed Versus Purchased Assessment Tools

Assessments can be locally constructed or purchased from commercial vendors. Each of these sources has advantages and disadvantages. Both may be important in a comprehensive assessment program. Among the advantages of commercial products are their convenience in being immediately available, in some cases with a scoring service. The sometimes significant costs of commercial assessments must be balanced against the opportunity costs of developing a local design. Furthermore, commercial products usually benefit from expert design and therefore have high technical quality. However, commercial assessment products for any one purpose are limited in number and may not align with your curricular goals and thus be incapable of supporting valid inferences about learning. It may be relatively easy to use them, and doing so may make you feel good and satisfy an outside stakeholder because you have engaged in an assessment activity. However, you may discover little about your students' learning, waste resources, and alienate faculty and staff who understand the activity has little meaning.

Student Motivation and Validity

Student motivation during assessment is a primary contributor to the relative usefulness of the results for making valid inferences. Students must work hard and perform at their highest level if the results are to reflect their abilities. Assessment planning must explicitly address ways to motivate students. High-stakes assessment, where students are directly affected by their assessment results, such as being able to graduate, is one such strong motivator.

Too Much Data

Assessment should provide evidence to answer important questions. An infinite number of variables can be assessed in a college or university. Every assessment has costs, including student, faculty, and staff time. Research questions should be chosen carefully to produce useful evidence about outcomes that are important to society or input and process variables known to be central to learning. It is time consuming and costly to process information, and a blizzard of data can bury important relationships and prevent people from seeing patterns. What do you need to know, and how can you learn it as effectively and efficiently as possible?

COMMUNICATING ABOUT LEARNING: THE LIMITATIONS OF GRADES

Aside from a handful of institutions, American colleges and universities testify to student learning and achievement through course grades and grade point averages. Grades are used to judge the rates at which students are permitted to advance through their curricula and to determine which students are qualified for degrees. Often they form the basis for conferring awards and honors. An examination of the genesis of grades, however, suggests they need to be used with care. Grades may serve well as a bureaucratic convenience for keeping records and sorting students from one another. But based on various factors such as classroom tests, attendance, class participation, and projects of many sorts, all too often grades represent a ragout of unknown processes and outcomes. Even when grades are based on paper-and-pencil tests, these assessments often are heavily biased toward memorized facts unconnected to any larger meaning and do not reflect higher-order cognitive skills (Milton, 1982). Most users of grades have little or no information about their origins or validity, and therefore, their meaning.

A more useful way to represent knowledge and skill to certify completion of both courses and curricula, and thus qualify for graduation, is mastery of clearly defined competencies as described by a curriculum's or course's intended outcome goals and objectives and assessed in a valid and reliable way. Students get more useful guidance on their learning, and employers and graduate schools find specific information on developed abilities that is of far greater value than grades whose meaning they do understand. The K–12 sector is moving toward certification on the basis of assessments aligned with state standards. Some colleges and universities—for example, Alverno College and Western Governors University—already certify graduates on the basis of their assessed competencies, not grades.

SOME GUIDELINES

The following guidelines can be helpful when using assessment to manage learning. They follow from this chapter's discussion and have emerged from the collective experience of many institutions.

Make Sure Every Unit and Program Formulates High-Quality Outcome Goals and Objectives

Be sure the intended outcome statements are consistently and properly used everywhere for planning, implementing, and assessment.

Insist on Valid, Reliable, Appropriate Assessment at Every Point

Be certain that every assessment is fully aligned with the intended outcome objectives. Reward high-level professional skill in designing, implementing, and interpreting the results of assessment. Encourage experimentation and willingness to take risks.

Be Sure Assessment Results Are Available

All those who need the results should have them available in an easily understood format. Everyone in the institution should expect assessment results to be made available on a timely basis. Filing assessment results away without disseminating them puts your institution at risk: people do not know what to do. Assessment data will often indicate areas where change is necessary. Improving quality, after all, is the main reason for monitoring results. If results are negative, they indicate conditions that must be changed; changed conditions will provide opportunities to increase quality. Hiding results and covering up problems is unprofessional and unethical and only compounds the problems. It is the antithesis of good management and reveals a lack of leadership. Make it clear that you want to hear bad news, you want to hear it quickly, and you will not punish its bearers. Then you will be able to respond promptly to address problems. If people fear punishment for bringing unpleasant news, they will keep it from you. Then you will be managing blindly.

Refusing to share information with your people to hide inconvenient facts or shield them from bad news is treating them like children and shows a lack of respect (Brock, 1987). They are not partners in the learning effort; you are limiting their ability to do their jobs and risk damaging your relationship with them. Because they are likely to become aware of this subterfuge, you risk their withholding the high effort required to produce learning.

Be Sure Assessment Results Are Used to Improve Learning

The purpose of assessment is understanding for improvement. From assessment results students discover how effectively they are learning so they can improve the quality of their learning. Teachers use assessment results to improve their own teaching to help their students learn more effectively, and program planners study their students' learning outcomes and their educational processes to improve these processes. Conducting assessment research but not using the results to improve learning is a waste of resources: money; student, faculty, and staff time; and goodwill. All individuals should understand that you expect them to use assessment results in an expeditious manner to effect changes in processes that are needed, and that you are interested in the outcomes of these changes and will follow up to ensure that assessment data have been used.

Take Responsibility for Using Assessment Results Yourself

The 85:15 rule states that an individual—for example, a faculty member—can only control about 15 percent of the variables affecting his or her work, with the other 85 percent being system variables and therefore belonging to managers (Seymour, 1992). The rule suggests that everyone in a managerial role that affects teachers' work needs to use information carefully to ensure teachers teach effectively. The responsibility for a large number of organizational variables rests on your shoulders. You need to understand your organization and act to facilitate learning everywhere.

Provide Resources Adequate to Do the Job Well

There are costs involved in assessment: for developing expertise, designing and implementing assessments, converting data to information, and disseminating and using assessment results. You must invest the resources necessary for a high-quality process.

Work with All Stakeholders to Ensure Acceptance of the Process

Some academicians unfamiliar with modern assessment fear and resist it; they see it as a stalking-horse for an administrative attack on the faculty or unnecessary interference with their work. Faculty evaluation is a separate process from the one discussed in this chapter; see Chapter Sixteen for a discussion of leadership in faculty evaluation. Assessment is wholly consistent with academic values of research and high-quality evidence as a basis for thought and action, concern for learning and student welfare, professional craftsmanship, and institutional pride. The purpose of assessment is to understand the institution and improve it and its capacity to enhance learning. Involve faculty and staff members and students from the beginning in all phases of assessment so they can understand and shape it and enthusiastically use its results.

Develop Leadership for Assessment Throughout the Institution

Everyone should have a stake in accomplishing the mission. All should come to view themselves as leaders, and senior administrators should actively develop the campus culture and the necessary knowledge and skills among the staff to cultivate leadership everywhere (Tichy, 1997). To assume a leadership role, everyone needs information about how the institution's processes are working.

Develop a Culture of Evidence

A culture of evidence in an organization permits management of learning "by fact." Guesswork, hunches, and hope are the alternatives. These vapors are ubiquitous in higher education, a stunning contrast to our vaunted emphasis on research. How is it that, although we have highly developed research skills, we rarely use them to understand ourselves and inform our stakeholders?

Be Sure There Is a Center of Assessment and Evaluation Skills on Campus

This expertise may be in your office of assessment, institutional research, or faculty development, or it may reside elsewhere. Campus constituents must have somewhere to go for professional advice and technical assistance.

Acquaint Yourself with the Professional Assessment Literature

Assessment is a key tool of management and leadership. You cannot function at a high level without it. You cannot leave it to your office of institutional research or a faculty committee. You must lead the assessment effort, and therefore, you must be knowledgeable. Take responsibility for your own continuous professional development.

Develop Faculty and Staff

High-level professional development of faculty and staff is essential for effective assessment. Modern assessment design, like the work involved in defining intended outcomes, designing curricula, instruction, and other complex aspects of academic work, requires deep understanding not only of disciplines but also of student development and the conventions and skills of the professional areas required to make it happen. Furthermore, like other disciplines, these areas are constantly changing as research advances and new methods are developed. Continuous professional development is important for all faculty members in all colleges and universities.

Most current faculty and staff never studied research and best practice related to their work as educators, and new members are constantly joining the academic community who are unlikely to be familiar with the diverse professional literature relevant to their duties. They may not be getting accurate information about their students' learning and their own effectiveness as educators because of limitations of current assessment activities at all levels in your institution. Creating an effective faculty development program is an urgent need. (For more on this see Chapter Fourteen.)

In Public Relations, Substitute Honest Evidence for Hype

Assessment information can provide powerful evidence for public information. Rather than depending on puffery or the speculations and ratings of popular magazines to inform your stakeholders of your institution's academic quality, enhance their understanding of the institution—and its reputation for candor—by publishing accurate information on your graduates' levels of learning and the value the institution has created by using real data. This is about the concept of "value added."

Remember That What You Assess Reflects Your Organization's Values

Your willingness to engage in vigorous assessment research, the variables you choose to assess, the results you distribute and to whom you provide them, and your expectations for their use says much about what your institution values. Do your assessment practices specifically and directly enhance important types of learning and development, or are they focused on enhancing institutional prestige? Do you and your staff serve society or yourselves?

Lead

The lives of many students can be transformed by a college or university that is effectively managed for the right kinds of learning. Those institutions that apply available research competently and consistently to their work also stand the best chance of surviving and thriving in a competitive environment. Lead quality improvement and change.

References

Anderson, L. W., & Krathwohl, D. R. (Eds.). (2001). *A taxonomy for learning, teaching, and assessing: A revision of Bloom's taxonomy of educational objectives*. White Plains, NY: Longman.

Bloom, B. S. (Ed.). (1956). *Taxonomy of educational objectives: Vol. 1. Cognitive domain*. White Plains, NY: Longman.

Brock, P. (1987). *The empowered manager: Positive political skills at work*. San Francisco: Jossey-Bass.

Drucker, P. F. (1974). *Management: Tasks, responsibilities, practices*. New York: HarperCollins.

Drucker, P. F. (1990). *Managing the nonprofit organization: Practices and principles*. New York: HarperCollins.

Harrow, A. J. (1972). *A taxonomy of the psychomotor domain: A guide for developing behavioral objectives*. White Plains, NY: Longman.

Kotter, J. (1996). *Leading change*. Cambridge, MA: Harvard Business School Press.

Krathwohl, D. R., Bloom, B. S., & Masia, B. B. (1964). *Taxonomy of educational objectives: The classification of educational goals: Handbook II. Affective domain*. White Plains, NY: Longman.

Milton, O. (1982). *Will that be on the final?* Springfield, IL: Charles C. Thomas.

Seymour, D. T. (1992). *On Q: Causing quality in higher education*. New York: American Council on Education–Macmillan.

Tichy, N. M. (1997). *The leadership engine: How winning companies build leaders at every level*. New York: HarperBusiness.

Tyler, R. W. (1934). *Constructing achievement tests*. Columbus: Ohio State University.

Resources

This section offers a wide variety of helpful resources, by topic area.

Learning Outcomes

Ideas for intended outcomes for a program can come from many sources, including other institutions' outcome statements, reports of national and disciplinary commissions, and of course, the faculty. One of the best sources is the professional literature in higher education that describes societal needs and professionally accepted research-based practice. For example, see the books by Astin (1993), Gardiner (1996), and Pascarella and Terenzini (1991) listed in the resource section of Chapter Seven. National reports critiquing current practice in higher education and calling for reform are another good source. For example, see Study Group (1984), also listed in Chapter Seven, or the following two works:

Project on Redefining the Meaning and Purpose of Baccalaureate Degrees. (1985). *Integrity in the college curriculum: A report to the academic community.* Washington, DC: Association of American Colleges. (ERIC Document Reproduction Service No. ED 251 059)

Wingspread Group on Higher Education. (1993). *An American imperative: Higher expectations for higher education.* Racine, WI: Johnson Foundation.

Two additional works that contain many ideas for outcomes are the following:
Anderson, L. W., & Krathwohl, D. R. (Eds.). (2001). *A taxonomy for learning, teaching, and assessing: A revision of Bloom's taxonomy of educational objectives. Complete edition.* White Plains, NY: Longman.
A revision of the Bloom Taxonomy of Educational Objectives in the Cognitive Domain (Bloom, 1956), this book evaluates the professional literature about the taxonomy published over the last half-century and revises the taxonomy based on this research and practitioners' experience with it. For taxonomies for affective and psychomotor (motor) outcomes see Krathwohl, Bloom, and Masia (1964) and Harrow (1972), respectively.

Gardiner, L. F. (1989). *Planning for assessment: Mission statements, goals, and objectives.* New York: Author. (ERIC Document Reproduction Service No. ED 403 809)
Originally developed for use and distributed by the New Jersey Department of Higher Education statewide outcome assessment program, this is a handbook for using mission statements, goals, and objectives in colleges and universities.

Grading

Milton, O., Pollio, H. R., & Eison, J. A. (1986). *Making sense of college grades.* San Francisco: Jossey-Bass.
Based on a large national study of grades and a review of the professional literature, this book discusses the history of grades, attitudes toward grades, learning to earn grades versus learning for knowledge, the differences in behavior of learning-oriented and grade-oriented students, and suggestions concerning grading.

General

Astin, A. W. (1991). *Assessment for excellence: The philosophy and practice of assessment and evaluation in higher education.* Phoenix: Oryx Press.
This book discusses the philosophy and logic of assessment in higher education and uses a system model showing how to think about and assess education outcomes, inputs, and environments. Other topics include using results of assessment, constructing a database, equity, public policy for assessment, and assessment's future. A useful appendix of almost sixty pages discusses the statistical analysis of longitudinal assessment data when applying the system model.

Gardiner, L. F., Anderson, C., & Cambridge, B. L. (Eds.). (1997). *Learning through assessment: A resource guide for higher education.* Washington, DC: American Association for Higher Education
Perhaps the most comprehensive directory of assessment resources available, this book includes the AAHE Principles of Good Practice for Assessing Student Learning, an "Assessment Library" section that describes assessment-related periodicals and includes an annotated bibliography of over three hundred publications, and descriptions of assessment-related associations and organizations, conferences, instruments, and Internet and multimedia resources. An assessment glossary concludes the book. See also http:/www.aahe.org for more information.

Jacobs, L. C., & Chase, C. I. (1992). *Developing and using tests effectively: A guide for faculty.* San Francisco: Jossey-Bass.
This handbook for classroom test design and use describes how to plan tests, the concepts of validity and reliability, how to use various item formats, alternative ways of using tests, administration, computer-assisted testing, item analysis, and grading.

Palomba, C. A., & Banta, T. W. (1999). *Assessment essentials: Planning, implementing, and improving assessment in higher education.* San Francisco: Jossey-Bass.
A basic handbook on assessment in higher education, this book discusses, among other topics, how to develop goals and assessment plans and encourage people to be involved in assessment; selecting assessment methods; how to use measures of performance and portfolios; classroom assessment; assessing general education, major fields, and campus environments and students' experiences; and reporting and using the results of assessment.

Case Studies

These two volumes describe numerous specific examples of assessment of various sorts in diverse institutions.

Banta, T. W., & Associates. (1993). *Making a difference: Outcomes of a decade of assessment in higher education.* San Francisco: Jossey-Bass.

Banta, T. W., Lund, J. P., Black, K. E., & Oblander, F. W. (1996). *Assessment in practice: Putting principles to work on college campuses.* San Francisco: Jossey-Bass.

Conferences

American Association for Higher Education Conference on Assessment. [http://www.aahe.org/assessment/].
This national conference, held annually in June since 1985, is the nation's oldest assessment conference. This is the place to interact with the largest number of assessment theoreticians and practitioners. Numerous sessions of various formats address a wide range of assessment issues.

Assessment Institute. [http://www.jaguars.iupui.edu/plan/confernc.html].
This limited-attendance annual national conference, held in November in Indianapolis, is sponsored by Indiana University-Purdue University Indianapolis. Workshops led by nationally prominent assessment experts, sessions led by practitioners from various institutions, and other activities introduce participants to a diverse array of issues and methods in assessment.

Electronic Resources

The sites listed here are notable for the value of the assessment resources they contain. A search for assessment information generally, specific types of information, and the sites of specific colleges and universities will yield additional information.

American Association for Higher Education Assessment Forum. [http://www.aahe.org/assessment/].
The AAHE has provided national leadership in assessment since the beginning of the current assessment movement. The Assessment Forum's Web site contains various assessment resources, including readings, the AAHE Principles of Good Practice for Assessing Student Learning, and a list of Internet discussion lists related to assessment.

Internet Resources for Higher Education Outcomes Assessment. [http://www2.acs.ncsu.edu/UPA/assmt/resource.htm#gen].
This site contains links to a comprehensive array of international assessment resources, including discussion lists, accrediting agencies, glossaries, the Bloom Taxonomy, journals, assessment rubrics, survey data, assessment pages of individual colleges and universities and organizations, including their assessment handbooks, student assessment and evaluation of courses and faculty members, and assessment in student affairs.

Internet Resources for Institutional Research. [http://airweb.org/links/].
Sponsored by the Association for Institutional Research, this site is designed to provide institutional researchers with useful resources. In addition to numerous assessment links, the site also has links relating to administration, data, publications, government, institutional research, quality improvement, student affairs, teaching and research, and technology.

ASSESS.
ASSESS offers a general assessment discussion. To subscribe send a message to LISTSERV@LSV.UKY.edu, with this command in the message body: SUBSCRIBE ASSESS.

CHAPTER 9

Curricula and Courses
Administrative Issues

ROBERT M. DIAMOND

The purpose of the curriculum is to foster a learner's development consistent with the mission of the institution and program. . . . [It] is a plan that integrates intended learning outcomes, content, learning process, and assessment. . . . [To] be effective it requires integration at the course, program, and institutional level. Curriculum development should be a dynamic process that involves planning, consideration of stakeholders, and plans for feedback and adjustment.

—Ann Austin-Beck, Minnowbrook, July 1998

Because learning is the primary mission of all colleges and universities, curricular strength and suitability most directly influence the outcomes of higher education. Great teaching, creative uses of technology, strong off-campus experiences, and well-designed courses do not in themselves, however, create an excellent educational experience. The combination of these aspects into an orchestrated student experience will determine how effectively an institution will reach its educational goals. Unfortunately, if there is one element in our academic program that tends to be overlooked, it is the design and assessment of this road map for learning: the curriculum and its constituent courses. In this chapter we will first focus on the broader curriculum-related issues and then move to your role in supporting course design and improvement. In the final section, we will provide an overview of course and curriculum design models that your faculty can use.

CURRICULUM DESIGN: THE BASICS

Calls for curriculum reform have been around for decades. After studying the curricula of twenty-nine institutions, Ernest Boyer reported "a lost sense of mission, disciplinary fragmentation, divided loyalties, and competing priorities" (1987, p. 6). A 1984

135

National Institute of Education report emphasized the need for institutions to show demonstrable improvements in students' knowledge, capacities, skills, and attitudes between admission and graduation. A decade later the concerns were similar. In a 1995 report for the Education Commission of the States, Roy Romer, then governor of Colorado, wrote in the Introduction: "For all its rich history, there are too many signs that higher education has not taken seriously its responsibility to maintain a strong commitment to undergraduate learning: to be accountable for products that are relevant, effective, and of demonstrable quality; and to provide society with the full benefits from investment in research and public service" (p. 2). In his review of the literature, Lion Gardiner observed, "The curriculum has given way to a marketplace philosophy: it is a supermarket where students are shoppers and professors are merchants of learning. Fads and fashions, the demands of popularity and success, enter where wisdom and experience should prevail" (1996, p. 25). In short, the primary structure of the educational experience at many if not most institutions requires review, repair, and a major restructuring. As Abbott (1996) concluded, "We continue to get graduates who think narrowly, are teacher-dependent, and have too little ability to tackle challenges or embrace change. . . . [The] need may be less for 'reform' than for fundamental redesign of the system"(p. 6). Unfortunately, many parents and students would agree.

Calls for academic reform, the growing emphasis by accreditation agencies on learning outcomes, increased competition, and the significant changes in the competencies needed by graduates will combine to make curriculum reform a top priority at most institutions in the years ahead. Engaging faculty in this crucial work is not an easy task. Curriculum design is challenging, and it usually results in very different resource needs, departmental priorities, and faculty assignments and roles.

The Curriculum and Your Role as an Academic Leader

Although faculty have the disciplinary knowledge for curriculum review, academic leaders have a number of key responsibilities. The board, trustees, and the president must recognize the importance of curriculum review, provide the necessary resources, and ensure that success is recognized and rewarded. The chief academic officer, working with his or her deans, must set priorities, and with the support of the chief financial officer, ensure that adequate funds are available. The dean, in collaboration with department chairs, must develop the specific charge to faculty, be responsible for ongoing review of the process, and see to it that a representative group of faculty be involved from the very beginning. Like any other important institutional initiative, the effort must be a priority at all levels of the institution. Fortunately, we have models to follow and experiences on which to build.

There Are Three Levels of Learning Goals

The learning goals at any institution exist on three levels: broad educational goals—those competencies that every graduate should have; program or major goals—those competencies that every student in a major or minor should obtain; and course-level goals—those competencies that are the desired outcomes of electives selected by each student.

Curriculum Design Is Just the First Step

At the end of the design process you will have a clear picture of the instructional flow of each program. Instructional goals should be made explicit, and how and where they will be assessed should be determined. You should also know the following: how credits will be distributed; which courses will be required and which will be electives for each major and minor; which courses are prerequisites for others; how unique needs of students will be met (prerequisites, advanced skills, and so on); where diagnostic testing and student evaluation will take place; which courses will be retained as they are, or be modified, eliminated, or entirely new; when and where internships and other nonclassroom activities will fit into the program; how achievement at the end of a course of study will be determined; what your staffing needs will be; and what your space needs will be.

Although changes in the overall design are inevitable as work progresses, the design process should provide you with a clear picture of how the various components of the curriculum fit together, how student needs will be met, and how the learning goals of the program will be realized. It should also give academic leaders a clear picture of what the next steps toward implementation should be.

Funding Curriculum Reform

Do not rely on outside funding. Although foundation or alumni support for curriculum reform does happen, it is the exception rather than the rule. As important as these efforts are, funding agencies and donors are far more willing to support innovations in technology (it is glamorous) or building construction or the endowment of a chair (they can have their names on them) than to support a process such as curriculum reform. As a result, funds must be set aside for this purpose in your budget. We are not talking about huge amounts, but financial support will be key to a successful initiative. More on this later.

A Task Force or Committee Should Be Appointed

The key first step is to appoint the task force or faculty committee that will be responsible for implementation. If there is a point in the process where hidden pitfalls exist, this is it. Campus politics, turf issues, and survival instincts all come into play when curriculum review is under way; thoughtful selection of faculty leadership can minimize potential problems. (Notice, we do not say *eliminate.*)

Usually the dean, in consultation with department chairs, establishes this team. Making sure that the committee represents the various constituencies present in the faulty is important to ensuring that the final product serves the interests of all students rather than those of a powerful faction. Because curricular requirements affect enrollment and staffing and thus have budget implications, one of your greatest challenges is to ensure fairness and openness in the design process.

Choose a Neutral Party as Chair

Select as the chair a neutral party who does not represent any one course or academic area, or in interdisciplinary programs, a single discipline. You need someone who has strong process skills and who will be viewed by faculty both on and off the committee as fair and impartial. You may want to consider a respected faculty leader from another academic area or a professional staff member from an academic support center. You can anticipate some objections from faculty to this approach, but dealing with potential political problems before work begins will pay off later on.

Select Team Members Carefully

Your faculty team must be representative of *all* the major academic elements that will be included in the program. In addition, consider representation of key administrators whose offices may be significantly affected—perhaps a curriculum committee member, a representative from an academic unit that cross-lists your courses, or alumni or employers of your graduates. If not on the committee itself, such individuals should be consulted or involved from the beginning. If possible, consider including a member of your board of trustees or board of visitors on this committee, if this individual can represent the viewpoint of an employer or practitioner. This type of involvement can pay major dividends later on.

Make Sure Appointees Have the Time

Make sure that all appointees are onboard not only the project but also the process that will be followed and that they are willing to devote the time necessary. In some cases, an individual who is perceived as resistant to change is appointed, and as you might anticipate, problems may occur. It is important that you involve reluctant individuals in such a way that ownership evolves.

Build the Needed Resources into the Base Budget

Curriculum design should be viewed by the entire institution as part of the ongoing commitment to a strong academic program. Although the dollars required will obviously vary considerably by the size of your institution and the scope of the project itself, you will need funds to support a number of activities.

- *Release time or summer employment for the chair and perhaps committee members:* Although not always necessary, sometimes it is essential to ensure that enough time is available.
- *Travel funds for team members to visit programs at other institutions or attend professional meetings where curriculum innovations are being discussed:* Travel of this sort should *not* compete for funds with other faculty travel needs.
- *Clerical assistance for chair and committee members.* Although this may be provided by one academic office or another, make sure it is not an add-on to an already overworked staff person.
- *Texts and other resources:* One of the committee's responsibilities will be to provide detailed guidelines for the development of new courses or for the revision of existing ones. Building on exemplary materials developed elsewhere is always encouraged.
- *Luncheon and breakfast meetings:* Providing pleasant, comfortable occasions for faculty to meet and talk about their work is well worth the expense. Such events can help to bridge the gaps between individuals and strengthen collegiality and mutual understanding.

- *Consultants:* Consultants are often invaluable. Make sure that funds are budgeted so as to provide the most flexibility in their use. The dean or department chair should approve all requests for discretionary funds from the chair.

Educate Your Committee Chair

Do not assume that your chair knows much about curriculum design, assessment, research on teaching and learning, or associated issues that must be addressed. One of the chair's main responsibilities will be to educate the committee. Before the process begins, meetings should be held with the committee chair to review priorities, clarify the charge to the committee, and review any data that have been collected to identify problems and concerns. This discussion will usually begin the process of identifying this individual's commitment and familiarity with the design process. Several sources are referenced at the end of this chapter that can support the chair through the design process. Good models do exist to assist you.

Encourage Thinking in the Ideal

As part of your charge to the committee, encourage them to think outside the box. Rather than start by focusing on what exists, the committee should begin by envisioning the ideal curriculum. Later in the process, this design will be adjusted to accommodate existing limitations of space, staff, and resources. This approach provides a far better product by making sure that options remain open long enough to be explored. Thinking in the ideal also makes the process more interesting and energizing for the committee.

Ensure That the Process Is Open

Throughout the design process, committee members should report on their progress and solicit feedback from all interested parties. Drafts of the proposed design should be widely circulated for comments and a significant effort should focus on collecting information and data. The best results are based on good information. This information-based approach will improve the quality of the final design and circumvent problems when the report is presented to the faculty for approval or when requests for support are forwarded to key academic offices.

Keeping lines of communication open and involving all key stakeholders are important to successful change. For example, if changes are proposed in credit structures or time lines, make sure your registrar is in the loop early. In any curriculum review there will be conflict between the various content areas as they vie for student time in the new program. With new technology, an expanding knowledge base, and significant changes in what is expected of graduates, you can anticipate that there will always be conflicting demands for credit and class time during program design. On some campuses the desire to move toward greater experimentation with nontraditional courses will increase tensions between faculty who prefer traditional courses and those who support more offerings on the Web. Although people will always have different points of view, a fair and open process can reduce conflict and make the design effort a positive experience.

Features tof a Strong Curriculum Proposal

In this section we focus on several features that you should look for in any curriculum proposal.

Does It Offer Outcome or Goal Statements for All Levels of the Curriculum?

Historically, the curriculum has been described in terms of content to be covered rather than anticipated student learning. Demands for accountability make this approach less than desirable. Measurable (assessable) outcomes should be stated for programs as well as for courses. Chapter Eight discusses writing functional outcome statements.

Does It State Basic Outcome Goals for All Students?

Whether it is a core program or a major or minor concentration, there should be a clear statement of the competencies (knowledge and skills) that every student should have upon graduation. For example, in an undergraduate core program, if there is a social science requirement, what is the anticipated skill or knowledge level for graduates *no matter which* sequence of courses they take to meet this requirement? Exhibit 9.1 lists common competencies found in outcome statements for undergraduate programs. Although structure, order, and groupings vary from institution to institution, there is considerable consistency among all when it comes to core competencies. (Samples of outcome statements from a number of institutions, disciplines, and programs can be found in Diamond, 1998, *Designing and Assessing Courses and Curricula*.)

EXHIBIT 9.1. **Some Basic Curricular Competencies.**

Communications	Ethics*
Writing	Interpersonal skills
Speaking	Interviewing skills
Listening	Learning skills
Reading	Leadership*
Basic mathematics	Problem solving
Basic statistics	Resource utilization
Computer literacy	Respect for diversity*
Conflict resolution	Scientific method
Critical thinking	Willingness to take risks*

* Competencies receiving greater attention in recent years.

Does It Ensure That Goals Will Be Reached?

Look for specific assignments of competencies to courses and for their development in the total learning experience. For example, if interpersonal skills and leadership are to be developed, where are these skills introduced and where are they developed? Do all students, no matter which tracks or options they take, have the opportunity to develop speaking, critical-thinking, and problem-solving skills? This type of sequenced development does not happen by chance; it has to be built into the curriculum.

Does It Address Prerequisites and Advanced Students?

Usually, faculty find students in their courses and programs who lack the competencies they need for success. This is a common problem in mathematics, where basic skills with word problems, reading charts and graphs, and understanding elementary statistics, fractions, and algebra are required in a variety of introductory courses. At the same time, we find at both the undergraduate and graduate levels that some students have already taken courses or have related work experience that makes it possible for them to receive advanced credit or to take other electives. Does the curriculum address these two issues?

Does It Address New Technologies, Community and Professional Experiences, Internships?

A wide range of new and effective pedagogical options are now available to faculty. How does the new curriculum propose to build these approaches into the instructional sequence?

Are Student Assessment and Program Evaluation Ongoing?

A curriculum's success can only be determined by the students' performance and success after graduation. Is there a capstone course to measure their ability to meet the goals that have been identified? Is there a protocol to review the impact of the new curriculum on attrition and retention, enrollment, job placement, and so on?

Is There a Rationale for Specific Changes?

Based on the goals of the program and the course sequence that is proposed, is it clear why it has suggested new, revised, eliminated, and maintained courses?

Should You Go Ahead?

The decision to proceed with any resource-intensive initiative should be based on the response to three basic questions: Is there a need for the project? Is there a good chance the project will be successful? Given competing demands for resources, how high is this project on your priority list, how significant is it in light of your institution's mission, vision, and priorities?

Exhibit 9.2 offers a list of factors that can be considered in determining need. They are divided into two broad categories—information collected from outside the institution and information that should be available inside your college or university from students, faculty, your office, or other administrative units.

Note that there must be an institutional commitment to support and protect those faculty who will be devoting extensive time to the project. As discussed in Chapter Seventeen, "The Mission-Driven Faculty Reward System," curriculum design can satisfy all the criteria for scholarship.

EXHIBIT 9.2. Establishing the Need: Information to Be Collected.

	Yes	No	Need more data
External factors:			
1. The existing program meets the present and long-term needs of your students.			
Alumni feedback	——	——	——
Employer feedback	——	——	——
Recruiter feedback	——	——	——
2. Graduates of the program are successful in finding a job or being accepted into graduate school.	——	——	——
3. The curriculum meets accreditation standards (if appropriate).	——	——	——
4. The curriculum is up-to-date and sensitive to changing needs in the field.	——	——	——
Internal factors:			
5. Attrition rate is acceptable.	——	——	——
6. Enrollment is stable or increasing.	——	——	——
7. Quality of students is stable or increasing.	——	——	——
8. More students are transferring in than transferring out.	——	——	——
9. Faculty like the existing program.	——	——	——
10. Students are pleased with the existing program.	——	——	——
11. Core learning outcomes are clearly stated for all students.	——	——	——
12. Discipline-specific learning outcomes are clearly stated for majors and required courses.	——	——	——
13. Students are assessed on their ability to meet these goals.	——	——	——
14. Tests and other evaluation protocols emphasize higher-order competencies.	——	——	——
15. Every student has the opportunity to receive the instruction and reinforcement necessary to meet these goals.	——	——	——
16. There is a capstone or comprehensive assessment at the end of the program.	——	——	——

Source: *Designing and Assessing Courses and Curricula* (p. 38) by Robert M. Diamond, Copyright (c) 1998. Reprinted by permission John Wiley & Sons, Inc.

COURSE DESIGN: THE BASICS

The heart of any academic institution is its courses—the basic components of the teaching-learning experience. It is in the courses that ideas are exchanged and knowledge broadened through a variety of experiences that provide students with an opportunity to question and to grow. It is in the context of this educational experience that the work of an institution is measured.

Earlier in this chapter we stated that courses need to be viewed as part of a planned sequence to reach articulated and measurable goals. Although course options should exist, it is the role of the curriculum to provide a road map for learners to follow. In the curriculum, courses determine the quality of the day-to-day learning experience. Yet higher education has paid less attention to the process of course and curriculum design and assessment than it has to other concerns. Faculty are rarely trained in the course design process, and consequently, the structure and content of many courses are determined more by textbooks than any other factor. Although the last several decades have seen the number of faculty development programs aimed at improving teaching grow, little attention has been paid to supporting faculty in the course design process. Thus, a fundamental question: What good is improving the quality of teaching if course content needs to be updated, key instructional goals are overlooked, or the instructional sequence is not developmentally solid?

Over the next decades we can expect to see increasing emphasis on course and curriculum design. Demands for improved academic programs and greater student retention, the move to learning outcomes assessment by accreditation agencies, new instructional options, greater use of nontraditional methods of instruction, and the development of new fields and interdisciplinary concentrations will all contribute to an increased concern about what is taught and how. Although you will probably not be directly involved in the course design process, you do have an important role to play. As an academic leader you help establish a climate that supports course and institutional improvement, and collecting and using data on teaching and learning, as accepted and encouraged practices. If you are an academic vice president, provost, dean or department chair, you will also find yourself being asked to make decisions about whether a specific initiative should be undertaken. The questions you ask faculty and the work required to answer them can provide faculty with a structure for their course design efforts.

Supporting a Climate for Course Innovation

Strong faculty are always in the process of improving their courses. Content is added or dropped, objectives are modified, and new instructional approaches are incorporated whereas others are abandoned. Although much of this work is done in the context of everyday teaching, at some point the redesign and redefinition effort may move from what can be accomplished as part of regular teaching to a more fundamental effort that requires additional time, new resources, and the support of the academic unit, department chair, and dean.

Course design is complex, time-consuming work, but its intrinsic rewards can be great. There are a number of actions you can take to encourage faculty to make the commitment.

Course Development Should Be Viewed as Important Faculty Work

Like any other initiative, the activity should be directly related to the institution's mission and priorities. Improving quality, increasing enrollment and retention, and improving job or graduate school placements can all be powerful forces for change.

Course Development Should Be Viewed as Scholarly Work

New course design or major modification of existing programs should, when the criteria are met, be viewed as scholarly work. When done well, course design implementation and revision have all the elements required of a scholarly activity (see Chapter Seventeen). It is important that your faculty reward criteria clearly articulate and support this concept.

A Small Grants Program to Support Innovation and Design Should Be Established

A program of this type does not require a great deal of money, but it can have a significant impact and publicize the initiative, its importance, and its impact. Awards of $2,500 to $3,500 to provide assistance for faculty, travel funds, or purchase of software can have far more impact than you might expect. You should also have available an additional discretionary fund ($10,000 to $20,000 minimum) to support important initiatives with release time, summer employment, or media support or production. Here are some suggestions. Establish the course innovation program through your academic support center or in the academic affairs office, with the selection process controlled by a campuswide faculty committee. Take care to ensure that the committee is both representative and credible. Then build the selection process around the design process that you are encouraging faculty to use. Suggestions for these criteria are offered later in this chapter.

If possible, explore the use of summer employment or release time to support the development of technology applications and other instructional materials. There will be instances when new materials will have to be developed; often this requirement is not recognized until the course design activity is well under way and most resources have already been committed. For this purpose, as noted earlier, we suggest the establishment of a discretionary innovation fund in the academic affairs office.

Successful Initiatives Should Be Recognized

Encourage activities that recognize the work that has been accomplished—perhaps luncheon meetings where faculty report to other faculty on their projects, news releases in your institutional newspaper and local press, or formal published reports. You may support faculty travel to disciplinary or other national meetings where they can make presentations about the projects. The more you recognize the work that has been done as significant and scholarly, the more important the activity will become to the college or university community.

Important Principles

The resources section of this chapter lists publications that can assist faculty with the course design process. Here, however, we review a number of important principles that are consistent in all effective design models and approaches.

Course Design Should Be a Sequential Process

Good design requires that a number of questions be asked and decisions made. This process should follow a sequence, with decisions building on one another. For example, you cannot select a teaching approach and the technology to use until the instructional goals and student characteristics are clearly defined and the entire range of available options has been identified.

Collecting and Using Data Are Integral Parts of the Process

Disciplinary developments, changing needs of society, the knowledge, skills, and attitudes students bring to the program, their ability to meet assumed prerequisites, attitudinal information, data on student learning—all are essential elements in the design process. Data collection and use will often make the difference between success and failure.

Major Course Design Should Not Be an Independent Activity

Although only one faculty member may be involved in teaching a particular course, involving someone else in the design process can be extremely helpful. A staff member from your academic support center or a faculty member from another discipline can be invaluable in the process by testing assumptions or helping to explore options. These individuals can put themselves in the role of the student, something that the faculty teaching the course as a subject matter expert simply cannot do. The more discussions that take place during the design process and the more alternatives explored, the better the final project will be.

People Should Be Encouraged to Think Outside the Box

All too often faculty begin the course design process by focusing more on which textbook to use and which topics they wish to cover than on the institutional goals for the course. As a result, key options may never be explored and questions about content or students never raised. Just as with curriculum design, encourage people to begin by thinking in the ideal: If they had the best possible course, what would it look like? Perceived barriers may not be real barriers at all. At one institution the faculty found that it was possible to offer courses for a range of credits and on flexible time lines, which created new and highly effective institutional options. Thinking outside the box also brings a level of excitement and intellectual challenge to the design process itself.

Faculty Should Be Protected

Make sure that faculty involved in course and curriculum innovations are supported by their dean and other key faculty. Many faculty involved in innovation find themselves at professional risk because the work they have undertaken has not been supported by their colleagues.

Those Involved Should Understand the Basics

Ensure that faculty are aware of what is known about student learning, teaching, assessment, the use of technology, and the design process itself. Many faculty involved in course design work in total isolation without the knowledge required to rethink the intellectual process and structure of their courses. In this context, a comprehensive knowledge of the disciplines is simply not enough. The chapters in Part Three of this *Field Guide* will provide faculty with basic first steps in developing this knowledge including uses of technology and research on teaching and learning. Before work begins, the faculty involved should have a clear picture of the process they will follow, the questions they will ask, and the information they need to collect.

Some Common Problems

As an academic administrator one of your challenges will be to ensure that each of your academic programs meets the accreditation requirements at regional and professional levels. Although standards are still evolving, there is little question that the focus of the new standards will be on learning outcomes and the ability of students to meet stated criteria. You can anticipate reluctance (that is, avoidance) on the part of many faculty to articulate publicly the learning outcomes of their courses, yet the new standards may leave few options. Unfortunately, some of the most common problems relate directly to this issue.

Student Outcomes in Measurable Terms Are Not Clearly Stated

As noted in Chapter Eight, vague words such as "appreciate" and "understand" are common in the list of outcomes for many courses. The emphasis here must not only be on clarity but also on assuring that the outcome statements aim for a higher level of learning than recall and recognition. It is important to note that it is not that faculty lack goals for their students' learning. More often they are reluctant to state these goals. Keep in mind that once these statements are developed and publicized, the institution, the faculty member, and the student become accountable . . . as well they should.

Outcome Statements Do Not Match What Is Taught or How Students Are Evaluated

All aspects of the instructional program must work together. Students must realize that their evaluation will relate directly to the outcome-performance statements of the individual course or program. If the three key elements—outcomes, content, assessment—do not line up, then major course redesign becomes imperative. Also keep in mind that the most widely used testing techniques—multiple choice, true and false, and matching—focus on the least significant goals of any course: recall and recognition.

Faculty Do Not Test Their Assumptions About Their Students

Whether we say it or not, every one of us makes certain assumptions about our students on the first day of class. We, and the authors of the textbooks we use, believe that our students bring to class certain knowledge and skills. This is true at every level of instruction, from kindergarten to postgraduate work. Unfortunately, more often than not, we are wrong. The problem is complicated even further because many faculty are not even aware that they are making assumptions, and because there will always be students in that same classroom who know less than the faculty assume and others who know more. To develop an effective course, it is essential that faculty state their assumptions and then, early in the course, test their appropriateness.

Courses Are Designed and Taught in Isolation

Even though most courses are part of a learning continuum faculty rarely discuss outcomes and learning issues with those who teach required prerequisite courses or the courses that follow in the sequence. What do faculty teaching the next course expect students who have completed the prerequisite course to be able to do on the first day of class? Quite often the expectations are unrealistic. Until these issues are addressed, students are likely to fail. There is a need for increased communication across programs and courses.

Instructional Methodologies Are Not Fully Explored

We tend to teach as we were taught . . . not a particularly exciting concept. Lecturing, as it was twenty-five, fifty, and one hundred years ago, is still the predominant instruction method on most campuses. As noted earlier, most faculty have little knowledge of the research on teaching and learning or their instructional options. With advances in technology, faculty members today need to spend far less of their time as presenters of information. It is your responsibility to ensure that your faculty are aware of the research, know about the resources available to them, and understand that innovation is encouraged. Do not assume that faculty know all about teaching. They may be most knowledgeable in their discipline and their research, but unless they were involved in one of the few comprehensive TA training programs or made the individual effort, their knowledge about teaching and learning will most likely be quite limited.

Should You Go Ahead?

Remember that there will be two levels of course development on your campus. First, there is the ongoing process in which faculty members who see a problem address it as part of their routine teaching responsibility. This approach, taken by most concerned faculty, rarely will come to your attention. Yet it can have a significant impact on the quality of your academic program. Second, when curricular problems are identified, institutional resources and additional faculty time will be needed to design entirely new courses or to redesign existing ones. These are the times when you will be asked to commit resources. Because discretionary funds are always scarce, it is important that you ask a number of key questions before doing so.

As you might expect, good course design requires a great deal of faculty time and energy. It represents a major commitment by your institution and therefore should not be entered into without a discussion of need and priorities. Before making the decision to go ahead, ask the same two fundamental questions as you would in evaluating a request to begin a curriculum initiative. Although the questions are generally the same, many of the specifics will be quite different. Does need exist? Are there good reasons to believe that if a project is begun it will be successful?

Once these issues are addressed you may decide to support or not to support the initiative, delay implementation until the needed support, time, or resources are available, or support the initiative with the understanding that risks are involved. There will, for example, be times when the need is great and the investment is worth making, and yet the chances for success are questionable. Exhibits 9.3 and 9.4 can guide your decision about when to give your support to a course design initiative.

Exhibit 9.4 examines a second important question. Assuming that the need for change does exist, are the required conditions in place so that the investment you will make in the effort is wise?

EXHIBIT 9.3. Course Design: Is There a Need for a Major Effort?

1. Consider a new course if:
   - Specific needs are unmet by existing courses.
   - A new course would permit the elimination of several existing ones, reducing duplication.
   - A new course would introduce a new content area with a new, expanded set of learning outcomes.

2. Consider redesigning an existing course if:
   - There is a high failure or dropout rate.
   - Students cannot meet the learning goals that have been established.
   - The course does not prepare students well for the course or courses that follow.
   - There is a high level of student dissatisfaction.
   - The need exists but enrollment is declining.
   - A significant portion of the content of the course is outdated or key content is missing.
   - The course is not well designed.
   - No clear statement of intended outcomes exist.
   - The student evaluation criteria do not mesh with intended outcomes.
   - The primary method of instruction is the lecture.
   - The course uses an inappropriate number of resources.
   - If taught as a multisection course, there are big differences in stated goals or student outcomes across sections.
   - The course does not meet the goals that have been established for it in the curriculum.

THE DESIGN PROCESS: MODELS AND PROCEDURES

Before the course or curriculum design process begins, faculty must have a clear picture of the problems they are addressing, the questions they must ask, and the general process they will follow. Fortunately, there are a number of design models that can save them considerable time and effort while at the same time improving the quality of the final product. Although these models have much in common (they are sequential, they emphasize the need for clearly articulated instructional goals, and they stress the importance of evaluation), they do differ in terms of entry point, level of detail, or specific

EXHIBIT 9.4. Course Design: Indicators of Potential Success.

- There is unit-level support for the effort (chair and dean).
- The administrators supporting the project will be in place for two years.
- If the course is to be taught by more than one faculty member, everyone involved (or all key faculty) are willing to participate.
- Faculty working on the project have enough time to do it well.
- Nontenured faculty participating in the initiative will either have the effort count as a scholarly activity (if conditions are met) or the tenure clock will be stopped during the design, implementation, and evaluation period (agreements also in writing).
- Administrators are willing to allow sufficient time for design, field testing, and revision.
- The design process that will be followed has been selected by participants and includes data collection, design, and evaluation.
- No major curriculum design is under way that would affect either the content or sequences of the course.
- If resources (equipment, space, faculty release time or summer employment, material purchase or development) are required, they are available and have been or can be committed.
- If new instructional materials (media, computer software, texts, student manuals) are to be developed, an institutional copyright document has been signed by all involved.
- A staff member or faculty member from another academic unit has agreed to serve as project facilitator.

process. Some, for example, are broader in scope; others may provide much more depth in selection of technology, student prerequisites, or the writing of learning outcomes themselves. Some also focus more directly on higher education than others.

After reviewing the various models, faculty should select an approach that will be most helpful to them based on the kind of course they are working on and their comfort level with the approach itself. The following paragraphs offer a guide to a number of the more useful course and curriculum models, identifying the focus and strengths of each.

Since the mid-1960s a number of instructional experts have been developing models. In their book *Survey of Instructional Development Models* (1997), Kent L. Gustafson and Robert M. Branch grouped these models into three main categories:

- *Classroom models* focus on instruction in a single classroom with a single instructor.
- *Product development models* focus on a modest amount of instruction requiring several hours or perhaps several days. The emphasis is on the design of a specific unit of study.
- *System design models* focus on an entire course and curriculum and may involve several faculty and require additional resources.

As with any classification system there will be some overlap. For example, faculty involved in the design of a new course could, after using a systems design model, turn to a product design approach when they reach the point when they will be designing, producing, and evaluating a specific lesson. What is important is that faculty realize that these models exist and that using them will save time and make the design process a lot easier.

Because it is one of the more comprehensive models and is designed specifically for use in higher education, a good place to start is with *Designing and Assessing Courses and Curricula* (Diamond, 1998). It provides examples from a variety of disciplines, a clear process to follow, and a wide variety of useful tools, techniques, and resources. If faculty are interested in reviewing a wider range of approaches, the Gustafson and Branch publication just described is another good starting point.

CONCLUSION

Although paying attention to cohesiveness and quality of courses and curricula is rarely among your day-to-day priorities, it is the foundation of your institution's academic program. It is therefore important that time and resources be set aside to ensure that development and assessment are ongoing and that continued educational improvement becomes institutionalized. You have a key role to play in ensuring that these crucial activities take place.

References

Abbott, J., interviewed by T. Marchese. (1996). The search for next-century learning. *Wingspread Journal, 18*(3), pp. 4–8.

Austin-Beck, A. (1998, July). An Overview of the Curriculum. Paper presented at Minnowbrook Conference, Blue Mountain Lake, New York.

Boyer, E. L. (1987). *College: The undergraduate experience in America.* New York: HarperCollins.

Diamond, R. M. (1998). *Designing and assessing courses and curricula.* San Francisco: Jossey-Bass.

Gardiner, L. F. (1996). *Redesigning higher education: Producing dramatic gains in student learning.* Washington, DC: George Washington University, Graduate School of Education and Human Development. (ERIC Document Reproduction Service No. ED 394 442)

Gustafson, K. L., & Branch, R. M. (1997). *Survey of instructional development models* (3rd ed.). Syracuse, NY: Syracuse University.

Romer, R. (1995). *Making quality count in undergraduate education.* Denver: Education Commission of the States.

Resources

Astin, A. W., & Astin, H. S. (2001). *Leadership reconsidered: Engaging higher education in social change.* Battle Creek, MI: Kellogg Foundation.
Provides a sound rationale for adding leadership competencies to the list of goals for any curriculum. Details the competencies required for transformative leadership that would be helpful in designing a core curriculum for an institution or a specific academic field.

Diamond, R. M. (1998). *Designing and assessing courses and curricula.* San Francisco: Jossey-Bass.
Focusing specifically on the process of curriculum design for higher education, this book presents a model for the design process, outlining the steps that should be followed. It also includes a number of case studies, evaluation instruments, and protocols.

Gustafson, K. L., & Branch, R. M. (1997). *Survey of instructional development models* (3rd ed.). Syracuse, NY: Syracuse University.
Provides an excellent overview of various instructional design models, ranging from strategies for approaching total curriculum design to smaller projects such as courses or individual projects.

Lunde, J. P., Baker, M., Buelow, F. H., & Hayes, L. S. (1995). *Reshaping curricula: Revitalizing program at three land-grant universities.* Bolton, MA: Anker.
Do not let the land-grant and agriculture focus dissuade you from reading this book. The problems and processes the authors discuss are generic, and the writing of outcome statements, the use of technology, and writing across the curriculum are addressed. If nothing else, get a copy of the "lessons learned" section on pages 242 to 245. It is loaded with good insights.

Mentkowski, M., & Associates. (2000). *Learning that lasts: Integrating learning, development, and performance in college and beyond.* San Francisco: Jossey-Bass.
This well-documented volume focuses on the work done at Alverno College in Milwaukee to develop a curriculum that prepares students for long-term success after graduation. The conception of learning that was developed by the faculty has implications for anyone involved in curriculum design. Although not an easy read, it is worth the effort.

Mestenhauser, J. A., & Ellingboe, B. (1998). *Reforming the higher education curriculum: Internationalizing the campus.* Phoenix: Oryx Press.
Discusses the importance of broadening a curriculum to include an international emphasis. Provides case studies from a variety of disciplines and concludes with a section on evaluation of outcomes. Discusses various instructional strategies; has a strong chapter on technology.

Nelson, M., & Associates. (2000). *Alive at the core: Exemplary approaches to general education in the humanities.* San Francisco: Jossey-Bass.

Describes creative programs in the humanities at thirteen colleges and universities. The focus is on the principles and strategies used to design these cross-disciplinary models, where technology and out-of-classroom activities were integrated.

Oblinger, D. G., & Venville, A. (1998). *What business wants from higher education.* Phoenix: Oryx Press.

This book focuses on how the learning environment must change to prepare students for the workplace of tomorrow. Encourages increased cooperation between higher education and the business community in educational planning. An American Council of Education publication.

Rhodes, F.H.T. (2001, September 14). A battle plan for professors to recapture the curriculum. *Chronicle of Higher Education,* pp. B7–B10.

In this article, condensed from a forthcoming book, the former president of Cornell University argues for a curriculum that is based not on courses that universities require but on the qualities they want to develop in students. Rhodes's list includes openness and ability to communicate, self-confidence and curiosity, a sense of proportion and context in science and nature, delight in the variety of human experience and expression, passion in one chosen area, commitment to responsible citizenship, and a sense of direction and self-discipline.

Romer, R. (1995). *Making quality count in undergraduate education.* Denver: Education Commission of the States.

A report from the governor's task force that focuses on the educational experience. This report not only presents a solid case for change but provides a clear picture of why many individuals in public leadership roles are frustrated with the condition of American higher education and the lack of institutional leadership.

Stark, J. S., & Lattuca, L. R. (1997). *Shaping the college curriculum: Academic plans in action.* Needham Heights, MA: Allyn & Bacon.

Provides a history of the evaluation of the American curriculum and highlights the forces for change and associated issues. Also discusses the role of the disciplines and how students and academic leaders can both support and impede change efforts, assessment, and technology. The going will not always be easy, but decision makers and the administrators to whom they report will find some extremely useful suggestions in Chapters Eight through Thirteen.

Tobias, S. (1992). *Revitalizing undergraduate science: Why some things work and most don't.* Tucson: Research Corporation.

Takes a hard look at science education reform at the undergraduate level. Case studies from a number of institutions provide some guidelines for successful approaches. Calls for major rethinking of both structure and process and a willingness on the part of academic leaders to learn from the experience of others.

CHAPTER 10

Teaching Strategies for the Twenty-First Century

JAMES EISON

Providing students with excellent instruction is central to the mission of every institution of higher education. Although faculty members have primary responsibility for designing and delivering courses to promote the types of learning needed by students for success in a rapidly changing world, institutions are most likely to be effective in fulfilling this mission when academic leaders (that is, department chairpersons, deans, academic vice presidents, and higher) are themselves knowledgeable about current best practices in instruction and are appropriately supportive of faculty efforts to enhance teaching and learning.

Much is now known about promoting student learning through effective teaching practices. This chapter reviews briefly three highly regarded and widely cited descriptions of characteristics of effective teaching. Ten popular instructional approaches or strategies currently being used to apply these principles to classroom practice are then highlighted. Alternative action steps that academic leaders can take to promote the use of teaching strategies for improved undergraduate education follow. Last, a collection of especially helpful print and electronic resources for additional information are identified.

STRATEGIES THAT IMPROVE UNDERGRADUATE EDUCATION

A variety of well-researched scholarly publications (for example, Association of American Colleges Task Group on General Education, 1988; Donovan, Bransford, & Pellegrino, 1999; Engelkemeyer & Brown, 1998; Study Group on the Conditions of Excellence in American Higher Education, 1984) spanning over fifteen years provide both faculty and academic administrators with a clear, consistent, and comprehensive description of instructional strategies for enhanced student learning. For illustrative purposes here, the findings and recommendations of three such reports will be mentioned briefly.

Seven Principles of Good Practice in Undergraduate Education

The single best known description of teaching practices that promote student learning is Chickering and Gamson's (1987, 1991, 1999) "Seven Principles of Good Practice in Undergraduate Education." First published in an article in the March 1987 *AAHE Bulletin,* the authors' provocative and pithy review of the research literature was later reproduced by the Johnson Foundation and over 150,000 copies were distributed. Subsequently, several articles and texts based on this landmark document, along with helpful instruments to assess instructor and institutional effectiveness in each of these seven areas, have been created (Gamson & Poulsen, 1989). These assessment inventories can be found in Chickering and Gamson (1991) and Hatfield (1995). The seven principles of good practice are these:

- *Encourages contact between students and faculty.* Frequent student-faculty contact in and out of class is the most important factor in student motivation and involvement.
- *Develops reciprocity and cooperation among students.* Learning is enhanced when it resembles a team effort rather than a solo race.
- *Encourages active learning.* Learning is not a spectator sport. Students must talk about what they are learning, write about it, relate it to past experiences, and apply it to their daily lives. They must make what they learn part of themselves.
- *Gives prompt feedback.* Knowing what you do and do not know focuses learning. Students need appropriate feedback on performance to benefit from courses.
- *Emphasizes time on task.* Time plus energy equals learning. There is no substitute for time on task.
- *Communicates high expectations.* If teachers expect more they will get more.
- *Respects diverse talents and ways of learning.* There are many roads to learning. Students need the opportunity to show their talents and learn in ways that work for them.

Other Best Practices

Angelo (1993) similarly articulated for faculty and administrators a well-supported list of "fourteen general, research-based principles for improving higher learning."

- Active learning is more effective than passive learning.
- Learning is more effective and efficient when learners have explicit, reasonable, positive goals, and when their goals fit well with teachers' goals.
- High expectations encourage high achievement.
- Motivation to learn is alterable; it can be positively or negatively affected by the task, the environment, the teacher, and the learner.
- Learning requires focused attention and awareness of the importance of what is to be learned.
- To be remembered, new information must be meaningfully connected to prior knowledge, and it must first be remembered in order to be learned.
- Unlearning what is already known is often more difficult than learning new information.
- Information that is organized in personally meaningful ways is more likely to be remembered, learned, and used.
- To be most effective, teachers need to balance levels of intellectual challenge and instructional support.
- Mastering a complex skill or body of knowledge takes great amounts of time and effort.
- Learning to transfer, to apply previous knowledge and skills to new contexts, requires a great deal of directed practice.
- The ways in which learners are assessed and evaluated powerfully affect the ways they study and learn.
- Interaction between teachers and learners is one of the most powerful factors in promoting learning; interaction among learners is another.
- Learners need feedback on their learning, early and often, to learn well; to become independent learners, they need to become self-assessing and self-correcting.

Among the more recent analyses of how instructors can be most helpful in facilitating student learning is the report of the Joint Task Force on Student Learning, created by the American Association of Higher Education, the American College Personnel

Association, and the National Association of Student Personnel Administrators. This document articulated ten principles of learning and identified a large number of actions and initiatives that have been used on various campuses to implement these principles (Engelkemeyer & Brown, 1998). The ten principles of learning are these:

- Learning is fundamentally about *making and maintaining connections*: biologically through neural networks; mentally among concepts, ideas, and meanings; and experientially through interaction between the mind and the environment, self and other, generality and context, deliberation and action.
- Learning is enhanced by *taking place in the context of a compelling situation* that balances challenge and opportunity, stimulating and using the brain's ability to conceptualize quickly and its capacity and need for contemplation and reflection upon experiences.
- Learning is an *active search for meaning* by the learner—constructing knowledge rather than passively receiving it, shaping as well as being shaped by experiences.
- Learning is *developmental,* a cumulative process *involving* the *whole person,* relating past and present, integrating the new with the old, starting from but transcending personal concerns and interests.
- Learning is done by *individuals* who are intrinsically *tied to others as social beings,* interacting as competitors or collaborators, constraining or supporting the learning process, and able to enhance learning through cooperation and sharing.
- Learning is *strongly affected by the educational climate* in which it takes place; the settings and surroundings, the influences of others, and the values accorded to the life of the mind and to learning achievements.
- Learning requires *frequent feedback* if it is to be sustained, *practice* if it is to be nourished, and *opportunities to use* what has been learned.
- Much learning *takes place informally and incidentally,* beyond explicit teaching or the classroom, in casual contacts with faculty and staff, peers, campus life, active social and community involvement, and unplanned but interesting, complex situations.
- Learning is *grounded in particular contexts and individual experiences,* requiring effort to transfer specific knowledge and skills to other circumstances or to more general understandings and to unlearn personal views and approaches when confronted by new information.

- Learning involves the *ability of individuals to monitor their own learning,* to understand how knowledge is acquired to develop strategies for learning based on discerning their capacities and limitations, and to be aware of their own ways of knowing in approaching new bodies of knowledge and disciplinary frameworks.

BUILDING ON THE PRINCIPLES: TEN INSTRUCTIONAL APPROACHES

Although the administrative responsibilities of most academic leaders leave relatively little time for classroom teaching, it is important for all levels of leadership in higher education to understand and support faculty efforts to teach in ways that have been shown to enhance student learning. In contrast to all-too-familiar "talk-and-chalk" teaching methodologies, the following approaches are consistent with the research-supported principles and strategies described in the preceding section.

Active Learning

Active learning strategies "involve students in doing things and thinking about the things that they are doing" (Bonwell & Eison, 1991). In a broad sense, active learning approaches include a wide range of alternative instructional strategies that engage students *either* in individual work (for example, solving a problem set, completing a research assignment, preparing a written paper, working on a computer-based assignment) or in collaborative work with fellow students (using cooperative learning structures to help master course content, preparing a group presentation). In addition, faculty can employ such active learning strategies for either in-class activities or out-of-class assignments. To learn more about active learning, see Bean (1996), Bonwell and Eison (1991), Brookfield and Preskill (1999), and Myers and Jones (1993).

Learning Groups

"Effective learning groups seem to have two major elements: first, an active learning process promoted by student conversation in groups; second, faculty expertise and guidance provided through structured tasks. That is, it is not sufficient to increase discussion among students, and it is not sufficient to replace listening to lectures with problems for students to work on. Both elements—structured tasks and interaction among peers—seem to be necessary for the true power of learning groups to be realized" (Bouton & Garth, 1983, p. 73). Helpful resources on learning include Bouton and Garth (1983), Garth (1999), and Tiberius (1990).

Collaborative Learning

"In collaborative learning, students work on focused but open-ended tasks. They discuss issues in small consensus groups, plan and carry out long-term projects in research teams, tutor one another, analyze and work problems together, puzzle out difficult lab instructions together, read aloud to one another what they have written, and help one another edit and revise research reports and term papers. Collaborative learning gives students practice working together when the stakes are relatively low, so that they can work effectively together later when the stakes are high. They learn to depend upon one another rather than depending exclusively on the authority of the teacher" (Bruffee, 1993, p. 1). To learn more about collaborative learning, see Bruffee (1993, 1995, 1999), Goodsell, Maher, Tinto, Smith, and MacGregor (1992), and Kadel and Keehner (1994).

Cooperative Learning

"Cooperative learning is the instructional use of small groups so that students work together to maximize their own and each other's learning. . . . Many educators who believe that they are using cooperative learning are, in fact, missing its essence. A crucial difference exists between simply putting students in groups to learn and in structuring cooperation among students. Cooperation is not having students sit side by side at the same table to talk with each other as they do their individual assignments. It is not assigning a report to a group of students where one student does all the work and the others put their names on the product as well. It is not having students do a task individually with instructions that the ones who finish first are to help the slower students. . . . To be cooperative, a group must have clear positive interdependence, members must promote each other's learning and success face-to-face, hold each other personally and individually accountable to do his or her fair share of the work, use appropriately the interpersonal and small-group skills needed for cooperative efforts to be successful, and process as a group how effectively members are working together. These five essential components must be present for small group learning to be truly cooperative" (Johnson, Johnson, & Smith, 1991, pp. iii–iv). Helpful resources on cooperative learning include Johnson, Johnson, and Smith (1991, 1998) and Millis and Cottell (1998).

Team Learning

"The primary features of team learning include: (1) permanent and purposeful heterogeneous work groups; (2) grading based on a combination of individual performance, group performance, and peer evaluation; (3) the majority of class time devoted to small group activities (necessitating a shift in the role of the instructor from dispenser of information to manager of a learning process); (4) a six-step instructional activity sequence, repeated several times per term that makes it possible to focus the vast majority of class time on helping students develop the ability to use concepts as opposed to simply learn about them" (Michaelsen, 1992, p. 109). To learn more about team learning see Michaelsen and Black (1994), Michaelsen, Black, and Fink (1996), Nuhfer (1997), and Stein and Hurd (2000).

Learning Communities

"A learning community is any one of a variety of curricular structures that link several existing courses—or actually restructure the curricular material entirely—so that students have opportunities for deeper understanding and integration of the material they are learning, and more interaction with one another and their teachers as fellow participants in the learning enterprise" (Gabelnick, McGregor, Matthews, & Smith, 1990, p. 19). Helpful resources on learning communities include Cross (1998), Gabelnick et al. (1990), Lenning and Ebbers (1999), and Matthews (1996).

Case Method Teaching

"Case teaching involves the interactive, student-centered exploration of realistic and specific narratives. The students engage in the intellectual, and emotional, exercise of facing complex problems and making critical decisions within the constraints imposed by reality—for example, limited time and information and pervasive uncertainty. Considering them from the protagonist's perspective, which calls on analysis to inform action, the students strive to resolve questions that have no single right answer. In their effort to find solutions and reach decisions through discussion, they sort out factual data, apply analytic tools, articulate issues, reflect on their relevant experience, and draw conclusions they can carry forward to new situations. In the process, they acquire substantive knowledge, as well as develop analytic, collaborative, and communication skills" (Boehrer, 1997). Helpful resources on case method teaching include Christensen and Hansen (1981), Hutchings (1993), and Silverman, Welty, and Lyon (1992).

Problem-Based Learning (PBL)

"PBL is an approach to learning in which problems serve as the stimulus for students to gain course concepts and content as well as metacognitive skills. Generally PBL problems are ill structured, based upon real situations, and have more than one 'right' answer. Students work in teams to define the nature of the problem, to identify what additional resources they need, and to find viable solutions. Faculty members act as facilitators by asking questions and monitoring group processes as students actively pursue viable solutions. Faculty members also guide students to resources" (Major, 1999, p. 7). To learn more about problem-based learning, see Albanese and Mitchell (1993), Duch, Groh, and Allen (2001), Mierson and Parikh (2000), and Wilkerson and Gijselaers (1996).

Service Learning

Although definitions of service learning vary, Weigert (1998, p. 5) has identified several characteristics that help differentiate service learning from volunteerism, community service, and other forms of experiential learning. These include, on the community side, "the student provides some meaningful service (work), that meets a need or goal, that is defined by a community (or some of its members)," and on the campus side, "the service provided by the student flows from and into course objectives, is integrated into the course by means of assignments that require some form of reflection on the service in light of course objectives, and the assignment is assessed and evaluated accordingly." Helpful resources on service learning include Eyler and Giles (1999), Honnet and Poulen (1989), Kendal et al. (1990), Rhoads and Howard

(1998), and Zlotkowski (1998). See also the eighteen-volume series published by the American Association for Higher Education Service Learning Project that explores community-based learning in and through the individual academic disciplines (the Web site appears in the annotated list of sites at the end of this chapter).

Classroom Assessment and Research

Influenced by the compelling thinking, speaking, and writing of K. Patricia Cross and Tom Angelo since the mid-1980s, many faculty have become classroom researchers actively engaged in studying and improving student learning in the courses they teach, often using techniques known as *classroom assessment.* As described by Cross and Steadman (1996), *classroom research* encourages faculty to use their classrooms as research laboratories and may be defined as "ongoing and cumulative intellectual inquiry by classroom teachers into the nature of teaching and learning in their own classrooms." The related notion of classroom assessment refers to alternative methods "faculty can use to collect feedback, early and often, on how well students are learning what they are being taught. The purpose of classroom assessment is to provide faculty and students with information and insights needed to improve teaching effectiveness and learning quality" (Angelo, 1991). Helpful resources on classroom assessment and research include Angelo (1991, 1998), Angelo and Cross (1993), Cross (1990), and Cross and Steadman (1996).

THE ROLE OF ACADEMIC LEADERS IN PROMOTING TEACHING EXCELLENCE

K. Patricia Cross (1989) has persuasively argued that "the biggest and most long-lasting reform of undergraduate education will come when individual faculty or small groups of instructors adopt the view of themselves as reformers within their immediate sphere of influence, the classes they teach every day." Academic leaders can, however, exercise a strong and visible influence on creating a campus climate that supports faculty efforts. Unfortunately, surprisingly little has been written to assist academic leaders in this important undertaking. Two excellent texts that address directly this issue are Cochran (1989) and Seldin and Associates (1990).

For example, Madeline Green (1990), writing in Seldin and Associates (1990), offers academic leaders many insights and recommendations, including the following seven points: (1) make good teaching a leadership priority, (2) become a partner in the venture, (3) have faculty lead the charge, (4) put your money where your rhetoric is, (5) reward good teaching in ways that matter, (6) make good teaching an institutional responsibility and not simply an individual one, and (7) make teaching ability a criterion for hiring faculty.

Cochran (1989) astutely observed that the leadership challenge associated with elevating the status of teaching, "is complex and cannot be accomplished by a singular action or in a haphazard fashion. Substantive reform requires a calculated change initiative that is coherently planned, organized, and implemented." To assist campus leaders in such efforts, in 1987 Cochran conducted a national survey of chief academic officers from over thirteen hundred four-year degree-granting institutions to assess their overall commitment to instructional effectiveness in terms of twenty-five specific items organized in five major categories, their satisfaction levels with their institutional performance in each of five instructional improvement categories, and their satisfaction levels with the amount of personal attention they have devoted to each of five instructional improvement categories. The five main categories addressed in this study, and for which Cochran (1989) offered numerous practical "ideas for action," were instructional development activities, instructional enhancement efforts, employment policies and practices, strategic administrative actions, and campus environment and culture.

After a careful and detailed analysis of survey results and articulation of a vast array of action steps that chief academic leaders might pursue to reestablish the importance of teaching in higher education, Cochran urged that "administrators must be willing to take bold stands to support teaching, energetically support new teaching initiatives, and create imaginative ways to enhance the basic instructional function. Administrators must build an attitude and environment that fosters quality teaching." In this pursuit, other helpful resources include Donald (1997), Gibbs (1995), Lazerson, Wagener, and Shumanis (2000), and North (1995).

One of the many recognized hallmarks of outstanding teachers is remaining current in their field. Academic leaders should similarly allocate some of their own professional development time to staying current in their knowledge of the scholarly writing and research on teaching practices that most effectively promote student learning. As a starting point, one's reading time might include current issues of the *AAHE Bulletin, Change: The Magazine of Higher Learning,* and the *Chronicle of Higher Education.* Other especially helpful periodic series are the ASHE-ERIC Higher Education Reports and New Directions for Teaching and Learning, both published by Jossey-Bass.

CONCLUSION

Supporting teaching and learning is among the many responsibilities of administrators. Being knowledgeable about educational research and emerging pedagogies is an ongoing challenge. Maintaining high expectations for faculty is important, but equally high standards need to be set for all academic administrators. Change and innovation are important aspects of academic life. Students need to be prepared for life and work in a changing world. Traditional methods of instruction will not suffice, and today's innovation can quickly fade as a fad or become tomorrow's "traditional." Ongoing learning at all levels of the institution is what higher education needs in order to do its most important work.

References

Association of American Colleges Task Group on General Education. (1988). *A new vitality in general education.* Washington, DC: Association of American Colleges.

Albanese, M. A., & Mitchell, S. (1993). Problem-based learning: A review of literature on its outcomes and implementation issues. *Academic Medicine, 68*(1), 52–81.

Angelo, T. A. (1991a). Ten easy pieces: Assessing higher learning in four dimensions. In T. A. Angelo (Ed.), *Classroom research: Early lessons from success.* New Directions for Teaching and Learning, no. 46. San Francisco: Jossey-Bass.

Angelo, T. A. (Ed.). (1991b). *Classroom research: Early lessons from success.* New Directions for Teaching and Learning, no. 46. San Francisco: Jossey-Bass.

Angelo, T. A. (1993, April). A teacher's dozen: Fourteen general, research-based principles for improving higher learning in our classrooms. *AAHE Bulletin,* 3–7, 13.

Angelo, T. A. (Ed.). (1998). *Classroom assessment and research: An update on uses, approaches, and research findings.* New Directions for Teaching and Learning, no. 75. San Francisco: Jossey-Bass.

Angelo, T. A., & Cross, K. P. (1993). *Classroom assessment techniques: A handbook for college teachers* (2nd ed.). San Francisco: Jossey-Bass.

Bean, J. C. (1996). *Engaging ideas: The professor's guide to integrating writing, critical thinking, and active learning in the classroom.* San Francisco: Jossey-Bass.

Bonwell, C., & Eison, J. A. (1991). *Active learning: Creating excitement in the classroom* (ASHE-ERIC Higher Education Report No. 1). Washington, DC: George Washington University.

Bouton, C., & Garth, R. Y. (1983, June). Students in learning groups: Active learning through conversation. In C. Bouton & R. Y. Garth (Eds.), *Learning in groups.* New Directions for Teaching and Learning, no. 14. San Francisco: Jossey-Bass.

Brookfield, S. D., & Preskill, S. (1999). *Discussion as a way of teaching: Tools and techniques for democratic classrooms.* San Francisco: Jossey-Bass.

Bruffee, K. A. (1993). *Collaborative learning: Higher education, interdependence, and the authority of knowledge.* Baltimore, MD: Johns Hopkins University Press.

Bruffee, K. A. (1995). Sharing our toys: Cooperative learning versus collaborative learning. *Change, 27*(1), 12–18.

Bruffee, K. A. (1999). *Collaborative learning: Higher education, interdependence, and the authority of knowledge* (2nd ed.). Baltimore, MD: Johns Hopkins University Press.

Chickering, A. W., & Gamson, Z. F. (1987, March). Seven principles for good practice in undergraduate education. *AAHE Bulletin, 39*(7), 3–7.

Chickering, A. W., & Gamson, Z. F. (Eds.). (1991). *Applying the seven principles for good practice in undergraduate education.* New Directions for Teaching and Learning, no. 47. San Francisco: Jossey-Bass.

Chickering, A. W., & Gamson, Z. F. (1999). Development and adaptations of the seven principles for good practice in undergraduate education. In M. D. Svinicki (Ed.), *Teaching and learning on the edge of the millennium: Building on what we have learned.* New Directions for Teaching and Learning, no. 80. San Francisco: Jossey-Bass.

Christensen, C. R., & Hansen, A. J. (1981). *Teaching and the case method.* Boston: Harvard Business School.

Cochran, L. H. (1989). *ACT: Administrative commitment to teaching.* Cape Girardeau, MO: STEP UP.

Cross, K. P. (1987, March). Teaching for learning, *AAHE Bulletin,* 3–7.

Cross, K. P. (1989, Fall). Reforming undergraduate education one class at a time. *Teaching excellence: Toward the best in the academy.* Professional and Organizational Development Network in Higher Education, 1–2.

Cross, K. P. (1990). Classroom research: Helping professors learn more about teaching and learning. In P. Seldin & Associates (Eds.), *How administrators can improve teaching.* San Francisco: Jossey-Bass.

Cross, K. P. (1998, July-August). Why learning communities? Why now? *About Campus, 3*(3), 4–11.

Cross, K. P., & Steadman, M. H. (1996). *Classroom research: Implementing the scholarship of teaching.* San Francisco: Jossey-Bass.

Donald, J. G. (1997). *Improving the environment for learning: Academic leaders talk about what works.* San Francisco: Jossey-Bass.

Donovan, M. S., Bransford, J. D., & Pellegrino, J. W. (Ed.). (1999). *How people learn: Bridging research and practice.* Washington, DC: National Academy Press.

Duch, B. J., Groh, S. E., & Allen, D. E. (Eds.). (2001). The power of problem-based learning. *A practical "how to" for teaching undergraduate courses in any discipline.* Sterling, VA: Stylus Press.

Education Commission of the States. (1996, April). What research says about improving undergraduate education. *AAHE Bulletin, 48*(8), 5–8.

Eyler, J., & Giles, D. E. (1999). *Where's the learning in service-learning.* San Francisco: Jossey-Bass.

Engelkemeyer, S. W., & Brown, S. C. (1998, October). Powerful partnerships: A shared responsibility for learning. *AAHE Bulletin, 51*(2), 10–12.

Gabelnick, F., McGregor, J., Matthews, R. S., & Smith, B. L. (Eds.). (1990). *Learning communities: Creating connections among students, faculty, and disciplines.* New Directions for Teaching and Learning, no. 41. San Francisco: Jossey-Bass.

Gamson, Z. F., & Poulsen, S. J. (1989). Inventories of good practice: The next step for the seven principles for good practice in undergraduate education. *AAHE Bulletin, 47*(3), 7–8, 14.

Garth, R. Y. (1999, Winter). Group-based learning. In M. D. Svinicki (Ed.), *Teaching and learning on the edge of the millennium: Building on what we have learned.* New Directions for Teaching and Learning, no. 80. San Francisco: Jossey-Bass.

Gibbs, G. (1995, May-June). Promoting excellent teaching is harder than you'd think: A note from an outside observer of the roles and rewards initiative. *Change, 27*(3), 17–20.

Goodsell, A., Maher, M., & Tinto, V., with Smith, B. L., & MacGregor, J. (1992). *Collaborative learning: A sourcebook for higher education.* University Park: The Pennsylvania State University, National Center on Postsecondary Teaching, Learning, and Assessment.

Greene, M. K. (1990). Why good teaching needs active leadership. In P. Seldin & Associates (Eds.), *How administrators can improve teaching.* San Francisco: Jossey-Bass.

Hatfield, S. R. (Ed.). (1995). *The seven principles in action: Improving undergraduate education.* Bolton, MA: Anker.

Honnet, E. P., & Poulen, S. J. (1989). *Principles of good practice for combining service and learning.* A Wingspread Special Report. Racine, WI: Johnson Foundation.

Hutchings, P. (1993). *Using cases to improve teaching: A guide to more reflective practice.* Washington, DC: American Association for Higher Education.

Johnson, D. W., Johnson, R. T., & Smith, K. A. (1991). *Cooperative learning: Increasing college faculty instructional productivity* (ASHE-ERIC Higher Education Report No. 4). Washington, DC: The George Washington University, Graduate School of Education.

Johnson, D. W., Johnson, R. T., & Smith, K. A. (1998). Cooperative learning returns to college: What evidence is there that it works. *Change, 30*(4), 27–35.

Kadel, S., & Keehner, J. A. (1994). *Collaborative learning: A sourcebook for higher education* (Vol. II). University Park: The Pennsylvania State University, National Center for Postsecondary Teaching, Learning, and Assessment.

Kendal, J. C., & others. (Eds.). (1990). *Combining service and learning.* Raleigh, NC: National Society for Internships and Experiential Education.

Lazerson, M., Wagener, U., & Shumanis, N. (2000, May-June). What makes a revolution: Teaching and learning in higher education, 1980–2000. *Change, 32*(3), 12–19.

Lenning, O. T., & Ebbers, L. H. (1999). *The powerful potential of learning communities: Improving education for the future* (ASHE-ERIC Higher Education Report, 26(6). Washington, DC: George Washington University.

Major, C. H. (1999, March). Connecting what we know and what we do through problem-based learning. *AAHE Bulletin, 51*(7), 7–9.

Matthews, T. (1996, Summer). Learning communities: A structure for educational coherence. *Liberal Education, 82*(3), 4–9.

Michaelsen, L. K. (1992). Team learning: A comprehensive approach for harnessing the power of small groups in higher education. In D. Wulff & J. D. Nyquist (Eds.), *To improve the academy* (Vol. 11, pp. 107–122). Stillwater, OK: New Forums Press and the Professional and Organizational Development Network in Higher Education.

Michaelsen, L. K., & Black, R. H. (1994). Building learning teams: The key to harnessing the power of small groups in higher education. In S. Kadel & J. A. Keehner (Eds.), *Collaborative learning: A sourcebook for higher education* (Vol. II, pp. 65–85). University Park: The Pennsylvania State University, National Center for Postsecondary Teaching, Learning and Assessment.

Michaelsen, L. K., Black, R. H., & Fink, L. D. (1996). What every faculty developer needs to know about learning groups. In L. Richlin (Ed.), *To improve the academy* (Vol. 15, pp. 31–58). Stillwater, OK: New Forums Press and the Professional and Organizational Development Network in Higher Education.

Mierson S., & Parikh, A. A. (2000, Jan.-Feb.). Stories from the field: Problem-based learning from a teacher's and a student's perspective. *Change, 32*(1), 21–27.

Millis, B. J., & Cottell, P. G. (1998). *Cooperative learning for higher education faculty.* Phoenix: Oryx Press

Myers, C., & Jones, T. B. (1993). *Promoting active learning.* San Francisco: Jossey-Bass.

North, J.D.G. (1995, Oct). Read my lips: The academic administrators role in the campus focus on teaching. *AAHE Bulletin, 48*(2), 3–6.

Nuhfer, E. (1997). Student management teams: The heretic's path to teaching success. In W. E. Campbell & K. A. Smith (Eds.), *New paradigms for college teaching* (pp. 103–126). Edina, MN: Interaction Book.

Pascarella, E. T., & Terenzini, P. T. (1991). *How college affects students.* San Francisco: Jossey-Bass.

Rhoads, R. A., & Howard, J.P.F. (Eds.). (1998). *Academic service learning: A pedagogy of action and reflection.* New Directions for Teaching and Learning, no. 73. San Francisco: Jossey-Bass.

Seldin, P., & Associates. (1990). *How administrators can improve teaching.* San Francisco: Jossey-Bass.

Silverman, R., Welty, W. M., & Lyon, S. (1992). *Case studies for teacher problem solving.* New York: McGraw-Hill.

Stein, R. F., & Hurd, S. (2000). *Using student teams in the classroom: A faculty guide.* Bolton, MA: Anker.

Study Group on the Conditions of Excellence in American Higher Education. (1984). *Involvement in learning: Realizing the potential of American higher education.* Washington, DC: National Institute of Education.

Tiberius, R. (1990). *Small group teaching: A troubleshooting guide.* Ontario: OISE Press/Ontario Institute for Studies in Education.

Weigert, K. M. (1998). Academic service learning: Its meaning and relevance. In R. A. Rhoads & J.P.F. Howard (Eds.), *Academic service learning: A pedagogy of action and reflection.* New Directions for Teaching and Learning, no. 73. San Francisco: Jossey-Bass.

Wilkerson, L., & Gijselaers, W. H. (Eds.). (1996). *Bringing problem-based learning to higher education: Theory and practice.* New Directions for Teaching and Learning, no. 68. San Francisco: Jossey-Bass.

Zlotkowski, E. (Ed.). (1998). *Successful service-learning programs: New models of excellence in higher education.* Bolton, MA: Anker.

Resources

The following resources are organized by type.

Print Material

Angelo, T. A., & Cross, K. P. (1993). *Classroom assessment techniques: A handbook for college teachers* (2nd ed.). San Francisco: Jossey-Bass.

This text, written for faculty interested in becoming more reflective and effective classroom instructors, offers detailed descriptions of fifty classroom assessment techniques and illustrates nicely their use with brief case studies across the disciplines.

Bonwell, C. C., & Eison, J. A. (1991). *Active learning: Creating excitement in the classroom* (ASHE-ERIC Higher Education Report No. 1). Washington, DC: George Washington University.
This text critically synthesizes published writing and research on active learning focusing on such issues as these: What is active learning and why is it important? How can active learning be incorporated in the classroom? What are the barriers? What conclusions should be drawn and recommendations made?

Bruffee, K. A. (1999). *Collaborative learning* (2nd ed.). Baltimore, MD: Johns Hopkins University Press.
This second edition of a now-classic text on collaborative learning offers readers three new chapters and an updated look at "the relationship between college and university professors and students: the learned and the learning" (p. xi).

Christensen, C. R., & Hansen, A. J. (1981). *Teaching and the case method.* Boston: Harvard Business School.
This work offers both neophytes and experienced case method teachers valuable insights into the excitement and challenges of case teaching. Based on experiences at Harvard Business School, the book contains text, a collection of teaching cases with instructor notes, and readings.

Cochran, L. H. (1989). *ACT: Administrative commitment to teaching.* Cape Girardeau, MO: STEP UP.
This book offers administrators a vast array of examples and "tangible research-based insights on how to make a stronger commitment to teaching" (p. v).

Eylers, J., & Giles, D. E. (1999). *Where's the learning in service-learning?* San Francisco: Jossey-Bass.
This exciting text offers readers a research-based look at ways to design academically effective service learning courses and programs.

Millis, B. J., & Cottell, P. G. (1998). *Cooperative learning for higher education faculty.* Phoenix: Oryx Press.
This text explores the practical application of cooperative learning instructional approaches in higher education. The authors provide a comprehensive and scholarly look at the underlying rationale for cooperative learning and summarize the research base that supports its ever-increasing use in college and university classrooms.

Seldin, P., & Associates. (1990). *How administrators can improve teaching.* San Francisco: Jossey-Bass.
This outstanding volume includes eleven provocative chapters examining key influences on teaching quality, the administrator's role in strengthening instructional quality, and making teaching excellence an institutional priority.

Web Sites

Active Learning Bibliography [http://www.cte.usf.edu]
This comprehensive listing prepared by Jim Eison and colleagues at the University of South Florida's Center for Teaching Enhancement identifies thousands of published articles describing the

use of active learning strategies in higher education. These references have been organized into eight broad-based discipline areas (business and computer science, communication, general works, humanities, mathematics, nursing and health-related fields, science, and social science) and then by fifteen categories of different active learning instructional approaches. To get to this bibliography, click first on "Resources," then click on "Index of All Bibliographies," and finally, click on "Active Learning Bibliography."

Charles C. Bonwell's Active Learning Site [http://www.active-learning-site.com]
This site supports the scholarship of teaching by providing research-based resources designed to help faculty use active learning successfully in college and university classrooms. Of special note is the active learning bibliography (identifying published articles from 1995 to 1998) and several concise article summaries

The Instructional Innovation Network [http://www.bestpractice.net]
The Instructional Innovation Network is a network of both human and electronic resources devoted to improving teaching and learning in higher education through cooperative learning and case teaching.

Collaborative Learning Small Group Learning Page [http://www.wcer.wisc.edu/nise/cl1]
This site, maintained by the National Institute for Science Education College Level One Team at the University of Wisconsin, supports the work of a nationwide community of postsecondary science, mathematics, engineering, and technology (SMET) faculty, education research disseminators, and students. On this site are a series of practical tips on integrating cooperative learning structures into courses (found under "Doing CL"); a meta-analysis of studies on undergraduate SMET education demonstrating that various forms of small group learning are effective in promoting greater academic achievement, more favorable attitudes toward learning, and increased student persistence (found under "Resources"); and an outstanding annotated bibliography (also found under "Resources").

The American Association of Higher Education Service Learning Project [http:// www.aahe.org/service/srv-lrn.htm]
This site describes AAHE's initiative to support the integration of service learning across the disciplines including an eighteen-volume series designed to provide resources to faculty wishing to explore community-based learning in and through the individual academic disciplines.

Service-Learning [http://csf.colorado.edu/sl/]
This site offers a virtual guide to, and library of, service learning in higher education. The primary components include a Guide to College and University Service-Learning Programs, Courses, and Syllabi; the Service-Learning Discussion Group archives; a Guide to Service-Learning Organizations, Networks, Venues and Resources; and an on-line library of Service-Learning Syllabi (by discipline).

National Service-Learning Clearinghouse (NSLC) [http://www.servicelearning.org]
   The clearinghouse site, which is funded by the Department of Service Learning, Corporation for National Service, supports Learn and Serve America grantees, as well as other programs engaged in service learning, through the collection and dissemination of information and materials.

IDEA Center [http://www.idea.ksu.edu]
   This site, maintained by Kansas State University's IDEA Center, now offers free access to the well-known series of IDEA papers. Many of these well-researched and highly readable papers have addressed the skillful use of active learning instructional strategies such as "Improving Discussions" (No. 15), "Improving Student Writing" (No. 25), "Answering and Asking Questions" (No. 31), and "Focusing on Active Meaningful Learning" (No. 34).

The Samford Problem-Based Learning Initiative [http://LR.Samford.edu/PBL]
   This site, maintained by Samford University's Problem-Based Learning Project and funded by the Pew Charitable Trust, provides helpful information about a PBL project to redesign key areas of the undergraduate curriculum.

Problem-Based Learning at the University of Delaware [http://www.udel.edu/pbl]
   This site, maintained by the University of Delaware Problem-Based Learning Project and funded by the National Science Foundation, offers article reprints, illustrative PBL problems (general problems as well as problems from disciplines such as biology, chemistry, criminal justice, and physics), sample course syllabi from over a dozen courses, and links to other PBL sites.

CHAPTER 11

Technology in the Learning Process

WALLACE HANNUM

One of the more obvious changes on university campuses in recent years is the use of technology. Courses previously taught by lecture and discussion now include on-line activity, such as discussion forums, links to on-line readings, and group exercises. Some courses are taught entirely on-line at a distance, with faculty and students never coming together in the same place or even at the same time. Green (2000) reports a rising use of technology on campuses. Almost a third of all college courses now have a Web page, 60 percent of all classes use e-mail, 40 percent of all college courses include Web resources on the syllabus, and 55 percent of universities offer some on-line courses.

Mention technology on campus today and many people immediately think of students and faculty working with computers and the Internet. Of course, computers and the Internet are examples of technology, but they are not the only examples. Technology in education extends beyond the application of computer and communications hardware to include the processes used for designing and delivering instruction. Adding technology to the instructional mix without considering any other change in instruction may yield some benefits, but they will be negligible. Technology is best considered more broadly, such as when faculty members rethink how to teach a course rather than take what they have always done and simply do it with technology. Just shifting teaching practices and materials to some form of technology delivery—placing old lecture notes on a Web site, for example—is the lowest form of the use of technology in instruction (Gilbert, 1996).

STATUS OF TECHNOLOGY APPLICATIONS

Exhibit 11.1 lists reasons for using technology to deliver instruction:

EXHIBIT 11.1. Reasons for Using Technology in Instruction.

Reason	*Comments*
Learning	When used appropriately and thoughtfully, technology enables students to learn more than they learn sitting in lecture classes.
Economics	Over time, you lower costs of providing instruction by shifting from a labor-intensive system, where faculty deliver lectures in a classroom, to a technology-based approach, where students receive instruction on-line whenever they like.
Job relevance	Because you are preparing students for a world in which technology is ubiquitous—especially the work world—you should make extensive use of technology on campus. When universities use technology widely, they better prepare students for their futures.
General acceptance	Technology is so accepted in our society that parents and students alike expect universities to use technology widely in their programs. Employers also expect students to have used technology in school.
Quality	When instruction is carefully designed and delivered with technology, it is of higher quality—whether PowerPoint presentations are used in the classroom, computer simulations are given as homework, or classes are offered entirely on-line.
Quantity	Technology improves the quantity of instruction available to students. On-line classes can be available twenty-four hours a day, and when the Internet is involved the sheer quantity of information to which students have access increases dramatically.
Access	Technology provides more access to instruction, especially in the case of distance education. Distance education through technology brings the instruction available in the university to many people who would otherwise not have such access. On campus, use of technology also makes instruction available outside of regular class times.
Instructional model	If employed in a thoughtful way, technology will alter the dominant instructional model from students passively receiving information to their engaging actively with knowledge. Technology changes the roles of instructors as information dispensers and learners as information repositories. It allows students to engage with learning and enhance their understanding of subject matter knowledge.
Modes of representation	Technology allows students to gain access to knowledge in more than one mode. Reading and listening to lectures are both highly symbolic activities, removed from the events and objects they describe. Through technology, students can interact with representations of the material they are studying, seeing and hearing phenomena and controlling interactions, as in simulations.
Deep processing and understanding	When students learn with technology, it enhances their deep processing of content and provides a richer understanding. Technology shifts the learning from rote memorization of facts presented in textbooks or lectures to a deeper interaction with the content and a richer understanding of concepts and principles.

Depending on your needs and interests, consider including technology applications to instruction for one or more of the reasons shown in the exhibit. However, remember that although proponents argue for increased technology use on campus, opponents argue against it, especially distance education. They contrast information, which they claim can be acquired through technology, with understanding, which they suggest cannot be easily acquired through the use of technology. In their view, faculty members interacting with students on campus do much more than simply dispense information, which some say is all that happens in distance education.

Although widespread instructional use of technology may be a recent phenomenon on many campuses, by no means is it without precedent. There is a substantial history of technology use in education and a rich research base for us to understand its use. Hundreds of empirical studies of instructional uses of technology appear in the literature. Although some findings are mixed, in general these studies support the proposition that instruction delivered by technology is at least as good as traditional instruction and often results in greater learning. But there is one caveat: the research suggests that *how* technology is used to deliver instruction matters much more than *what* technology or even *whether* technology is used.

Simply adding technology to courses without making any other modifications in how the course is taught will not add much instructional value. Combining technology with careful design to profit from instructional strategies that have strong effects on learning will add considerable value. In short, there is no magic in the technology itself.

Common Problems

Some of the problems with instructional uses of technology are predictable and preventable. Most stem from a rush to use technology or a failure to think through why and how it should be used. We create problems when we

- Start by assuming we will use technology, rather than start with questions about course purpose and design
- Focus on the technology because it appears glamorous and sophisticated, rather than keep the focus on learning and instruction
- Rely exclusively on technology advocates and outside vendors to guide us
- Fail to consider providing time and support for faculty to use technology in meaningful ways in their instruction

- Fail to consider the development and use of technology as valued faculty work in promotion and tenure reviews
- Fail to consider the costs of maintaining and continuing technology-based projects
- Do not make arrangements for technical assistance to faculty and students who use technology

Approaches to Using Technology

It is tempting for administrators and faculty to embrace technology, then convert existing instruction to use technology and assume they have enhanced learning. Decades of evidence suggest that this repurposing of instructional materials—such as putting a syllabus on the Web or videotaping a lecture class and then putting that on the Internet as streamed video—adds little instructional value. Instead, faculty must redesign their courses to take full advantage of instructional possibilities offered by technology. Nowhere is this more clear than in distance education classes offered over the Internet. Unfortunately, some faculty just post their lecture notes and readings on a Web site and consider this to be on-line instruction. This does not represent the potential of on-line instruction. This is using the Internet as a post office to send lecture notes—much as was done more than half a century ago, when lecture notes were mailed to students taking correspondence courses. The instructional content and the pedagogy are not modified to take advantage of the possibilities that technology offers. Improving instruction through technology requires first considering what makes for good instruction. Then we can build these qualities into technology-delivered instruction.

Supplemental Uses

Faculty can use technology to supplement what they were doing before. For example, rather than drawing a diagram of a process on a blackboard, faculty can use computers with presentation software to project the diagram on a screen. Rather than making copies of the course syllabus to pass out in class, they can put it on a Web page. Rather than placing a required reading on reserve in the library, they can place links to it on a course Web site. Rather than lecturing in the classroom, they can videotape a classroom lecture and convert this into streamed video for Internet delivery. Rather than coming to class and reading from their lecture notes, they may place their notes on a course Web site. While these uses may offer some benefits, they fail to take full advantage of technology.

Do these common uses of technology in higher education actually improve instruction? Probably not. Doing the same instructional activities while changing their display or delivery format is likely not adding any significant instructional value, nor should it. The learners hear and see essentially the same thing whether it is displayed by presentation software or an instructor at the blackboard.

Still, this supplemental use of technology might make more efficient use of instructional time because faculty do not have to spend class time constructing complex diagrams on the blackboard. Students might also be freed of the burden of trying to write down everything the faculty member says because they can gain access to that on the class Web site whenever they wish.

Faculty can also use technology to do things they were not able to do before. For example, when using technology as a supplement, they can

- Use a computer simulation to show changes in an archeological site over a period of centuries
- Use real-time computation of data from a space shuttle to explore physical forces
- Have students interact with complex engineering models to learn how to design electrical power plants
- Use virtual reality to have students learn about chemical compounds by "walking" through them
- Use patient simulations to allow students to learn about diagnosis and treatment of diseases
- Use videoconferencing to bring authorities from around the world into their classrooms to interact with their students
- Have students produce multimedia projects rather than written term papers
- Connect their students with students at other universities for group efforts
- Introduce a rich variety of content into their classrooms through the Internet rather than being bound to the textbook

In these examples, the technology is a supplement to the classroom experience. In essence, it is added to the traditional classroom mix.

Replacement Uses

Technology can also be much more than just a supplement to a traditional classroom experience. Courses taught with technology could change the role of faculty as dispensers of instructional content by placing students directly into contact with the material. Courses formerly taught through campus lectures according to a fixed schedule have become on-line courses taught over the Internet at the time and place of the students' choosing. Distance education, especially on-line or e-learning, offers ways for technology to replace the traditional classroom. Some argue that e-learning will eventually replace the traditional university.

Although e-learning itself is new, the arguments about technology replacing instruction are old. Different technologies have long had the ability to replace much, or possibly all, that some faculty do in classrooms. Lectures can be printed in books, recorded on audiotape or videotape, broadcast as radio or television, or streamed over the Internet. Early correspondence study replaced traditional classrooms. Distance education courses that are taught through broadcast television are still used instead of traditional courses. More recently, courses taught over the Internet are used as replacements for traditional classes.

Internet-Based Learning

Faculty may take one of two views on the use of the Internet. In the *publishing view,* the Internet is thought of as a means to distribute materials. From this point of view, on-line learning is a way to distribute instructional materials to learners who are removed from the faculty member in both space and time. In the *communications view,* the Internet is thought of as a means of bringing people together to exchange thoughts and ideas. On-line learning becomes a way to enable faculty and learners to communicate and interact although they may not be together in the same space at the same time. Based on these two views of the Internet, Hannum (1999) has suggested a number of different instructional modes for on-line learning.

- In the *library mode* on-line learning consists mainly of links to instructional resources such as on-line encyclopedias, journals, and books, and other Web sites offering relevant content. The links to other sites can be organized by topic to help learners find desired information. Links can be annotated, allowing learners to review information about a site before deciding to visit it. The library mode may supplement a regular course or an on-line course.

- The *textbook mode* provides learners with on-line access to instructional materials, such as a course syllabus, lecture notes, slides, and video or graphics used in class. The textbook mode is appropriate as the main way to deliver content in an on-line learning course. It can also be used as a supplement to a regular class.
- The *interactive instruction mode* allows learners to interact over the Internet with interactive multimedia or computer-assisted instruction lessons that previously were distributed on CD-ROM. This can be very rich instructionally, extending considerably beyond drill-and-practice computer-assisted instruction. The interactive instruction mode uses the World Wide Web to distribute interactive multimedia. It is appropriate for stand-alone instruction when an instructor is not available. It also can be used as a supplement to a regular class when assignments require learners to acquire some content on their own.
- Whereas the previous on-line learning modes are based on the publishing view, the *computer-mediated communications mode* is based on the communications view. The purpose of the computer-mediated communications mode is to facilitate communications between instructor and students or among students (Berge, 1995). There are a variety of levels of computer-mediated communications (Trentin & Benigno, 1997). At the simplest level, computer-mediated communications consist of e-mail between instructor and student. Another option is to use a listserv to allow any participant to post a message to all other participants. If discussion forums are added, the computer-mediated communications mode could allow a "class" of learners to carry on an asynchronous discussion about topics. The computer-mediated communications mode could also include synchronous computer conferencing using desktop video or chats.
- On-line learning designers can combine features of the publishing modes with the computer-mediated communications mode to form a *hybrid mode* of on-line learning. For example, teachers could create an on-line learning course that uses both the textbook mode and the computer-mediated communications mode. Because it combines features of several on-line learning modes, the hybrid mode can offer a rich learning experience.
- The final on-line learning mode is a combination of all the features of the other on-line learning modes to create a virtual classroom (Saltzberg & Polyson, 1995). The *virtual classroom mode* uses technology to create an on-line classroom that comes close to duplicating what is possible when instructors and

learners are physically in the same room. Instructors and learners communicate in real time by desktop videoconferencing, assignments and class notes are distributed on a Web site, interactive multimedia materials are shown as lecture supplements, and learners discuss issues in real-time chats or in asynchronous discussion forums.

GUIDELINES FOR USING TECHNOLOGY

Whether faculty wish to use technology to supplement their classroom activity or replace it, certain guidelines should be followed to ensure that the result will be high-quality instruction. First of all, be sure that acceptable principles for good instruction are followed when using technology. The first set of guidelines that follows suggests how technology may be used to provide instruction consistent with principles for good undergraduate instruction. Next, be sure that important factors that affect successful technology application are recognized and controlled. The second set of guidelines offers questions to ask to determine if technology is being used well in light of these factors.

Seven Principles for Good Practice

Chickering and Gamson (1991) specified seven principles for good practice in undergraduate instruction. These principles have been widely recognized in higher education as representing our best practices. Thus, it should not be surprising that some suggest applying these principles to teaching on-line. Both Chickering and Ehrmann (1997) and Hannum (1999) have suggested how these principles could be useful in on-line teaching. When the features of the Internet are used to implement these known good practices, the instructional experience is very likely to be effective. The following paragraphs suggest how to implement each of the seven principles in a technology-based learning environment.

Principle 1. Good Practice Encourages Student-Instructor Contact

Student-instructor interaction is essential to a high-quality learning environment. This principle can be implemented on-line as follows:

- E-mail can be used as a means of student-instructor interaction in Web-based courses. The quality of the interaction will depend on the instructor's willingness to respond meaningfully and promptly to many e-mail messages each week.
- Listservs allow instructors to communicate easily with a group of students. In essence, a listserv is a form of group e-mail in which one message is sent from any member of the group to all others. An instructor may serve as moderator to make sure the messages are relevant to the class.
- Web pages allow instructors to distribute materials to students and support interactivity through forms, scripts, and applets. Interactive Web pages, like interactive courseware, take time to create and are technically challenging and expensive, but they promote better interactions.
- Chat rooms are similar to discussion forums but happen in real time. The discussion occurs immediately as students and teachers interact at the same point in time.
- Desktop videoconferencing allows students and instructors to interact over the Internet in real time, seeing and hearing each other. This is a low-cost form of interactive distance learning.

Principle 2. Good Practice Encourages Cooperation Among Students

Learning environments are enhanced when students work cooperatively rather than competitively. This principle can be implemented as follows:

- Web pages can give students a shared workspace that might include each one's contribution to a group project, the resources he or she found useful to the group project, a time line for the project, and specific assignments. Individual students can update their work on the site for the other students to see and use.
- E-mail may be used as a means of student-student interaction in Web-based courses. Students can collaborate with each other on a course assignment such as a case study. They can also share work products or other resources, such as reference materials, with other students by attaching them to e-mail transmissions. This allows them to work cooperatively on group projects.
- Threaded discussion forums can provide a Web-based mechanism for asynchronous group conversation about course topics with many responses possible for each topic or thread. The instructor can assign questions or discussion

topics and have students post their responses in the discussion forum; students can read and respond to their peers' postings. Because discussion forums are asynchronous, students can read and respond when they wish. This quality reduces the immediacy of the exchange but may promote more thoughtful replies.

- Chat rooms allow students to interact in real time on some aspect of courses they are taking. Students can use chat rooms to work cooperatively on a case study, develop a group paper, create a group presentation, discuss questions that have been asked, or do almost any other activity that requires group interaction.
- Desktop videoconferencing allows students to interact in real time to carry on discussions or make plans for a project. A shared whiteboard, or shared screens, allow all participants to view the same information for planning or critiques. Desktop videoconferencing can be used to create virtual work teams or study groups among students in a course.
- Collaborative projects involve constructing multimedia resources to document and communicate what was learned. Students might create Web sites in a collaborative fashion, which allows them to interact for knowledge construction and communication.

Principle 3. Good Practice Encourages Active Learning

When students are actively engaged in learning activities they learn more. This principle can be implemented as follows:

- Web pages can provide exercises for students to complete or problems for them to solve. This requires their active participation in construction of responses.
- Hyperlinks allow students to control navigation through the Web environment. This learner control promotes active involvement and lets learners choose what they want or need to see.
- With independent learning environments, students are no longer passive listeners with instructors functioning as the source of all information. Students can be actively involved in and guided through their learning by instructions on Web pages. They can work independently on problem-based learning assignments. When necessary, they can contact the instructor or other students for assistance.

- Using computer simulations engages students in exploring complex physical and social phenomena so they can understand them.

Principle 4. Good Practice Gives Prompt Feedback

Providing prompt feedback to students facilitates their learning. This principle can be implemented as follows:

- E-mail provides students with a mechanism for asking questions and getting individual feedback. Instructors can use e-mail to provide students with feedback on assignments.
- Listservs allow instructors to communicate easily with a group of students and provide feedback on projects and other group activities.
- Threaded discussion forums allow any subscriber to provide feedback on any comment made in the forum. Thus, both instructor and other students can offer feedback.
- Computer-assisted instruction programs such as tutorials give immediate feedback to students based on their responses to questions.

Principle 5. Good Practice Emphasizes Time on Task

When students are directly focused on and engaged with the learning task for a greater amount of time, they learn more. This principle can be implemented on-line as follows:

- Web sites providing the course syllabus can contain explicit directions for students to proceed through the course. All assignments and expectations are clearly stated and available for reference at any time. This allows students to focus their time appropriately on learning tasks.
- Flexible mastery learning allows learners to invest the amount of time they need to learn the material. Students who joined the class with good knowledge of the subject matter may spend little time, whereas students with less prior knowledge may need more time to read and process the same information to complete assignments.
- E-mail allows students to ask for guidance at any time, if they are getting off-track or confused.

- Hyperlinks with annotations help students keep on task by guiding them to essential sites. Students may become distracted or diverted when following external hyperlinks.

Principle 6. Good Practice Communicates High Expectations

When instructors have high expectations for their students and communicate them, their students learn more. This principle can be implemented as follows:

- A Web site with a course syllabus may state the instructor's expectations. The students' roles and responsibilities can be clearly communicated through information offered on the site.
- Expectations about the quality of their learning and their work can be made explicit through objectives, examples, and practice examinations.
- Listservs also allow faculty to communicate their expectations to students. Careful advising is particularly important in Internet-based courses to make sure students understand course requirements and directions for completing course assignments.

Principle 7. Good Practice Respects Diverse Talents and Ways of Learning

Students have different talents and different ways of approaching learning tasks. When instructors take this into account, they can enhance learning. This principle can be implemented as follows:

- Multimedia environments incorporate text, graphics, audio, animation, and video, appealing to multiple senses and different learning approaches. An Internet-based learning environment is multimedia-oriented, giving students freedom to learn as they wish.
- Independent learning environments allow students to participate in a class when it is most convenient for them, when they have the time and energy for learning. An Internet-based learning environment is independent of time and place, so students have freedom to access instruction when and where they wish.

These guidelines for technology use are based on important principles for undergraduate instruction that are likely to result in high-quality instruction and enhanced student learning. They help ensure that technology use is planned and implemented to produce the desired high-quality learning environment. The focus must be on what causes or supports student learning, not on the technology itself.

Questions to Ask When Choosing Technology Applications

As an academic leader you will receive many proposals for technology application on your campus. In reviewing these proposals, you should consider several questions to decide on the appropriate course of action. Exhibit 11.2 offers a set of questions to ask.

EXHIBIT 11.2. Questions to Ask.

Topic	*Questions*
Access	What provisions have been made for appropriate access to the technology?
	Are some subgroups likely to have less access?
	Will individuals be able to gain access when and where they wish?
Quality	How will the project ensure an acceptable level of instructional quality?
	How will the technology help learners reach instructional goals?
Need	Does the technology address a recognized need or is it being used as an end in itself?
	What purpose will be served through technology use?
Objectives	Is the instructional intent of the project clear?
	Does the intent focus on stated objectives?
	Are the objectives reasonable in light of the needs?
Value added	How does including technology add value to the instructional process?
Appropriate focus	Does the project focus on enhancing student learning rather than on the use of technology for its own sake?
Interactivity	Is the technology use designed so that learners can interact with and control the technology?
	Is the technology used primarily for one-way presentation of information or to support interactions among students, faculty, and subject matter?
Sustainability	Can the project be sustained over time?
	Is this likely a onetime occurrence that will disappear without additional outside resources and support?

EXHIBIT 11.2.   **Questions to Ask.** (continued)

Topic	Questions
Student support	How will the project provide support and assistance for students?
	Will students have sufficient support for using the technology?
	Will students find support for what is expected of them as learners in a different situation?
Faculty support	How will the project provide support and assistance for faculty who use the technology?
	Will faculty have sufficient support for using the technology?
	Will faculty find support for what is expected of them as instructors in a different situation?
Infrastructure	Does the campus have the requisite infrastructure to support the project, including adequate connectivity, hardware, software, and training and user support?
Cost	Does the project have an estimate of the costs of creating and maintaining it?
	Are funds available to support the true costs of implementing the project (faculty time, support staff time, space, hardware and software)?
	Can the project be accomplished just as well at a lower cost?
Scalability	Will the project scale to accommodate more courses, more faculty, and more students?
Maintenance	Does the campus have the ability to maintain the technology?
	Can faculty maintain courses delivered via technology?
	Can hardware and software upgrades be acquired?
	Can new technology be acquired and used?

CONCLUSION

Not every technology project will be successful for a variety of reasons. As an academic leader, you must learn how to identify those that are likely to succeed and then support them. You must also learn to recognize those projects that have flaws that will limit their success and remedy the flaws during the design stage. Asking appropriate questions before embarking on technology-related projects is essential to achieving academic success.

There are many reasons to expect that when technology is appropriately used in instructional environments, it will have strong effects on student learning. But there is little reason to expect that merely adding technology will have more than minimal effects on student learning.

References

Berge, Z. (1995). Facilitating computer conference: Recommendations from the field. *Educational Technology, 35*(6), 22–30.

Chickering, A. W., & Gamson, Z. F. (Eds.). (1991). *Applying the seven principles for good practice in undergraduate education.* New Directions for Thinking and Learning, no. 47. San Francisco: Jossey-Bass.

Chickering, A. W., & Ehrmann, S. C. (1997). Implementing the seven principles: Technology as lever. [http://www.aahe.org/technology/ehrmann.htm].

Gilbert, S. (1996, March-April). Making the most of a slow revolution. *Change, 28*(2), 10–23.

Green, K. C. (2000). *The campus computing project.* Encino, CA: Campus Computing. [http://www.campuscomputing.net/summaries/2000/].

Hannum, W. (1999, March 1–4). *Creating Internet-based learning environments.* Paper presented at the Society for Information Technology and Teacher Education 10th International Conference, San Antonio, TX.

Saltzberg, S., & Polyson, S. (1995). Distributed learning on the World Wide Web. *Syllabus, 9*(1) 10.

Trentin, G., & Benigno, V. (1997). Multimedia conferencing in education: Methodological and organizational considerations. *Educational Technology, 37*(5), 32–38.

Resources

American Federation of Teachers, Higher Education Program and Policy Council. (2000, May). Distance education: Guidelines for good practice. [http://www.aft.org/higher_ed/downloadable/distance.pdf].
Proposes a set of quality standards for higher education distance courses based on a survey of faculty who teach such courses.

Alessi, S. M. (1996). Seeking common ground: Our conflicting viewpoints about learning and technology. [http://itech1.coe.uga.edu/itforum/paper11/paper11.html].
Discusses technology use in the future and its relationship to intellectual property, individualism and collectivism, just-in-time learning, instructional design, and equity. Argues for using technology to embed education in our everyday uses of computer and communications technology.

American Distance Education Consortium. (2001). ADEC guiding principles for distance learning. [http://www.adec.edu/admin/papers/distance-learning_principles.html].
Suggests distance learning guidelines organized into four areas: design for learning, support for learners, infrastructure, and organizational commitment.

Australian National Training Authority. (1998). Pedagogical issues emerging from this project. [http://www.tafe.sa.edu.au/lsrsc/one/natproj/tal/pedissues/pedaiss.htm].
Reviews pedagogical issues that emerged from several technology-based projects. A good summary and discussion of issues in using technology for instruction along with suggestions.

Bourne, J. R., & Moore, J. C. (2001). *On-line education: Vol. 2. Learning effectiveness, faculty satisfaction, and cost effectiveness: Proceedings of the 2000 Sloan Summer Workshop on Asynchronous Learning Networks.* Needham, MA: Sloan Center for Online Education.
Presents the proceedings of a summer workshop on on-line learning, including case studies describing effectiveness, faculty satisfaction, and cost-effectiveness of asynchronous learning environments.

Downes, S. (2001). The future of on-line learning. [http://www.atl.ualberta.ca/downes/ future/welcome.htm]
Examines changes in technology and education that will influence the future use of on-line learning.

Ehrmann, S. C. (2000, Fall). Technology and revolution in education: Ending the cycle of failure. *Liberal Education, 40–49.*
Reviews factors that have inhibited the application of technology in education, discussing six barriers. Offers suggestions for how to overcome these problems, which have limited the use of technology in higher education.

Frayer, D. A., & West, L. B. (2001). Creating a new world of learning possibilities through instructional technology. [http://horizon.unc.edu/projects/monograph/CD/Instructional_Technology/Frayer.asp].
Discusses appropriate instructional uses of technology and factors influencing faculty acceptance of it. Includes Web sites and articles related to pedagogical uses of technology.

Golas, K. (2001). Guidelines for designing online learning. [http://www.aero.swri.org/pub/ 2000ITSEC_ON-LINELEARNING.htm].
Suggests specific guidelines for designing on-line learning. Could be used to evaluate on-line courses or to review proposals for on-line courses.

Graham, C., Cagiltay, K., Craner, J., Lim, B., & Duffy, T. M. (2000). Teaching in a Web-based distance learning environment: An evaluation summary based on four courses (Center for Research on Learning and Technology Technical Report No. 13–00), Indiana University.
Reports on an evaluation of several on-line courses using Chickering and Gamson's seven principles of good practice as basis for judging effectiveness. Also examines design, organization, navigation, and aesthetics of course sites. Provides good suggestions for what to look for when creating or evaluating on-line courses.

Hall, R. H. (2000). Instructional Web site design principles: A literature review and synthesis. *Virtual University Journal, 2*(1), 1–13.
Summarizes the literature on Web site design and suggests some principles for effective Web-based instructional design.

Hazemi, R., Hailes, S., & Wilbur, S. (1998). *The digital university: Reinventing the academy.* New York: Springer.
Describes asynchronous collaboration in a learning environment, including challenges, tools to use, and the virtual classroom.

Indiana Higher Education Telecommunication System. (2001). Guiding principles for faculty in distance learning. [http://www.ihets.org/learntech/facprinc.html].
Presents specific suggestions to faculty for teaching distance learning courses. A comprehensive look at requirements for effective distance education.

Inglis, A. (1999). *Delivering digitally: Managing the transition to the new knowledge media.* London: Kogan Page.
Presents the issues and recommended strategies for managing the shift to technology in the delivery of higher education. Discusses the background of technology use, social forces, learning in an electronic environment, costs, infrastructure, support staff, and evaluation.

Institute for Higher Education Policy. (2000). Quality on the line: Benchmarks for success in Internet-based education. [http://www.ihep.com/Pubs/PDF/Quality.pdf].
Reports on a study of forty-five benchmarks for quality in Internet-based education. Using empirical data, suggests a set of benchmarks for establishing quality for courses delivered over the Internet.

Katz, R. M. (1999). *Dancing with the devil: Information technology and the new competition in higher education.* San Francisco: Jossey-Bass.
Presents a series of articles to frame the questions of technology in higher education. Discusses issues associated with change, new competition, and renewal.

Katz, S. N. (2001, June 15). In information technology: Don't mistake a tool for a goal. *Chronicle of Higher Education Review,* pp. B7–B9.
Places educational technology applications in historical context and raises concerns about the impact of technology on universities.

Lau, L. K. (2000). *Distance learning technologies: Issues, trends, and opportunities.* Hershey, PA: Idea Group Publishing.
Presents the theoretical foundations for distance learning and discusses the practical-conceptual aspects, strategies for using distance learning, issues, and technologies. Offers several cases of practical implementation.

Oblinger, D., & Kidwell, J. (2000, May-June). Distance learning: Are we being realistic? EDUCAUSE, pp. 31–39.
Discusses the role of distance education in higher education, including the rationale for it, learners, readiness, alternative models, and partnerships. Gives a good understanding of distance education options for higher education.

Oblinger, D., & Rush, S. (1997). *The learning revolution: The challenge of information technology in the academy.* Bolton, MA: Anker.
Describes the challenges faced by higher education in the information age, presents several projects as case studies, and discusses the future.

Oblinger, D., & Rush, S. (1998). *The future-compatible campus: Planning, designing, and implementing information technology.* Bolton, MA: Anker.
This collection of essays about using technology in higher education presents information about the rationale for using technology, strategic planning and common errors, student services, and learning environments.

Paulsen, M. F. (1998). The online report on pedagogical techniques for computer-mediated communication. [http://www.emoderators.com/moderators/cmcped.html#15].
Reviews literature on teaching techniques in adult learning and in computer-mediated learning. Suggests various teaching techniques that can be used in on-line courses.

Petrides, L. A. (2000). *Case studies on information technology in higher education: Implications for policy and practice.* Hershey, PA: Idea Group Publishing.
Presents a group of case studies about the application of technology in higher education. Subjects are organized into four areas: planning and management, impact on people and culture, teaching and learning, and reflections on a changing environment.

Van Dusen, G. C. (1997). *The virtual campus: Technology and reform in higher education.* Washington, DC: George Washington University, Graduate School of Education and Human Development.
Presents a synthesis of research on virtual campuses. Examines assumptions, offers conclusions and recommendations. Discusses new roles, quality issues, interactions, on-line scholarship, and governance.

Van Dusen, G. C. (2000). *Digital dilemma: Issues of access, cost, and quality in media-enhanced and distance education.* San Francisco: Jossey-Bass.
Discusses issues of access, cost, and quality in media-enhanced and distance education.

Weiss, R. E., Knowlton, D. S., & Speck, B. W. (2000). *Principles of effective teaching in the on-line classroom.* San Francisco: Jossey-Bass.
Presents a series of articles about teaching on-line including the theoretical framework, suggestions for course design, interacting on-line with students, and evaluation of students.

CHAPTER 12

Improving Academic Advising

Issues and Action Areas for Campus Leaders

FRANKLIN P. WILBUR

Academic advising is certainly one of higher education's sacred cows: nearly everyone acknowledges its importance, yet many campuses do not sufficiently commit to it or organize it in a manner that ensures it is effective for all students. The way an institution carries out academic advising reveals a lot about its character: what it values, how well it communicates its expectations, and what it really wants for its students. Putting the necessary commitment, leadership, and infrastructure in place to provide for a quality system of academic advising can have a dynamic impact on retention, campus climate, and overall student academic success. In this chapter, I will describe the elements of a quality academic advising system and what you will need to consider when building, strengthening, maintaining, and assessing various aspects of advising on your campus.

DEFINING ACADEMIC ADVISING

Academic advising is all about helping students explore their educational environment, make informed choices in planning their course of study, and take responsibility for their own learning; it sets the stage for them to become effective lifelong learners. Richard Light writes, "Good advising may be the single most underestimated characteristic of a successful college experience" (2001, p. 81).

There is a rich and extensive literature on the subject of advising, often referred to as student developmental advising. Here is one definition offered by authorities in the field: "Developmental academic advising is defined as a systematic process based on a close student-adviser relationship intended to aid students in achieving educational, career, and personal goals through the utilization of the full range of institutional and community resources. It both stimulates and supports students in their quest for an enriched quality of life. . . . [It] reflects the institution's mission of total student development and is most likely to be realized when the academic affairs and student affairs divisions collaborate in its implementation" (Ender, Winston, & Miller, 1984, p. 19).

EVALUATING YOUR CURRENT SYSTEM OF ADVISING

With this general definition in mind, let us consider how you might go about evaluating the system of advising that is in place on your campus and the type of time commitment and resources that would be required to get you from where you are now to where you would like to be. This shift will likely require changes in campus culture, strong leadership, and information in order to chart progress.

Centralized Versus Decentralized Structures

Centralized and decentralized structures are the two main models to consider for the delivery of advising services. A centralized advising structure usually uses an advising center staffed by full-time professional advisers. The centralized structure allows for consistency in the advisers' approach and training, as well as greater availability. But it costs more to operate, and advisers will not have the expertise on particular programs that faculty who teach in the programs do.

A decentralized advising structure usually consists of faculty and staff who provide advising services to students at the departmental level. Although this approach allows the advising services to be in close proximity to the students' courses in their particular departments, and can be operated at a low cost, it has the disadvantage of not offering a consistent level of advising services across the schools and colleges.

Often a combination of the two models can be crafted to meet the needs of your campus in the best way. For a more in-depth discussion, see "Organization Models for Academic Advising" by C. Pardee in *Academic Advising: A Comprehensive Handbook* (Gordon & Habley, 2000).

Faculty Versus Professional Advisers

You must also consider how advising will be delivered on your campus. Will professional, full-time staff advisers provide student advising or will the faculty workload include advising assignments as part of their responsibilities? The advantage of using professional advisers is that advising is their main focus, so students benefit from both their availability and their commitment to advising. In addition, the level of training and the knowledge of campus rules and regulations are likely to be more consistent among professionals than among faculty advisers. Finally, an advising professional's global knowledge of the university or college is particularly helpful to students with undeclared majors.

Faculty advisers also have advantages. They can offer students more in-depth knowledge about the particular majors in their area of expertise. They also offer students an additional opportunity to connect in a meaningful way with a faculty member. But faculty have teaching responsibilities and office hours for their classes, so they are not as accessible. They are also less familiar with programs outside of their school or college. In addition, unless campus leadership appropriately recognizes and rewards faculty advising, it is likely to be a low priority in relation to other commitments.

Understanding Need

Every campus has its own unique history, mission, climate, and aspirations. Different institutions have very different student populations and structures, requiring a wide variety of advising services and support strategies. Although U.S. higher education focuses most of its academic advising on undergraduates, including part-time and non-residential students, other populations have critical advising needs as well, such as graduate students and students enrolled primarily through distance learning programs. Effective academic advising depends, among other things, on a campus's ability to foster meaningful, trusting, and caring relationships between and among its students, staff, and faculty.

In conversations with your students, you will almost certainly hear praise for the efforts of some advisers, but you will also hear that there are some faculty and staff who are not available when students need them, do not have the information needed to advise effectively, are difficult to talk to about issues outside of their areas of subject matter expertise, and so on. Conversations with the advisers may reveal that students often do not keep appointments, arrive unprepared, or expect advisers to make decisions for them.

Assessing Effectiveness

In assessing the effectiveness and organization of academic advising on your campus, begin by examining the data you routinely collect (such as student surveys, course assessments, exit interviews, postgraduate or alumni surveys, parent questionnaires) to see what students and others have to say about academic advising and the quality of the support students receive throughout their programs of study at every step and milestone. Talk to students and those engaged in advising and listen to what they have to say about their experiences together. Organize focus groups of students, faculty, and administrators, or send out special campus surveys to gather information on various aspects of advising. The National Association for Academic Advising (NACADA; http://www.nacada.ksu.edu/) and American College Testing (ACT; http://www.act.org/) offer instruments for collecting such information from the student and staff-faculty perspectives. Or you may wish to develop your own instruments. Questions should probe the expectations of students, faculty, and staff concerning academic advising, including services, relationships, and outcomes, and compare such expectations to their actual experiences. You will want answers to questions such as the following:

- What aspects of advising do students, staff, and faculty feel are working well?
- Where does the advising system fail to meet student needs?
- Do students and advisers have the information they need when they need it, so that they can have meaningful conversations about program options and class schedules and make decisions or referrals?
- Does the campus electronic communication network as it currently stands facilitate or impede communications between students and advisers and monitoring academic progress?

In addition, you will want to look at how faculty regard their academic advising roles by having them answer questions such as these:

- What exactly is my role as an academic adviser? What is expected of me?
- How do I keep in contact with the students assigned to me?
- What information do I need to know, particularly about options outside of my department?

- What information resources will be available to me and how do I use them?
- Is advising considered important by my students, my peers, and those in administrative positions?
- Does advising really "count" in the campus reward system?
- Is my advising effective? How can I know? How can I improve?

Candid information from those involved in the advising process, combined with a clear sense of mission, vision, and direction for the institution, will help you to prioritize and shape the action plan for improving advising on your campus. Initiatives may require changes in procedures that challenge traditional ways of doing things, call for a reassignment of people to new roles, or require realignment of existing resources—all can be unsettling to an organization. Support and encouragement from campus leaders are essential throughout the process.

Assigning Leadership and Responsibility

Once you have a clear sense of the role of advising on your campus and the areas most in need of improvement, a specific mandate and charge must be given to develop a plan of action. Where possible, identify *one* campus faculty or staff member to be given the responsibility to lead a team effort to improve academic advising; this person should have the necessary resources and authority to organize, make decisions, and initiate action as appropriate. Choose an individual who is highly credible in the campus community and has solid leadership skills. Nothing really lasting in the way of change on campus is accomplished alone, so your campus leader must be able to rally support. Such support often comes from natural allies: advising professionals in offices around the campus, faculty who are well known for their commitment to advising, associate or assistant deans who often have to coordinate academic information and orientation sessions for students and faculty, and so on. A broad-based campus team, representing many if not all of the main academic and student support units on campus, should be able to construct a plan of action suitable for your campus environment.

Leadership is also required at the top. The chancellor, president, and provost must send the message to faculty that academic advising "counts" and will be recognized and rewarded appropriately. Advising on many campuses is specifically defined as an important aspect of teaching essential to student success. In 1993 Gershon Vincow, then vice chancellor for academic affairs at Syracuse University, clearly stated in his annual address to the faculty that appropriate recognition of advising and mentoring of students was essential to the improvement of advising. He stressed that advising contributions were to be evaluated with regard to faculty promotion and tenure (Vincow, 1993). During the semesters following this address, promoting and tenure guidelines were modified to reflect the renewed commitment to advising, giving weight to the old adage, "Say what you mean, mean what you say." This set the stage for a change in campus culture. Advising was prioritized at Syracuse, due in no small part to this leadership position. A national award for advising followed in the years ahead.

DEVELOPING AN ACTION PLAN

Based on data, discussion, and best judgment, each campus must decide where to focus its energies to improve the quality of advising. You may wish to consider incorporating some or all of the following practices into your campus's plan.

Construct or Revise an Official Campus Statement on Academic Advising

Every campus benefits from crafting and continuously publicizing a statement on what academic advising is supposed to be and what everyone has to do for it to work effectively. Although individual campus advising statements will reflect differences in philosophy, mission, and populations, every statement needs to address the necessary roles and responsibilities of various stakeholders. The statement must also describe the resources that will be provided at an institutional level; this decision affects the availability of timely, accurate information. Campus advising statements should be developed with broad community input and should ultimately receive an endorsement from the highest levels, including the faculty senate. Consider the following statement officially endorsed by the senate of Syracuse University:

> *Academic Advising* is an essential component of a Syracuse University education, and the University is committed to providing the individual advice and assistance that students need at every step throughout their degree program. A successful system of academic advising is highly dependent upon a shared commitment of faculty, staff, and students to the process and the availability of timely accurate information.

Students are responsible for scheduling, preparing for, and keeping advising appointments; seeking out contacts and information; and knowing the basic requirements of their individual degree programs. Students bear the final responsibility for making their own decisions based on the best information and advice available, and ultimately, on their own judgment.

Advisers are responsible for developing a thorough knowledge of the institution, including academic resources. Advisers are expected to involve students by encouraging them to ask questions, gather information, and explore options so that they may develop a meaningful academic plan. Advisers will be available to students on a regular basis, monitor their advisees' progress, assist in considering career options, and make appropriate referrals to other campus offices.

The *University,* through its schools and colleges, pledges to support a campuswide network of faculty, staff, and student peer advisers by providing them with a clear and firm foundation of information regarding policies, procedures, resources, and programs. The University is committed to help faculty and staff to develop effective advising skills, to evaluate its system of academic advising and support services, and to make improvements where necessary. The University also acknowledges the important contribution advisers make to the community through appropriate recognition with the institutional reward system. [Syracuse University, 2001]

This statement was crafted as the result of the efforts of many people across the campus. A subcommittee of faculty and staff drafted a preliminary statement and circulated it among all part- and full-time faculty members, encouraging them to edit it and send in their individual responses through e-mail or campus mail. Focus groups made up of a sampling of faculty from all schools and colleges then met to discuss the revised form. With the community input completed, a final draft of the statement was submitted to the vice chancellor for his approval before submission to the university senate, where it was subsequently approved. Although this process may seem arduous, it resulted in broad ownership and gave credibility to the institution's commitment to academic advising.

Such a statement is an institutional pledge that advising will be supported, assessed, and recognized as an important educational activity. It is very helpful to a campus leader charged with examining current practices and determining where improvement efforts need to be focused. Here are some additional campus advising statements and Web sites at which they may be accessed: University of Texas at Austin's mission statement (http://uts.cc.utexas.edu/~acadv/standards/appendixa.html), University of Wisconsin at Madison (http://www.cals.wisc.edu/students/advisor/missionstatement.htm), Fort Hayes State University, Kansas (http://www.fhsu.edu/acad-adv/handbook/part1.html), Pennsylvania State University (http://www.psu.edu/dus/cfe/impadv.htm).

Take Inventory, Share, and Reflect on Current Practices

Do not reinvent—look to build on existing institutional strengths. Take stock of what you have in place, share that information, and have an open debate on strengths and deficiencies. A good way to start is by collecting all published advising materials, including handbooks, training manuals, Web-based statements, policy manuals, degree progress checklists, and so on. Assemble several collections, in print or electronically, for all academic offices to examine what other units are doing and how they are communicating policies and procedures to students, parents, staff, and faculty. Simply sharing these materials often has the desired effect of improving the weaker documents and practices in the campus community. You can also compare and contrast what you are now doing, or could be doing, with the advising services at similar institutions nationally, through information and publications provided by NACADA (http://www.nacada.ksu.edu/).

Develop an Accessible Advising Database

It is very helpful for advisers to have an always-available on-line list of current advisees, complete with contact information. Listings need to be kept up-to-date. Often the update process can be simplified by linking advising databases to other information systems so that changes in phone numbers, addresses, class schedules, and so on may be captured automatically. Students, too, appreciate easy access to contact information for their advisers, various advising resources, and office hours for scheduling appointments. Because students often have more than one adviser (for example, a dual-major honors student who is also an athlete), it is also important for advisers to be able to communicate among themselves on student needs and progress. (See the later section on building integrated student information systems for more details on information technology as it relates to these issues.)

Provide Networking Opportunities

Encourage designated staff or faculty in each academic area to explore exemplary advising practices from other institutions, including the design of handbooks and guides, for possible adoption. Campus administrators should consider funding multiple memberships in NACADA. This organization provides easy access to best practice information through its Web site (http://www.nacada.ksu.edu/), newsletters, books, journals, and regional and national meetings, and offers valuable peer interaction. NACADA also has a consultant referral service, adviser training materials, a national clearinghouse on adviser information, and an annual summer institute on academic advising.

Provide Adviser Training

Everyone involved in student advising needs to have ongoing support and training for this challenging role. Whether they are new to the faculty or staff or veterans of many years, training helps advisers share techniques that work, discuss difficult problems that may arise, exchange information, receive updates on new policies and program requirements, and become more comfortable in working with students one-on-one. Campuses need to consider the duration, scheduling, format, and content of training sessions carefully and decide whether adviser training will be required or optional for existing faculty and staff. New faculty training should incorporate adviser training as a formal element. A specific office or program of your institution should be charged with this responsibility.

The following list shows topics to cover in training programs, by subject area:

- *Administration topics:* Academic rules and regulations, record keeping, using campus electronic resources
- *Communication topics:* Listening skills, communicating with students, communicating with other advisers for students with more than one adviser
- *Development topics:* Handling a student in crisis, helping students in transition, knowing when and how to make referrals, assisting students with special needs, helping with time management and study skills, understanding the role of learning communities
- *Academic topics:* Intrainstitutional transfer, minors and dual majors, internships and study abroad programs, career information, academic support services

Publicize and Celebrate Academic Opportunities

You will need to determine how campus media can be best used to communicate academic advising information. Special fall editions of campus newspapers might feature academic advising, what it is, how it works, whom to consult with questions, and special support services. Web sites and campus television programming are also vehicles to get the word out.

Consider holding a special event, perhaps an "academic opportunities information fair," so that students can go to one location to learn about academic programs, support services, service learning, study abroad, and so on. This kind of event eliminates the need for students to make special appointments with individuals across campus and exposes them to opportunities they may never have considered. Some colleges use student centers, gymnasiums, or conference facilities and run events much like convention exhibit halls. Students, faculty, staff, and alumni are stationed to hand out information, answer questions, and demonstrate activities associated with their particular field. Students are able to have thoughtful conversations with many different knowledgeable people in one convenient location as they consider changing majors, adding a minor, joining a club or program, or enhancing their programs of study in other ways.

Institute Rewards and Recognition

Wherever academic advising works well, you will find practices in place to recognize and reward advisers—whether staff, faculty, or peers—for their efforts and effectiveness. "Adviser of the Year" programs are frequently sponsored by an entire institution or initiated by individual academic units. Some campuses have funding available for students to take an adviser out to lunch or provide other opportunities to interact informally. For faculty, tenure and promoting policies that consider accomplishments in the advising arena are another very important way for an institution to make advising really matter. For examples of two campuses with stated policies linking advising to tenure and promotion, see Oregon State University's criteria (http://www.orst.edu/staff/faculty/handbook/promoten/spromoten.htm) or Michigan State University's College of Education policy on tenure (http://ed-web3.educ.msu.edu/college/college-policy/tenure.htm).

Other reward strategies could include funding for travel to conferences, priority teaching assignments, recognition ceremonies that are attended by students, gifts such as notebook computers, and various administrative and technical supports. In addition to rewarding individuals, you can reward units for collective work with base budget increases. When advising is shown to be valued in tangible ways, it is much easier to get faculty and staff to take training seriously and work to improve their skills, and to become more knowledgeable about academic and residence life opportunities, campus policies and procedures, support services, and degree requirements.

Build Integrated Student Information Systems

All academic advising activities and services are enhanced when students, faculty, and staff have access to and are trained to use a well-integrated campus information system. Many campuses already have, or are working to build, systems that allow students and advisers to do the following:

- Explore course syllabi and program descriptions
- Build schedules, access class schedules, and register on-line
- View their academic records and track progress toward degree requirements (degree audit capabilities)
- Communicate with their advisers for advice or to set up appointments
- Request learning support services or referrals
- Allow several advisers working with one student to stay in close communication and share notes
- Access grades as soon as they are posted
- Access financial and scholarship information
- Determine requirements for intrainstitutional transfer
- Access all institutional electronic publications
- Access library and other information resources, including campus e-mail directories
- Evaluate transcripts
- Submit course and advising evaluations
- Subscribe to academic listservs
- Access career planning information and alumni networks

When such information is readily available to students and their advisers, it gives all parties a greater sense of control of the academic planning and monitoring process and helps campuses to coordinate advising resources. When properly designed, integrated systems can relieve students and advisers of much of the trivial paperwork involved in building schedules and tracking requirements. Information is available more quickly, and frequently more accurately, and often costs less. Unlike paper publications that may contain outdated information as soon as they are printed, electronic information resources can be kept up-to-date and be distributed at a fraction of the cost of traditional hard copy. One site worth taking a look at is Penn State's (http://www.psu.edu/ advising/), which contains daily updates. Touch-tone phone systems are often used to allow students and advisers to obtain a wide array of academic information, including registration and tuition payment, without Web access. Information kiosks strategically located around campus are also part of the strategy to make information easily and immediately accessible. *Transforming Academic Advising Through the Use of Information Technology* (Kramer & Childs, 1996), a NACADA publication, is a highly recommended resource for campus leaders who want to understand the human-technical information interface in advising.

Link First-Year Programs

Establishing meaningful, comfortable advising relationships early in a student's career should be a priority for all campuses. Advisers may telephone students over the summer and meet them and their parents during opening weekend to begin developing a relationship. Many campuses have initiated special programs and residence hall arrangements for first-year students. Some organize small-group freshman forums and seminars led by faculty members who agree to serve as the primary academic adviser for their groups. These types of small-group interactions, which often include advisers and students attending cultural events and having meals together, significantly enhance the quality of the advising relationship. Professors get to know students personally, and students do not view their advisers simply as people who sign a course registration form. Other first-year experiences that encourage a good advising relationship include learning communities, summer previews for students and parents, and themed living or learning centers.

First-year programs can powerfully enhance any advising model, which can be further strengthened when linked to formal learning communities and special support services. The National Resource Center for the First-Year Experience and Students in Transition (http://www.sc.edu/fye/) provides comprehensive information on many types of approaches designed to integrate students into campus life and facilitate their academic success.

Gather Information for Continuous Improvement

Advising needs to be assessed for effectiveness and continuous improvement at every level: student, faculty, staff, department, and institution. In particular, advisers need to receive individual feedback, both for their own improvement and to document advising for tenure, promotion, and salary increments, depending on your institution's reward system. When choosing from the variety of techniques for collecting information, keep in mind the need for honesty, simplicity, and multiple sources. Data collection methods include surveys (in-person, through the mail, over the phone, on the Web), peer review and field observations, student and adviser self-evaluations, focus groups and individual interviews, alumni feedback, and teaching portfolios.

Obviously, the more comfortable individuals are with the way the data are collected and used, the more honest, forthright, and helpful they will be. NACADA offers a wide variety of resources on the effective assessment of advising, including sample evaluation forms, survey instruments, and links to institutional Web sites. For a specific example, see the Web site of Indiana University-Purdue University Indianapolis (http://www.imir.iupui.edu/imir/ar/adv99/entadv99.htm) site for its 1999 advising survey; it includes extensive information on all aspects of the assessment process, including instruments and results.

TAKING STOCK: DETERMINING AREAS FOR ACTION

Although it is by no means comprehensive, the checklist in Exhibit 12.1 summarizes many of the points covered in this chapter, and I hope will help you develop initiatives that can have both immediate and long-term impact on your campus's system of advising services.

CONCLUSION

Given high-quality academic programs, students who are eager to learn and well-matched to the institution, and a caring, knowledgeable, and supportive staff and faculty, academic advising can be a source of great pride, satisfaction, and accomplishment for the entire community. What students usually remember most about their college experience is their direct contact with individuals who cared about their success—people who asked

EXHIBIT 12.1. Checklist for Building an Effective Campus Academic Advising System.

	Yes	No	To some degree	Don't know
1. Does your institution have an official statement defining its position on academic advising and explaining the various roles and responsibilities of students, faculty, and staff?	___	___	___	___
2. Are formal practices in place to recognize and reward those who excel in advising?	___	___	___	___
3. Is advising recognized on your campus as an important aspect of teaching or service and are expectations for advising competence articulated in tenure and promotion guidelines?	___	___	___	___
4a. Is the effectiveness of academic advising assessed regularly, at the individual faculty and staff level as well as at the department, school or college, and institution levels?	___	___	___	___
4b. Are data collected from all sources (campus surveys, alumni surveys, focus group discussions) used as part of the continuous improvement process for advising?	___	___	___	___
4c. Is advising assessment information reported as part of the institution's self-study plan for accreditation?	___	___	___	___
5a. Does your campus information system facilitate the availability for advising purposes of timely, accurate information on students' academic progress, support services, and academic options?	___	___	___	___
5b. Using your campus student information system, is it possible for advisees and advisers to conduct degree audits and to experiment with what-if scenarios when exploring such options as changing majors, enrolling in a study abroad program, adding a minor or additional major, and so on? Is an adequate technical infrastructure in place for such information flow?	___	___	___	___
6a. Is there training in place, offered on a regular basis, for all faculty, staff, and students (peer advisers) who are assigned to advising roles?	___	___	___	___
6b. If training is in place, is its adequacy regularly assessed?	___	___	___	___

EXHIBIT 12.1. **Checklist for Building an Effective Campus Academic Advising System.** (continued)

	Yes	No	To some degree	Don't know
7. Does your campus have effective communications and coordination between and among advisers from academic and student affairs?	—	—	—	—
8. Are advisers aware of campus student support services and knowledgeable and comfortable with making referrals?	—	—	—	—
9a. Do you have adequate campus leadership in place to monitor continually and work to improve the quality of academic advising?	—	—	—	—
9b. Has a clear administrative mandate been given to the individual or team charged with improving advising?	—	—	—	—
9c. Are goals for advising realistic, specific, and measurable?	—	—	—	—
10a. Do recognized leaders in academic advising from your campus have access, through organizational memberships, to national advising resources?	—	—	—	—
10b. Is their involvement with regional and national meetings supported?	—	—	—	—
11. Do you regularly provide coverage through campus media (newspapers, magazines, television, campus recruitment videos, radio) of academic opportunities, support services, and the role of advisers in helping students explore options?	—	—	—	—
12. Does your campus sponsor academic opportunities fairs or other events that enhance student awareness of various programs and provide forums for sharing information?	—	—	—	—
13. Is academic advising integrated into special programs for first-year students, such as learning communities, freshman forums and seminars, and summer preview events?	—	—	—	—
14. Do you feel confident enough about the quality of academic advising services on your campus to highlight them in your admissions materials?	—	—	—	—
15. Should you consider establishing or enhancing a professional advising center or centers to supplement faculty and staff advising?	—	—	—	—

probing questions, provided support and encouragement, expected them to take responsibility for their own learning, helped them to see the big picture, and provided some direction when it was most needed. Just ask alumni of your institution what they recall from their years on your campus; they most often will cite meaningful, caring relationships they established with faculty and staff. The most active, engaged, and supportive alumni feel as they do and contribute as they do in part because of the guidance they received at critical times when they were students. Academic advising, particularly developmental advising, linked closely with extracurricular learning experiences, provides a safety net and a foundation for the entire academic experience. It allows learners to work, play, explore, make mistakes, and experience the satisfaction of success while in a supportive and encouraging environment. A campus with a strong advising system has leaders who understand just how critical fostering advising relationships is for student growth and success, and who are willing to work to build the necessary infrastructure to allow relationships between advisers and advisees to flourish as a natural and important part of the total learning environment.

References

Ender, S. C., Winston, R. B. Jr., Miller, T. K. (1984). Academic advising reconsidered. In R. B. Winston, Jr., T. K. Miller, S. C. Ender, T. J. Grites, & Associates (Eds.), *Developmental academic advising* (pp. 3–35). San Francisco: Jossey-Bass.

Gordon, V. N., & Habley, W. R. (Eds.). (2000). *Academic advising: A comprehensive handbook.* San Francisco: Jossey-Bass.

Kramer, G. L., & Childs, M. W. (Eds.). (1996). Transforming academic advising through the use of information technology. *NACADA Monograph* (Series No. 4).

Light, R. J. (2001). *Making the most of college.* Cambridge, MA: Harvard University Press.

Syracuse University. (2001). Statement on academic advising. [http://sumweb.syr.edu/registrar/AdvisingMinors.html].

Vincow, G. (1993, January). *Annual address to the faculty.* Syracuse University, Syracuse, NY.

Resources

American College Testing. (2001). Evaluation/survey services. [http://www.act.org/ess/ index.html]. Lists available ACT evaluation and survey services to aid administrators in obtaining comprehensive information about postsecondary students' attitudes, opinions, needs, and development.

Beck, R. J. (2002). *Undergraduate academic advising.* Tufts University, Center for Academic Excellence. [http://ase.tufts.edu/cte/occasional_papers/advising.htm]. This reference site for advising offers links to a wide variety of advising resources, including ERIC, professional organizations, books, and videotapes. It also offers a comprehensive bibliography.

Center for Excellence in Academic Advising, Pennsylvania State University. (2001). The mentor: An academic advising journal. [http://www.psu.edu/dus/mentor/].
This site for an on-line journal focused on higher education advising includes an advising forum for on-line discussions, current articles, and three months of archived articles on a range of topics such as helping students handle bad news and legal aspects of advising.

Frost, S. H. (1991). *Academic advising for student success: A system of shared responsibility* (ASHE-ERIC Higher Education Report No. 3). Washington, DC: George Washington University, School of Education and Human Development.
Reviews research on the correlation between positive, meaningful contact between advisers and students and its impact on persistence in college. Main categories include faculty-student contact as a contributor to student success, shared responsibility between students and advisers, and the advising relationship as it relates to students' needs.

Glennen, R. E., & Vowell, F. N. (Eds.). (1995). Academic advising as a comprehensive campus process. *NACADA Monograph* (Series No. 2).
Provides information for implementing advising programs and on the role of an institution in addressing advising. Topics are divided into three main areas: administrative support service, academic advising services and student support services, and the ways people throughout an institution can serve as advisers.

Gordon, V. N., & Habley, W. R. (Eds.). (2000). *Academic advising: A comprehensive handbook.* San Francisco: Jossey-Bass.
This excellent reference offers an in-depth overview of advising, including historical background, current issues, research, theory, and best practices in the field. Offers an introduction to many of the researchers and experts in the field of advising.

Kramer, G. L. (Ed.). (1995). Reaffirming the role of faculty in academic advising. *NACADA Monograph* (Series No. 1).
A variety of authors examine how to engage faculty in advising, discussing training, accountability, evaluation, and recognition and rewards for better practice.

Kramer, G. L., & Childs, M. W. (Eds.). (1996). Transforming academic advising through the use of information technology. *NACADA Monograph* (Series No. 4).
Writings by a variety of practitioners deal with the development and application of information technology systems for the enhancement of campus advising.

Kramer, G. L., & Childs, W. M. (Eds.). (2000). The "e" factor in delivering advising and student services. *NACADA Monograph* (Series No. 7).
Provides an overview of key issues and current practices for Web-based advising. Includes chapters on planning, designing, and integrating advising services for delivery over the Web. Provides examples of best practices.

Kramer, G. L., & Upcraft, M. L. (Eds.). (1995). First-year student academic advising: Patterns in the present, pathways to the future. *NACADA Monograph* (Series No. 3).
Focuses on helping professionals understand first-year students and discusses the adoption of successful strategies for ensuring their success.

National Academic Advising Association. (2000). Homepage. [http://www.nacada.ksu.edu/].
The NACADA site provides links to a wide range of advising resources, including national and regional conferences, award programs, the consultants bureau, publications such as the NACADA journal and newsletter, national advising standards, statement of core values in advising, results of the 2000 national advising survey, and a variety of other professional resources.

National Clearinghouse for Academic Advising. (2001). Advising mission statements. University College: Ohio State University. [http://www.uvc.ohio-state.edu/chouse/ MISSTATE.html].
This NACADA site links to a sampling of advising mission statements from institutions around the United States.

Productivity, Quality, and Outcomes Implementation Committee. (1998, March). *Report of the PQO task force on advising: The university advising plan—A comprehensive, collaborative proposal.* Montana State University-Bozeman. [http://www.montana.edu/aircj/report/pqo/PQOAdvisingPlan.html#Exec].
This detailed account of MSU's comprehensive plan reviews the process from beginning to end. Includes national retention and advising research, surveys, the proposed plan, and a bibliography of resources. Illustrates how the university built on existing processes to create a clearly defined integrated approach to advising.

Ramos, B., & Vallandingham, D. (Eds.). (1997). Advising students with disabilities. *NACADA Monograph* (Series No. 5).
Chapters discuss issues that academic advisers face in meeting the needs of students with disabilities, and offer strategies and practical advice.

Winston, R. B. Jr., Miller, T. K., Ender, S. C., Grites, T. J., & Associates. (1984). *Developmental academic advising.* San Francisco: Jossey-Bass.
Authored by experts in the field of developmental academic advising, chapters cover a range of topics in the categories of advising strategies, organization and administration of advising programs, and translating theory to practice.

CHAPTER 13

Faculty Development
An Investment for the Future

MARILLA SVINICKI

hange. Accountability. Technology. The graying of the faculty. Student demographics. Consumerism. Deteriorating working conditions for the faculty. Competition from other entities.

Anyone who is an administrator today already knows the kinds of challenges that higher education is facing. They have been chronicled repeatedly over the decades, from Jerry Gaff's original book on faculty renewal (Gaff, 1975) to more recent listings by AAHE's president, Yolanda Moses (2001), and others (Gumport, 2001; Schuster, 1990). You are much more likely to be interested in hearing about where to spend your institution's time and resources in coping with these forces. I am going to try to interest you in spending it where you will get the best return on your investment: the human capital of every institution, its faculty.

If you spend time and resources in faculty and staff development, you will get a huge return on your investment in terms of creativity, productivity, morale, and self-renewing energy. This was the argument that Jerry Gaff made in his seminal work on faculty development. He argued that institutions already made a huge investment in the faculty over the course of their careers, so it was only logical to maintain the quality of that investment by keeping it alive with development funding. To get an idea of the size of the investment an institution might make, take a look at the cost of a faculty member over the course of a thirty-year career. If she starts at $45,000 and gets only a 3 percent raise each year, the total reaches almost $2.3 million in salary alone. Figure in benefits, training, auxiliary support such as student and staff help and you could well go further into the millions.

Are you unconvinced or even offended by the financial argument in favor of faculty development? Then consider this: college and universities are about the preservation, transmittal, and proliferation of civilization. Civilization is advanced not by things

211

but by people thinking about, talking about, and tinkering with things, and also teaching others to think, talk, and tinker. Resources devoted to professional development produce the energy and capacity to continue those advances. Remember that the faculty are more than repositories of knowledge; they are models of the intellectual life for their students. If students see someone who is invested in the pursuit of learning and understanding, it is a great motivator for them to adopt that same attitude and value set. This can then help an institution become more attractive to high-quality students, who will also be more likely to stay if their teachers manifest a commitment to the institution. Investing in one faculty member's quality of life is multiplied many times over in each student he or she touches. Think how many students are affected by one teacher in the course of a thirty-year career.

There are, of course, many other arguments that can be made in favor of investing in faculty development. For example, faculty whose institution exhibits a concern for their development are more likely to stay and give back to that institution. They become a community, working together toward a common cause. They become part of the larger community in which the institution exists and help to build bridges between the institution and its neighbors. Political arguments, pragmatic arguments, altruistic arguments, and sociological arguments can be offered in favor of faculty development. But like the issues forcing change, these arguments have been discussed elsewhere and probably more convincingly than I could do here. Suffice it to say that money invested in human capital is a self-renewing investment.

Research on faculty vitality by Bland and Schmitz has shown that it is based on an interplay of faculty and institutional forces (Bland & Schmitz, 1990). Faculty must perceive that their institution supports their development in order to feel invested in it. Ward (1995), in reviewing research on teaching improvement and faculty change, reported that one of the most important factors influencing improved teaching was the faculty's perception of a positive institutional climate for change. An active and vital faculty development program creates just such an institutional climate.

FACULTY AND INSTRUCTIONAL DEVELOPMENT

Traditionally, the term *faculty development* was associated with development in the discipline, and included such standard practices as sabbaticals, research support, and travel grants. In the late 1960s and early 1970s that focus began to change, with more attention focused on the quality of teaching (Lewis, 1998). An important work published in the mid-1970s made very good arguments in favor of shifting the focus of faculty development to a better balance between teaching and disciplinary scholarship (Gaff, 1975). This idea has grown into today's more common practice of including a wide range of faculty and institutional activities under the umbrella term faculty development.

Faculty and instructional development programs have many different goals today. Programs that are termed *faculty development* tend to focus primarily on the faculty member and his or her development. They emphasize improved teaching through developing the skills and resources of the faculty member. These programs also sometimes expand their focus beyond the faculty member as a teacher to deal with the individual's wider professional and personal development.

When the preferred designation of the program is *instructional development,* it is more likely to focus on the course or the curriculum as a unit of analysis and the interplay between faculty and students, rather than on the faculty member alone. These programs emphasize the design of effective instruction through clear goals, the selection of appropriate instructional strategies to achieve those goals, and the design of adequate assessment strategies to determine if the goals have been met. Programs of this type also often work at a higher organizational level, such as the department or curriculum. Some programs even work toward institutional renewal by focusing on organizational development issues, such as the work and reward structure of the institution, the strategies for implementing and sustaining change, the methods used to evaluate performance, and so on. Although some functions of these programs are the same on most campuses, the type of faculty and instructional development program appropriate for your institution should have goals that are relevant to its mission and its traditional processes and structures. For example, institutions that are primarily focused on teaching would be best served by programs that support faculty attempts to develop teaching skills and innovations. Institutions with a more varied mission, such as comprehensive institutions, might need programs that have a wide variety of offerings, some focused on teaching, others on professional development of faculty. Institutions that pride themselves on taking a holistic approach to student development may want to include a similar focus in their faculty development programs. They would, therefore, offer programs that support personal development. Finally, large institutions with a wide range of disciplines represented or a decentralized governance structure may find that programs that accommodate disciplinary differences or are based in departments will better fit their needs.

Perhaps the best faculty and instructional development program is flexible yet stable enough to respond to the changing needs of the faculty and the institution while maintaining a set of core values that are in line with the institution's mission. In addition, the recent movement in higher education toward building self-renewing communities suggests that when faculty are involved in all aspects of programming and encouraged to look at this kind of development as a scholarly activity, they are more likely to experience sustainable transformation.

TYPES OF PROGRAMS

Because a wide variety of institutions offer programs with an equally wide variety of resources available, there are several different structures to accommodate these situations.

Faculty-Led Programs

These programs are based on contributed time by faculty who are interested in or charged with responsibility for faculty development. For institutions with few resources or for small, relatively homogeneous institutions, this type of program offers the benefits of low overhead and more faculty input. Its primary disadvantages are, of course, an increased workload for the involved faculty and sometimes less continuity if the faculty leaders change regularly.

Stand-Alone Offices Run by a Designated Faculty Member

In these programs an individual faculty member has actually been assigned the responsibility of developing the program as part of his or her workload. This structure works well at midsize institutions because it has the advantage of continuity and focus of control in one individual, which make for more stable programming. The disadvantages include the limited time and skills that any one individual can bring to the job, necessitating the drawing in of other faculty to help with programming.

Professionally Staffed Offices

These programs have full-time staff with advanced training in faculty development; their sole responsibility is this program. The advantages of this structure are the intensity with which the individuals can approach their task, the ability of such individuals to stay current in the field, and the continuity and organization of services because the staff do not turn over regularly. The disadvantages are the costs and bureaucracy that come with a permanent, dedicated office, the possibility of faculty rejecting anyone not considered a peer, and the potential for programming to become too set in its ways.

Department- or Unit-Based Structures

Some large institutions have been successful in operating at something less than an institutionwide level. A particularly effective fulcrum for faculty development of all types is the department. Most faculty at large institutions do not really identify with the institution as a whole; they identify more readily with their department or discipline. Programs at this level tap into this interest as a source of intrinsic motivation. The department chair is the administrator with the best sense of each faculty member's potential and needs, making him or her a logical broker of faculty development efforts for the individual members. In addition, the department is the focus of most curricular issues, making it a logical place for instructional and organizational development as well. For more information on this approach, consult Lucas (1989, 2000).

Collaborative, Distributed Network Structures

It may not be necessary for an institution to create a discrete entity for development programming. Sometimes pockets of development are interspersed throughout the institution in departments and colleges. Coordinating the efforts of these entities without actually combining them structurally is appealing because it means less bureaucracy and more local responsiveness. For example, departments with special needs in media support because of the nature of the discipline (for example, art or history) could develop well-designed and supported facilities that could also be tapped into occasionally by other types of departments in exchange for expertise from those disciplines. Such a system has the potential for a much greater sense of institutional community and makes more efficient use of resources. Resources are concentrated in the departments where they are most needed, rather than all departments trying to meet a common standard. The disadvantages are mostly in coordinating such efforts. Under this structure there is still a need for some entity to act as broker among the different components. Communication throughout the campus community is critical. For an example of such a system, see Watson and Grossman (1994) or Baiocco and DeWaters (1995).

PROGRAM COMPONENTS

It is not possible in this brief overview to list the specific offerings that you might consider for your program. Several sources describe program offerings and strategies; they are listed in the resource section of this chapter. It is also probably not appropriate for any single administrator to be overly concerned with the specific components offered. Component selection should be one of the steps taken during program formation, and it should be done with consideration of the institution's mission and resources and with the input of, preferably, the leadership and the faculty. However, generally program components fall into one of the following categories:

- *Consultation with individual faculty:* one-on-one or small-group intense review of faculty's questions about their teaching
- *Formal training opportunities:* workshops, seminars, on-line modules on various topics of interest
- *Less formal training methods:* mentoring, apprenticeships, support groups, study groups, resource support (books, newsletters, media support)
- *Programs to support innovation:* small grants, classroom research, staff support for new projects
- *Grant programs:* offering grants to faculty or working with faculty to find outside funding for instructional and curricular innovation and development
- *Evaluation of teaching:* support for student feedback, peer observation, portfolio development
- *Preparation programs for promotion and tenure decisions or posttenure review:* individual consultation, workshops on portfolio development, career management, or revitalization
- *Advocacy for teaching and instructional issues:* service on committees on teaching, production of white papers on topics under consideration

ADMINISTRATIVE SUPPORT

Administrative support for faculty development efforts is critical to their productivity and success. Fortunately, there are things beyond offering more money (although that is desirable) that administrators can do to be a partner in these efforts. I polled the directors of centers of a number of major institutions of higher education around the United

States about their own experiences with administrator support. They had much to say, including pointing out that we can learn a lot from both negative and positive examples of support. Their views, along with the views of the best writers in the field, are summarized as follows:

- Provide visible as well as behind-the-scenes support for development programs.
- Locate the program in the reporting line that addresses significant faculty issues, generally under the office of the president or provost.
- Provide the program with a stable funding base in the institution's permanent budget structure, and staff it with well-trained and well-respected individuals who reflect the best models of continuous development in their own careers.
- Establish a fundraising priority for faculty development initiatives, such as alumni or parent groups who wish to support course improvement and innovation, or major donors who wish to sponsor annual programs for faculty.
- Be personally knowledgeable about the program's activities, and participate in more meaningful ways than just showing up and saying how important the program is (and then leaving for a more important event). Be an active participant and even a presenter at events sponsored by the program organizers.
- Acknowledge the positive impact of the program in private as well as public discussions about institutional priorities with faculty, other administrators, the public.
- Lend your support by writing to and lobbying key faculty and administrators to enlist their participation in and support of development programs.
- Appoint development representatives to key committees, even asking them to chair the committees as neutral parties with no departmental biases.
- Work with faculty and staff to set clear goals and expectations for the development programs that are tied to the institutional mission and goals. These goals should be reviewed regularly with extensive faculty input. Keep expectations focused and avoid "mission creep."
- Make sure that administrators at all levels are trained for and attuned to initiating and supporting faculty development opportunities in their sphere of influence—especially chairs, who are most likely to influence faculty and curricular decisions. Be a model of this value by providing for your own development as well as theirs.

- Keep those in charge of the program up-to-date on institutional priorities and changes so that the program can be ready to support the institution and the faculty as change occurs. Work in partnership with program leaders to create a learning organization.

PROGRAM ASSESSMENT STRATEGIES: QUESTIONS TO ASK

Of course, as a responsible administrator you want to support a development program as much as you possibly can. But you also have to be mindful of the bottom line: Are you getting a good return on your investment? Given the complex nature of the phenomenon of faculty development, it is hard to offer an exact measure of its effectiveness, but here are some key questions to ask to help you decide if your program is succeeding or has the possibility of succeeding.

Structure and Process Measures

- Is the program located administratively so it can be seen as central to the mission of the institution?
- Is the program located administratively so it can respond to changing institutional priorities relevant to its mission?
- Does the program have stable funding, personnel, and administrative oversight?
- Are the program's goals clearly tied to the mission and goals of the institution?
- Do the activities offered have a direct connection with the overall program goals?
- Is there a pattern of ongoing review of goals and provision for input from faculty and other constituencies?
- Does the program have a sufficient variety of offerings to serve the needs and learning preferences of the faculty?
- Does the program have a history of an ability to change and grow in response to the changing needs of faculty and the institution?
- How well does the program understand and make use of campus structure and resources in support of its offerings? How well connected is it to other programs on campus?

- Does the program evaluate its offerings in terms of faculty satisfaction and behavior change, morale, and retention?
- Does the program evaluate its offerings in terms of impact on student learning and satisfaction; retention of students in courses, programs, and at the institution; student attitudes about their courses and the institution?
- Does the program evaluate its offerings in terms of the impact on other institutional functioning, such as program review, curriculum change, organizational change?
- To what extent do program staff members maintain their own development as professionals?

Outcomes

- How well known is the program among its target audiences?
- How well regarded is the program among its target audiences?
- What is the level of participation in the program by the target audiences? How does it compare with participation in other campus programs of a similar nature? How does it compare with participation in programs at other, similar institutions?
- Do faculty and others who participate in the program's offerings experience positive changes in their situation as a result of that participation?
- To what extent do faculty see the program as a valuable resource for information and guidance in the areas targeted by its goals?
- What does the program contribute to the growth of the institution and the advancement of its mission?

CONCLUSION

Faculty and instructional development programs have the potential to stimulate growth for their institutions if they have the right combination of goals, support, and staff. However, it is important for you to understand that the kind of change being targeted by such programs will not come quickly. Like most changes in higher education, this one will be gradual and incremental. Therefore, perhaps the most important thing an administrator can do to support faculty and instructional development is to *be patient!*

Like a large ship, an institution of higher education is usually hard to start, hard to steer, and hard to stop. On top of that, most development programs do not have much control over the rudder or the engine; they have to make changes through the work of others. When as a relatively new faculty developer I bemoaned the lack of progress our center had made, a seasoned faculty member said to me, "What are you complaining about? You've only been doing this for five years! You can't expect change in such a short time."

So although the possibility for change is great, the pace is slow. That may be the hardest part of your task in supporting faculty development: having the patience to wait and see the process through to the end.

References

Baiocco, S. A., & DeWaters, J. N. (1995). Futuristic faculty development: A collegiate development network. *Academe, 81,* 38–39.

Bland, C., & Schmitz, C. (1990). An overview of research on faculty and institutional vitality. In J. Schuster & D. W. Wheeler (Eds.), *Enhancing faculty careers: Strategies for development and renewal* (pp. 41–61). San Francisco: Jossey-Bass.

Gaff, J. (1975). *Toward faculty renewal.* San Francisco: Jossey-Bass.

Gumport, P. J. (2001). Restructuring: Imperatives and opportunities for academic leaders. *Innovative Higher Education, 25*(4), 239–251.

Lewis, K. G. (1998). Instructional improvement in higher education. In G. R. Firth & E. F. Pajak (Eds.), *Handbook of research on school supervision* (pp. 721–737). New York: Simon & Schuster-Macmillan.

Lucas, A. (1989). *The department chairperson's role in enhancing college teaching.* San Francisco: Jossey-Bass.

Lucas, A. (2000). *Leading academic change: Essential roles for department chairs.* San Francisco: Jossey-Bass.

Moses, Y. (2001). Scanning the environment: AAHE's president reports on trends in higher education. *AAHE Bulletin, 53*(10), 7–9.

Schuster, J. (1990). The need for fresh approaches to faculty renewal. In J. Schuster, D. W. Wheeler, & Associates (Eds.), *Enhancing faculty careers: Strategies for development and renewal* (pp. 3–19). San Francisco: Jossey-Bass.

Ward, B. (1995). Research for faculty development. In E. Neal (Ed.), *To improve the academy* (Vol. 14; pp. 27–42). Fort Collins, CO: POD Network.

Watson, G. G., & Grossman, L. (1994). Pursuing a comprehensive faculty development program: Making fragmentation work. *Journal of Counseling and Development, 72,* 465–473.

Resources

General Discussions of Faculty Development

Schuster, J., Wheeler, D., & Associates. (Eds.). (1990). *Enhancing faculty careers: Strategies for development and renewal.* San Francisco: Jossey-Bass.

If you can only read one book, read this one. It has excellent chapters on all aspects of faculty development, including its history (Schuster, "The Need for Fresh Approaches to Faculty Renewal"), research on faculty vitality (Bland & Schmitz, "An Overview of Research on Faculty and Institutional Vitality"), and the concept of faculty development itself (Wheeler & Schuster, "Building Comprehensive Programs to Enhance Faculty Development").

Lewis, K. G. (1998). Instructional improvement in higher education. In G. R. Firth & E. F. Pajak (Eds.), *Handbook of research on school supervision* (pp. 721–737). New York: Simon & Schuster-Macmillan.
A fairly comprehensive look at the history and practices of faculty development from its earliest days to the current state of the art.

Heppner, P., & Johnson, J. (Eds.). (1994, May-June). *Journal of Counseling and Development, 72*(5).
This special issue of the journal devoted to the faculty development concept includes an overview by Millis ("Faculty Development in the 1990s: What It Is and Why We Can't Wait"), which offers a quick review of some of the pressures leading to the need for faculty development and what might be done about them. It also includes specific articles on program components, such as programs for new faculty (Sorcinelli, "Effective Approaches to New Faculty Development") and the chair's place in faculty development (Reich, "Developing Faculty Development Programs: A View from the Chair").

Gillespie, K. (2002). *A guide to faculty development: Practical advice, examples, and resources.* Bolton, MA: Anker.
The Professional and Organizational Development (POD) Network in Higher Education is by far the most influential organization in the areas of faculty and instructional development. It includes faculty developers from around the world and is where most faculty developers get their training and continuing ideas. This guide, produced under POD's auspices, compiles the best ideas about programming from that wide array of individuals and institutions.

Programs and Practices

Even though you may not be directly involved in designing programming for your unit, you might want to be able to point your selected leaders toward resources that will help them plan programs.

To improve the academy. (published annually). Fort Collins, CO: POD Network.
In addition to its *Handbook for New Practitioners* cited earlier, the POD Network compiles an annual book of readings that focuses on the latest issues in faculty development. Authors describe best practices as well as new ideas, making this publication a very rich resource for programming.

Innovative Higher Education.
This journal publishes several special-topic issues concerning faculty and instructional development. Cited in this chapter is the issue on faculty development itself (Gumport, 2001), but the journal has also published editions on peer review, posttenure review, and many other topics of interest to developers and faculty alike.

PART FOUR

Assessment

Comprehensive or transformational change requires holistic and integrated thinking about the institution. Rethinking undergraduate education is not just about changing course content or course offerings. It requires new approaches to student services, faculty development, assessment, and community involvement.

—Peter Eckel, Barbara Hill, Madeleine Green, and Bill Mallon,
On Change—Reports From the Road: Insights on Institutional Change,
American Council on Education, 1999, pp. 1–2

CHAPTER 14

Evaluation and Assessment
An Institutional Context

MICHAEL THEALL

ollecting and using good data are key elements in the success of any higher education organization. Data are necessary in reporting to boards of trustees, accrediting agencies, government offices, parents, and the general public, but they are perhaps even more important for internal purposes, especially helping individuals, units, and the institution grow and improve. Every office on your campus has a need for accurate and timely information. Units dealing with students, faculty, and academic matters have a dual responsibility: to keep certain information secure while efficiently sharing other information so that units and individuals can see how well they are doing and how they might improve.

As an institutional leader of assessment and evaluation efforts, you have six critical responsibilities: to identify and use the talents of people with appropriate expertise and skills; to create conditions that allow these individuals to lead information-gathering efforts effectively; to provide the resources they need to collect, analyze, and report information; to model standards for accurate interpretation and appropriate use of data; to ensure that the various efforts are coordinated and that the data are productively used; and to oversee the development of complex systems for handling different but interrelated types of information.

KEY DIFFERENCES BETWEEN EVALUATION AND ASSESSMENT

There are many kinds of data collection for many purposes, but when we think of institutional data needs and evidence of quality, we often think of two terms—assessment and evaluation. These are frequently considered to be equivalent and interchangeable, but although they are closely related they are not identical. *Evaluation* is an older concept described by Michael Scriven (1967) as "the gathering and combining of performance data with a weighted set of goal scales" for the purpose of "the estimation of merit, worth, value, etc." (p. 41). To be consistent in this chapter, I will use the word evaluation to mean just that; a process whose goal is always to provide information about an activity, program, individual, or group for the purpose of making decisions about merit or worth. Evaluation should not be confused with *measurement,* which is nonjudgmental and simply involves the collection of data.

Assessment is a newer conception with a somewhat different focus and is often connected to a broad effort (the "assessment movement") to improve the methods used to determine learning and other educational outcomes. Gray (1991) says that the assessment movement has a "long-term focus on a range of techniques used to gather a variety of information in support of instructional, programmatic, and institutional change" (p. 54). To be consistent in this chapter, I will use the word assessment to mean any process primarily intended to gather and use information for purposes of improvement or change, without necessarily having the attending goal of making final decisions about merit or worth.

Scriven also coined two terms for the roles of evaluation: *formative* (evaluation for ongoing revision and improvement) and *summative* (evaluation for making terminal decisions about merit or worth). These terms are very useful and are found in both evaluation and assessment. Unfortunately, their use further blends the two concepts, making precise definition difficult. Evaluation and assessment can both be formative or summative, thus confounding attempts to distinguish the two. One could easily say that assessment is formative evaluation, whereas evaluation is summative assessment. Scriven also noted that the instruments used to collect data could focus on *instrumental* data (information about process) or *consequential* data (information about outcomes). Assessment and evaluation can legitimately consider both types of data, and again the result is a blending of the two definitions.

Ultimately, at most institutions the differences between assessment and evaluation are most easily understood by considering the functions of the units that do the work. Assessment offices usually collect data for accreditation and may support individual teachers or programs with classroom efforts to determine what students learn. Evaluation offices most often coordinate the collection, analysis, and reporting of data from student ratings of instruction but do not take part in other aspects of faculty evaluation or in measuring learning. An important responsibility of leaders is to help their institutions develop unambiguous and locally applicable definitions of these terms and the missions and functions of the units charged with carrying out the efforts.

CREATING A GOOD SYSTEM

Assessment and evaluation do not have to be threatening. For example, Angelo and Cross (1993) define classroom assessment as "an approach designed to help teachers find out what students are learning in the classroom and how well they are learning it" (p. 4). Thus, assessment can be an essentially private activity that informs classroom process in support of better learning, or by extension, an activity that informs unit and institutional process in support of better performance. This seems reasonable enough, so why are assessment and evaluation such sensitive issues? In part, because these processes, even when confidential, open individuals to inspection and judgment by others. Yet in higher education we consistently make such judgments.

All faculty assess their students and are evaluated by them. All students are graded by teachers and asked to provide information and opinions about their teachers and courses. And all academic administrators review performance data and make decisions, and their performance is reviewed by their supervisors, and in many cases, by the faculty as well. The immediacy and reciprocity of such judgments can result in defensiveness or hostility, and literally every student, faculty member, and academic administrator has a powerful, personal story to tell. Unfortunately, these stories and the conclusions drawn from them are often negative because few people enjoy being evaluated and the consequences of negative evaluation are severe. In truth, such stories can reflect everything from simple misunderstanding to actual abysmal practice to outright myth.

Why are so many efforts incomplete and inappropriate and what has this to do with leadership? An underlying reason for the problems we face is the haphazard way in which systems for evaluation and assessment are developed, operated, and managed. The most appropriate solutions to the problems lie in shared commitment to and responsibility for good practice. Such commitment and responsibility require leadership from all those involved in the process. Leadership here means proactive efforts to build trust, avoid problems, rely on established research and standards for good practice, and create conditions for success.

KEY TOPICS FOR INSTITUTIONAL LEADERS

There are three important assessment and evaluation topics for institutional leaders to consider.

Key Issue: Quality of Data Collection and Use

How can leaders ensure quality? Leadership is required from all those involved in assessment and evaluation. Successful administrative leaders create conditions that support, promote, and motivate others to assume leadership roles among their peers and support good practice.

Key Resources: Local Expertise and Infrastructure

How can leaders best use resources? Expert advice is always useful and often critical to initiating and reviewing assessment and evaluation processes and activities. But the success of ongoing operation depends on those who use the systems. Successful leaders must know whom and what to ask and must find ways to increase both participation and efficiency.

Key Dangers: Apathy, Haste, Politics, Tunnel Vision

How can leaders avoid problems and pitfalls? Assessment and evaluation are sensitive matters, threatening to many because they involve evidence of performance and important personal and institutional decisions. They are intended to promote both stability and change; we gather information to determine what works as well as what to do to change and improve what appears not to work. Clearly, the stakeholders who have political power, influence, or resources will desire stability in the form of evaluation data that support the status quo. Those in positions of lesser influence will see more benefit from change and seek evaluation results that challenge the current process and structures and suggest reallocation of power and resources.

But despite their importance, assessment and evaluation are often undersupported or thrown together as last minute responses to external pressures. Successful leaders understand timing and the institutional political dynamics, and can introduce ideas, programs, and even policies when these have the best chance for success. But that is not all. Leaders must also bring a *gestalt,* a clear and supportive vision, to everything from the first dialogues on assessment and evaluation to the decisions that are made and the ongoing validation of the systems used.

Leadership is a human activity requiring action and interaction. This chapter will consider the issues by concentrating on a conception of quality that is closely connected to, first, the stakeholders, or those who are involved or affected by evaluation and assessment, and second, the systems that can facilitate effective assessment and evaluation. I will stress the interactions of these people and systems rather than the details of psychometrics, the methodologies of evaluation and assessment, the technologies used, or the administrative requirements of day-to-day operations. I will outline important considerations underlying valid, reliable, and accepted systems and focus on how effective leadership can ensure their success by supporting these activities and those who enact them. The stakeholders are the people who can and must be involved in the development, implementation, and oversight of the comprehensive systems necessary for effective evaluation and assessment.

MEASURING EDUCATIONAL QUALITY

How do we measure educational quality in higher education? The debate over the validity and accuracy of nationally publicized lists of so-called best colleges demonstrates that there is much disagreement about how to measure the quality of higher education institutions. But with respect to our basic educational mission, we measure quality by considering both the process (teaching) and its outcomes (learning). One of the most widely circulated process guides is Chickering and Gamson's (1991) seven principles for good practice in undergraduate education, which encourage student-faculty contact, cooperation among students, active learning, prompt feedback, time on task, high expectations, and mutual respect. These are useful indicators, but not guarantors of success. Evaluation and assessment efforts are needed to fill in the picture of institutional quality, but although evaluation and assessment are useful processes that can provide valuable information, they are also sometimes incomplete and inaccurate and can result in personal discomfort, poor decision making, strife, professionally damaging consequences, even litigation.

For example, one of the most common errors in evaluation is the assumption that a single data collection process (for example, a student ratings system), once in place, is sufficient and will serve its purpose indefinitely. Underlying this false assumption is an even more basic error: incomplete consideration of the complex and numerous data needs and subsystems that are required for successful practice. In assessment, a common error has been to impose a requirement for assessment plans without providing faculty with reasonable justification for the work or sufficient training and support to develop meaningful plans. To avoid such problems, the key areas of practice must be closely interrelated and cyclical. That is, by their very nature, these processes require constant attention, regular review, and frequent revision to accommodate changes brought about by internal and external forces. Leaders must support good practice as an ongoing and dynamic effort that is sensitive to change.

Without such support, the task becomes yet another bureaucratic requirement divorced from day-to-day teaching and other aspects of faculty work. In both of these cases, effective leadership can make the difference between accepted, productive practice and extra work that holds little value for anyone. Therefore, assessment and evaluation can succeed only if they are perceived as meaningful, relevant, and useful activities. Leaders must demonstrate the importance, relevance, and need for the processes.

The best definition of quality is the one that reflects the reality of the institution. Furthermore, the definition must be widely shared and commonly understood. Internally, this means that leaders must involve all institutional stakeholders in dialogue and consensus-producing activities. But institutions do not exist in isolation. There are others whose opinions must be considered because they can influence the definition of quality. Leaders must interact in different ways with stakeholders to assure them that the institution is living up to an acceptable standard. The first step for the leader is recognizing the stakeholders.

Determine the Stakeholders

There are three principal groups of stakeholders in higher education evaluation and assessment: faculty, academic administrators, and students. But many other individuals and groups also have vested interests. These are stakeholders who are more distant from ongoing activity and whose involvement in decisions, need for information, participation in day-to-day process, and influence gradually decrease as a result.

In Figure 14.1, faculty, students, and academic administrators form the nucleus (Level I) of an atomic model. There is regular interaction among these stakeholders, but there are other circles of influence and these can interact and affect each other as well as the nuclear participants. As the arrows indicate, there are interlevel as well as intralevel interactions. Nonetheless, ongoing practice is most influenced by the inner core of stakeholders.

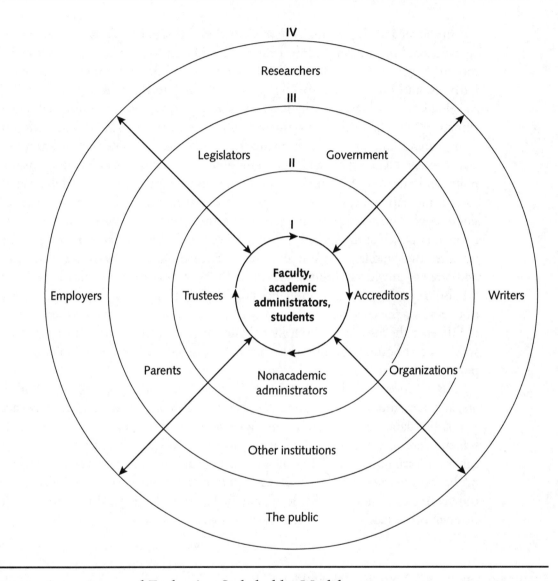

FIGURE 14.1. **Assessment and Evaluation Stakeholder Model**

In the second ring around the nucleus (Level II) are boards of trustees, accrediting agencies, and institutional administrators in addition to those who directly review performance; all of these people need and use evaluative information on a frequent or regular basis, and their impact can be specific, strong, and immediate. The next ring of stakeholders (Level III) includes local and state legislative and governmental bodies concerned with public institutions, the federal government, other higher education institutions, parents, and professional organizations and societies. The first two groups in this level have oversight responsibilities and the ability to exert direct influence on institutional policy and practice. Other higher education institutions can be involved in general ways, such as the national dialogue on teaching and learning, but also at more specific levels. For example, the institutions in a state university system may have input about common evaluation policy in the system. The latter two groups have specific interests in the quality of teaching and learning but less direct influence. Parents, always as concerned parties and often as providers of tuition payments (especially at public institutions, where they are also taxpayers), can exert influence both directly by personal contact with the institution and its representatives, and indirectly by contacting legislators or others in a position to influence the institution. Professional associations can affect broad issues such as licensure and certification and influence curriculum, standards, and even evaluation in disciplinary areas.

At the outermost ring (level 4), employers, researchers, journalists and other writers, and sometimes even the general public may be concerned with and have access to evaluation data, but most often these are aggregate data, and instances in which these stakeholders are directly involved at the institutional level are less frequent. Employers can exert local influence on curricular matters, such as education versus training needs in the local market and the qualities of graduates who best suit employer needs. The impact of stakeholders at this level may be felt more in general matters or indirectly through other stakeholders, such as legislators.

Encourage Leadership from All Stakeholders

For the most part, leadership in evaluation must come from the three primary stakeholder groups because they have the immediate responsibilities of developing, implementing, and operating the assessment and evaluation systems and they use the data that result.

But for evaluation and assessment to be effective, leadership must come from all the principal stakeholders. Furthermore, that leadership must take the form of a constant demand and expectation that any process will be based on the best evidence guiding practice, coupled with a clear understanding of the specific needs of the institution and the individuals concerned.

In determining leadership, we can isolate faculty, students, and academic administrators as principals because of their regular involvement in evaluation, but they do not (nor could they) have the entire responsibility for and authority over evaluation practice. Outside this nucleus there must be an expectation for high standards of practice, an acknowledgment that best practice is sensitive to local context, and a willingness to let best practice be guided by established evidence and decided on by those who must operate, maintain, and use the systems. Imposing irrelevant external regulation and making unreasonable demands will not improve evaluation but only create resistance. Only the stakeholders can ensure best practice, and the core stakeholders can do much to influence those at the outer levels of the model. Connolly (2000), in a discussion of academic freedom, warned against constructing arguments that "are just so much window dressing meant to disguise entrenched privilege" (p. 75).

In sum, we can think of leadership in evaluation and assessment as an effort by all concerned to create, sustain, and improve the systems we use to determine merit and worth. If these systems are well-constructed and supported, they can efficiently and effectively provide the raw material for valid and reliable decision making. If they are left to chance, the result will be chaos. What has been lacking is leadership that promotes seven critical activities. This leadership must come from all the primary stakeholders. A basic set of principles can be phrased in terms of those things that effective leadership should model and promote.

SEVEN PRINCIPLES FOR EFFECTIVE LEADERSHIP

There are seven principles for effective leadership in evaluation and assessment:

- Include all stakeholders and strive for public dialogue and consensus from the outset.
- Determine the most appropriate roles and goals at the outset.
- Understand the substantial literature of the field; accept established findings and ignore unsubstantiated anecdotes or opinions.
- Develop, adapt, or adopt a system suited to the context and serving all stakeholders.

- Establish, maintain, and ensure standards of quality in the system.
- Ensure fair and accurate interpretation and use of evaluation results.
- Couple evaluation with resources for recognition, reward, improvement, and development.

GUIDELINES FOR PRACTICE

Here are some basic guidelines and specific behaviors that can support the seven principles and lead to fair, accurate, and accepted practice.

Demand and Defend Good Practice

- Use expert opinion and advice. Rely on the established literature base but include contextual considerations that make the system relevant to local needs.
- Reject unreasonable demands for data, particularly when the data may be misinterpreted or misused.
- Train those who provide, handle, interpret, use, and make decisions with evaluation data.
- Do not make ad hoc changes in the system.
- Build in the capability to investigate unusual situations and to protect individuals and the institution from errors and the resulting dissension and suspicion.
- Recognize and reward examples of best practice.

Support a Quality Evaluation Effort

- Hire qualified staff; faculty evaluation is too important to trust to novices.
- Provide human and material resources as needed.
- Regularly re-analyze data and make necessary revisions, particularly of any norms used in formative or summative decision making.
- Build a database of institutional information that serves the needs of the involved units as well as the concerned constituencies. Developing a data-sharing synergy among the units that deal with assessment, evaluation, insti-

tutional research, student affairs, admissions, alumni affairs, and institutional development will lead to more thorough analysis and more informed decisions.

- Provide fiscal and other incentives to exemplary units and individuals.

Build Trust in the System

To build trust, work to have evaluation and assessment accepted as valid, reliable, fair, relevant, useful, and productive.

- Initiate and continue open discussions about general and specific issues.
- Include stakeholders early, and publicly involve those who exemplify good practice.
- Use local examples of success to promote relevance and encourage modeling.
- Establish a clear grievance procedure.
- Use pilot tests of process and systems, and review and revise them before formal implementation.
- Take sufficient time to evaluate the systems before they are used for summative evaluation.
- Regularly evaluate the evaluation system and the evaluators.
- Review evaluation needs when other changes occur in teaching, learning, or the conditions in which they take place, and develop new processes or systems to meet new needs.

Create a Positive Image (and Reality)

- Use motivational techniques and strategies that keep stakeholders invested and interested.
- Create an ongoing dialogue and faculty forum.
- Ensure that resources for support and improvement are closely connected to evaluation.
- Connect classroom assessment and research to the scholarship of teaching and to the reward system.

- Be prepared to react to changes in assessment or evaluation practice and have a person on campus who knows the literature of the field and can guide the change process in a systematic way.
- Make assessment and evaluation part of an agenda for excellence.
- Involve new and experienced faculty, and keep student leaders engaged.
- Publicize positive results inside the institution and outside to all stakeholders.
- Connect assessment and evaluation efforts with other institutional, department, and individual priorities.

Create an Efficient Data Management Process

The last suggestion of the preceding section requires a brief additional note. Institutions ordinarily need many kinds of information and support many units that collect or handle information. Usually, these units deal with teacher-course evaluation, assessment, institutional research, alumni affairs, development, admissions, registration, computing, and special projects such as accreditation. Often there are similarities in the kinds of information required, and two inefficiencies are the result: duplication of effort and cost, and missed opportunities to capitalize on good information. Institutions should make a concerted effort to develop comprehensive data management systems that can streamline data collection and provide many users with access to the array of information collected by the various units. With a systematic approach to design and a relational database strategy, current technology makes this entirely possible. This is not a wholesale exchange of information, but a carefully developed sharing of relevant data that supplements the individual capabilities of each unit. Some factors to be considered by each unit in developing such sophisticated systems and an institutional data management plan are mission and function, information needs, data sources, constituencies, analysis and reporting issues, interpretation and uses of data, confidentiality and security issues, existing data sharing process, resource needs (including institutional infrastructure, database design and management), the users' need for simple and efficient systems, individual protection, and oversight.

For example, a simple, two-way exchange of classroom assessment and course evaluation data could enhance the comprehensiveness of what each unit could collect alone; provide a more complete understanding of teaching and learning for individuals, units, and the institution; identify excellent practice and explore how the benefits from such successes could be transferred to other situations; and support faculty classroom research and work in the realm of the scholarship of teaching. Now, add to this entry-exit assessment data, admissions and alumni data, and grade profiles, and you can see how such an array could support reaccreditation efforts, responses to governing bodies, and public information efforts. Perhaps most important, this kind of coordinated effort has to include active student participation. Engaging students in this dialogue as an ongoing part of institutional improvement would enhance the quality and depth of responses and would make students partners in excellence while providing a rich diversity of information for meaningful dialogue among core stakeholders.

CONCLUSION

Because of the many pressures on higher education, we may have lost sight of our common bond: the pursuit, sharing, integration, and application of knowledge. The definition of a college, after all, is a body of persons having a common purpose or common duties. A colleague is defined as one chosen to work with another. Those who choose to work with each other toward the common purpose of higher education must make the purpose a priority and focus on processes that engender success. Isolation, compartmentalization, and elitism have no place here, and all stakeholders have equal responsibility for ensuring success.

References

Angelo, T. A., & Cross, K. P. (1993). *Classroom assessment techniques: A handbook for college teachers* (2nd ed.). San Francisco: Jossey-Bass.

Chickering, A. W., & Gamson, Z. F. (Eds.). (1991). *Applying the seven principles for good practice in undergraduate education.* New Directions for Teaching and Learning, no. 47. San Francisco: Jossey-Bass.

Connolly, J. M. (2000). The academy's freedom, the academy's burden. *NEA Higher Education Journal, 16*(1), 69–82.

Gray, P. J. (1991). Using assessment data to improve teaching. In M. Theall & J. Franklin (Eds.), *Effective practices for improving teaching.* New Directions for Teaching and Learning, no. 48. San Francisco: Jossey-Bass.

Scriven, M. (1967). Methodology of evaluation. In R. Tyler, R. Gagne, & M. Scriven (Eds.), *Perspectives of curriculum evaluation.* Skokie, IL: Rand McNally.

Resources

Angelo, T. A., & Cross, K. P. (1993). *Classroom assessment techniques: A handbook for college teachers* (2nd ed.). San Francisco: Jossey-Bass.

This widely read text is derived from work by the National Center for Research into Postsecondary Teaching and Learning at the University of Michigan. The book offers extensive description and application of various strategies for gathering and using information to assess student learning.

Arreola, R. A. (2000). *Developing a comprehensive faculty evaluation system* (2nd ed.). Bolton, MA: Anker.

This is the best practical guide to developing and implementing a comprehensive evaluation system. It contains a thorough overview, grounded discussion of operational issues, samples of instruments and processes, and proven techniques for generating dialogue and consensus. If you can have only one book to guide faculty evaluation, this should be it.

Birnbaum, R. (1988). *How colleges work: The cybernetics of academic organization and leadership.* San Francisco: Jossey-Bass

Birnbaum, R. (1992). *How academic leadership works. Understanding success and failure in the college presidency.* San Francisco: Jossey-Bass.

Birnbaum, R. (2001). *Management fads in higher education: Where they come from, what they do, and why they fail.* San Francisco: Jossey-Bass.

All of Birnbaum's books are clear, insightful, realistic, and very readable. They provide many examples, and the work is grounded in a substantial and broad literature base.

Bloom, S. (1998). Structure and ideology in medical education: An analysis of resistance to change. *Journal of Health and Social Behavior, 29,* 294–306.

This is an interesting view of the change process and a sobering description of reform without change—that is, the futility of responding to the need to alter or improve something without implementing any long-lasting or meaningful changes. In conjunction with Birnbaum's text on fads, this work alerts readers to the need for making change relevant and connecting to stakeholder frames of reference.

Boyer, E. L. (1990). *Scholarship reconsidered: The priorities of the professoriate.* San Francisco: Jossey-Bass.

This short work has had a tremendous impact in the decade since its publication, generating dialogue and action on campuses of all types. It is reconceptualization of scholarship, particularly the introduction of the scholarship of teaching as an equal partner with discovery, integration, and application, that has led to numerous projects and attempts to broaden the roles of faculty.

Chickering, A. W., & Gamson, Z. F. (1987). Seven principles for good practice in undergraduate education. *Wingspread Journal, 9,* 1–4.

The seven principles have been used as guidelines for assessment in traditional and even on-line instruction, and there has been widespread use of the faculty, student, and institutional inventories devised to measure implementation of the principles on campuses.

Cross, K. P., & Steadman, M. H. (1996). *Classroom research: Implementing the scholarship of teaching*. San Francisco: Jossey-Bass.
This work expands on Cross's work in classroom assessment to incorporate Boyer's definitions of scholarship. It provides teachers with strategies for conducting classroom research that supports better understanding of classroom process and also is rigorous enough to be incorporated into more traditional outlets for scholarship.

Farmer, D. W. (1988). *Enhancing student learning: Emphasizing essential competencies in academic programs*. Wilkes Barre, PA: Kings College Press.

Farmer, D. W. (1999). Institutional improvement and motivated faculty: A case study. In M. Theall (Ed.), *Motivation from within: Approaches for encouraging faculty and students to excel*. New Directions for Teaching and Learning, no. 78. San Francisco: Jossey-Bass.
Farmer's work as an academic administrator and leader in change processes is summarized in the New Directions chapter and his specific efforts at Kings College are discussed in detail in the book. Both works are useful for those in a position to effect change through leadership.

Feldman, K. A., & Paulsen, M. B. (1998). *Teaching and learning in the college classroom* (2nd ed.). New York: Simon & Schuster.
This is the most comprehensive collection of readings on this topic. It is broad and substantial, and includes landmark items like Boyer's definitions of the four kinds of scholarship and Chickering and Gamson's seven principles. It also incorporates some of Feldman's studies of college teaching and Paulsen and Feldman's work on creating a campus teaching culture. This is probably the best single compendium of the research on college teaching.

Glassick, C. E., Huber, M. T., & Maeroff, G. I. (1997). *Scholarship assessed: Evaluation of the professoriate*. San Francisco: Jossey-Bass.
This work continues where Boyer's text leaves off, providing discussion and guidelines for evaluating and documenting scholarly work, particularly in the realm of the scholarship of teaching. Completed after Boyer's death, it nonetheless includes a prologue by Boyer.

Pescolozodi, B., & Aminzade, R. (1999). *The social worlds of higher education: Handbook for teaching in a new century*. Newbury Park, CA: Pine Forge Press.
This is a very interesting collection of works by sociologists and considers a range of higher education issues. Its treatment of higher education as a sociological microcosm is unique and worthwhile.

Scriven, M. (1967). Methodology of evaluation. In R. Tyler, R. Gagne, & M. Scriven (Eds.), *Perspectives of curriculum evaluation*. Skokie, IL: Rand McNally.
If there is a seminal article on modern evaluation, this is it. Scriven's terminology and approach are the basis for contemporary evaluation and assessment.

Theall, M., & Franklin, J. (Eds.). (1990). *Student ratings of instruction: Issues for improving practice.* New Directions for Teaching and Learning, no. 43. San Francisco: Jossey-Bass.

This is one of the first discussions of evaluation to focus on context and the systematic nature of evaluation and the requirements it imposes. Several aspects of evaluation, from ethical issues to disciplinary differences, are presented.

CHAPTER 15

Academic Program Review

JON F. WERGIN

See if this scenario describes what happens in the typical department at your institution: Units come up for a formal program review every five to seven years. It is an event that does not inspire much enthusiasm among the faculty. There is plenty of busywork as the self-study is prepared, and a lot of grumbling about wasted time and bureaucratic intrusion. Despite administrative admonishment that program review is *really* for the purpose of departmental improvement—not summative assessment—everyone's goal is to get through the process with a minimum of aggravation. When it is over, nothing much changes, and you are left with at best a vague sense of dissatisfaction with the process. This whole pageant is repeated, with minor variations, for regional and specialized accreditation, student outcome assessment, and various ad hoc strategic planning initiatives.

BARRIERS TO EFFECTIVE EVALUATION

If all this seems distressingly familiar, you are not alone. There is more evaluation in higher education today than ever before, but it has had remarkably little impact on student learning, as several studies (Ewell, 1997; Gray & Banta, 1997; Angelo, 1999) have shown. As Joseph Burke (1999, p. 4) asks in what he calls the *assessment anomaly,* "If everyone's doing it, why isn't more getting done?" There are two usual suspects in this sorry state of affairs: the complexity of measuring student learning outcomes, and the old standby, faculty resistance. I will take up each of these in turn.

Before we begin, note that in this chapter I use the term *department* in a structural sense, to mean the smallest academic unit in the institution having its own budget. I use the term *program* in a functional sense, to mean a collection of activities (such as a course of study) with clearly defined purposes, goals, and responsibilities. Programs, therefore, can be completely contained in departments or can cross departmental lines.

Two Usual Suspects: Measurement and Faculty Resistance

The argument for measurement as a barrier goes like this: The thrust of the assessment movement has been to shift the focus from "inputs," such as resources and capacities, to "outcomes," namely effects on student learning. This is all well and good, but the problem is that we do not know how to measure student learning very well, and certainly not in the aggregate. So if the point of student outcome assessment is to reveal what students as a group have gained from their college experience, and to do so in a way that leads to some comparability across programs and institutions, the measurement challenges become horrendous. Besides, to continue the argument, "real" learning has certain ineffable qualities anyway, which defy any of our crude attempts at measurement.

The argument for faculty resistance as a barrier to useful assessment (or for that matter, to virtually any campus initiative), goes like this: Faculty members treasure their autonomy and are not about to give it up just because some administrator talks about the need to become more accountable. More than any other part of their work, their teaching is their domain, and faculty feel as if they have proprietary rights to their courses. Student grades are sufficient evidence of learning; demanding any more evidence than that presents a potentially serious threat to academic freedom.

Both of these barriers are real, and the arguments that present them have some merit. However, these are not the real culprits, in my view. The central reasons why program assessment has not been more effective lie elsewhere.

A Compliance Mentality

The questions driving many program reviews, as well as other forms of program evaluation, are "theirs," not "ours." The review is on someone else's agenda: higher administration, governing board, accrediting commission. Most faculty accept the necessity of program review but do not see it as a process that will affect their own professional practice, at least not in a positive way. Thus, the self-study is given over to selected staff and a few faculty members who, if they are lucky, will be given some release time to conduct it and write the report. The process becomes tedious, time consuming, and too often ultimately of little or no consequence. Because the focus is backward (on what has already happened) rather than forward (on what is possible), the review is a ritual, a special event that is not integrated into the work of the faculty. The opportunity for critical reflection—a chance to put our strong academic values of systematic inquiry and questioning of assumptions to use—is lost in the desire to get the thing done.

An Individualistic Culture

Organizational guru Peter Senge (2000) has called the academic culture the most individualistic among all professions. Another anonymous pundit has said this: "Academic departments are clans of arrogant experts seeking to sustain individual privilege at the expense of institutional goals." An overstatement? Sure. But I will bet that it is not much of a stretch to identify departments like this at your own institution. The problem is that in cultures like these, evaluation devolves to the individual, not to the academic unit. Faculty are rewarded on the basis of their contributions to their profession or discipline, not to their institutions.

Furthermore, as Fairweather (1996) has pointed out, when units *are* evaluated, they are normally judged on the basis of the sum of the performances of individual faculty—scholarly productivity, for example—not by measuring the unit's contributions to the larger good. The emphasis continues to be on individual merit, not collective value to the institutional mission. As a consequence, there is little faculty investment in activities that require collective action.

Neglect of Existing Resources and Instruments

Ask the staff of any institutional research office whether all the information they collect is put to good use and the answer will likely be a resounding "No!" Most institutions, even small ones, collect a great deal of information about themselves, their faculty, and their students, with much of it potentially useful for helping the institution know itself better. But far too much of it lies inert in a computer file or in someone's office. The problem is not that institutions collect too little information of use for program assessment but rather that too much energy goes into collecting that information, at the expense of analysis, interpretation, meaning making, and ultimately, informed decision making.

Consequential Validity

Consequential validity is a term made popular by Lee Shulman of the Carnegie Foundation for the Advancement of Teaching to refer to a phenomenon that is ignored far too often. Shulman suggests that besides the traditional ways to assess the validity and reliability of evaluation measures, we need also to consider evaluation's effect on behavior. For example, suppose that the police department in your town were evaluated, and publicly held accountable, on the basis of the number of arrests its officers made. Would the arrest rate go up or down? And what would this indicate about the quality of police work in town? Or to take an example from academe, suppose that teaching quality were judged on the basis of student ratings of instruction. Faculty would feel significant pressure to increase their student ratings and so would be tempted to do whatever was necessary to achieve this outcome. They would end up chasing the measures, thus making them the surrogate goal. Student ratings are at least somewhat manipulable, and in ways that might have little to do with teaching quality. Worse, focusing on ratings could actually serve as a *disincentive* to doing quality work if faculty felt that making changes in their courses would not be worth the almost-certain (albeit temporary) drop in student ratings that would follow. At the institutional level, the mentality of the marketplace has created a rush of institutions wanting to improve their tier status as defined by *U.S. News* rankings. The rankings have themselves become the goal, even if the criteria that define them have little to do with the true missions of the institutions. Ignoring the unintended consequences of using program and institutional measures has far-reaching—and mostly pernicious—effects.

PRESENT STATE OF PROGRAM ASSESSMENT: THE PEW STUDY

With all this in mind, and with the generous support of The Pew Charitable Trusts, my associate Judi Swingen and I set out to assess the state of program assessment in the United States. We reviewed the literature, called on personal networks of informants, and sent a mass-mailing to all campus provosts, inviting them to share examples of effective evaluation practice with us. (In our view, *effective evaluation* informs judgments of quality, which then lead to improved departmental functioning.) We eventually studied 130 institutions across the Carnegie categories, from community colleges to research universities. From some we merely collected information on paper, for others we conducted telephone interviews with key campus participants, and for eight institutions we wrote extensive case studies based on two-day visits to their campuses. A full account of this research study may be found in our 2000 monograph *Departmental Assessment: How Some Colleges Are Effectively Evaluating the Collective Work of Faculty* (Wergin & Swingen, 2000). A summary of this study follows, leavened somewhat by a distance of two years.

The bottom line: we found the state of program evaluation in higher education to be dismal indeed. Although there was plenty of evaluation going on, discontent with its usefulness was widespread. Among several roots of campus unhappiness, one was most striking: *most departments and most faculty failed to see the relevance of program evaluation and assessment to the work they did.* Our suspicions proved correct: *departmental assessment was largely a ritualistic and time-consuming affair, mandated from above, with few real consequences for the lives of the faculty.*

Despite this rather bleak landscape, we found some notable exceptions, places where unit evaluation informed judgments of worth and improved departmental functioning. So we studied them carefully to try and discern what made them stand out from the pack. We found it most useful to cut the analysis in three ways: first, the *necessary conditions* for effective evaluation; second, the institutional policies and practices that served as the *best predictors* of effectiveness; and third, the issues that remained *most problematic,* even at the exemplary institutions. I have expanded on each of these points briefly in the following paragraphs.

Necessary Conditions for Effective Evaluation

Certain institutional features seemed essential. Although they alone did not guarantee effective evaluation practice, they were necessary for it. We found examples of campuses where evaluation went nowhere, even with otherwise exemplary policies, and we traced the barriers to the lack of effective leadership in central academic administration, academic departments, or both. Campuses with successful practices concerned themselves first with building an institutional climate that supported quality improvement. For example, when the provost at a private research university with a history of successful program review was asked how he would go about initiating evaluation in another institution, he said this: "First I'd take a measure of the institution and its vision for the future. Is there ambition for change? I would try to find ways of articulating a higher degree of aspiration; if there weren't a strong appetite for this, then program review would be doomed to failure."

The following were the elements of a quality institutional climate as suggested by the institutions we reviewed:

A Leadership of Engagement

Leaders were able to frame issues clearly, put clear choices before the faculty, and were open to negotiation about what would inform these decisions. Of all the elements of organizational climate, this one was the most important.

Engaged Departments

Departments asked very basic questions about themselves: "What are we trying to do? Why are we trying to do it? Why are we doing it that way? How do we know it works?" In essence, these departments had created a climate for reflection.

A Culture of Evidence

There was a spirit of reflection and continuous improvement based on data, an almost matter-of-fact acceptance of the need for evidence as a tool for decision making. We found that a culture of evidence bore little if any relationship to the *amount* of evidence collected on campus; the key lay in what the institution *did* with the information collected.

A Culture of Peer Collaboration and Review

Common criteria and standards for evaluation had been negotiated based on a shared understanding by departmental faculty of one another's work. Successful departments had a truly collaborative culture: it was not necessarily that they all worked together, but rather that they had a clear sense of what their colleagues did, how the collection of individual work created a coherent whole, and how their own work contributed to that collective. (For an interesting discussion about these two conceptions of collaboration, see Bensimon & O'Neil, 1998.)

A Respect for Difference

Faculty roles had become differentiated, leading to a shift in focus away from work judged by standards external to the unit (merit) and toward the contribution of the faculty member to the mission of the unit (worth). This distinction between merit and worth is key to understanding the difference between the rampant specialization that has plagued academic departments in the last half-century and true role differentiation, which takes the departmental context into account.

Evaluation with Consequence

There was a tangible, visible impact on resource allocation decisions. This principle seems so obvious as to be almost not worth mentioning, yet it is amazing how something so obvious is so often ignored. We discovered also that "consequence" has its limits: the process cannot be *so* consequential that it turns into a high-stakes political exercise. When this happens, incentives for improvement are lost in the rush to look good.

Best Predictors of Effectiveness

The evidence could not be more clear: *what made program assessment effective in some places and not others was the extent to which institutional policies were flexible and decentralized.* We have all had this experience: we finish a study, put it away for a while, and then go back to it and find new insights. Such was the case here. We had become so engrossed in the details of our study that we missed this unmistakable fact, which was there all along: among the institutions meeting the necessary conditions just described, this one factor distinguished those where program review was effective from those where it was not. In these institutions, units were invited to define for themselves the critical evaluation questions, the key stakeholders and sources of evidence, and the most appropriate analysis and interpretation procedures.

A perfect example of this was a small private university that had been laboring under a traditional program review policy for years, one that mandated a comprehensive self-study for the department under scrutiny, completed according to criteria provided by the institution, and followed up by a visit from an external review team. No one at this institution was happy with the paltry return on investment of all this time and money, including the administration, so they decided to try something different: a "focused" program review, in which departments up for evaluation would first submit a proposal identifying the key issues they faced as a department and a plan for studying these issues. As negotiated with the department's dean, this proposal would serve as the basis for the department's self-study. The only institutionwide requirement was that departments include in their study an analysis of how they were contributing to the mission of the institution. After two years' experience with this experimental policy, the results were clear: departments taking the focused approach made significant changes to their collective work, whereas those taking the traditional comprehensive approach did not. Some administrators at this institution remained skeptical, suggesting first that the differences could be due to nothing more than the Hawthorne effect (that is, the units employing the experimental approach changed because of the attention they received from it), and then later that weak departments would use the focused approach merely to avoid scrutiny of their problems. It turned out that just the opposite was true: the strong departments were those that opted for the focused approach because they had a clearer sense of collective mission and saw in the new policy an opportunity to collect information that would help them become stronger.

There is a lesson to be learned from this story. Institutions should focus less on accountability for achieving certain predetermined results and more on how well units conduct evaluations for themselves and use the data these evaluations generate. Rewards then accrue to units that can show how they have used the assessment to solve problems and resolve issues. This notion is similar to "academic audit" procedures currently in widespread use in Western Europe and Hong Kong. Rather than attempting to evaluate quality itself, the focus instead is on processes believed to *produce* quality (Dill, 1999).

Remaining Problems

Criteria are the kinds of evidence collected as markers of quality, *standards* are the benchmarks against which the evidence is compared. We found many problems with the use of evidence, even in the most exemplary cases. It was not that institutions lacked information that could lead to judgments about departmental quality; our database contained examples of more than a hundred quality indicators, and these were distributed fairly evenly across input (faculty qualifications, FTEs), process (curriculum quality, demands on students), and output (faculty publications, student learning) criteria. The problem was that we found not a single case in which institutional procedures called for examining the quality of the evidence *itself*—not one! Instead, the underlying assumption seemed to be that the more information collected, the better, and that some kind of invisible hand would guide them to true and valid conclusions. This assumption can lead to bizarre consequences. Here is a particularly egregious example. At one flagship university, in order to allow for comparability with peer institutions the assessment of quality of instruction includes these criteria: number of full-time faculty (undergraduate and graduate), total students per full-time faculty (undergraduate, master's, and doctoral), and degrees awarded per faculty (baccalaureate, master's, and doctorate). How, one might ask, do these indices qualify as markers of instructional quality? What do they have to do with the quality of student learning?

Further, we found a widespread lack of clarity and agreement about what the standards should be. For example, what is the most appropriate standard for departmental research productivity? Departmental goals negotiated earlier with the dean? Last year's performance? The extent to which the scholarship fits in with school priorities or the university's strategic plan? Or how well the department stacks up against its peer departments in other institutions? Standards considered important or credible by one stakeholder group may not be considered important at all by another; thus, departmental quality will always be in the eye of the beholder. Just as it is dangerous to ignore issues of data quality, it is also risky to assume that all involved have the same implicit standards.

Similarities to Accreditation

At this writing (late 2001) I am engaged in another Pew-funded project, this one aimed at integrating reforms in how the eight regional accrediting associations assess the educational effectiveness of member institutions, particularly with respect to the use of student learning outcomes. Accreditors wrestle with many of the same issues that institutions face with program review. See if these barriers to effective accreditation practice, identified by regional accreditation staff and commissioners, look familiar when applied to program review:

- Institutions have not internalized the importance of assessing student learning outcomes. They do not think about creative ways of documenting student learning or about how good assessment is in their best interest. Assessment for the purpose of an institution's self-study is a mechanistic process and not part of the organic curriculum.

- There is widespread discomfort with defining the nature and role of professional judgment, and in particular a shared understanding of peer review.
- It is not clear what evaluation teams should look for. "Good" evidence does not exist for many important qualities—for example, whether good institutional decisions are being made.
- Accreditation is not sufficiently faculty-centered, and there are few rewards for faculty engagement. There is little collective responsibility for the curriculum, especially the general education curriculum.
- Conversation about outcomes has become political; measures have become surrogate goals. There is a tendency to back away from tough questions and move toward things that are easier to measure.
- Some institutions are too dependent. They want explicit standards, they interpret guidelines as tacit standards, and they wait to be told what the results of the accreditation review are.
- Assessment is often placed in the hands of those in the institution who know little about it.

RECOMMENDATIONS FOR GOOD PRACTICE

Some clear lessons emerge from these studies. Perhaps the clearest is that the most substantial barriers to educational quality and its improvement have to do with how we think about evaluation. As long as we maintain an "outside-in" focus, in which evaluation and assessment occur only when mandated externally, and a compliance mentality, which encourages a rote, get-it-over-with approach to evaluation, we will never become truly reflective about the work we do or achieve an academic culture in which attention to quality is part of the fabric. A second and equally important lesson is that good evaluation does not spring solely from a healthy organizational climate and thoughtful policies. Good evaluation practice, such as using evidence and standards appropriately, is a learned professional skill like any other. Third and finally, program review must be faculty-centered, focusing primarily on the most critical questions faculty have about the work they do. If the principal function of program review is the improvement of educational practice, then real change, deep change, must happen with the faculty. They are the ones ultimately responsible for maintaining academic integrity.

These recommendations suggest several important steps you can take to improve program review practices at your institution.

Consider Program Review an Integral Part of the Institution's Business

Communicate this forcefully. Do not pitch review as a strictly formative exercise, one that will have no bearing on budget decisions. Faculty will not believe that. Besides, program review has to be consequential if it is to be taken seriously. Just be sure that the review is not *so* consequential that the whole thing turns into a high-stakes political game. Be direct about how program review fits into the larger scheme of priority setting and resource allocation. Be as clear and open about this as you possibly can, particularly the kinds of evidence that will inform decision making and the role of program review as a source of evidence.

Make Program Review Policies as Flexible and Decentralized as Possible

Make sure these policies respect the wide variation in departmental missions and resources. Avoid any process that looks like a cookie-cutter approach to evaluation, one in which departments and programs all have to work from the same template. Adopt focused program review procedures, in which programs identify key questions and issues they most want to address. Be as flexible as possible with these, while at the same time being clear that departments must also address how they are adding value to the institution and otherwise contributing to institutional priorities.

Avoid the Five-to-Seven-Year Lapse

Avoid making program review something that departments and programs only think about every five to seven years. Although periodic and episodic reflection is a good thing, the temptation will be strong to return to business as usual after the review period is over. A much better plan is to consider program review as part of a more continuous round of program self-assessment. A formal periodic review becomes the basis for an action plan negotiated between the department and the dean. In subsequent years the department's annual report then takes the form of an abbreviated self-study, reporting on progress made on the action plan, unexpected opportunities or challenges, and ways the plan should be revised accordingly. This way, when the department or program comes up for its periodic formal review, the self-study could take the form of a somewhat more elaborate annual report, revisiting critical issues and identifying new ones.

Gain the Perspectives of an External Review Team

Maintain the practice, currently used by most institutions, of embellishing the departmental self-study with the perspectives of an external review team. With the rush to self-assessment and the use of outsiders primarily as "auditors" of departmental processes, something useful and special about peer review has been lost. The Latin root of *assessment* is *assidere,* or "to sit beside" (Braskamp & Ory, 1994). The function of external reviewers is indeed "to sit beside" the department, using their academic expertise to provide other perspectives and to invite their colleagues to see themselves—and their strengths, weaknesses, and opportunities—differently. They are not there to pronounce judgments but to ask questions and provoke discussion and reflection. Focus their work by giving them a list of questions in advance and identifying the evidence that might be available to them.

Appoint Faculty to Oversee Program Review Procedures

Maintain another widely used practice of appointing a faculty body to oversee program review procedures on campus and to receive and comment on departmental reports. Do not, however, fall into the trap of assuming that this group will be able to fulfill its responsibilities without training. There are two areas in particular where training will likely be needed: evaluating the quality of the evidence presented, and maintaining a systems view—that is, looking at a department or program not just for its own merits but also for the extent to which it adds value to the institution. Review committees also need to be clear that different programs add value in different ways, and thus use different standards and evidence.

Meet with the Department to Discuss Follow-Through

This is an absolutely critical step if the review process is to have any credibility or integrity. Invite members of the department to give their own interpretations of the review and what it means, and discuss as candidly as you can what you think its implications are. Discuss as well the process by which the review will be negotiated into a departmental action plan, including likely targets, responsibilities, and consequences. Use this forum as an opportunity to reinforce the value of the department to the institution, what you see as its main contributions, and how you are prepared to help it move forward.

CONCLUSION

The ultimate purpose of program review should be to create a learning organization, a place where what we do and how we do it gets as much attention as other kinds of learning. We need to be careful that we define *learning organization* in a way that fits the culture of the academy. Unlike the for-profit sector of society, higher education is not strictly about the business of continuous improvement—that is, change for the purpose of increasing productivity. Productivity is not solely what the academy is about. We are, however, about the business of critical reflection, where cultural and substantive change results from questioning the status quo. As Parker Palmer (1998) has written, a hunger exists among faculty for a genuine intellectual community, a setting that promotes reflection and intellectual discourse. At its best, program review can be the grist for these conversations.

References

Angelo, T. A. (1999, May). Doing assessment as if learning matters most. *AAHE Bulletin.* [www.aahe.org/bulletin/angelomay99.htm].

Bensimon, E. M., & O'Neill, H. F. Jr. (1998). Collaborative effort to measure faculty work. *Liberal Education, 84*(4), 22–31.

Braskamp, L. A., & Ory, J. C. (1994). *Assessing faculty work: Enhancing individual and institutional performance.* San Francisco: Jossey-Bass.

Burke, J. C. (1999, July-August). The assessment anomaly: If everyone's doing it why isn't more getting done? *Assessment Update, 11*(4), 4.

Dill, D. D. (1999). *Implementing academic audits: Lessons learned in Europe and Asia.* Unpublished manuscript, University of North Carolina, Chapel Hill.

Ewell, P. (1997, December). Organizing for learning. *AAHE Bulletin, 50*(4), 3–6.

Fairweather, J. S. (1996). *Faculty work and the public trust: Restoring the value of teaching and public service in American academic life.* Needham Heights, MA: Allyn & Bacon.

Gray, P. J., & Banta, T. W. (Eds.). (1997). *The campus-level impact of assessment: Progress, problems, and possibilities.* San Francisco: Jossey-Bass.

Palmer, P. J. (1998). *The courage to teach.* San Francisco: Jossey-Bass.

Senge, P. M. (2000). The academy as learning community: Contradiction in terms or realizable future? (pp. 275–300). In A. F. Lucas & Associates (Eds.), *Leading academic change: Essential roles for department chairs.* San Francisco: Jossey-Bass.

Wergin, J. F., & Swingen, J. N. (2000). *Departmental assessment: How some colleges are effectively evaluating the collective work of faculty.* Washington, DC: American Association for Higher Education.

Resources

Berberet, J., & McMillin, L. (Eds.). (2002). *A new academic compact: Re-envisioning the relationship between faculty and their institutions.* Bolton, MA: Anker.
A comprehensive look at faculty work in the Associated New American Colleges, based on the findings of task forces on professional development, institutional citizenship, and faculty workload. Includes several case studies at member institutions. Faculty-centered, with a refreshing absence of the usual warmed-over recommendations.

Dickeson, R. C. (1999). *Prioritizing academic programs and services: Reallocating resources to achieve strategic balance.* San Francisco: Jossey-Bass.
A different resource altogether from the Berberet and McMillin book. Here is presented a hard-nosed approach to making difficult decisions, based on ten criteria, with centrality to mission at the core. Useful as a way to think about quality indicators, less so for its assumptions about quantitative formulas and rational decision making.

Eckel, P., Green, M., & Hill, B. (1999–2001). *On change* (Vols. I–V). Washington, DC: American Council on Education.
If you have time to read only one source on change in higher education, this should be it. These five occasional papers are all based on an in-depth analysis of change at twenty-six diverse institutions, isolating forces for change in the academy, characteristics of institutions successful in undertaking change, and needed leadership qualities.

Ferren, A. S., & Slavings, R. (2000). *Investing in quality: Tools for improving curricular efficiency.* Washington, DC: Association of American Colleges and Universities.
The authors tackle one of the most difficult questions that academic administrators face today: How can we improve academic quality and cut costs at the same time? Includes chapters on financial modeling and tool development. Insightful and practical.

Kuh, G. D. (2001, May-June). Assessing what really matters to student learning: Inside the national survey of student engagement. *Change, 33*(3), 10–17.

A useful summary of what promises to be one of the most useful, if indirect, measures of student learning at the institutional level.

Massy, W. (2001, July-August). Making quality work. *University Business,* p. 44.
In this article Massy argues for adding a fourth responsibility to the usual trio—teaching, scholarship, and service—what he calls *quality work.* This model keeps the responsibility for maintaining academic integrity squarely in the hands of the faculty, but also requires them to be responsible for academic oversight.

Tierney, W. G. (1999). *Building the responsive campus: Creating high-performance colleges and universities.* Thousand Oaks, CA: Sage.
In this remarkable book, Tierney responds to the multiple demands for reform in higher education with fresh ideas, all based on research, and all bold.

CHAPTER 16

Leadership in Faculty Evaluation

MICHAEL THEALL

hapter Fourteen of this book discussed institutional leadership in evaluation and assessment, acknowledging the sensitivity of the issues and the complexities of initiating and maintaining best practice. I will not repeat the general guidelines outlined there. Rather, in this chapter, we will look specifically at perhaps the most sensitive and contentious area of evaluation in higher education: evaluation of the performance of faculty and its most thorny subtopic, the use of student ratings of instruction. These present a set of issues and problems in addition to those general concerns outlined earlier, but they also present a special set of opportunities. We will deal primarily with summative faculty evaluation as a matter of policy and practice, concentrating on the three groups of stakeholders most heavily involved in the process and on the systems necessary for effective faculty evaluation. The focus will be on effectively leading the complex process of making rational and fair decisions about the work of faculty and on the positive potential of combining evaluation with resources for improvement and development.

Evaluation without development is punitive. Development without evaluation is guesswork. Neither one works very well alone. Perhaps the most important overall consideration is to ensure that comprehensive systems for evaluation are developed, maintained, and properly used. *Comprehensive* systems incorporate policy, process, personal protection, and resources for development, along with public dialogue and all the human and machine resources required for efficient and effective data management. They also take into account the need to train those who interpret and use evaluative data. And in comprehensive systems, the operation, stability, and accuracy of the process itself is regularly assessed.

Comprehensive systems are based on a common understanding and the acceptance of five essential ingredients:

- There are institutionally and individually relevant underlying reasons for evaluation.
- The roles and goals of evaluation are appropriate.
- Mechanisms used to serve the administrative and data needs of the process are valid.
- The functions of the system are not punitive.
- The people involved are trustworthy.

Theall and Franklin (1990a, 1990b) argued for a systems approach over a decade ago and continue to believe that best practice can be achieved only through careful consideration of all the factors influencing evaluation. The best single source currently available on how to build such systems for faculty evaluation is Raoul Arreola's (2000) *Developing a Comprehensive Faculty Evaluation System,* and the processes and techniques outlined in that text apply to broader efforts as well. Interestingly, Arreola makes specific note of two main obstacles to effective faculty evaluation: faculty resistance and administrator apathy. He says that "of the two threats to success, administrator apathy is the more deadly" (p. 21). Leadership in faculty evaluation requires active participation and support from top administrators as well as their willingness to let others become leaders. Leaders are willing to invest the time and effort necessary to understand and promote good practice.

If the sensitive nature of evaluation and the impact of institutional differences were not enough, there are serious technical and operational issues that can strengthen or destroy evaluation. Many writers have raised questions about the uneven psychometric quality of evaluation instruments and have provided guidelines for sound practice that would help to avoid problems (for example, Arreola, 2000; Braskamp & Ory, 1994; Centra, 1993). There has also been active exploration of the impact of certain widely discussed variables on student evaluations (for example, the work of Greenwald & Gillmore, 1997, and others on grades and ratings), the misuse and misinterpretation of evaluation data (for example, Franklin & Theall, 1989; Theall & Franklin, 1990a, 1990b), and the impact of context on evaluation (Feldman, 1998). Though the conclusions of this research are similar and support the case for sound evaluation based on established research, theory, and practice, these same results, because they legitimately present cautions, have unfortunately been seen by some as evidence against any and every kind of evaluation.

When you add to this the intensely personal nature of teaching, the admitted difficulties in precisely defining or representing excellent performance (as opposed to adequate, fair, or poor performance), and the power of evaluation to influence careers and professional advancement, it is easy to understand the extent of the dialogue, debate, and dissension over the past four decades as faculty evaluation and the collection and use of student-provided data have become ubiquitous. Ironically, while rigorous research on evaluation and student ratings has increasingly shown these data to be reliable, valid, and useful (for example, Marsh, 1987), the tone of anti-evaluation personal opinion has become more and more strident and the anecdotes more frequent (for example, Sproule, 2000), often without any substantial evidence (as documented in Theall, 1998).

Many issues arise. Some, like the quality of instruments used or the usefulness of the reports provided, are legitimate, practical issues. Other complaints have less merit. There have been arguments against ratings as a violation of academic freedom (Haskell, 1997) although rebuttals have quickly been offered (Theall, 1997). I have even encountered a person who claimed that evaluation was a violation of his constitutionally guaranteed freedom of religion. The frequency of his religious activities, he said, made it impossible to hold office hours. Because the evaluation form contained an item about the instructor being "punctual in meeting classes and keeping office hours" and students had provided negative feedback about his absences, he felt his religious freedom was in jeopardy. Connolly (2000, p. 75) in a discussion of academic freedom has warned against constructing arguments that "are just so much window dressing meant to disguise entrenched privilege." The same caveat applies here but in this case it is to avoid such arguments against faculty evaluation. Such excesses only serve to damage efforts to improve practice, and leadership in this case involves public refutation of this kind of claim by all stakeholders.

Colleague Jennifer Franklin has often said that she has never had a faculty member come to her office to complain about his or her high ratings, saying that they were invalid and unreliable or that students were incapable of providing useful information. Conversely, many of my colleagues in evaluation and I have had faculty voice complaints about others' high ratings, suggesting they were the result of leniency, mere popularity, making learning "fun," and various other sins against hallowed tradition. One person with whom I worked on a teaching awards committee even expressed the conviction that nominations of two faculty members should be dismissed because their grade profiles were too high—such profiles being indisputable indications of bad teaching. Such arguments may never disappear, but their importance is that they are symptoms of deeper problems.

POTENTIAL PROBLEM AREAS AND SUGGESTIONS FOR AVOIDING THEM

In order to promote good practice, leaders must be aware of potential problems, and in faculty evaluation, there are many. Awareness of these potential difficulties can help leaders to take preventative actions such as opening a dialogue, involving key stakeholders, and building trust.

Differing Views of General Evaluation Roles and Goals

To succeed, any system must be based on common understanding and consensus about basic issues among the primary stakeholders. Thus, knowing who the stakeholders are and bringing them together for open discussion of these issues is a critical first step. Leaders must convene and guide productive discussion among stakeholders with the clear objective of reaching consensus about basic issues.

Poor Definition of What Will Be Evaluated

The traditional triumverate of teaching, scholarship, and service is probably insufficient given the complexity of contemporary faculty work. Not only do these domains need clear definition; other areas of evaluation also need clear description. Entrepreneurship, grant support, technology involvement, the scholarship of teaching, and community service are just a few of the ill-defined areas. As research on the scholarship of teaching (Kreber, 2001) has shown, there is little agreement about what these areas are and how they can be measured or evaluated. Leaders must emphasize clear local definition of the areas to be evaluated so that process and practice can be relevant, meaningful, accurate, and accepted.

Too Hasty Adoption of Process, or the Not-Invented-Here Syndrome

This is a corollary to the preceding problem. Effective faculty evaluation must reflect local context and conditions, but it must not be so insular or parochial that it ignores principles of good practice. For example, institutions often make one of two common methodological errors: adopting a commercial or other institution's student ratings questionnaire without changing it or creating an entirely local questionnaire without validation. In either case, the validity of the instrument is in question. Leaders at all levels must balance the need for incorporating local context with reliance on established research, theory, and practice.

Overreliance on Student Ratings of Teaching

As Seldin's research (for example, 1999) has shown, student ratings are now used at well over 90 percent of U.S. institutions. Often, these results are the only data used to make summative decisions about teaching. A wide range of data is necessary to inform these decisions properly, and even if such data are properly collected and used, they present only part of the overall faculty evaluation picture. Leaders must ensure that sufficient and appropriate information about each aspect of faculty performance is gathered.

Invalid or Unreliable Interpretation and Use of Data

Even the best data can be misinterpreted and misused. Franklin and Theall (1989) studied faculty and administrators' knowledge, opinions, and attitudes about student ratings. They found a significant lack of knowledge about information basic to correct interpretation of typical ratings reports. In addition, they found that negative attitudes about evaluation, ratings, and students were significantly correlated with this lack of knowledge. Faculty evaluation cannot succeed if those who interpret and use data make technical or conceptual errors. Leaders must promote training or other activities that both stress established research and theory and prepare decision makers to use the information generated by the local system correctly.

Poor Data Management, Analysis, and Reporting Formats

As a corollary to the preceding point, it is critical to have technical and human systems that ensure top-quality data collection and handling, appropriate and complete analysis, compilation of understandable and useful reports, and regular review of the systems themselves. A standardized process for data collection, development of a complete database, establishment of norms or performance criteria, attention to security and control of confidential information, and training of the individuals involved are some of the ways you can prevent problems. Leaders must view evaluation as a systematic and cyclical process that relies on quality control, regular review and revision, and constant attention to detail, and they must assign qualified people to the tasks.

Misinformation, Mythology, and Mistrust

There are several layers of complexity here. As the public debate on evaluation, and particularly student ratings, has shown, critics ignore several decades of rigorous and replicated research in favor of weak individual studies and personal opinions about evaluation (for details, see Theall, 1998, 1999b; Theall, Abrami, & Mets, 2001). Misinformation breeds mistrust of the intent of evaluation, and such mistrust can be exacerbated by poor institutional decision making and related behaviors. For example, department chair requests for reports of ratings results to the third decimal place (received by myself and colleagues) suggest gross overinterpretation of the precision of the data and a willingness to make arbitrary decisions about merit. When lip service is given to teaching but reward systems are inclined toward research and publication, it quickly demonstrates which is the more important. Leaders must demand knowledgeable use of evaluative information, require fair and equitable rewards for performance, and model informed and rational decision-making processes.

Insufficient Resources

Questionnaires and computers are not enough. Most important to effective practice is the combination of supportive administrators, committed faculty, and expert practitioners, *all of whom have leadership responsibilities.* Because the field is faculty evaluation, the person most responsible for coordinating the system should possess deep knowledge of the research and theory that underlie the field. That person should constantly be able to interact with faculty and students, provide training and support to users, work with stakeholders to arrive at decisions about policy and practice, make revisions and improvements in the system, and represent the needs of the system to top administrators. *Leaders must commit to shared leadership and the provision of resources necessary to preserve and protect good practice.*

STAKEHOLDERS IN FACULTY EVALUATION

Our general stakeholder model (see Figure 14.1 in Chapter Fourteen) places faculty, academic administrators, and students at the core of assessment and evaluation. In faculty evaluation, they are even more intimately and regularly involved in developing, operating, and using the systems that provide data for decision making. In an interesting parallel to established research in communications, the stakeholder model resembles Rokeach's (1964) model of human belief systems, an atomic structure in which "primitive" beliefs are at the core and "peripheral" and "inconsequential" beliefs are in the outer rings. Primitive beliefs are the result of social consensus or deep personal experience (for example, "The object you are now looking at is called a book" or "I am a good person") and are extremely resistant to change. But if they are changed, the individual's entire belief system can be affected. Peripheral and inconsequential beliefs are often easily changed (for example, one's loyalty to a brand of bottled water), and such changes do not affect the entire belief system.

As we approach the core of the model, we find more and more "primitive" stakeholder beliefs that are formed by immersion in a social context with shared opinions (for example, opinions arising from an individual being a member of the university, a department, or the professoriate) as well as by personal experience. However, it is often the case that easily changed peripheral beliefs of those less involved with day-to-day practice can result in process, policy, and procedures being forced on those who hold the strongest beliefs about evaluation, those who are most intimately involved with it. This leads not to smooth operation or productive change but rather is a prescription for disaster. The least destructive outcome is often what Bloom (1998) has called *reform without change.* Human effort and fiscal expenditure lead to little more than frustration and the increasingly sure sense that any and all evaluation efforts are an intrusive waste of time. The essential point about this parallel is that it demonstrates both the position and the strength of beliefs of various stakeholders. Failure to recognize the dynamic nature of the models can seriously affect regular and productive practice. *Effective leaders work across the levels of stakeholders while maintaining the autonomy necessary to ensure locally acceptable practice, and they must strive to maximize the positive impact while minimizing waste and pointless conflict.*

Stakeholders at the outer levels of the model are much less involved in day-to-day process. Exhibit 16.1 indicates the degree or level of involvement of the stakeholder groups. Faculty, administrators, and students are regularly involved in, and responsible for, the evaluation process. Trustees, accreditation agencies, and other institutional administrators have some degree of involvement, but only in certain areas. At levels 3 and 4, there is little consistent participation, but there is always the potential for a significant impact.

PRINCIPLES FOR EFFECTIVE FACULTY EVALUATION

In Chapter Fourteen, I presented seven principles for effective leadership in evaluation. These seven principles are repeated here, but with specific suggestions for their application to the development and success of faculty evaluation systems.

Include Stakeholders in the Dialogue, Strive for Public Dialogue and Consensus

Pay special attention to the three primary stakeholders (faculty, administrators, students) because day-to-day practice is the province of these groups. As much as possible, find out the interests and needs of other stakeholder groups in order to build into the system some means of responding to their needs. For example, develop the ability to combine evaluation and assessment data for accreditation purposes and develop and maintain a substantial database for analyses requested by trustees (see Exhibit 16.1).

Determine the Most Appropriate Roles and Goals for Evaluation at the Outset

These are the starting points for any successful system. The roles and goals must be consistent with institutional history and directions and must serve individual, unit, and institutional needs. They are, so to speak, the preamble to the evaluation constitution. *Never initiate a system claiming that its purpose is formative only to move it gradually into summative use.* It is entirely possible for one system to serve both purposes well, but the distinction must be made clear and the integrity of formative data never violated.

Understand the Literature, Accept Its Findings, Ignore Anecdote

Not everyone involved must be an expert, but a failure to rely on genuine internal and external expertise opens the system to error, subsequent misinterpretation and misuse,

EXHIBIT 16.1. **Stakeholder Degree of Responsibility for Evaluation Activities.**

	Inclusion of Stakeholders	Evaluation Roles, Goals	Knowledge of Literature	Developing Process	Ensuring Standards	Data Use, Interpretation	Resources for Improvement
Level 1 stakeholders:							
Faculty	5	5	5	5	5	5	5
Administrators	5	5	5	5	5	5	5
Students	4	3	2	3	4	3	4
Level 2 stakeholders:							
Trustees	4	3	2	2	4	3	4
Accreditors	3	3	4	1	4	3	2
Other administrators	3	3	2	2	3	3	4
Level 3 stakeholders:							
Local and state legislators	2	2	2	1	2	1	2
Other institutions	1	2	3	1	2	1	2
Parents	1	2	1	1	2	1	1
Federal government	1	1	1	1	2	1	1
Organizations	1	1	1	1	2	1	1
Level 4 stakeholders:							
Employers	1	1	1	1	1	1	1
Researchers (in fields excluding evaluation)	1	1	1	1	1	1	1
Journalists, writers	1	1	1	1	1	1	1
The public	1	1	1	1	1	1	1

Note: 5 = extensive; 4 = frequent; 3 = regular; 2 = occasional; 1 = infrequent and a lack of credibility that will ultimately destroy the opportunity for productive use of the system.

Develop, Adapt, Adopt a System That Serves All Stakeholders

This is not an overnight process. Rather, it is iterative and cyclical with several stages of approval and oversight along the way. Field tests of instruments and process are critical, and reports of these tests must be presented to stakeholders to ensure that they accept the system. Anything less than an open discussion of system performance can be seen as hiding an ulterior motive.

Establish, Maintain, and Ensure Standards of Quality in the System

Regular validation and reanalysis of data are critical not only to maintain current and accurate norms but also to demonstrate a commitment to continuous quality. This applies not only to ratings data but to the mechanisms and procedures used to evaluate all other aspects of faculty performance. Develop standards for judging research, service, and other factors along with teaching.

Ensure Fair and Accurate Interpretation and Use of Evaluation Results

Training is critical. Students should be informed about how and why their input is important and how to represent their opinions most accurately. Peers need training on reliable and valid processes for classroom observation or other methods of recording their observations. Administrators and those on decision committees need to use properly both quantitative data and—even more so—the kinds of qualitative data found in teaching portfolios.

Couple Evaluation with Resources for Recognition, Reward, Improvement, Development

Individual teaching awards are appropriate, but equally important is recognizing effective practice at the unit level. Evaluation data can also identify generally excellent teachers and those who are especially skilled at certain techniques. These teachers can be recognized and share their expertise in new faculty or mentoring programs. They can work with the staff of teaching centers or similar units to develop workshops and other activities that support faculty, teaching assistants, and even courses on teaching and learning. Such practices build an institutional repertoire of teaching excellence that serves all constituencies and is a tangible demonstration of the use of evaluation for improvement. Faculty are generally individuals who have strong intrinsic motivation (Theall, 1999a). Rewarding their performance by asking them to share their skills is often a more powerful motivator than a financial reward.

CONCLUSION

In sum, leadership in faculty evaluation, as in any other arena, requires all concerned to commit to rigorous inquiry, public consensus, and standards of quality and to accept the right of others to express their opinions about individual performance. The systems that are put in place should not drive evaluation efforts but should be their servants. If these systems are well-constructed and supported, they can efficiently and effectively provide the raw material for valid and reliable decision making. If they are combined with resources for improvement, they can be powerful agents for change and excellence. If they are left to chance, the result will be chaos. Faculty, students, institutions, and higher education deserve no less than the best systems and the best practice.

References

Arreola, R. A. (2000). *Developing a comprehensive faculty evaluation system* (2nd ed.). Bolton, MA: Anker.

Bloom, S. (1998). Structure and ideology in medical education: An analysis of resistance to change. *Journal of Health and Social Behavior, 29,* 294–306.

Braskamp, L. A., & Ory, J. C. (1994). *Assessing faculty work.* San Francisco: Jossey-Bass.

Centra, J. A. (1993). *Reflective faculty evaluation: Enhancing teaching and determining faculty effectiveness.* San Francisco: Jossey-Bass.

Connolly, J. M. (2000). The academy's freedom, the academy's burden. *NEA Higher Education Journal, 16*(1), 69–82.

Feldman, K. A. (1998). Reflections on the effective study of college teaching and student ratings: One continuing quest and two unresolved issues. In J. C. Smart (Ed.), *Higher education: Handbook of theory and research.* New York: Agathon Press.

Franklin, J., & Theall, M. (1989, March 31). *Who reads ratings? Knowledge, attitudes, and practices of users of student ratings of instruction.* Paper presented at the seventieth annual meeting of the American Educational Research Association, San Francisco. (ED 306 241).

Greenwald, A. G., & Gillmore, G. R. (1997). Grading leniency is a removable contaminant of student ratings. *American Psychologist, 52*(11), 1209–1217.

Haskell, R. E. (1997). Academic freedom, tenure, and student evaluations of faculty: Galloping polls in the twenty-first century. *Educational Policy Analysis Archives, 5*(6). [http://olam.ed.asu.edu/epaa/v5n6.html].

Kreber, C. (Ed.). (2001). *Scholarship revisited: Perspectives on the scholarship of teaching.* New Directions for Teaching and Learning, no. 86. San Francisco: Jossey-Bass.

Marsh, H. W. (1987). Student evaluations of university teaching: Research findings, methodological issues, and directions for future research. *International Journal of Educational Research, 11,* 253–388.

Rokeach, M. (1964). Images of the consumer's mind on and off Madison Avenue. *ETC: A Review of General Semantics, 21*(3).

Seldin, P. (1999). *Changing practices in faculty evaluation.* San Francisco: Jossey-Bass.

Sproule, R. (2000). Student evaluation of teaching: A methodological critique of conventional practices. *Education Policy Analysis Archives, 8*(50). [http://epaa.asu.edu/epaa/v8n50.html].

Theall, M. (1997). On drawing reasonable conclusions about student ratings of instruction: A reply to Haskell and to Stake. *Education Policy Analysis Archives, 5*(8). [http://epaa.asu.edu/epaa/v5n8c2.html].

Theall, M. (1998). Colloquy, colloquia, colloquiarum: A declining form, a questionable forum. *Instructional Evaluation and Faculty Development, 18*(1&2) [http://www.uis.edu/~ctl/sigfed.html].

Theall, M. (Ed.). (1999a). *Motivation from within: Approaches for encouraging faculty and students to excel.* New Directions for Teaching and Learning, no. 78. San Francisco: Jossey-Bass.

Theall, M. (1999b). Why student ratings? *Advocate, 1*(3), 5–8.

Theall, M., Abrami, P. C., & Mets, L. (Eds.). (2001). *The student ratings debate: Are they valid? How can we best use them?* New Directions for Institutional Research, no. 109. San Francisco: Jossey-Bass.

Theall, M., & Franklin, J. (1990a). *Student ratings of instruction: Issues for improving practice.* New Directions for Teaching and Learning, no. 43. San Francisco: Jossey-Bass.

Theall, M., & Franklin, J. L. (1990b). Student ratings in the context of complex evaluation systems. In M. Theall & J. Franklin (Eds.), *Student ratings of instruction: Issues for improving practice.* New Directions for Teaching and Learning, no. 43. San Francisco: Jossey-Bass.

Resources

Arreola, R. A. (2000). *Developing a comprehensive faculty evaluation system* (2nd ed.). Bolton, MA: Anker.

This is the best practical guide to developing and implementing a comprehensive evaluation system. It contains a thorough overview, a grounded discussion of operational issues, samples of instruments and process, and proven techniques for generating dialogue and consensus. If you can have only one book to guide faculty evaluation, this should be it.

Bloom, S. (1998). Structure and ideology in medical education: An analysis of resistance to change. *Journal of Health and Social Behavior, 29,* 294–306.

This is an interesting view of the change process and a sobering description of reform without change—that is, the futility of responding to the need to alter or improve something without implementing any long-lasting or meaningful changes. In conjunction with Birnbaum's text on fads, it alerts readers to the need for making change relevant and connecting to stakeholder frames of reference.

Braskamp, L. A., & Ory, J. C. (1994). *Assessing faculty work.* San Francisco: Jossey-Bass.

Centra, J. A. (1993). *Reflective faculty evaluation: Enhancing teaching and determining faculty effectiveness.* San Francisco: Jossey-Bass.
These are two of the most substantial recent books on the general topic of faculty evaluation. They are comprehensive and discuss a range of issues. Although more theoretical than the Arreola text, they are excellent additions to a basic library on the topic.

Feldman, K. A. Research syntheses in *Research in Higher Education.*
In a series of over a dozen articles published from 1976 through 1998, Feldman has provided the most in-depth reviews of specific issues relating to faculty evaluation and student ratings of instruction. These definitive works have explored all of the main issues raised as potential biases to faculty evaluation.

Feldman, K. A., & Paulsen, M. B. (1998). *Teaching and learning in the college classroom* (2nd ed.). New York: Simon & Schuster.
This is the most comprehensive collection of readings on the topic. It is broad and substantial, and includes landmark items like Boyer's definitions of the four kinds of scholarship and Chickering and Gamson's seven principles, and also incorporates some of Feldman's studies of college teaching and Paulsen and Feldman's work on creating a campus teaching culture. This is probably the best single compendium of the research on college teaching.

Marsh, H. W. (1987). Student evaluations of university teaching: Research findings, methodological issues, and directions for future research. *International Journal of Educational Research, 11,* 253–388.
This review of the faculty evaluation literature remains the most cited work of its kind. Its depth and breadth are unusual and its conclusions are supported by virtually all major researchers in evaluation.

Miller, R. I. (1987). *Evaluating faculty for promotion and tenure.* San Francisco: Jossey-Bass.
This text lists ten useful characteristics of effective systems that were the basis for many of the recommendations in this chapter. It covers legal issues and administrative roles, and discusses promotion and tenure procedures.

Ryan, K. E. (Ed.). (2000). *Evaluating teaching in higher education: A vision for the future.* New Directions for Teaching and Learning, no. 83. San Francisco: Jossey-Bass.
This recent volume looks ahead to possible changes in practice based on issues such as the increasing demand for distance and on-line learning and the effects of new definitions of validity.

Scriven, M. (1967). Methodology of evaluation. In R. Tyler, R. Gagne, & M. Scriven (Eds.), *Perspectives of curriculum evaluation.* Skokie, IL: Rand McNally.
   If there is a seminal article on modern evaluation, this is it. Scriven's terminology and approach are the basis for contemporary evaluation and assessment.

Theall, M., & Franklin, J. (1990). *Student ratings of instruction: Issues for improving practice.* New Directions for Teaching and Learning, no. 43. San Francisco: Jossey Bass.
   This was one of the first discussions of evaluation to focus on context and the systematic nature of evaluation and the requirements it imposes. Several aspects of evaluation from ethical issues to disciplinary differences are presented in the chapters of this New Directions volume.

CHAPTER 17

The Mission-Driven Faculty Reward System

ROBERT M. DIAMOND

An institution's greatest asset is its faculty. In order for any important institutional change to occur, it is imperative that faculty be actively involved from the planning stages through implementation. Faculty bring creative, culturally sensitive ideas to the planning process, and as key change agents they ultimately must participate in any sustainable institutional change. Many administrators struggle with the challenge of engaging faculty time and interest in institutional change initiatives.

How do we tap the energy and insights of our best faculty for the purposes of institutional improvement? We know that a key determinant in how faculty allocate their time and energy is the institution's reward system. Although there will always be exceptions, most faculty devote their professional energies to those activities that are recognized and rewarded by their institution, their colleagues, and their discipline. Unfortunately, higher education has a long tradition of saying one thing and doing another with respect to faculty rewards. For example, although teaching figures prominently in the mission and vision statements of every college and university, research and publication ("scholarship") have been the primary basis of promotion and tenure decisions at most institutions. National studies have shown that faculty consider the reward system on their campus to be woefully out of balance and in need of refocusing (Gray, Froh, & Diamond, 1992; Gray, Diamond, & Adam, 1996). In general, three specific contradictions are evident in faculty reward systems and practices on most campuses:

- There is a disconnect between what colleges and universities say is important and the activities that are rewarded in their tenure and reward systems.
- Many forms of scholarly work are not recognized as such.
- Much of what has been recognized as scholarship has had little demonstrable impact in significance or in moving the field ahead—two characteristics that most experts agree are essential to scholarly work.

Important curriculum reform, innovation in discipline-based pedagogy, application of new technologies, and community outreach are not activities that can be undertaken and completed in short periods of time. They require an extended commitment on the part of the individual faculty member and the full support of the institution. That support includes recognizing such activities in the faculty reward system, given certain conditions and qualifications. As an academic leader, it is one of your most important responsibilities to ensure that the passion and energy of your faculty are invested in areas of priority for your institution. You can do this most directly by carefully structuring the faculty reward system to reinforce your institutional mission and vision.

In this role you have a number of responsibilities. If change is required, it is the role of the appropriate administrator to take several steps: place the needed revision on the institutional agenda; propose a change process; facilitate the development of appropriate mission and priority statements at all institutional levels; understand the important roles that faculty, department chairs, and academic disciplines play in the change process; and develop an active process that systematically reinforces the goals and criteria that are developed.

This chapter will discuss the characteristics of a mission-driven faculty reward system, identify a number of key issues you will need to consider, and provide you with a framework for describing scholarly work. A checklist to help you determine how well your present faculty reward system supports the mission and vision of your institution is provided along with an annotated bibliography of useful resources.

CHARACTERISTICS OF THE MISSION-DRIVEN FACULTY REWARD SYSTEM

The mission-driven faculty reward system has several key characteristics.

Institutional Priorities and Mission Are Directly Supported by System Criteria

All promotion, tenure, and faculty review guidelines and policy documents should clearly relate the criteria and the weighting of activities to the institutional mission and vision. This kind of linkage requires individual schools, colleges, and departments to have clearly articulated mission and priority statements that fit into and reinforce the institutional mission and vision. Relating rewards directly to institutional priorities suggests that both will change over time but that they will necessarily change together and in an acknowledged, public fashion.

Features of the Reward System Are Always Consistent

The mission-driven reward system's characteristics should be consistent whether for annual review, promotion, tenure, or posttenure review. The professional evaluation of faculty should be an ongoing process, with all phases interrelated and mutually supporting. Consistent criteria and characteristics can reduce the work of documentation for faculty and eliminate contradictions in the review process.

All Institutional Documents Relating to Faculty Rewards Are Consistent and Integrated

The initial document on which others build is the institutional policy guidelines. It is here that the mission, vision, and priorities of the institution are articulated and related to faculty rewards. Important ground rules are established at this level. For example, definitions of scholarly, professional, and creative work might appear in these guidelines. As policy guidelines move from the institution to the school or college, and finally to the department level, they become more detailed and discipline-specific. Sample documents can be found in Diamond (1999), *Aligning Faculty Rewards with Institutional Mission: Statements, Policies, and Guidelines,* and Trower (2000), *Policies on Faculty Appointment.*

The Reward System Is Sensitive to Differences

Several important differences should be recognized:

- *Different strengths of faculty.* Increased complexity in academic units requires a synergy of different interests, strengths, and expertise. Increased specialization coupled with more interdisciplinary work means that differences between faculty will increase.
- *Differences between the disciplines.* Faculty practice, theories about knowledge, and understanding of scholarship differ in important ways from discipline to

discipline. Although some fields are comfortable with scholarship in a scientific context, others are more devoted to outreach activities, practice, or pedagogy. Statements on faculty work from over twenty-five disciplines can be found in *The Disciplines Speak* (Diamond & Adam, 1995, 2000), a two-volume series published by the American Association for Higher Education.

- *Different missions and priorities in individual academic units.* The priorities of a department or program are determined by the nature of the institution in which the unit exists, the disciplines represented, and the historical focus or strength of the unit. For the faculty reward system to be coherent, it is crucial that each department develop its own mission and priorities in the context of the school or college and institutional statements and that the policies developed at all levels acknowledge and make room for individual differences.

SOME GUIDANCE ON CREATING A MISSION-DRIVEN REWARD SYSTEM

Here are some principles to guide your creation of a mission-driven faculty reward system.

Avoid Formulas

There is no set pattern for how faculty should divide their time between teaching, research, and service activities. The common approach of 40:40:20 does not allow for faculty specialization, differences between the disciplines, recognition of individual faculty strengths, and the fact that the scholarly, professional, and creative work of faculty (scholarship) can take place in the context of teaching, service, or outreach.

Make Faculty Central in Revising the Reward System

Faculty must be key developers of the revised faculty reward system and should participate actively in developing school, college, and departmental and program mission statements as well as the guidelines and standards on which they will be judged in relation to these statements.

Explore the Establishment of Part-Time Tenure Line Appointments

There is little question that the six- to seven-year tenure time frame creates difficulties for many young faculty—particularly women—because it tends to coincide with the time when they are starting families. Under these circumstances, the problems of balancing a professional career with a personal life can be extremely difficult. Data show (Williams, 1999) that men are more likely than women to be granted tenure. Although women's tenure rate was the same in 1992 as it was in 1975, there was a 56 percent increase in the tenure rate for men over the same period. In a *Change* magazine article, "A Half-Time Tenure Track Proposal," Robert Drago and Joan Williams (2000) presented a strong case for the option of a part-time tenure line position as well as specific guidelines for such a policy. With this option, a faculty member could request less than a full-time position for a period of time. The tenure line would be modified accordingly. For example, such faculty members might be asked to pay an appropriate portion of their health benefits, with the salary money that they would release going to the academic unit to cover staff replacement costs.

This approach makes sense for both the faculty member and the institution; it allows for professional continuity and supports young faculty while maintaining their institutional commitment. In addition, as Drago and Williams (2000) so clearly point out, "Current practices artificially reduce the talent pool by eliminating a hefty percentage of qualified candidates (most mothers) from reaching for or achieving tenure" (p. 49).

Educate Faculty Serving on Promotion, Tenure, and Faculty Review Committees

All too often faculty serving on these committees are unaware of key institutional priorities, especially if they have been recently rearticulated or refocused. Education is crucial when guidelines are changing. The guide *Serving on Promotion, Tenure, and Faculty Review Committees* (Diamond, 2002) can assist you.

Anticipate Resistance

You can expect that any effort to expand the scope of scholarly work and modify the reward system will be challenged by some faculty. Simply put, some faculty have benefited from the traditional model. It is important that faculty in these fields (primarily in the sciences) understand their role in determining the priorities of their academic unit. If traditional research is an important activity to their mission, the existing emphasis will most likely remain in place. Also expect that some faculty may resist implementation of new policies. Because some resistant faculty may be assigned as mentors to junior faculty or may be asked to serve on promotion and tenure committees, their resistance must be dealt with directly. In some cases this may require removing these individuals from key leadership roles.

Help Faculty Prepare for Professional Review

Advising faculty of institutional mission, vision, priorities, and professional review practices should begin with the interviewing process and continue through orientation and across the academic career. A number of publications are available to help faculty document their activities and prepare for review. These are described later in this chapter.

PROMOTION AND TENURE POLICIES AND PRACTICES

As colleges and universities face increased demand to reduce costs and at the same time improve the quality of academic programs and services, the tenure system has been a key discussion point. Perceived by critics as the device by which inefficiency is maintained and incompetence is tolerated, tenure will continue to be a lightening rod in the foreseeable future. In one way or another you will undoubtedly be involved in the debate.

Many of the perceptions on which the debate is based are myths and misconceptions. Certainly, the fact that department chairs, deans, and chief academic officers have failed to make hard personnel decisions in the past has not helped, but misinformation and misunderstanding about tenure abound. In a presentation at the 2001 Conference on Faculty Roles and Rewards sponsored by the American Association for Higher Education (AAHE), Steven G. Olswang, Cheryl A. Cameron, and Edmond Kamai, building on an extensive review of the legal history of tenure, identified a number of tenure facts and fictions (see Exhibit 17.1.).

EXHIBIT 17.1. What Tenure Does and Does Not Do.

What Tenure Does
- Provide protection of academic freedom (intellectual expression and inquiries)
- Provide for employment security through a conditional employment contract
- Facilitate the employment of highly qualified people in a highly competitive market

What Tenure Does Not Do
- Protect against termination
- Allow faculty to say anything they want in the classroom
- Protect against a salary reduction
- Allow faculty to research any topic they choose
- Guarantee adequate space or equipment for research
- Permit faculty unrestricted authorization to submit requests for external funds
- Allow faculty unrestricted speech at faculty meetings
- Protect faculty from being punished for public statements about an institution
- Give faculty ownership in everything developed in the course of employment
- Give faculty the right to engage in unlimited outside consulting
- Allow faculty to determine the courses they will teach
- Give faculty the exclusive right to determine the content of their courses

Source: Olswang, Cameron, & Kamai, 2001.

As you become involved in discussions about tenure, keep in mind that regardless of whether your institution calls it tenure or not, it must have a way of protecting and facilitating scholarship, a system by which it will evaluate its faculty, and a means by which it will retain its best faculty. These are the basic functions of a tenure system.

The tenure process is a powerful socializing force. What an institution requires at tenure time in the way of productivity and merit speaks volumes about its values and priorities. To ensure future success and vitality, institutions need to work hard to support the very best faculty through the tenure process. Promotion and tenure policies and practices should address a number of factors:

Stopping the Tenure Clock

There needs to be a procedure that allows the tenure clock to be stopped when a faculty member is asked to participate in an important institutional initiative or to assume an administrative position that would preclude him or her from completing all the requirements for tenure in the specified time. As discussed earlier, a provision for a part-time tenure option can also serve when there are life situations that place special demands on the faculty member, such as family emergencies or new responsibilities.

Citizenship and Collegiality

Determination of how effectively a faculty member works in his or her department and with other faculty must be based on clear criteria, standards, and documentation. Balancing departments' prerogative to select candidates who are good departmental or institutional citizens with individuals' rights is a delicate matter. Judgments about a candidate's interactions with others can be part of promotion and tenure deliberations if expectations are made clear and if solid evidence is provided for decision making.

Interdisciplinary or Collaborative Work

Policy statements should enumerate the criteria that will be used and the range of information that should be presented. This is particularly important with the anticipated growth in interdisciplinary work and other kinds of collaboration.

A Grandfather Clause

Because policies and criteria change, it is unfair to modify the standards and procedures for faculty already in the system without providing them with an opportunity to remain under the system in place at the time of hiring. This is particularly true for faculty in the final years of the tenure cycle.

Information Received While Review Is in Process

Quite often materials are published, reviews are obtained, or information about the candidate's work is received during the review process. Because this information, whether positive or negative, can be extremely important, policies for handling it should be established.

SOME GUIDANCE ON THE TENURE ISSUE

Here are some principles to guide you in your consideration of the tenure issue.

Be Familiar with the Work of Boyer and Rice

Although not all institutions or disciplines are comfortable with the four forms of scholarship described in Ernest Boyer's (1990) *Scholarship Reconsidered,* the Boyer-Rice model has made an important contribution to our thinking about scholarship and is in use on many campuses and in most disciplinary statements. Building on the work of Eugene Rice, Boyer proposed four general forms of scholarship:

- *Discovery:* advancing knowledge through original research
- *Integration:* synthesizing and reintegrating knowledge to reveal new patterns and relationships
- *Application:* using new knowledge in professional practice
- *Teaching:* transforming knowledge

Do Not Start from Scratch

Although each institution must develop its own faculty reward criteria and procedures, a wide range of resources are available that can make the process easier. These include checklists for framing policy statements, sample institutional policy statements, and guides for review committees and candidates (see the Resources at the end of this chapter).

Be Sure That Promotion and Tenure Guidelines Are Accurate

Promotion and tenure guidelines should describe the criteria that will be used to judge scholarly, professional, and creative work. Although academic disciplines may not agree about what to call the work of faculty (some use *scholarship,* others professional or creative work), there is fairly consistent agreement about the characteristics of scholarly work. Building on our earlier work and that of Eugene Rice and Ernest Boyer and of Charles Glassick, Mary Taylor Huber, and Gene Maeroff (1997), we propose a definition that can be easily modified for inclusion in institutional, school or college, and department or program statements. This descriptive approach has the advantage of providing a base on which all statements are developed, ensuring coherence and coordination of standards.

An activity or work will be considered scholarly if it meets the following criteria:

EXHIBIT 17.2. Criteria for Scholarly Activity.

- It requires a high level of discipline-related expertise.
- It is conducted in a scholarly manner with clear goals, adequate preparation, and appropriate methodology.
- The work and its results are appropriately and effectively documented and disseminated. This reporting should include a reflective critique that addresses the significance of the work, the process that was used, and what was learned.
- It has significance beyond the individual context.
- It breaks new ground or is innovative.
- It can be replicated or elaborated on.
- The work—both process and product or result—is reviewed and judged to be meritorious and significant by a panel of one's peers.

It will be the responsibility of the academic unit to determine if the activity or work itself falls within the priorities of the department, school or college, discipline, and institution.

Cultivate an Assessment-Rich Culture on Your Campus

Developing a campus climate that is committed to collecting and using data and information is another contemporary leadership challenge. Assessment and evaluation are an integral part of institutional improvement and professional growth. For faculty members data collection and use are key activities for ongoing excellence in teaching and scholarship. Although greater attention may be paid to assessment activities at career points such as promotion, tenure, or contract renewal, assessment for continuous improvement has come to be viewed as an ongoing activity throughout the professional career.

Exemplary teachers constantly collect and use information about how well instructional goals are being met, about students' degree of preparation and motivation to learn, about student attitudes and persistence, and about changes that are taking place in disciplinary pedagogy. This practitioner knowledge helps teachers to identify (and, ideally, avoid) potential problems, but the process serves two other functions as well. First, assessment data can provide documentation for a faculty member's professional portfolio. Second, information and data can contribute to the faculty member's development in the area of the scholarship of teaching.

Use Student Course Ratings as One Component in Teaching Evaluation

When they were first introduced, student rating instruments were designed to provide faculty with information that they could use to improve courses while still under way. They were *not* designed to serve as the primary means for measuring teaching effectiveness or determining merit pay awards. As an evaluative tool, student ratings have a number of inherent limitations:

- They measure student learning only from the perspective of the student.
- They are usually administered at the end of the semester, after many unhappy or unsuccessful students have dropped the course.
- Mean ratings on all items tend to be above average.
- Many items assume traditional forms of teaching, such as the lecture.
- They may not be sensitive to the challenges faced by faculty teaching difficult or unpopular courses with large numbers of underprepared students.

On many campuses student ratings are overused (every course, every semester). When students see little evidence of change in response to their evaluations, they may not invest the time to provide useful or specific information. Students should be informed about how the information they provide will be used, and if specific actions are taken as a result of the information, what they are.

Although student ratings offer valuable information about students' perceptions, they should not be the only or most important source of information about a faculty member's teaching. You will find a number of excellent resources on evaluating teaching referenced in Chapter Sixteen.

CREATING A MISSION-DRIVEN FACULTY REWARD SYSTEM: GETTING STARTED

The initial, crucial step in revising the faculty reward system on your campus is addressing the relationship between your institutional mission and vision and the policies and practices by which faculty are rewarded for carrying them out. Whether or not activities are already under way, a good place to start is in the review of present perceptions and procedures. The checklist shown in Exhibit 17.3 has been designed for this purpose. It may also prove helpful to trustees and presidents who are considering questions they wish to ask about the present status of the faculty reward system at their institutions.

CONCLUSION

The importance of the faculty reward system and how well it supports the vision and mission of an institution cannot be overestimated. Without a close relationship between the two, the quality of your academic programs and teaching will suffer, faculty will feel they are caught between a rock and a hard place, morale will suffer, resources will be wasted, and improvement will be impossible to accomplish.

Fortunately, there now exists a wide body of literature and experience on which to build. Accreditation agencies, disciplinary associations, and professional groups are also actively supporting efforts to make the tenure, promotion, and faculty reward systems more fair and appropriate at institutions and for each faculty member. There is no single model. What makes sense for one institution may be totally inappropriate for another. Although we know fairly well what makes a quality system, it will be up to you to ensure that the reward criteria you use are the right ones for your institution.

In this chapter we have outlined the characteristics to look for, identified many of the available resources, and listed important questions to ask. As you move ahead, keep in mind that a key to developing a quality system is faculty involvement in its development. For a system and process to work, faculty *must* have ownership. Develop it from the beginning.

EXHIBIT 17.3. **Institutional Priorities and Faculty Rewards Checklist.**

	Yes	No	To some degree	Don't know
1. Does the institution's mission statement clearly identify its priorities and unique characteristics?	——	——	——	——
2a. Do administrators, faculty, and staff believe in and support the statement?	——	——	——	——
b. Were they actively involved in its development?	——	——	——	——
3. Do individual units or departments have clearly articulated mission statements that identify their specific priorities?	——	——	——	——
4. Do such statements mesh with and support the institutional mission statement?	——	——	——	——
5a. Do the members of the unit support its mission statement?	——	——	——	——
b. Were they involved in its development?	——	——	——	——
6a. Are the priorities of the institution and the department understood by new faculty?	——	——	——	——
b. Are they clearly articulated at every point in the hiring process?	——	——	——	——
7a. Are units evaluated on how well they meet the specific goals defined in their mission statement?	——	——	——	——
b. Are resources and awards allocated accordingly?	——	——	——	——
8a. Does the faculty reward system (promotion, tenure, and merit pay) actively support the articulated mission statements of the institution and of the unit in which faculty work?	——	——	——	——
b. Is good teaching important in the equation?	——	——	——	——
c. Are there clearly defined requirements for determining good teaching?	——	——	——	——
9a. Do faculty understand the criteria by which they will be judged?	——	——	——	——
b. Are they assisted in preparing the necessary documentation of their work?	——	——	——	——
c. Are faculty provided with a clear statement addressing faculty rewards procedures, requirements, and criteria?	——	——	——	——
10. Is there a mentoring system for new faculty?	——	——	——	——
11. Is the faculty reward system sensitive to the differences among the disciplines?	——	——	——	——

EXHIBIT 17.3. Institutional Priorities and Faculty Rewards Checklist. (continued)

	Yes	No	To some degree	Don't know
12. Is the faculty reward system sensitive to the differences in the strengths of individual faculty?	—	—	—	—
13. Is the faculty reward system sensitive to the differences in departments?	—	—	—	—
14. In the faculty reward system, does the weight given to the same activity differ among individual faculty?	—	—	—	—
15. In the faculty reward system, does the weight given to the same activity differ between units?	—	—	—	—
16. Does the system recognize the range of important activities that faculty in specific units perform?	—	—	—	—
17. Does the system allow individual faculty reward criteria to be modified based on assignment?	—	—	—	—
18. Do faculty and unit heads consider the evaluation process fair?	—	—	—	—
19a. Are data provided to faculty throughout their careers to help them identify areas of strength and those in need of improvement?	—	—	—	—
b. Is a formal procedure in place to provide assistance and support when needed?	—	—	—	—
20. Do faculty who are assigned specific instructional or service projects (curriculum design, community support) receive guidance about how these activities will be reviewed and recognized by the faculty reward system?	—	—	—	—

References

Boyer, E. L. (1990). *Scholarship reconsidered: Priorities for the professoriate.* Princeton, NJ: Carnegie Foundation for the Advancement of Teaching.

Diamond, R. M. (1999). *Aligning faculty rewards with institutional mission: Statements, policies, and guidelines.* Bolton, MA: Anker.

Diamond, R. M. (2002). *Serving on promotion, tenure, and faculty review committees: A faculty guide* (2nd ed.). Bolton, MA: Anker.

Diamond, R. M., & Adam, B. E. (Eds.). (1995). *The disciplines speak: Rewarding the scholarly, professional, and creative work of faculty* (Vol. I). Washington, DC: American Association for Higher Education.

Diamond, R. M., & Adam, B. E. (Eds.). (2000). *The disciplines speak: Rewarding the scholarly, professional, and creative work of faculty* (Vol. II). Washington, DC: American Association for Higher Education.

Drago, R., & Williams, J. (2000, November-December). A half-time tenure track proposal. *Change,* pp. 47–51.

Glassick, C. E., Taylor Huber, M., & Maeroff, G. I. (1997). *Scholarship assessed: Evaluating the professoriate.* San Francisco: Jossey-Bass.

Gray, P. J., Diamond, R. M., & Adam, B. E. (1996). *A national study on the relative importance of research and undergraduate teaching at colleges and universities.* Syracuse, NY: Syracuse University.

Gray, P. J., Froh, R. C., & Diamond, R. M. (1992). *A national study of research universities on the balance between research and undergraduate teaching.* Syracuse, NY: Syracuse University.

Olswang, S. G., Cameron, C. A., & Kamai, E. (2001, February). *The new tenure.* Presentation made at the American Association for Higher Education's Conference on Faculty Roles and Rewards, Tampa, FL.

Trower, C. A. (Ed.). (2000). *Policies on faculty appointment: Standard practices and unusual arrangements.* Bolton, MA: Anker Publishing.

Williams, J. (1999). *Unbending gender: Why family and work conflict and what to do about it.* New York: Oxford University Press.

Resources

Administrative Issues: Policies and Guidelines

American Council on Education. (2000). *Good practice in tenure evaluation: Advice for tenured faculty, department chairs and academic administrators.* Washington, DC: American Council on Education, American Association of University Professors, and United Education Insurance. A practical guide to issues that should be addressed and the characteristics of a quality review process. Includes a number of checklists and a section on supporting unsuccessful candidates.

Arreola, R. A. (1995). *Developing a comprehensive faculty evaluation system.* Bolton, MA: Anker. A practical handbook of protocols, worksheets, and assessment instruments that can be used in developing a faculty evaluation system. Also includes a number of case studies and a formula for determining merit pay.

Chait, R., & Trower, C. (1997). *Where tenure does not reign: Colleges with contract systems.* Washington, DC: American Association for Higher Education.
Provides a good overview of institutions using alternate forms of faculty contracts and includes a discussion of policy implications and impact.

Connell, M. A., & Savage, F. G. (2001). The role of collegiality in higher education, tenure, promotion, and termination decisions. *Journal of College and University Law, 27*(4), 833–858.
An excellent review of arguments for and against considerations of collegiality in higher education employment. Includes a review of relevant case law.

Diamond, R. M. (1999). *Aligning faculty rewards with institutional mission: Statements, policies, and guidelines.* Bolton, MA: Anker.
A practical guide to what should be included in institutional, school or college, and departmental promotion and tenure guidelines, as well as in union contracts. Addresses the issues of institutional mission and vision statements. Examples from numerous institutions throughout.

Diamond, R. M., & Adam, B. E. (Eds.). (1993). *Recognizing faculty work: Reward systems for the year 2000.* New Directions in Higher Education, no. 81. San Francisco: Jossey-Bass.
Provides a model for relating the faculty reward system to institutional priorities as they are enacted at the level of the academic unit. Includes a number of campus case studies and discusses intrinsic rewards and the professional portfolio.

Elman, S. E., & Marx Smock, S. (1985). *Professional service and faculty rewards: Toward an integrated structure.* Washington, DC: National Association of State Universities and Land-Grant Colleges.
Addresses issues related to recognizing professional service in the faculty reward system. Provides a rationale for including this work in the recognition system and describes the range of faculty activities that falls in this area.

Seldin, P. (1993). *Successful use of the teaching portfolio.* Bolton, MA: Anker.
Primarily for administrators, from department chairs to presidents. This volume presents the use of the teaching portfolio in an institutional context. Discusses implementation of a campuswide portfolio assessment plan for faculty as an integral part of the reward system. Includes sample portfolios.

Seldin, P., & Associates. (1990). *How administrators can improve teaching.* San Francisco: Jossey-Bass.
Thirteen nationally prominent educators talk about improving teaching by developing institutional policies and practices that support and reward good teaching.

Tierney, W. G., & Rhoads, R. A. (1993). *Enhancing promotion, tenure and beyond: Faculty socialization as a cultural process* (ASHE-ERIC Higher Education Report No. 6). Washington, DC: George Washington University.
Discusses how faculty values are shaped and how these values are reflected in faculty roles. Discusses promotion and tenure as part of a socialization process.

Wergin, J. F. (1994). *The collaborative department: How five campuses are inching toward cultures of collective responsibility.* Washington, DC: American Association for Higher Education.
Includes five detailed cases illustrating different approaches to shifting the focus of incentives and rewards from the individual faculty member to the department. Pulls together central issues that the five institutions—Kent State University, Rochester Institute of Technology, Syracuse University, University of California-Berkeley, and University of Wisconsin-Madison—confront in dealing with collective responsibility.

What Is Scholarship?

Boyer, E. L. (1990). *Scholarship reconsidered: Priorities for the professoriate.* Princeton, NJ: Carnegie Foundation for the Advancement of Teaching.
An ideal introduction to rethinking the definition of scholarly or professional work. This work has provided a basis for much of the change in thinking about scholarship at colleges and universities. An excellent volume for launching campus discussion.

Diamond, R. M., & Adam, B. E. (Eds.). (1995). *The disciplines speak: Rewarding the scholarly, professional, and creative work of faculty* (Vol. I). Washington, DC: American Association for Higher Education.

Diamond, R. M., & Adam, B. E. (Eds.). (2000). *The disciplines speak: Rewarding the scholarly, professional, and creative work of faculty* (Vol. II). Washington, DC: American Association for Higher Education.
These two volumes include statements from twenty-five scholarly and disciplinary associations describing the range of faculty work in their fields.

Glassick, C. E., Taylor Huber, M., & Maeroff, G. I. (1997). *Scholarship assessed: Evaluating the professoriate.* San Francisco: Jossey-Bass.
The follow-up to Ernest Boyer's *Scholarship Reconsidered* focuses on definitions and documentation of scholarship. Includes results from the 1994 survey on institutional change in the faculty reward system.

Preparing for Review: Faculty Guides

Diamond, R. M. (1995). *Preparing for promotion and tenure review.* Bolton, MA: Anker.
Designed to help faculty prepare for promotion and tenure review. Makes recommendations about questions to ask and materials to provide. Includes a number of examples on preparing documentation.

Gelmon, S., & Agre-Kippenhan, S. (2002). Promotion, tenure, and the engaged scholar: Keeping the scholarship of engagement in the review process. *AAHE Bulletin, 54*(5).
Provides excellent and down-to-earth advice to faculty preparing for tenure and promotion review. The suggestions are practical and would be helpful to anyone in the process. Get it out to your faculty.

National Education Association. (1994). *Entering the profession: Advice for the untenured.* Washington, DC: National Education Association.

Designed for faculty on unionized campuses, this guidebook pays particular attention to the formal appeal process.

Licata, C. M., & Morreale, J. C. (1997). *Posttenure review: Policies, practices, precautions.* Washington, DC: American Association for Higher Education.

An excellent introduction to the topic. Includes a number of specific case studies and a set of useful recommendations.

Lynton, E. A. (1995). *Making the case for professional service.* Washington, DC: American Association for Higher Education.

Discusses the importance of professional service and describes how and under what conditions this work should be considered scholarly. Five case studies are included.

Morreale, J. C., & Licata, C. M. (1997). *Posttenure review: A guidebook for academic administrators of colleges and schools of business.* St. Louis: AACSB—The International Association of Management Education.

Although as the name implies this work focuses on schools of business and management, much of it would be useful to any institution developing a posttenure review system.

Seldin, P. (1997). *The teaching portfolio: A practical guide to improved performance and promotion/tenure decisions* (2nd ed.). Bolton, MA: Anker.

This faculty guide describes a rationale for the use of a teaching portfolio and provides detailed recommendations for assembling such a dossier. Includes a number of representative samples.

Whicker, M. L., Kronenfeld, J. J., & Strickland, R. L. (1993). *Getting tenure.* Thousand Oaks, CA: Sage.

Traces the steps in the traditional promotion and tenure process. The authors emphasize the politics of promotion and tenure.

Serving on Promotion and Tenure Committees

Braskamp, L. A., & Ory, J. C. (1994). *Assessing faculty work.* San Francisco: Jossey-Bass.

Describes the expanding role of faculty assessment and the limitations of present practices, examines how assessment can be used to improve the quality of teaching and learning. A discussion of the scholarly nature of faculty work is followed by useful sections on relating institutional expectations to assessment and on collecting and organizing evidence of teaching effectiveness.

Centra, J. A. (1993). *Reflective faculty evaluation: Enhancing teaching and determining faculty effectiveness.* San Francisco: Jossey-Bass.

An extension of his 1979 publication on determining faculty effectiveness, with a significant addition in the area of teaching portfolios, self-reporting, and the role of colleagues and department chairs in teaching evaluation. Includes an in-depth review of specific techniques and sources of information.

Diamond, R. M. (2002). *Serving on promotion and tenure and faculty review committees: A faculty guide* (2nd ed.). Bolton, MA: Anker.

A handbook for faculty, this guide outlines problem cases and provides committees with procedural recommendations designed to make the process fair to the candidate and easier on the committee. Includes procedures for addressing a number of issues from collegiality to joint appointments and other nontraditional assignments.

Edgerton, R., Hutchings, P., & Quinlan, K. (1991). *The teaching portfolio: Capturing the scholarship in teaching.* Washington, DC: American Association for Higher Education.

Provides a rationale for the teaching portfolio and discusses documents that might be presented. Includes examples of teaching-related materials and reflective statements and discusses the process of getting started in the use of this approach to documenting teaching.

Hutchings, P. (1993). *Campus use of the teaching portfolio: Twenty-five profiles.* Washington, DC: American Association for Higher Education.

Offers detailed accounts of what twenty-five campuses are doing with teaching portfolios. Each profile answers the same set of questions, including what the portfolio consists of, how it is evaluated, and the impact the portfolio process has had on teaching and learning. Includes public and private institutions of various sizes and missions.

Recommended Web Sites

American Association for Higher Education. Faculty roles and rewards. [http://www.aahe.org/FFRR/ffrrnew2.htm].

Provides an overview of the American Association for Higher Education's Faculty Role and Rewards initiative. The site includes program and conference announcements, publications, and contact information.

Ohio State University. (1999). Faculty handbook. Academic administration: TIU administration. Appointments, promotion, and tenure document. [http://oaa.ohio-state.edu/handbook/i_apt-doc.html].

Describes the criteria and procedures for faculty appointment, advancement, and rewards at Ohio State. It includes a prototype document outline for use by departments and an outline of what should be included in a departmental mission statement.

Ohio State University Board of Trustees. (1996, March). Actions of the board of trustees. [http://www.osu.edu/osu/newsrel/Archive/96–05–03_Trustees:_Actions_of_the_Ohio_State_University_Board_Trustees].

Of particular interest are the comments of Nancy Rudd, vice provost, and Sebastian Knowles, associate professor of English, about the intent and anticipated effects of the revised rules.

Ohio State University Board of Trustees. Criteria for appointment, reappointment, and promotion and tenure. [http://trustees.ohio-state.edu/rules47/ru47–02.html].

A statement from the board of trustees that relates faculty appointments, promotion, and tenure to the mission of the institution and provides basic guidelines.

Oregon State University. Faculty handbook: Promotion and tenure guidelines. [http://osu.orst.edu/staff/faculty/handbook/promoten/spromoten.htm].

Oregon State's promotion and tenure guidelines. These include a discussion of faculty responsibilities in light of the mission of the institution, an expanded definition of scholarship, and an outline of the review process.

Oregon State University Faculty Senate. (1998). Task force on posttenure review: Final report. [http://osu.orst.edu/dept/senate/tfoptr.report.htm].

An excellent report by a task force on posttenure review. You will find brief reviews of related Oregon State Board of Education policies and of the existing faculty review system (PROF) as well as a summary of posttenure review at five other institutions. The report also discusses academic freedom, lists the desired characteristics of an effective posttenure review system, and makes recommendations.

Portland State University Office of Academic Affairs. (1997). Promotion and tenure guidelines. [http://www.oaa.pdx.edu/OAADOC/PTGUIDE/Introduction/introduction.html].

An example of a recently revised set of promotion and tenure guidelines. Of particular interest is the section on scholarship.

Syracuse University. Self-study: Report 1—Faculty roles. [http://syracuse.edu:80/selfstudy/report1/facultyroles.html].

Syracuse University was one of the first research institutions in the country to revise its mission and faculty reward system to reflect a balance between research and teaching. Report 1 identifies topics addressed in the action plans required from all schools and colleges and provides interesting reports on how different populations (faculty, chairs of promotion and tenure committees, department chairs, and deans) perceive the impact of these initiatives.

Syracuse University. Self-study: Report 2—Faculty. [http://syracuse.edu:80/selfstudy/report2/faculty.html].

Sets forth the steps of the revision process and provides insight into what has been accomplished and what yet needs to be done.

University of Southern California. The Project on Faculty Performance and Compensation. [http://www.usc.edu/dept/education/fpc/].

The project aims to develop alternative models, aligned with school and college missions, for evaluating tenured faculty performance and for compensation and incentives. Links to publications, presentations, current projects, and a survey instrument. Codirectors of the project research team were Estela Mara Bensimon and Linda Serra Hagedorn.

Vincow, G. (1994, January). Annual report to the faculty. [http://syracuse.edu:80/acadaff/1994faculty.html#modify].

This link takes you directly to Section K, "Modifying Faculty Roles and Rewards." The entire report is of interest, however. It details the process that Syracuse University followed to change institutional priorities and describes the conception of a student-centered research university.

Initiatives are described in detail and the attributes of a student-centered course, the role of assessment, and the relationship of research scholarship to undergraduate instructors are all addressed. The report concludes with a list of changes (outcomes) that can be anticipated if this shift in institutional goals is successful. A number of useful citations and references are included.

Virginia Commonwealth University. Faculty roles and rewards policy. [http://www.vcu.edu/ireweb/policies/facroles.htm].
This extremely useful document provides the rationale behind a revised faculty roles and rewards policy. It includes the goals of the system and the guidelines that are to be followed at the school, college, and department levels.

PART FIVE

Other Issues

If the next generation of citizen leaders is to be engaged and committed to leading for the common good, then the institutions which nurture them must be engaged in the work of the society and the community, modeling effective leadership and problem solving skills, demonstrating how to accomplish change for the common good.

A.W. Astin and H.S. Astin. *Leadership Reconsidered: Engaging Higher Education in Social Change,* Battle Creek, MI: W.K. Kellogg Foundation, 2000, p. 2.

CHAPTER 18

Supportive Financial Systems

SUSAN STETSON CLARKE

As a leader in higher education, you are doubtless engaged in continuing institutional change, including the transformation of learning experiences and the elements that support such transformation. Key among these elements is the institution's financial system, which has an essential role in quantifying institutional goals and measuring progress toward them. Financial systems begin with the people who use and manage them and include budgets and their components, financial and managerial reports (particularly the measures used to track institutional change), and audited financial statements.

Institutional change depends in part on the working relationships between financial professionals and those in academic areas, student affairs, and development, all of whom operate in different contexts and often do not have positive images of one another. Because of the nature of their work, financial professionals have to be concerned with cost analysis and control, but others may perceive them as indifferent to teaching, learning, research, student concerns, donor relationships, and so on. For their part, financial professionals may perceive those in other roles as unrealistic and unwilling to concern themselves with costs and the institutional impact of policy decisions. *Successful change calls for leaders who are willing to seek solutions to mutual, complex problems and put aside professional territorialism, differences in jargon, misunderstandings, and fears.* Participants at a conference sponsored by the Association of American Colleges and Universities and the National Association of College and University Business Officers concluded that it is possible and in fact necessary to find common ground on which academic and financial leaders can meet.

This chapter identifies the components of financial systems and the characteristics that can help to promote, enable, and support sustainable institutional change. The characteristics do not depend on specific hardware or software but rather on the behavior of individuals, the decisions they make about the treatment of financial information, and their interactions with one another. Also included is a discussion of some issues currently of interest in financial and business operations related to ongoing changes in higher education. The chapter concludes with suggestions for effective working relationships.

FINANCIAL SYSTEM COMPONENTS

Financial systems contain several key components.

People

All systems are dependent on people to create, maintain, and adjust them. Financial professionals are those staff members who ensure that monetary transactions are accurately recorded and who create, manage, and prepare financial records. They may be on the central staff and report to the chief business officer, or they may be located in academic departments or administrative units; in the latter case they serve as the interface between the department and the central financial staff. Most work with faculty and others in the institution to develop budgets, monitor expenses, manage investments, arrange debt financing, and in general make sure that business transactions are appropriately conducted and accounted for.

It is a particular challenge to achieve successful working relationships between financial professionals and faculty and academic staff. This accomplishment can begin with a recognition of differences between faculty and staff when it comes to change. Faculty qualities that may help or hinder change include the following:

- They are loyal to their academic discipline, divisions, or other working groups, some of which may have their own endowments and external supporters.
- They see themselves as the heart and central driving force of the institution, as a community of scholars.
- They encourage change from within, fostered by collegial persuasion rather than external pressure or administrative direction or compliance.
- They evaluate outcomes based on flexible, subjective peer judgment that may not be measurable.
- They may not be generally aware of or concerned with the financial aspects of the institution and consequently may feel left out of financial decisions that can affect their projects.

Financial staff qualities that may help or hinder change are these:

- They are part of a workforce that has different expertise and plays different roles than faculty.
- They feel their work is important to the functioning of the institution and the well-being of students, faculty, and staff.
- They expect to respond to changes required or dictated by others.
- They expect centralized planning and regular administrative supervision, as well as quantitative outcome standards in making evaluative judgments.

In order for academics and financial professionals to work together successfully on behalf of the institution, each side must make clear, nonjudgmental, and respectful acknowledgment of the value of the other's very different approach. Both must also strive for creativity and modification of their usual working styles.

Budgets

Budgets are ways of quantifying institutional plans by identifying anticipated resources and allocating them in accordance with the plans and priorities of the institution. Budgets include annual operating plans and capital project budgets, such as plans to provide for buildings and equipment whose useful lives extend over several years. Budgets need to be adaptable to the changing needs of the institution yet adhere to basic principles established by the leadership, such as ensuring that expenditures do not exceed revenues.

Financial Reporting

Internal reports are tailored to the needs of the leadership for advancing their goals. They include expenditure reports, enrollment data, salary ratios, tuition revenues, and various comparisons and benchmarks that are key to measuring progress toward goals. Analyses may include, for example, percentage of the budget spent on programs that have high priority in the strategic plan, data on the courses and degree programs that generate resources and those that consume them, ratio of central expenditures compared with direct expenditures of academic programs, and percentages of professional graduates failing licensing examinations compared with other institutions. Other types of reporting are required for specific purposes, generally externally imposed—regulatory reporting, tax reporting, and charitable soliciting reporting.

Audited Financial Statements

Independent evaluations are made of the information contained in the financial reports, including whether significant aspects of operations are accurately represented, institutional policies are consistent, and generally accepted accounting principles are adhered to.

The standards for and scope of the external audits depend on whether the institution is independent or public and on the level of federal funds received. Many institutions arrange for financial statements to be audited by a certified public accounting firm in accordance with generally accepted auditing standards established by the American Institute of Certified Public Accountants, and they publish these statements with the auditor's opinion. Institutions with significant federal funds are required to be audited in accordance with Office of Management and Budget Circular A-133 and standards established by the Comptroller General of the United States. Some public institutions are not required to issue stand-alone financial statements because their financial and federal award information is included in the statements and reports issued for the higher education system or for the local or state government.

DESIRABLE CHARACTERISTICS OF FINANCIAL SYSTEMS

When you consider the financial systems at your institution, look to see if they have the ten characteristics described in this section. These are important for supporting the goals of the institution and the changes it has determined to make. If you find that your systems lack these qualities, work with the chief financial officer and others to change them so they will be more supportive of your institution's needs.

Effective Financial Professionals

Whether they are in the central office or departmental units, those who track financial records and perform analyses can play a significant role in academic reform and other changes. They can explore the interrelationships between the mechanics of operations and strategic initiatives, such as enrollment management and tuition pricing, stream-lined procedures and customer satisfaction, curriculum content and career placement, and so on. Their talent and creativity can be used to frame questions, perform analyses, and develop meaningful measurement. They can design and deliver reports that quantify the operational impact of various courses of action. Truly effective financial professionals should be customer-oriented and have consensus-building skills. They need to have the ability and willingness to adapt to new circumstances and changing needs. They should have an understanding of the big-picture issues and be eager to learn on a continuing basis.

One university with a retention problem for first-year students assigned a team of faculty and finance staff to determine what dropouts actually cost in foregone tuition revenue for subsequent years and develop a reasonable model for increased revenue with improved retention. Their collaboration resulted in the introduction of a voluntary first-year encouragement and seminar program. At the end of two years, the program had a positive outcome: a significant increase in retention and increased tuition revenue.

Less Competition, More Institutional Perspective

In effective financial systems, competition is discouraged and an institutional perspective is encouraged. Budgeting and financial reporting should be structured so that the institution's goals are advanced rather than those of any individual unit. For example, a university with a budgeting process that allocates funding to each department based on the number of students enrolled in its courses will have great difficulty in consolidating duplicative courses; the resource allocation system will need to be changed to reward collaboration and cooperation.

Openly Shared Financial Information and Guidelines

Financial information that is open and shared rather than hidden and personally brokered is essential to effecting change. This openness fosters organizational learning and results in better decision making. Likewise, the rules for budgeting and resource allocation should be open and widely understood and embraced. If rules are not articulated and known to many, it is difficult to address inequities and other dysfunctions, both real and perceived.

As part of greater sharing of information, many institutions are introducing software that enables people outside the financial staff to get answers to financial questions. Some systems are set up so that data and information can be input by a broad base of users. Departmental staff have the training, access, and authority to process transfers or enter financial commitments, thus increasing departmental control and redirecting accounting office staff efforts to more central matters.

A Central Database

Colleges and universities should be integrated by common accounting systems so that financial data reside in one database that is the source of all budget and financial performance discussions and decisions. Related to the database should be common definitions and use. Definitions should use widely accepted language and avoid business terms or academic idiosyncrasies.

Data warehouses are a relatively new form of central database. The software allows users to create the information they need to address current issues, rather than compile data from previous reports; ask questions and get facts immediately, rather than work with anecdotes; and gain a better understanding of the data structure and the interrelationships among various types of financial information.

If you use separate departmental financial record keeping—with different definitions, periods of time, and so on—to support individual positions, it may foster competition that is counterproductive to institutional interests. In contrast, shared data can foster understanding of what lies behind the numbers and help resolve opposing perspectives.

Consistency Between Financial Documents

Some institutions prepare budgets in one presentation format and internal reports in another. Then they have to convert year-end results to comply with accounting standards and presentation of financial statements. The language is simpler and communications are clearer when the same terms and formats are used in budgets and financial statements. Senior management and trustees can compare budgets with actual performance when the actuals are the same as the financial statements.

Avoidance of Netting

Netting is the presentation of the numbers that result after deductions. This practice can be misleading. For example, showing numbers for changes in tuition revenues that have scholarships deducted from them may not reveal changes in enrollment and financial aid, each of which has its own dynamic. Likewise, showing auxiliary revenues net of expenses, after deduction of expenses, gives no indication of the different markets for auxiliary services and the expenses associated with them.

Meaningful Measurements

Establishing appropriate measures for determining the extent of change is likely to be an iterative process. The question "What do we want to achieve?" has to be converted into a measure, which will also call for identifying the necessary data and which method to use to collect them. Collection will likely have to take place in a systematic and continuing way, with regular evaluation.

Measurements should have several important characteristics. They should be clearly connected to organizational goals and strategies; be objective, quantifiable, and measurable; be easily understood and communicated; use indicators that reflect what is envisioned and what has already occurred; be linked to databases and institutionwide information; and allow for comparisons with other organizations when relevant.

Accountability and Control

There must be accountability in a financial system. A reward system can only be meaningful if it makes clear who is to be praised and who should be blamed. Accountability should be consistent with responsibility, and individual performance should be assessed using accountability factors.

If there is widespread accountability, there is much less need for control across the institution. For example, with full accountability, accounting staffs do not have to verify availability of funds before purchasing departments place orders. In addition, purchasing staff can advise departments how they may place their own orders within "menus" of negotiated prices for "best buys." Information feedback can be accurate, rapid, and monitored after the fact. Processes can be simplified and trust reinforced.

Control and decentralization should be appropriate for the types of transactions and for the institution and its circumstances. Although the decentralized structure of higher education lends itself to persuasion by peers rather than top-down imposition of change, to implement priorities you may need to exert authority.

Appropriate Summarization

Data should be summarized to the extent necessary to convey significance and meaning, and the amount of detail should be geared to the user's level of responsibility. There is no need for data overload.

Adaptability and Flexibility

Like strategic plans, financial systems and their components should be reviewed and adapted on a regular basis. They should reflect the changing needs of the users and be flexible enough to incorporate change. Such change, however, should be accompanied by excellent communication, explaining reasons for it in a clear and understandable way.

EMERGING ISSUES AND APPROACHES

At the same time that they are supporting the transformation of the learning experience in their institutions, financial systems are also being transformed. Operational staffs are working to provide enhanced financial reporting based on more widespread acceptance of the qualities of effective systems noted in the preceding section, and on greater use of the technical capabilities of today's information age. One example is budgeting. It is moving away from historical, revenue-based models focusing on assets and dollars, with the focus shifting to objectives and performance measures, a link that heightens the likelihood of success in achieving change. Budgets are created first by defining objectives, then quantifying the resources required to achieve them. In many states there is either performance funding (which directly ties funding to achievements) or performance budgeting (which uses performance as a factor in funding decisions) for public colleges and universities.

Another example is the emergence of the portal, a mechanism that aggregates technology tools and software applications with internal and external information sources and databases. Moving beyond the Web site, it can serve as the gateway to the institution's resources and provide access to information and technology resources in a secure, consistent, and customizable manner. Just as distance education can contribute to the transformation of learning, the portal has the potential to give greater autonomy to users of financial systems. With appropriate content, the portal can provide users with information that helps them determine what to do and how to do it. It can guide them through a process on-line in a self-service model so they can operate without an intermediary. In many other ways, traditional approaches to financial operations are being revised to reflect new attitudes and new applications of technology. For example, information that was once closely held is more widely available. Judgments that were based on anecdotes are being made in a framework of newly available information. Transactions that once required approval are changing to encourage individual empowerment. Operations that were locally oriented are being institutionally aligned. Organizational structures that were vertical are changing into horizontal ones—campus units that were silos of specialization are being converted to one-stop shopping and organizational patterns that began with student-oriented services are being applied to new areas. Managers who began their careers in controlling modes are operating as facilitators. And finally, a culture of compliance is changing to a culture of trust.

WHAT YOU CAN DO TO HELP FINANCIAL OPERATIONS

To help integrate financial and other planning on your campus, it is important to identify and understand issues, get to know the people who operate financial systems, engage them in planning and strategizing, and demonstrate responsibility through your own behavior. You can foster understanding of academic, student affairs, and development attitudes, and enlist the aid of financial professionals to bring their quantitative perspective to many topics and issues.

Gather Data

One way to assess attitudes about the financial systems in your institution is to collect information on existing perceptions and report the data to key decision makers. Exhibit 18.1 shows a checklist developed by the National Academy for Academic Leadership. It may be distributed to members of the board of trustees who serve on relevant committees, key leaders in academic affairs and other important units, and senior staff in financial operations. Responses should be collected and reported by the institutional research officer of the institution or another neutral party, with all responses grouped to permit anonymity. The instrument has the value of bringing issues and concerns to the table and identifying specific problem areas, thus providing opportunity for their resolution.

Share Information

Look for ways that you and members of your department can be knowledgeable about the financial state of the institution. Set up sessions with the financial professionals so you can be briefed on their current issues. Arrange similar briefings for financial professionals on current events and plans in your department, particularly those that are likely to affect the institution's finances. Such arrangements can be as informal as including financial professionals in departmental meetings or as structured as an off-campus retreat.

Create Teams

Look for opportunities to create teams that include representatives of various interests to deal with current projects, including budgeting approaches, measurements, fundraising strategies, and criteria that relate decision making to the institution's priorities. Help the team members become aware of matters such as implications of research on teaching and learning, design of academic space, technology's impact on teaching and learning, attracting new students, and donor relationships.

Use the Institutional Database

Identify significant academic or other measures and look for ways to include them in the central database. If you feel a need for a separate departmental system, discuss it

EXHIBIT 18.1. **Budget, Resources, and Innovation Checklist.**

	Yes	No	To some degree	Don't know
1. Our institution has a provision for regular financial reporting and monitoring.	—	—	—	—
2. The reporting system makes clear the accountabilities for actions and results at specific milestones.	—	—	—	—
3. Financial data are presented in a way that promotes comparisons.	—	—	—	—
4. There is widespread understanding of our institution's financial picture.	—	—	—	—
5. The language used to describe financial issues is clear and understood.	—	—	—	—
6. Leaders have a clear understanding of such terms as operating funds, restricted funds, debt capacity, trustee constraints, labor costs, fixed costs, cross subsidies, and so on.	—	—	—	—
7. The resource allocation process is sensitive to institutional missions and priorities.	—	—	—	—
8. There is a system for aligning proposals for innovation with the mission or strategic plan of the institution.	—	—	—	—
9. Money to support innovation is available at any time (that is, availability is not tied to the budget).	—	—	—	—
10. Seed money for innovative projects exists.	—	—	—	—
11. There is a method for determining the true cost of proposed innovations and existing programs.	—	—	—	—
12. There is a process for determining how to meet the ongoing costs of innovative projects originally supported by seed money.	—	—	—	—
13. The resource allocation process encourages cooperation while discouraging competition (there are rewards for cooperation).	—	—	—	—
14. The reward system encourages risk-taking and allows for failure.	—	—	—	—

EXHIBIT 18.1. Budget, Resources, and Innovation Checklist. (continued)

15. The operational relationship between the financial offices and others at my institution is (please check):

____ strong.

____ cooperative.

____ neutral.

____ sometimes uncooperative.

____ sometimes hostile.

General comments on the relationship that you would like to make:

_____

_____

_____

_____

16. Your position:

____ Board member or trustee

____ Academic affairs

____ Student affairs

____ Development

____ Financial affairs

with the central financial professionals and make sure that your system uses the same starting numbers, definitions, periods of time, and so on. In the long run, if the system is shown to be important to institutional operation, it may become a part of the central database.

Take Financial Accountability Seriously

Make certain that your department's finances are handled appropriately. Use financial management as part of the performance evaluation of every person whose work involves financial decisions, including faculty members who are responsible for contracts and grants.

Demonstrate Acceptance

Show by your own behavior that you are aware of the financial systems. If you disagree with aspects of those systems, work to change them, but in the meantime show respect for them. One provost was present at a senior leadership discussion of current issues in purchasing, particularly the need to adhere to government regulations and ways to avoid or reduce costs. The very next day, in a letter agreement that was contrary to regulations on federal research funds, the provost ordered a computer at a price much higher than the purchasing office would have negotiated if the staff had known about the intention to purchase. The provost did not intend to be hostile to the financial systems; he simply felt that they had nothing to do with him or his role.

CONCLUSION

Sustainable institutional change calls for mutual understanding and inquiry, widely understood information (sometimes gained through new applications of technology), and a shared commitment to institutional goals. Effective financial systems that support and enable change are a function of these factors. Leaders should take steps to foster an environment that promotes respect, trust, and cooperation between financial staff and other institutional members. If it encourages creativity and contributions at all levels and moves to transactions based on trust and autonomy, higher education will be able to achieve a future of continuous improvement motivated by new visions with systems that help to realize them.

Resources

Curry, J. R. (2000). Budgeting. In C. M. Grills (Ed.), *College and university business administration* (6th ed.). Washington, DC: National Association of College and University Business Officers. This chapter offers a full description of the elements of budgeting, followed by highly useful "maxims to budget by." The book is the Bible for business officers, newly updated in its sixth edition.

Diamond, R. M., & Clarke, S. S. (2001, June). Closing the divide, or can this relationship be saved? *Business Officer*, pp. 26–29. Discusses characteristics of relationships within senior management to encourage innovation.

Folpe, H. (2000). Financial reporting. In C. M. Grills (Ed.), *College and university business administration* (6th ed.). Washington, DC: National Association of College and University Business Officers. This is a knowledgeable overview of general-purpose external financial reporting in higher education. Look here if you want to learn about GAAP, AICPA, GASB, FASB, and differences in reporting models.

Goldstein, L., Katz, R., & Terran, M. J. (2001, July). A new business architecture. *Business Officer*, pp. 34–41. A timely review of new trends in university business operations.

Hyatt, J. A., & Santiago, A. A. (1986). *Financial management of colleges and universities.* Washington, DC: National Association of College and University Business Officers. Although somewhat dated, this is a helpful description of procedures and strategies, including qualities needed for successful integration of planning and budgeting.

Klinger, D. J. (2001, July). A Gutenberg moment. *Business Officer*, pp. 44–46. This is a report of a symposium on higher education's use of the Internet and e-commerce based on sound business models.

Klinger, D., & Roberts, P. (2000, January). The newlywed game. *Business Officer*, pp. 32–35. NACUBO's report on a program sponsored by the Association of American Colleges and Universities (AAC&U) and the National Association of College and University Business Officers (NACUBO) on working relationships between academic and financial leaders.

Meisinger, R. J., Jr. (1994). *College and university budgeting: An introduction for faculty and academic administrators* (2nd ed.). Washington, DC: National Association of College and University Business Officers. Although perhaps more than you wanted to know on this subject (192 pages), this book offers a thorough description and discussion well-grounded in customary approaches.

Pappas, A. T. (1996). *Reengineering your nonprofit organization: A guide to strategic transformation.* New York: Wiley. A step-by-step procedural manual for assessing all aspects of an institution and for redesigning all facets to meet new challenges and purposes.

Puzon, B., Stevens, J., & Gaff, J. (2000, Winter). Quality and cost. *Liberal Education,* pp. 54–56.
AAC&U's report on a program sponsored by AAC&U and NACUBO on working relationships between academic and financial leaders.

Senge, P., Kleiner, A., Roberts, C., Ross, R., Roth, G., & Smith, B. (1999). *The dance of change:
The challenges to sustaining momentum in learning organizations.* New York: Random House.
A series of articles on methods for sustaining momentum in learning organizations.

Regents of the University of California. The new business architecture for the University of California. [http://uc2010.ucsd.edu/nbarch/financial.htm].
This is a report on strategies needed to manage growth effectively, control costs, improve the
overall work environment, and implement best business practices to accommodate increased
activity resulting from anticipated new growth at the University of California.

Warzynski, C. (2001, April). *How can the balanced scorecard improve performance at your institution?*
Presentation at the regional conference of the National Consortium for Continuous Improve-
ment in Higher Education, University Park, Pennsylvania State University.
A presentation on how to use a new, leading technique for measuring progress.

CHAPTER 19

Enhancing Student Learning Through Collaboration Between Academic Affairs and Student Affairs

GEORGE D. KUH, SARA E. HINKLE

There is a gap between what most colleges and universities say they are about and what they actually do. For example, most undergraduate catalogues assert that students should cultivate a broad array of intellectual, social, and aesthetic sensibilities. But the curriculum usually emphasizes a much narrower set of skills and competencies. It is also clear from decades of research that both the in-class and out-of-class experiences of students contribute to a wide range of desired outcomes of college. Yet few schools intentionally try to connect these two spheres of students' lives; out-of-class experiences are all but ignored by many faculty members and academic administrators when planning and delivering academic programs.

Whether you are a trustee, president, or academic dean, member of the curriculum committee, chair of the student life task force, or institutional advancement officer, one of your priorities must be to eliminate the unfortunate, unnecessary, and dysfunctional disconnect between academic affairs and student affairs. A great deal of research on student learning shows why collaboration between these groups is essential to enhancing the quality of the undergraduate experience. Fortunately, there are many instructive examples from colleges and universities in which effective academic and student affairs partnerships exist.

In this chapter we briefly review the research base that unequivocally shows why it is critical we intentionally stitch together the academic and student affairs functions on college campuses. We then describe the conditions that characterize productive, highly collaborative academic and student affairs units and suggest ways you can address the obstacles to their creation. Sprinkled throughout are examples of activities that are particularly suitable for collaborative efforts. Finally, the Resources at the end of the chapter feature some of the best and most accessible writing on this topic to allow you and your colleagues to pursue this critical subject in more depth.

WHAT RESEARCH TELLS US

Two streams of research findings are instructive for closing the gap between academic and student affairs in order to improve the quality of the undergraduate experience. The first line identifies educational practices that are generally effective with all types of students. This body of work shows that students learn more when they strive to meet high standards set by their teachers; get frequent, timely feedback on their performance; have ample opportunities to interact with their teachers and peers around substantive topics and issues; and apply what they are learning to real-life situations (Chickering & Gamson, 1991; Education Commission of the States, 1995).

The research also shows that the impact of college on students is cumulative, the result of many different kinds of experiences inside and outside the classroom over an extended period of time (Pascarella & Terenzini, 1991). For this reason *we must engage students in many types of effective educational practices during their studies so that they will benefit in the desired ways.*

The second line of research shows that high-performing organizations are mission-driven, client-centered, and have highly collaborative cultures (Collins & Porras, 1997; Peters & Waterman, 1982). In addition, they systematically learn and adapt to changing circumstances. These same characteristics can be found in educationally effective colleges and universities. Faculty members and student affairs professionals are the two groups that have the most contact with students. Therefore, they also can have the most immediate, direct influence on student learning. Faculty members and their academic administrative colleagues work primarily with students in the context of the formal curriculum during specified periods of time (classes, labs, studio work). Student affairs professionals usually see students in less formal settings outside the classroom. *The inescapable conclusion is that to create a learner-centered campus, these two groups—faculty members and student affairs staff—must work closely together to arrange students' in-class and out-of-class experiences, consistent with the research on college student development and effective educational practices.*

CONDITIONS THAT PROMOTE PRODUCTIVE COLLABORATIONS

Seven conditions characterize campuses that have established effective collaborative efforts between academic and student affairs. Any institution can cultivate these conditions, because they require institutional will—not money—to realize.

Consistently Articulated and Widely Shared Commitment to Student Success

Institutions committed to student success *focus* on student success. They state this often and periodically remind people that student success is the core business of the institution—an institutional value, a priority, a measurable goal. Student success is featured in the mission, philosophy, reward system, and culture. Institutions differ in how they define student success, but most definitions are generally consistent with the view we take in this chapter: student success is a combination of student satisfaction, persistence, and achievement at high but reasonable levels consistent with student background and aspirations.

Consider Kennesaw State University in Georgia where, under the leadership of Dr. Betty Siegel, a commitment to student success is noticeable in every corner. A constant symbolic and functional reminder of this commitment is an administrative structure called the Division of Student Success, which is a reconstitution of several student affairs and academic affairs functional units.

William Rainey Harper College (Illinois) is another example. At this two-year open-door college the vice presidents for academic affairs and student affairs established a joint Statement of Student Success. This articulation of institutional philosophy endorses two concepts: (1) all students have the right to succeed, and (2) the college has the right to uphold high standards for achievement. The college developed five standards of academic performance along with an "intrusive intervention" program administered by the student development staff. To help students meet the college's academic standards, they get frequent feedback on their progress. With guidance from faculty and staff members, they create personalized "success contracts" that emphasize academic skill development and other strategies that they need to make good decisions about college and career. As a result of these collaborative efforts, at-risk students in the program better understand the academic system, know what contributes to low grades, and have a plan and access to resources that can help them succeed (American Association for Higher Education, American College Personnel Association, National Association of Student Personnel Administrators, 1998).

An Enacted Institutional Philosophy That Values Seamless Learning

It is one thing for you to assert that certain goals and values are important; it is quite another to realize these goals in practice. Toward this end, a coordinated response on the part of faculty members, student affairs staff, and others is needed to create a seamless learning environment (Kuh, 1996) through which students' experiences inside and outside the classroom are complementary and consistent with the institution's educational mission and values. Some examples of seamless learning opportunities on a campus are service learning, study abroad, and internships. Another increasingly popular program is the residential learning community, an effort to link the in-class and out-of-class experience by coenrolling students in two or more courses and assigning them to live in the same residence. Examples are variations of the Freshman Interest Group (FIGs) at Indiana University Bloomington (http://www.indiana.edu/~figs/), Northern Illinois University, and the University of Missouri-Columbia.

Another example is the University of Maryland's College Park Scholars Program, a two-year living-learning experience for first-year and sophomore students (American Association for Higher Education, American College Personnel Association, National Association of Student Personnel Administrators, 1998; Shapiro & Levine, 1999). Students reside on floors corresponding to a thematically linked academic program and attend most of their classes in the residence hall. Participating commuter students are given access to common areas in the host residence hall. Residence life staff, faculty, and other program staff offices are also located in the hall in order to increase interaction between them and the students. Through weekly colloquia, discussion groups, and field trips the thematic program blurs the line between what is learned in and out of the classroom to create a seamless learning environment. (For more information about this scholars program see http://scholars.umd.edu/.)

A Common Language

A common language allows faculty members and student affairs professionals to communicate effectively. To cultivate a culture of evidence and high performance you must enlist the commitment, talents, and energy of everyone at all levels of your institution. To work effectively across organizational boundaries, you and your colleagues need to develop a lexicon that conveys common values and preferred interpretations of the meaning of daily events and institutional goals. Speaking a common language speeds up the collaborative process and makes it easier to recruit and teach others about the task at hand. One way to begin the process of developing a common language is to get your colleagues to examine the prevailing mental models of faculty, student affairs professionals, academic administrators, and other key personnel and their effects on policies and practices (Arnold & Kuh, 1999). Examining these differing mental models reveals what these groups value and why they devote time and energy to various activities. Most importantly, to facilitate productive cross-functional dialogue we must reorient our mental models to achieve a shared vision of learning.

The general education curriculum can be a vehicle for cultivating a common language and shared vision, because it usually is not the property of any specific group of faculty members and can be aligned both with academic affairs and the congenial holistic philosophy of student affairs (Brady, 1999). Furthermore, the skills and competencies associated with general education are usually developed and demonstrated both inside and outside the classroom (Kuh & Banta, 2000). Longwood College (Virginia) used general education as a springboard for academic and student affairs to work together on assessment (Kuh & Banta, 2000). A committee made up of faculty members and student affairs professionals designed an approach to assess student achievement of six institutionwide developmental goals of the general education program. A key feature of the effort was recognizing and measuring how students' experiences inside and outside the classroom contributed to each of the six goals. Longwood is a model in using general education revision as an opportunity to develop a shared language for talking about student learning and institutional improvement.

Knowledge and Consistent Use of Effective Educational Policies and Practices

The literature on best practices describes how educationally effective colleges and universities engage students (Education Commission of the States, 1995; Ewell, 1997; Kuh, Schuh, Whitt, & Associates, 1991; Pascarella & Terenzini, 1991). The seven principles for good practice in higher education are perhaps the best known set of engagement concepts (Chickering & Gamson, 1991). These practices are frequent student-faculty contact, cooperation among students, use of active learning techniques, prompt feedback, time on task, high expectations, and respect for diverse talents and ways of learning.

The Chapman Learning Community at Bowling Green State University (Ohio) enacts these principles. Chapman is a residential learning community that experiments with pedagogies and program structures to engage students at high levels in educationally purposeful in-class and out-of-class activities (Klein, 2000). Dubbed a "think tank for learning," Chapman uses teaching practices that emphasize and support interaction between students, faculty members, and residence life professionals, out-of-class learning experiences, and critical thinking. Small classes facilitate student-faculty interaction and lots of verbal and written feedback. As a result, Chapman students appear to make a smoother transition to college life and are more satisfied with their experience than their peers. (For more information about Chapman, see http://www.bgsu.edu/colleges/library/infosrv/lue/chapman.html.)

Collection and Use of Information

Systematic collection, widespread distribution, and routine use of high-quality information about the student experience are critical. What your institution measures is an expression of its values. Too few colleges and universities know enough about the undergraduate experience, especially how students spend their time and the extent to which they are engaged in good educational practices such as those described earlier. Moreover, without such information it is almost impossible to know where to invest institutional resources to improve student learning.

Since 1995 Wake Forest University (North Carolina) has periodically used the College Student Experiences Questionnaire (CSEQ) to assess the quality of undergraduate education. The institution first administered the survey to establish a baseline and subsequently to monitor institutional improvement. By comparing its students' responses with those at peer institutions, the university documents the impact of various institutional initiatives and identifies areas where additional efforts may be needed. One of these new initiatives is planning programs and events around an annual theme, such as "Year of Globalization and Diversity," in order to connect out-of-class activities more purposefully with course-related matters. In another initiative, faculty members now teach freshman seminar courses in the residence halls in order to make the student living environment more intellectually engaging, and this has substantially increased the amount of faculty-student interaction. Yet another is that student affairs staff now participate in new faculty orientation by presenting pertinent findings from the CSEQ data to focus on selected aspects of the Wake Forest student experience. Overall, CSEQ results have helped focus faculty members and student affairs professionals on ways to work together to link students' out-of-class experiences with the institution's curricular goals.

Strong Leadership and Commitment by Senior Administrators

A successful commitment to collaboration must begin at the top with the support and endorsement of senior administrators. As an institutional leader you must be a strong champion and advocate for innovation and change, and you must publicly encourage and support collaborative initiatives (Schroeder, 1999). *You must lead the way by modeling the desired behavior.* According to Tierney (1999), "when institutional participants incorporate in their own behavior the kind of work they desire from others they offer potent incentives for what they want" (p. 132). One of the criteria for evaluating leadership at the division and department levels should be the level of collaboration the unit has achieved with other groups and how these efforts contribute to an ethos of learning (Engstrom & Tinto, 2000).

In the mid-1980s the University of Wyoming formed the Academic Deans–Student Affairs Advisory Council, a twenty-four member group charged with developing partnerships between the academic and student support services. The council is made up of academic deans and student affairs directors who meet monthly to enhance communication and cooperation and solve common problems. Their accomplishments include the implementation and revision of myriad policies and practices related to general education, registration, advising, class schedules, honor degrees, and transfer student credits and assessments (Nutter & Hurst, 1988, in Brown, 1988; R. Abernethy, personal communication with authors, July 23, 2001).

Unwavering Focus on Encouraging Students to Profit from Learning Opportunities

Effective collaborative efforts concentrate on addressing issues and problems that inhibit student success. That is, collaboration is not an end unto itself. Rather, it is a necessary process that benefits both students and the institution. In their best form, partnerships between academic and student affairs applaud short-term successes while staying focused on the larger, long-term goal of improving the quality of the undergraduate experience for all students. Such efforts evaluate as they go, sharing information widely about the status of interventions and their effects on students with people at various levels, which helps people better grasp the implications of their work for institutional performance and student learning.

In the spring of 1997, personnel from the Indiana University Bloomington (IUB) Office of Academic Affairs, College of Arts and Sciences, Enrollment Services (admissions, financial aid, orientation), Campus Life Division, and Registrar formed a cross-functional team and began meeting regularly. The group called itself Frosh Up to reflect its commitment to develop campuswide policies and practices that would "lift up" all new students to the level required for academic and social success. Frosh Up met over a four-month period to identify opportunities to infuse effective educational practices into students' precollege and early college experiences that would be consistent with the university's academic mission and values. A host of new initiatives resulted. For example, staff members from admissions and student financial assistance now consistently highlight the institution's academic values and expectations in their communications with students and their families. The orientation program and materials have been updated to reinforce the same key messages that admissions and financial aid personnel were sending. And the fall welcome week has been restructured to have a more academic focus (Hossler, Kuh, & Olsen, 2001). Because the members represented different offices and programs spanning academic and student affairs, they were able to develop a comprehensive picture of the new student experience and implement their recommendations quickly.

WHAT YOU CAN DO TO OVERCOME OBSTACLES TO FRUITFUL COLLABORATION

If collaboration between academic and student affairs offers so many student and institutional benefits, why are not all colleges and universities doing more of it? The simplest answer is that obstacles to productive collaboration are firmly rooted in the cultures of most institutions of higher education (Austin, 1990; Caple, 1996). For this reason we must plainly describe the barriers "to bring to a conscious level the powerful forces that have made the task of developing relationships between faculty and student affairs so difficult" (Engstrom & Tinto, 2000, p. 426).

Concentrate Collaborative Efforts on Important Problems and Core Activities

Successful collaborative ventures start with defining high-priority tasks and problems that are consistent with the institution's mission and intuitively appeal to both faculty and student affairs staff. You must inspire your colleagues to create a sense of urgency *for doing something important and meaningful* that will improve the quality of the undergraduate experience. One key is bringing together people who have contact with students inside and outside the classroom who can link the various complementary programs and practices so that the sum of their impact on student learning and success will be greater than any single group or set of activities can be.

Demands for evidence of student learning are coming from every quarter. All the regional accreditation agencies and a host of other external authorities require data on the quality of the undergraduate experience. Disciplinary associations and professional societies also are featuring assessment workshops in their annual meetings and articles about assessing student learning in their publications. Thus, assessment is a natural venue for collaboration. Faculty members and student affairs professionals see the student experience from different vantage points and can complement one another's knowledge and expertise in designing and implementing assessments and in interpreting results. One way you can start is to establish a campuswide assessment committee made up of faculty members, student affairs professionals, and academic administrators.

Virginia Commonwealth University established such a committee to assess and improve the first-year experience (Banta & Kuh, 1998). First-year students taking English wrote brief anonymous responses each week for a period of fifteen weeks to questions about a variety of student issues. Faculty and student affairs professionals then read the responses, identified significant issues from the data, conducted followup interviews with students, and summarized the findings. Committee reports were incorporated into the university's strategic plan and spawned numerous initiatives on the campus in response to students' needs and concerns. For example, the university established a central advising center to assist students who had not declared a major, developed a more comprehensive advising handbook for faculty and staff, and appointed a new associate dean for student affairs to link academic and student affairs programming.

Provide Incentives and Minimize Disincentives

In order to reward and reinforce collaborative behaviors that promote student learning, institutions need a blend of both symbolic and fiscal incentives (Tierney, 1999) that are compatible with institutional priorities and goals (Engstrom & Tinto, 2000) and with the cultural traditions and mores of the campus (Kuh & Whitt, 1988; Tierney, 1999). Therefore, symbolic incentives will differ from campus to campus. Some common incentives include simple but heartfelt words of encouragement, awards, plaques, and ceremonies that publicly honor colleagues who have worked to promote the institution's mission.

Sooner or later, though, you have got to tie fiscal rewards to symbolic incentives. Paying lip service to the value of collaboration but not backing up such words with resources sends a very powerful but incorrect message about what really matters.

In addition, you must minimize *disincentives*—obstacles that dissuade faculty and staff members from taking up collaborative projects. Many faculty members feel that such efforts will take too much time and interfere with research and other teaching responsibilities that are clearly acknowledged in the reward structures. For example, assistant professors are often advised by senior colleagues and department chairs that involvement in such projects as service learning may reduce their productivity (Gray, 2000). If we are to "recognize and legitimize a broader, more inclusive view of scholarship" (Engstrom & Tinto, 2000, p. 446), then promotion and tenure policies must be revised so that faculty are not penalized for participating in such collaborative projects.

Recruit and Reward Like-Minded People

In the final analysis, institutional transformation and educationally effective colleges require a legion of informed, skilled, committed professionals who put what they know into action. Thus, a key step in creating a seamless learning environment is hiring and retaining faculty members and student affairs professionals throughout your institution who are knowledgeable of the higher education literature and are committed to student success. The goal is not to produce institutional hegemony but intentionally to seek out, select, and socialize colleagues with the needed expertise who share the seamless learning vision (Collins & Porras, 1997). The result will be to align institutional purpose and human energy, as individual and collective efforts get directed toward a shared vision that is a meaningful extension of each individual's personal vision (Senge, 1994). To leverage the positive impact of such efforts, regular meetings should be held including these leaders and their associates with an eye toward creating an organizational synergy that might not otherwise occur. Syracuse University in New York (Wright, 2001) is one institution that has done this with demonstrable success.

Visit Places Where Successful Collaborative Activities Are Under Way

One way to expand overnight the number of people who are primed for collaboration is to send a cross-functional team to visit model programs at other institutions. Such ventures are particularly powerful if the activities to be examined have direct implications for work back on your campus. For example, we took a core group of more than a dozen academic administrators, faculty members, and student affairs professionals from Indiana University Bloomington to the University of Missouri-Columbia to see and hear firsthand from people like themselves about the promising educational practices being implemented at the sister school. This was a key step toward understanding the practical applications of the research on and theory of undergraduate improvement efforts. Moreover, the participants on the trip were introduced to the vision and language of student success in ways that no series of on-campus meetings could accomplish, convincing key people that adopting promising practices was not only doable but preferable to the way the campus was currently operating (Hossler, Kuh, & Olsen, 2001).

Face Head-On the Inevitable Conflicts, Misunderstandings, and Status Issues

Collaborative ventures between academic and student affairs are almost never smooth sailing. It is imperative that you acknowledge the conflict and different points of view that are the hallmarks of difficult dialogues; these are legitimate, essential ingredients of a collaborative learning process (Senge, 1994). Dealing with these differences in an open, respectful way almost always strengthens and enriches partnerships (Schroeder, 1999). The collaborative process requires that roles continually are renegotiated, based on who has the requisite knowledge and experience to manage the issue or concern effectively (Engstrom & Tinto, 2000). And you have got to address status differences as well. At many institutions, student affairs professionals are not uniformly respected by faculty members and academic administrators. But respect can be earned, and collaboration is one of the more effective ways to demonstrate competence.

The Intensive Freshman Seminar (IFS; http://www.indiana.edu/~ifs/) is a transitional program for first-year students at Indiana University Bloomington that is a vehicle for collaborative dialogue. Although this student experience lasts only three weeks in the summer, the collaborative process needed to implement the program goes on year-round. Participating faculty and staff members meet five times a year to prepare and share various approaches they have found to be effective in enhancing student learning in and out of the classroom. The insights gained are frequently incorporated into learning approaches throughout the year, not only during IFS. For the IFS colleagues—the faculty and staff who collaborate on the program—this ongoing series of conversations has become a valued aspect of the IFS experience, almost as much as the actual three-week program.

CONCLUSION

Over the years there have been many calls for faculty members and student affairs professionals to work together. Always well intentioned, such efforts too often lack a warrant that both groups find persuasive. Today, from all quarters, higher education is being challenged to enhance student learning. Fortunately, years of research point to educational practices that both faculty members and student affairs professionals can use. In addition, we now have numerous examples of successful partnerships on which to build, some of which we have described in this chapter. The combination of these partnerships with the use of effective educational practices should help enhance the desired college outcomes.

But make no mistake: the partnerships we seek must spring from a deep resolve to strengthen institutional responsibility for learning and be rooted in an informed, authentic appreciation for what academic and student affairs contribute to the learning enterprise. This means that when orienting new students, reshaping the curriculum, or linking students' out-of-class experiences to the academic program, you must arrange the institutional structures and reward system to take advantage of the expertise of both faculty members and student affairs professionals. And you must over time carefully stitch into your institution's culture the values that support such partnerships. May the force for collaboration be with you. . . .

References and Resources

Understanding Academic and Student Affairs Cultures

Arnold, K., & Kuh, G. D. (1999). What matters in undergraduate education? Mental models, student learning, and student affairs. In E. J. Whitt (Ed.), *Student learning as student affairs work:*

Responding to our imperative. Washington, DC: National Association of Student Personnel Administrators.
Compares and contrasts the "mental models" of faculty, student affairs professionals, students, and external stakeholders in order to foster an understanding of what matters to these groups. Recommends cross-functional discussions of the importance of reorienting these mental models to achieve a shared vision of student learning.

Austin, A. E. (1990). Faculty cultures, faculty values. In W. G. Tierney (Ed.), *Assessing academic climates and cultures.* New Directions for Institutional Research, no. 68. San Francisco: Jossey-Bass.
Describes four primary cultures that influence faculty values and behaviors and suggests ways that institutions can build on these cultural values to enhance organizational performance.

Caple, R. B. (1996). The learning debate: A historical perspective. *Journal of College Student Development, 37*(2), 193–202.
Provides a brief history of the student affairs profession and offers a perspective on why it has been cast in a dualistic role with academic affairs. Emphasizes the importance of collaboration to promote student learning.

Kuh, G. D., & Whitt, E. J. (1988). *The invisible tapestry: Culture in American colleges and universities* (ASHE-ERIC Higher Education Report No. 1). Washington, DC: Association for the Study of Higher Education.
Examines how cultural perspectives can be used to understand and interpret events and actions at colleges and universities and provides implications for faculty and administrators.

Effective Educational Practices

Chickering, A. W., & Gamson, Z. F. (Eds.). (1991). *Applying the seven principles for good practice in undergraduate education.* New Directions for Teaching and Learning, no. 47. San Francisco: Jossey-Bass.
Summarizes the key research that underlies the seven principles for good practice in undergraduate education. Provides examples of how these principles are being applied at various institutions, as evidenced through feedback from faculty and institutional inventories for good practice.

Education Commission of the States. (1995). *Making quality count in undergraduate education.* Denver: Education Commission of the States.
Addresses the issue of quality in higher education from the perspective of various stakeholders, including students, state leaders, and society as a whole. Emphasizes the need for a shared agenda for quality undergraduate education involving key figures in the institution and community.

Kuh, G. D., Douglas, K. B., Lund, J. P., & Ramin-Gyurnek, J. (1994). *Student learning outside the classroom: Transcending artificial boundaries* (ASHE-ERIC Higher Education Report No. 8). Washington, DC: George Washington University, School of Education and Human Development.
  Describes what institutions, administrators, faculty, student affairs staff, and students can do to connect out-of-class experiences with the academic mission, thus promoting undergraduate learning and increasing institutional productivity.

Pascarella, E. T., & Terenzini, P. T. (1991). *How college affects students: Findings and insights from twenty years of research.* San Francisco: Jossey-Bass.
  This landmark volume synthesizes key research on how higher education affects students. Summarizes critical theories of development and examines the net affects of college on cognitive, attitudinal, value, psychosocial, and moral dimensions.

Creating a Collaborative, Learner-Centered Institution

American College Personnel Association (ACPA). (1994). *The student learning imperative: Implications for student affairs.* Washington, DC: Author. (Also available in the March 1996 issue of the *Journal of College Student Development,* pp. 118–122.)
  Addresses questions and challenges as to how student affairs can intentionally create conditions to enhance student learning and development.

Banta, T. W., & Kuh, G. D. (1998). A missing link in assessment: Collaboration between academic and student affairs. *Change, 30*(2), 40–46.
  Promotes the value of collaboration in assessment and cites specific examples of successful partnerships on various campuses.

Brady, S. M. (1999). Students at the center of education. *Liberal Education, 85*(1), 14–21.
  Offers reflections on the conference "To Enhance Student Learning by Increasing the Effectiveness of Faculty Work" of the Associated New American Colleges, from the perspective of a student affairs professional. Emphasizes how to improve collaboration between student and academic affairs.

Brown, S. S. (Ed.). (1988). [Special edition]. *NASPA Journal, 26*(1).
  This entire edition is devoted to the issue of collaboration between student and academic affairs. The twelve featured articles address such topics as barriers to collaboration and means to overcome them; specific examples of successful partnerships are provided.

Collins, J. C., & Porras, J. I. (1997). *Built to last: Successful habits of visionary companies.* New York: HarperCollins.
  Identifies characteristics of eighteen visionary corporations, including Wal-Mart, Walt Disney, and Sony, in order to discern what has made them prosperous and different from their competitors. Emphasizes the importance of establishing a core ideology and assembling a team that espouses this ideology.

Ewell, P. T. (1997). Organizing for learning: A new imperative. *American Association for Higher Education Bulletin, 50*(4), 3–6.
Summarizes key concepts regarding what we know about learning and the need for collaboration in order to foster institutional change and improve undergraduate education.

Klein, T. (2000). From classroom to learning community: One professor's reflections. *About Campus, 5*(3), 12–19.
Offers thoughts and reflections on the value of the learning community from the director of Chapman Learning Community at Bowling Green State University.

Kuh, G. D. (1996). Guiding principles for creating seamless learning environments for undergraduates. *Journal of College Student Development, 37,* 135–148.
Presents six principles that link curricular and co-curricular experiences as a means of fostering student learning and personal development and explains their implications for practitioners and graduate preparation programs.

Kuh, G. D., Schuh, J. H., Whitt, E. J., & Associates. (1991). *Involving colleges: Successful approaches to fostering student learning and personal development outside the classroom.* San Francisco: Jossey-Bass.
Describes how the various institutional factors and conditions of fourteen "involving colleges" promote learning and development through high-quality educationally purposeful out-of-class learning opportunities.

Peters, T. J., & Waterman, R. H. (1982). *In search of excellence: Lessons from America's best-run companies.* New York: Warner Books.
Identifies eight basic principles of management that promote organizational excellence, as found in forty-three of America's successful companies.

Potter, D. L. (1999). Where powerful partnerships begin. *About Campus, 4*(2), 11–16.
Identifies principles of learning and how they can be applied to create learning-centered institutions through collaborative efforts.

Schroeder, C. C., & Hurst, J. C. (1996). Designing learning environments that integrate curricular and co-curricular experiences. *Journal of College Student Development, 37*(2), 174–181.
Describes conditions that optimize opportunities for student learning, including strong partnerships between academic and student affairs. Offers examples of programs that involve successful collaborations.

Schuh, J. H., & Whitt, E. J. (Eds.). (1999). *Creating successful partnerships between academic and student affairs.* New Directions for Student Services, no. 87. San Francisco: Jossey-Bass.
Includes seven articles on the topic of academic and student affairs collaborations. Highlights successful partnerships on various campuses, including service learning efforts, freshman interest groups, and a collaborative core curriculum.

Senge, P. M. (1994). *The fifth discipline: The art and practice of the learning organization.* New York: Doubleday.

Discusses the importance of learning organizations—that is, ones that continually increase their capacity to learn and reach their highest aspirations. Identifies five key ideas for creating a learning organization, as well as means for putting these ideas into practice.

Terenzini, P. T., & Pascarella, E. T. (1994). Living with myths: Undergraduate education in America. *Change, 26*(1), 28–32.

Identifies five commonly held myths about undergraduate education based on an extensive review of the literature. Emphasizes the need for a new mindset with regard to the work of faculty and student affairs in connecting classroom and out-of-classroom experiences to promote student learning.

Tierney, W. G. (1999). *Building the responsive campus: Creating high-performance colleges and universities.* Thousand Oaks, CA: Sage.

Critiques modern academe and proposes organizational changes to make institutions of higher education more high-performing and learning-centered. Addresses such issues as faculty roles and rewards, presidential leadership, strategic planning, and assessment and evaluation.

Vaill, P. B. (1998). *Spirited leading and learning: Process wisdom for a new age.* San Francisco: Jossey-Bass.

Contains a collection of essays on managerial leadership. Some of its key premises include leadership as learning, leadership of high-performing systems, and infusing spirituality into leadership.

Examples of Effective Academic-Student Affairs Partnerships

About Campus.

Published six times a year by Jossey-Bass and the American College Personnel Association (New York), this magazine is devoted to issues that serve as common ground for academic and student affairs. It offers an eclectic array of essays and articles in order to foster different approaches and ways of thinking about student learning and development.

Powerful partnerships: A shared responsibility for learning. (1998, June). Washington, DC: American Association for Higher Education, American College Personnel Association, & National Association of Student Personnel Administrators. [http://www.naspa.org/resources/partnerships.cfm]. Provides a list of principles about learning and their implications for pedagogy, curricula, learning environments, and assessment. Each principle is illustrated with a set of exemplary cooperative practices that involve partnerships between academic and student affairs.

Engstrom, C. M., & Tinto, V. (2000). Developing partnerships with academic affairs to enhance student learning (pp. 425–452). In M. J. Barr & M. Desler (Eds.), *Handbook on student affairs administration* (2nd ed.). San Francisco: Jossey-Bass.

Presents a thorough overview of the key issues involved with forming collaborative relationships between academic and student affairs.

Gray, M. J. (2000). Making the commitment to community service: What it takes. *About Campus, 5*(20), 19–24.
Provides practical information on what it takes to undergo a successful commitment to community service, based on some of the results of a national study on service.

Hossler, D., Kuh, G. D., & Olsen, D. (2001). Finding (more) fruit on the vines: Using higher education research and institutional research to guide institutional policies and strategies: Part II. *Research in Higher Education, 42,* 223–235.
Describes how higher education theory and research guided institutional policy and practice with regard to improving the first-year experience at Indiana University Bloomington.

Kuh, G. D., & Banta, T. W. (2000). Faculty-student affairs collaboration on assessment: Lessons from the field. *About Campus, 4*(6), 4–11.
Outlines the barriers to faculty and student affairs collaboration on assessment and suggests mean to overcome them by offering specific examples of successful partnerships.

Residential Learning Communities International Registry. [http://www.bgsu.edu/colleges/clc/rlcch/submissions/].
Serves as a clearinghouse devoted to the collection and dissemination of information about residential learning communities. Lists close to one hundred institutions that offer residential learning communities and provides detailed information about each program, including a brief summary of the program, contact information, sources of funding, description of faculty and staff involvement, courses offered, and information on the facilities and budget.

Schroeder, C. C. (1999). Forging educational partnerships that advance student learning (pp. 133–156). In G. S. Blimling & E. J. Whitt (Eds.), *Good practices in student affairs: Principles to foster student learning.* San Francisco: Jossey-Bass.
Establishes the importance of creating seamless learning environments for students. Presents constraints to collaboration and means to overcome them, and identifies specific opportunities for successful educational partnerships.

Shapiro, N. S., & Levine, J. H. (1999). Introducing learning communities to your campus. *About Campus, 4*(5), 2–10.
Offers specific strategies for the design and implementation of learning communities by using the University of Maryland-College Park as a case study.

Wright, B. D. (2001). The Syracuse transformation: On becoming a student-centered research university. *Change, 33*(4), 38–45.
Describes the intentional effort by Syracuse University to focus on undergraduate education through a series of initiatives, including fostering academic and student affairs partnerships.

CHAPTER 20

Dealing with Technology
Administrative Issues

STEVEN W. GILBERT, STEPHEN C. EHRMANN

Many of us have hopes for using information technology to improve teaching and learning, but we have no clear scientific proof of great educational benefits from making big investments in its academic uses. As a result, important decisions must be made in times of growing tension and uncertainty. The accelerated development of new applications of information technologies and the associated media hype fuel new visions and raise expectations. Meanwhile, proliferating instructional options are often restrained by limited resources, institutions that are structured for sedate change, and professionals who are unprepared for rapid change and multiple options.

As more faculty members and students are encouraged to use technology for teaching and learning, they expect to accomplish more and also discover that they need more help. The capacity of academic support services to provide that help usually lessens as expectations rise. Costs go up and the "support service crisis" gets worse (Gilbert, 2001).

At most colleges and universities there is no widely understood or supported strategy for improving teaching and learning through information technology. Instead, as a result of a series of decentralized decisions, many members of the community experience a process that can only be described as crisis-lurch, crisis-lurch. As an academic leader, you can help break this cycle, and there are good reasons to do so: better educational outcomes, positive responses to change, less paranoia, and so on.

Sadly, however, at most colleges and universities no single individual has the breadth of training, experience, expertise, and perspective to be a completely credible resource for significant policy, personnel, and funding decisions in this area. That applies to presidents, chief academic officers, chief information officers, faculty, and especially outside consultants. Fortunately, there are alternatives.

In this chapter we first describe some of the obstacles—both perceived and actual—that you face in advancing your institutional mission with technology, and then outline some of the goals you can most confidently expect to achieve. We conclude with a number of recommendations to assist you in developing a meaningful vision for the use of technology. We also suggest a number of questions that you can ask to get the information you need to make good decisions about technology.

OBSTACLES TO TECHNOLOGY

Although those hoping to use technology to improve teaching and learning and operational efficiency face many obstacles that are quite real, a number of others that are based on misconceptions can be even more formidable and distracting. As we visit institution after institution we find that many of the most important technology-based decisions are being made based on myths or fears rather than reality. Unfortunately, when this occurs the result is a great deal of frustration, disillusionment, and wasted time and resources.

Myths and Misperceptions

Some of the most common misconceptions are these:

- *The reductionist fallacy:* New technology can replace (all or most) old practices.
- *The irresistible bargain fallacy:* We cannot resist the bargain—"Such a deal . . . if we wait longer it will cost far more."
- *The just-do-it fallacy:* The technology *will* improve learning; once we start using it we will identify the benefits.
- *The past-less fallacy:* We can ignore history; we are different and the technology is different.
- *The champion fallacy:* If we support the advocates and champions, everyone else will follow.
- *The instant gratification fallacy:* The impact of technology is immediate.
- *The hard wire fallacy:* Just increase your technical capacity and all else will follow.
- *The you-will-be-toast fallacy:* If you do not start now you will miss the train entirely.

- *The caboose fallacy:* You are behind and will never catch up.
- *The confusing-courses-with-classroom fallacy:* Technology can replace courses and must be brought into all classrooms.

Real Obstacles

Although experience has shown that the preceding ideas are based on myth rather than reality, there are a number of real obstacles that must be dealt with directly if technology is to be used effectively and appropriately on your campus.

Lack of Achievable Visions

There is no focus on achievable visions and there are no feasible pathways to those visions or necessary support.

Contention and Diffusion

It is hard to get academic and administrative staff to agree on common visions, strategies, and support structures, even though such agreement is far more important with complex technology-related improvements than was the case in the past.

Lack of Collaboration

The academic culture at most colleges and universities has not encouraged people from different areas (academic departments, staff offices, administrative units) to communicate well or frequently, let alone work together toward shared, explicit goals. It is still rare and refreshing to find cheerful communication and skillful collaboration among key stakeholders, with all of them having the knowledge, experience, and control of resources they need to coordinate and achieve information technology's potential.

Changing Technologies

Technologies change far faster than our ability to change programs to take advantage of them.

Scarcity of Knowledgeable Academic Leaders

Few people old enough to be eligible for a senior position have been trained in or have experience with the new variety of technology options and their management. In fact, things have been changing so fast that almost no one can achieve and maintain a broad, balanced perspective and comprehensive knowledge of the available options.

Unavailable or Unprepared Professional Staff

It is difficult to find qualified staff, especially to provide technology support for educational applications. It is equally hard to find or train professional staff and faculty who have real insights into using technology for significant academic improvement at a reasonable cost.

Lack of Support Staff

Industry pays technology professionals more and needs more of them, so their salaries rise faster than those of their colleagues in academia. Consequently, many technical personnel leave for jobs in other sectors. Widespread integration of information technology into curriculum requires widespread changes in how faculty and other professionals think and act—a great educational challenge that cannot be addressed rapidly, easily, or cheaply. "Mainstream" faculty who do not have any fondness for innovation or information technology need more introductory and elementary training and more ongoing technical support than did the pioneers. And the pioneers need more help with more challenging projects as they move further ahead and dive more deeply into new technology options.

A Focus on Low-Level Outcomes

The emphasis on easily measurable outcomes leads many institutions to overlook more significant outcomes and the instructional skills of many faculty.

Little Understanding of Classroom Dynamics

Paradoxically, the increasing accessibility and capabilities of on-line options for enhancing extended instruction should increase the pressure to take full advantage of the unique assets of face-to-face student-faculty options, and increase the pressure to understand which conditions respond best to which combinations of technology, pedagogy, and personal engagement.

Pendulum Extremes as Solutions

Higher education seems to go from one extreme solution to another without considering anything in between. The pendulum swing du jour seems to be learning-centered or learner-centered education, perhaps combined with outcome assessment.

Too Much Hype

Expectations rise faster than the resources needed to achieve them. There is a tendency to overstate the pace of change but understate the time, effort, and resources needed, while wrongly claiming that other industries have been integrating technology more rapidly.

Not Enough Time

Faculty, support staff, and administrators are already busy with the traditional load of responsibilities that do not include coping with a growing array of instructional options and new technologies.

Demanding New Work Paradigms

Many faculty have difficulty adjusting to new work paradigms. They cannot find, select, adapt, and implement attractive new options without help, and support staff cannot integrate their work into new institutionwide systems without altering their procedures or making compromises with new systems and other offices.

Lack of Training, Tools, and Taxonomy for Instructional Options

Most faculty lack training, the vocabulary, and a conceptual framework of pedagogical and technological options, yet their involvement and ownership is essential in implementing any new educational use of information technology. In addition, very few staff members have the knowledge and experience necessary to provide professional development that covers all these areas.

Lack of Training, Tools, and Taxonomy for Assessment of Learner Needs and Achievements

Very few faculty are aware of even the primitive tools and taxonomies available for assessing and describing students' different learning needs, assessing and describing similar characteristics for instructional media and resources, and assessing and describing similar characteristics for faculty members. Nor are they aware of the tools for matching them and bringing them together.

BENEFITS OF USING TECHNOLOGY

Most people would agree that, with regard to new educational uses of information technology, higher education is far past the point of no return. In fact, use of information technology is well established. Kenneth C. Green's latest data (2001) further confirm that well over half of all courses make at least some use of e-mail, the Web, and so on. Even the ability to compete for students, faculty, and grants seems to depend in part on the visibility and success of your integration of new technologies into teaching and learning.

A rapidly growing number of students, faculty, staff, and alumni use word processing, spreadsheets, e-mail, presentation tools, the Web, and perhaps some form of multimedia. More and more of your colleagues are convinced that these and other technology applications allow faculty and academic support professionals to improve teaching and learning, enhance student recruitment, and increase student retention and success. Many institutions are even finding new ways to serve their alumni with telecommunications and computing. "No new technology" is no longer an option in academia. But there is far less clarity about what an institution stands to gain or what it risks losing when it is dealing with technology.

Institutions benefit from technology through:

Gains in Content

Some curricular goals depend on specific uses of information technology (on-line problem solving, digital media applications, using on-line resources in inquiry and research, and so on).

Gains in Access

The audience for the educational experience may be expanded as course locations and times become more flexible. The student population becomes more diverse with new populations being served, such as those with physical disabilities.

Gains in Effectiveness

Technology allows for more interaction between students and between students and faculty, a greater variety of instructional options and resources, and quicker response times. There is a greater ability to deal effectively with prerequisite problems and academic diversity among students.

Gains in Efficiency

Use of time and resources can be more efficient.

Gains from Standardization or Personalization

An institution can benefit from using information technology to standardize some kinds of instruction, but it can also benefit from using the technology to adapt available instructional resources and create courses reflecting each teacher's unique insights, knowledge, and abilities. Information technology can also be used to enable faculty and students to personalize their communications and relationships during courses. For example, communications technology can help people recognize and understand their differences and learn from the diversity in a group of students. Personalizing instruction with technology can also mean offering different variations or options to different learners in the same course, or offering different instructional options to different teachers, even those teaching different sections of the same course.

Gains in Productivity

An institution can be more productive by enabling large numbers of students to learn from the same materials or activities (and relatively fewer faculty). This approach seems to work best with content and skills that can be easily specified and with learners who are externally motivated and self-disciplined. The great success of the popular series of "dummies" books is perhaps a testament to the possibility of great numbers of people learning independently from relatively inexpensive instructional materials.

It is important to note that technology is not sufficient to do any of these things by itself. An institution also needs to have qualified faculty, appropriate facilities, interested students, and many other important ingredients. We mention this because some institutions ignore the need to budget for these other ingredients: they buy the technology and wait for the new content and the intended results to appear. We will talk more about professional development later.

A PORTFOLIO OF STRATEGIES FOR USING TECHNOLOGY EFFECTIVELY

No college or university has the resources necessary to engage every faculty member, every student, and every academic support professional immediately and fully in new educational uses of information technology. Choices will be made, whether intentionally or not. Of course, in today's environment of rapidly increasing complexity—more options, limited resources, ill-prepared institutions and individuals—choosing just one goal for improving teaching and learning with technology does not work. Nor does spreading your efforts evenly across all conceivable goals.

Most institutions find that the traditional five-year strategic plan fails to offer enough flexible guidance for the quick decisions that must be made with the pace of change in educational technology. Lack of planning and traditional strategic planning both fail to interrupt the continuing cycle of crisis-lurch decision making. Developing what may be called a *technology plan* may mean focusing on technology without taking into account the needs of the people who are likely to use it for academic purposes. A more useful approach is to develop a set of related strategies and working plans that can be frequently and easily revised to reflect significant unanticipated changes. These strategies and plans should be closely linked with implementation programs so that each influences the other.

It is also important to gain and keep the confidence of all constituents. A good way to do that is to provide a public description of a rational strategy from which everyone will eventually benefit, so that everyone can understand how and when some will be more deeply involved and supported than others. Do not overlook the ways in which many faculty members have already been improving courses and supporting their students' learning. There have been at least two successful models for integrating technology. Both are important to recognize and support—and they are not mutually exclusive! First, in *incremental change* faculty colleagues exchange ideas and materials, trying new technological bits and pieces and gradually refining their courses. Second, there are more structured team-based *instructional design* approaches to developing, testing, and improving entire courses, programs, or instructional units.

We recommend a *Portfolio of Six Strategies* for using technology effectively:

Develop a Vision

Have a well-articulated and widely shared educational vision including a definition of the institutional community that describes who is being served, and who is providing and supporting the service.

Explain Minimum Requirements

Provide well-developed descriptions of minimum requirements for the technology infrastructure—people as well as hardware, facilities, and other information resources—so that plans for achieving it are widely understood.

Offer Something for Almost Everyone, Every Year (Wide-Shallow)

Wide-shallow strategies often support making modest changes in instructional modules or materials in many individual courses. Some wide-shallow strategies are aimed primarily at enabling or permitting the achievement of commonly sought learning outcomes.

Offer More Focused, Extensive Programs for a Few (Narrow-Deep)

A narrow-deep strategy may enable faculty and students to make significant, visible changes in how they teach and learn in a few individual courses or an entire program that involves several courses. Many narrow-deep strategies have higher costs and higher risks than other strategies.

It should be noted that the terms *wide* and *narrow* refer to the number of people who are affected by a strategy. A narrow strategy would affect very few people; the narrowest change affects how one teacher teaches a single topic in a single course. The widest change makes an impact on all teaching and learning throughout the institution. *Deep* and *shallow* refer to the magnitude of the impact of the strategy on those involved: a shallow strategy would not cause much change in the behavior of the teachers and students involved.

Determine Review and Budgeting Processes

Establish criteria and mechanisms for reviewing and revising the strategies you develop and for supporting them through major resource allocation decisions.

Aim for Clarity, Openness

Enable anyone (who tries) to understand these processes.

BUILDING A PORTFOLIO OF STRATEGIES

The following paragraphs suggest ways to analyze your options and develop a portfolio of strategies that is appropriate for your institution, division, or department.

Develop the Vision: Purpose, Pace, and Risk

First, think about what you hope to achieve by integrating information technology more fully into teaching and learning on your campus. Consider distinctions among basic paradigms such as these:

- Using information technology to increase institutional productivity and access to education
- Using information technology to increase communication between faculty and students and to expand the content that can be taught

- Using information technology to support collaborative learning and community building

Determine the pace and risk you are willing to accept in conjunction with technological change. Which is the most appropriate overall position or strategy for your institution: leader, follower, or resister? Why? Do you need to be a leader? Can you afford to be? Are you more comfortable among those who delay the longest? How ready are you to jump into some of the most competitive new markets: (inter)national, purely on-line programs in general education or business, and so on?

Each institution should establish the context for shaping its own unique portfolio of change strategies for the educational uses of information technology by deciding whether it will be a leader, follower, or resister. Leaders are prepared to make the greatest investments with the greatest risk of failure but also with the excitement and potential payoff of being pioneers. Followers identify their peer institutions and watch them carefully, adopting any practice that about 20 percent of the cohort has already embraced. Resisters avoid all new practices except those for which nonparticipation becomes embarrassing. Note that your institution's overall strategy for educational uses of information technology needs to have nothing to do with its strategy in other areas, such as athletics, research, excellence in specific disciplines, and so on.

Determine the Minimum Requirements for Technology and Support

Establish the minimum levels for access, capacity, and use of hardware, software, and telecommunications. The technological foundation may also include minimum specifications for classroom equipment, laboratories, residence halls, and so on. Institutional subunits such as departments in a college or colleges in a university may set and achieve higher standards built on broader institutional requirements.

Ensure Access

Establish minimum levels of quality and ease of use of the hardware, software, and telecommunications. Then make sure that all students and faculty have access above those levels (for example, to e-mail and the Web). Students should not find it difficult or frustrating—whether they are in campus computer labs or their own residences or workplaces—to log on to get e-mail, to participate in a Blackboard-based course, or to find other information that is intended to be accessible to them. Be sure to consider various categories of students and faculty members when developing wide-shallow strategies: on-campus residents, commuters, students with easy home access to computing, students who had little access to computing before college, students with disabilities, faculty members who are uncomfortable with technology, faculty members who have been acquiring equipment through grants, and so on.

Again, permit institutional subunits such as departments or colleges in a university to set and achieve even higher standards. Review carefully the desirability and viability of maintaining a three-year "refresh" cycle for replacing obsolescent computers and software; determine criteria for eligibility for some people to be on a shorter cycle.

Consider Usage

Do you want to require all faculty to put basic course syllabus information on the Web in WebCT? Do you want to require all faculty to give their e-mail addresses to their students and to respond to all messages from students within thirty-six hours? What are your minimum infrastructure requirements for these educational uses? What is the minimum configuration of hardware, software, and connectivity you must provide for all faculty, students, staff, and so on, and how can you provide it? Which technological skills and knowledge—information literacy—do you want all your graduates to acquire? How will you provide the necessary training?

Consider Wide-Shallow Issues

Determine what percentage of all faculty use which of the most common computing, multimedia, or telecommunications utilities (e-mail, the Web, PowerPoint, course-management tools, video) in their courses and in their classrooms, and at what general levels. Determine current levels and set plausible goals for increasing them.

Consider Narrow-Deep Issues

Narrow-deep strategies enable smaller groups to explore more expensive and risky combinations of technology and educational approach—with the hope that what they learn will prove useful to others later.

For some institutions, a reasonable narrow-deep strategy might be to enable all faculty and students participating in upper-division courses in one department to conduct their course-related communication on the Internet and develop course-related information systems on it as well. This might be accomplished by providing laptop computers with built-in modems, paid-for accounts on a dial-in Internet service, and one-quarter time allocation for one academic year of the services of a computing support person and a librarian.

Another attractive narrow-deep strategy might be to establish an internal grant-making program in which a request for proposals (RFP) is distributed to all faculty members. The RFP might specify that half the grants will be made only to those who have never before used information technology in their teaching, and that pairs of faculty including one experienced and one inexperienced member will get special consideration. Further, each proposal may request a combination of a stipend of up to $500, hardware and software valued at up to $2,500, one course release time, and assignment of 10 percent each of a librarian and a technical support person and a faculty development professional. Those applying would be asked to explain how their proposed teaching approaches fit with the applications of technology and the kinds of support services they are requesting. They might also be asked to specify how they will evaluate their results and assess their progress. Finally, applicants could be told that the grantors favor projects permitting the teaching of important topics that would be difficult to cover through conventional methods.

Select a few course-related projects proposed by pioneers. Choose projects based on evidence that these faculty members will make exceptional efforts to use technology and to help their colleagues who might be willing to try something similar. Also, select a few program areas in which your institution is already strong or in which you are already building a new focus.

Look at Review and Budgeting Processes

What process will you use to facilitate the extension and modification of these strategies, programs, and goals? Establish criteria and mechanisms for changing those strategies and for making important resource allocation decisions. (See *collaborative change* programs at www.tltgroup.org.)

Maintain a Credible, Rational Balance

If your plan is not publicly explained and plainly implemented, many faculty members and others in the college or university community will assume the worst. Their erroneous assumptions may lead them to resist or disrupt institutional efforts to improve teaching and learning with technology. Consequently, having a portfolio of strategies that anyone who is faintly interested can understand and see as equitable is a good beginning! However, the technological infrastructure must also provide a foundation for positive experiences that support realistic expectations—expectations that match your goals.

A WORD ABOUT UBIQUITOUS COMPUTING

Wake Forest University was not the first institution to enable and require all undergraduate students and faculty to have the same computer, but it did one of the best jobs of preparing for such a significant commitment and it made the biggest splash. WFU calculated that it could permeate the environment with uniform computers and raise tuition approximately $3,000 per year per student at the same time and increase the quality of its student body. The circumstances surrounding that set of decisions are not likely to apply to many other institutions in the near future.

There are now dozens if not hundreds of colleges and universities that require or strongly urge every student to acquire a computer that is either identical or nearly the same in essential capabilities, software, network access, and other features. The decision to make this kind of commitment has many implications and should not be undertaken lightly or quickly. These are some of the key variables to consider:

- *Level of commitment.* Is the institution committed to being recognized as a leader in educational uses of information technology, information literacy, and so on?
- *Capacity to support almost universal usage of computing technology.* Is there institutional capacity for maintenance, training, instructional design, and so on?
- *Enthusiasm and tolerance.* Are the faculty, students, staff, governing board, alumni, and other stakeholders willing to make a major investment in technology, rather than considering other possible uses for the funds and their energy?
- *Financial resources of the institution and the student body.* How many can afford to pay their own way? Can the institution make up the difference *for everyone?*

- *Planning and assessment capacity.* Is the institution ready and able to make the commitment of planning resources and organizational resources to initiate and sustain such a large, complex undertaking?

OTHER ISSUES, OTHER QUESTIONS

Our recommendations are fairly simple to make but not so easy to carry out: if you want to improve education with technology, think on a time scale and dimensions that fit educational change, not just the technology. Aim for types of educational progress that are important to you and can be materially advanced by appropriate use of technology. Aim for types of progress that are likely to be both widely valued and quite visible. Consider the other ingredients that will be needed (for example, redesign of courses of study, faculty development, new ways of marketing your program, new organizational partnerships). Then patiently and persistently pursue that agenda for enough years (and through enough generations of technology) so that people can see and value the educational progress that has been made.

But any educational vision has another dimension, whether stated explicitly or not: the ways in which the institution intends to nurture the learning, experimentation, and growth of faculty and academic support professionals. The institution must provide an infrastructure that will support the less predictable progress that depends on individual faculty members' initiative, creativity, and dedication to improving teaching and learning with technology.

One reason why this approach to developing an institutional vision is easier said than done is that it involves several interdependent questions. Here are three of the most fundamental questions:

- What kinds of educational progress can and should you achieve with technology and what ingredients (in addition to technology) do you need to achieve such progress? In this effort to make progress, what do you want not to lose?
- Who are *you* (part A)? Who is included in your institutional identity? Who are the members of your community? How do your roles differ and interrelate?
- Who are *you* (part B)? How should you organize yourself? Who is primarily responsible for asking such questions as these? Who else has a right to be involved, and how? Who is responsible for carrying out the programs that

evolve from these discussions? Who should participate most actively, and in which phases? How rapidly?

Reconciling Conflicting Goals

Some people still think that *effectiveness goals* and *access goals* are in opposition. But using new technology enables certain kinds of gains to be made in both. For example, an on-line conversation can help individual learners open up and gain the wisdom of outside experts while also allowing access to students who could not otherwise participate because of their locations or schedules. Nonetheless, the increased use of technology to change educational processes will inevitably threaten certain aspects of access, quality, efficiency, and costs, just as, if we were to give up certain current uses of computers, that too would threaten certain aspects of access, quality, efficiency, and costs. Although gains always are accompanied by losses, some issues are worth special attention, because things may either improve or deteriorate depending on the details of how you use the technology.

Academic Community

Will your uses of technology connect people more than isolate them? Will they create loyalty and bonds more than they break such bonds? Will technology create better or more distanced communication between faculty and students, between faculty, administration, and alumni?

Budget Balance

Will you ramp up your uses of technology while carefully extending conventional budgetary limits, or will you jump over those limits in pursuit of the new?

Academic Freedom

Will the uses of technology free people to speak their minds and be heard more widely, or will they increase the degree to which they are under the observation and influence of others?

Relationships with Faculty Governance Organizations

Will new educational use of technology provide opportunities for better relationships between faculty governance organizations and administrative leaders or will it be the focus of increasing contention over ownership of course-related materials and intellectual work?

Role of Adjuncts

Will you give more dignity and support to part-time members of your communities, and enable them to contribute more fully to new approaches to teaching and learning that involve effective use of information technology? Or will you expect them to fit in with new initiatives as best they can?

Legal and Ethical Issues

As you develop your vision for educational technology, accessibility and ownership are two key areas that you will need to consider. What are the educational, ethical, and legal-economic consequences of investing more (or fewer) resources in making educational uses of information technology equally accessible to those who have disabilities? Are you planning and budgeting to take advantage of new ways of supporting previously excluded constituencies and to avoid legal liability for failing to comply with relevant legislation?

Have you examined the implications for ownership and control of the results of intellectual work of learners and teachers in the emerging digital environment? What policy decisions are you making about on-line behavior (acceptable use policies)—that is, about helping, sharing, and stealing on-line? What are your possible institutional liabilities and policies on plagiarism, control of course syllabi, and ownership of course materials, and so on? These questions need your full consideration.

Professional Support and Services

As we move from decades of limited instructional alternatives to many possibilities, and as expectations increase more rapidly than the resources available to meet them, the question of how best to use available resources comes to the fore. Today, most professional support units feel understaffed to meet faculty and student demands as they expand their uses of technology. Support personnel may panic when they realize the possible effects of efforts to encourage more faculty to use technology in their courses—and to encourage those who have already begun to continue and develop even more sophisticated uses of technology.

What will you do if current efforts to increase faculty interest in applications of information technology succeed? How are you measuring or estimating the future needs for professional development for faculty, staff, and administrators? How are you planning, reevaluating, and budgeting to meet those needs? It is important to plan for professional development.

Professional Development

Recognize the need for professional development resources and services to support educational uses of information technology. Create programs and resources that help faculty and support staff move beyond reconstructing traditional classroom or course structures. Emphasize training and support for "hybrid" courses, which involve both face-to-face and on-line interaction. Help everyone recognize that different groups, as well as different individuals, have different needs and can make different contributions. In particular, different topics and disciplines may work better on-line than others. Keep working to find ways to teach larger groups on-line (and in classrooms) while increasing quality and access.

It is unlikely that anyone can measure or prove the comparative cost-effectiveness of any single approach to professional development. Well-designed and well-led workshops can be effective for those who participate in them. Private "house calls" providing tutorials in faculty offices may be effective in reaching faculty who do not respond to anything else. The strategy likely to be most cost-effective in the long run is, once again, a hybrid—a combination of workshops for groups, tutorials for individuals, and programs that encourage and support small-group coaching-style efforts. In your planning consider the following:

- *Aim of efforts:* With current levels of faculty development and other support service resources, where should you focus your efforts? Should you meet continuing (growing) needs of faculty who are already committed to on-line instruction or encouraging and supporting people to develop new programs?

- *Focus of support services:* What is the risk that current or new, motivated faculty will be frustrated if support services are diverted to program development, which may not be intended for those faculty members? What are the likely consequences? The next wave of faculty to be receptive to new technologies in the classroom and distance instruction will not be as able and willing to do it as independently as the early adopters or pioneers were. The second wave is likely to be much larger than the first wave (especially if they are offered incentives and support). However, do not expect many of them to be self-starters or sustainers in this endeavor, because most will already be too busy with their traditional workload. In your efforts to support the interest of this new cohort of faculty members, do not undermine the commitment and energy of faculty and support service staff who have already found ways to work together to improve teaching and learning with information technology. Do not divert so many resources to the new wave that you impede the progress of the pioneers.
- *Use of student assistants:* In well-managed programs where students are trained and supervised and given opportunities for a variety of assignments—possibly including supervising their peers—the value of the support services they provide is usually dramatically greater than the costs of development and management. Students in such programs often acknowledge that they find their experience *educationally* enriching as well. Keep in mind that many students come to our institutions with extensive experience in technology and its applications. Do not overlook this resource.

OTHER RECOMMENDATIONS

As you develop your vision and support program for technology use, consider the following recommendations.

Develop New Collaborations Between Programs and Institutions

Look for and create new collaborations in the development, support, and use of teaching resources. (See http://www.tltgroup.org/OpenSource/Base.htm.)

Develop Incentives for Effective Use of Technology

Faculty, staff, and administrators are already working hard. Look at your reward system for individuals and programs; explore the use of special summer assignments or formal ways of recognizing outstanding accomplishments, for example.

Centralize Where It Makes Sense

Continue to develop and implement more consistent institutionwide standards for acquisition and support of hardware, software, course-management systems, and telecommunications, and more centralized coordination of support services for faculty use of technology. (Do not try too hard to standardize or centralize *fully*; current commitment to provide support only for WebCT for on-line courses may need to be expanded to include other platforms that could emerge in the near future and have features especially useful for certain subjects or teaching approaches.) Carefully analyze the costs and potential benefits—amount of training and length of transition time usually required, for example—of centralized resources, including an institutionwide campus portal. Do not simply listen to vendors.

Assign Responsibility

Put one individual in charge of leading your information technology initiatives. You need coordination and leadership. However, keep in mind that many individuals will be involved in different roles and with different responsibilities.

Collect and Use Data

Conduct evaluation or assessment studies of instructional uses of information technology to guide decisions about future uses. Compare retention patterns at your institution with national patterns. Be cautious in making assumptions about the needs and likely responses of students to changes in general education courses and programs. Do market research in advance, watch very carefully when making any changes, assess the results and pay attention to the information you collect, and be prepared to support efforts to change these centrally important programs.

Learn from Others and Watch Your Competition

Studies on the use and effectiveness of technology are constantly being undertaken and new developments are being reported on a regular basis. Assign someone the responsibility of keeping up with the research and what competitors are doing.

Develop a Replacement Policy

How will you maintain a short enough "refresh cycle" (maximum time between replacements of computer-related acquisitions) to meet faculty, staff, and student perceptions of obsolescence? Can you establish a system for distributing hand-me-down technology that will be perceived as fair and reasonable, especially by those near the bottom of the system?

Do Not Expect to Have All the Answers

There will always be more demands for resources than can be met as well as questions for which answers do not yet or may never exist. For example, how can you start a new initiative without risk? How do you expand what you are doing without new funding? What evidence is there that increasing on-line or distance activities will attract more students? There will be unrealistic questions, paradoxical questions, unwelcome questions and uncommon questions. Expect them all. When it comes to technology, nothing is easy.

CONCLUSION

In developing a comprehensive approach to technology on your campus, keep in mind that there are three major challenges:

- Establishing a vision for the institution and a practical plan for implementation
- Articulating and communicating the vision and plan to the entire campus community
- Determining the resources that will be required and providing them

What you are proposing must be realistic for your institution at this time in its history. That is, before committing to develop, implement, and support major programs involving many students and faculty, be sure your institution has people who have adequate, relevant experience with that particular technology and instructional approach and that you have real evidence that students will respond well—learning well and enrolling in and successfully completing courses that depend on this technology. Be careful about committing too fully to any one approach or platform, such as Blackboard, WebCT, or current configurations of two-way video electronic classrooms.

Your institution has already achieved much to be proud of in teaching, learning, research, and technology. There are likely still a few weaknesses in your infrastructure for supporting teaching, learning, and technology. Those parts of the infrastructure should be identified and strengthened. The institution should take advantage of previous strengths and build on the increasing willingness of faculty and staff to try new technologies and new approaches to teaching and learning.

A great effort will be necessary to keep expectations from further outdistancing available resources. As you engage more and more of your faculty, students, professional staff, and administrators in academic uses of information technology, you will be asking most of them to think and act in new ways, ways for which they are unprepared. Their need for training, technical support, and other forms of professional development will grow.

Most colleges and universities have barely begun to provide the level of professional development necessary to achieve the most attractive and reachable new goals. Most have barely begun to provide the level of professional development that is consistent with pragmatic selection of new technologies and new instructional approaches and their emerging educational missions. Most have barely begun to lay the foundation for professional development on which they will be able to frame and build the educational future.

Professional development *for everyone* can be the heart of the effort to achieve what is both possible and desirable with new technologies at your institution. Professional development in all its forms can help more of your stakeholders understand and embrace your institutional vision, and achieve elements of it both individually and collectively.

The greatest risk for your college or university when it comes to new technologies is to ignore them completely or to leap fully into on-line education without taking advantage of new opportunities to improve teaching and learning in traditional settings and with new combinations of face-to-face and asynchronous instruction. The most common mistake is to ignore the instructional possibilities inherent in the most widely accepted (that is, least newsworthy) applications. For example, the remarkably rapid rise in the number of faculty and students who use e-mail to communicate with each other opens new instructional options, many of which may be adopted with little fanfare, guidance, or support. Will your institution ensure that all students and faculty have access to e-mail and the Web at least above some plausible minimum level? Will your institution provide training and support for more efficient and instructionally rich uses of this increasingly popular tool? Will your institution develop ways of routinely reaching large groups of students through e-mail?

Every significant change brings new gains and new losses. In this time of rapid change, it is more important than ever to be clear about what you hope to gain and what you cherish and want not to lose. You can take advantage of the new discontinuity to improve education—in classrooms, on campus, on-line, in combination, everywhere. But as you look at new options and try to understand their consequences, what appears at risk of being lost? Many have responded to this question by saying that they fear that meaningful communications and connections among learners and teachers will be eroded by a growing dependence on sterile interaction with computers.

So in addition to the obvious learning goals enumerated earlier in this chapter, why not also use the integration of new applications of information technology as a means for developing more nurturing communities—communities in which all can grow and achieve, in which all learners, teachers, professional staff, administrators, and alumni are encouraged and enabled to support one another's efforts to surpass their own previous limits, communities in which everyone can learn, grow, teach, and help one another?

References

Gilbert, S. W. (2001, October 4). Why bother? [http://www.tltgroup.org/gilbert/WhyBotherLIST.htm].

Green, K. C. (2001, October). eCommerce comes slowly to the campus. [http://www.tltgroup.org/share/campuscomputing2001.htm].

Resources

Education, Technology, and Change

AAHESGIT. [http://www.cren.net:8080/guest/archives/aahesgit/].
TLT-SWG, formerly AAHESGIT, offers an ongoing on-line discussion of many issues related to education, technology, and change, with a strong emphasis on higher education. This is one of the largest, most highly moderated and edited Internet listservs. It began in 1993 and

averaged over ten messages per week at its peak (more recently about three per week). Several thousand subscribers and an estimated double or triple number of "pass-through" readers have made this one of the most long-lived, highly respected on-line discussion groups. The site offers an archive of the complete text of all messages.

Change. (1996, March-April).
This special issue of *Change: The Magazine of Higher Learning* is about the "slow revolution" under way in higher education as a result of new educational uses of information technology. It had the largest sales and distribution of any issue to that date. The lead article, "Making the Most of a Slow Revolution," offered a dozen recommendations, most of which still apply.

Chickering, A., & Ehrmann, S. (1996, October). Implementing the seven principles: Technology as lever. *AAHE Bulletin,* pp. 3–6.
Which kinds of technology use can help faculty and students implement Chickering and Gamson's seven principles of good practice in undergraduate education? This classic essay explains how technology can create educational value when it is used to help students to communicate, to get rapid feedback, to spend more time studying, and to carry out other activities that improve learning outcomes. (This essay also available at http://www.tltgroup.org/programs/seven.html.)

Chodron, P. [http://www.shambhala.org/teachers/pema/].
On this Web site Pema Chodron offers a variety of publications and other services and resources to help individuals cope with accelerating change and the confusion of daily life.

Ehrmann, S. (1995, March-April). Asking the right questions: What does research tell us about technology and higher learning? *Change, 27*(2), 20–27.
This essay gives a brief overview of the evaluation literature on teaching, learning, technology and costs. It is important reading for anyone who has ever been asked, "Where is the research about whether technology improves learning?" (See also http://www.learner.org/edtech/rscheval/rightquestion.html.)

Ehrmann, S. (1999, September). Access and/or quality: Redefining choices in the third revolution. *Educom Review,* pp. 24–27, 50–51.
Many assume that enlarging access to education (such as with distance learning) threatens the quality of outcomes while also assuming that investments in quality on campus are elitist, threatening access. But history suggests that during an educational revolution both access and quality improve in some ways while being damaged in others. This article argues that investments in technology, whether for distance learning or for on-campus purposes, should aim to improve both access to education and the quality of outcomes. (Also available on the Web at http://www.tltgroup.org/resources/or quality.htm.)

Ehrmann, S. (2001, January-February). Using technology to make large-scale improvements in the outcomes of higher education: Learning from past mistakes. *EDUCAUSE Review,* pp. 54–55.
Observers have been expecting a computerized transformation of teaching and learning in higher

education for almost forty years. Ehrmann argues that past efforts have often been frustrated by inappropriate strategies, not by the technology itself. This brief article outlines a five-part strategy for institutions, systems, and nations that want to use technology to make valuable, visible improvements in the outcomes of higher learning. (Also available on the Web at http://www.tltgroup.org/resources/Visions/Improving_Outcomes.html.)

Eisler, D. [http://weber.edu/deisler/campus_portals.htm].
David Eisler, the provost of Weber State University in Utah, has written several exceptionally helpful articles about campus portals. He has built a Web site that offers a well-organized and rich collection of information and insights about the important decisions surrounding the development of a single institutional portal that users can customize as the one best source of information from and about a college or university. See the site for more information and for references to his publications and presentations.

Gilbert, S. W. [http://www.syllabus.com/] and [http://www.tltgroup.org/].
Since mid-2000, Steven W. Gilbert has written a monthly column in *Syllabus* on observations, insights, and challenges about the instructional uses of information technology. Some of the columns can be found on the *Syllabus* and TLT Group Web sites shown here.
In addition, articles, workbooks, guidelines, and Web pages originally developed for teaching, learning, technology roundtables, and related collaborative change programs are available directly from the TLT Group (One Dupont Circle, Suite 360, Washington DC 20036).

Gilbert, S. W. (2001, October 4). Why bother? [http://www.tltgroup.org/gilbert/WhyBotherLIST.htm].
We have no clear proof of the major educational benefits from making big investments in academic uses of information technology. But as more faculty members and students are encouraged to use technology for teaching and learning, they expect to accomplish more, and they need more help. The capacity of academic support services to provide that help usually falls farther behind. The "support service crisis" gets worse. So, why bother? What are the different kinds of reasons for trying?

Gilbert, S. W., & Green, K. C. (1994, May-June). The new computing in higher education. *Change,* pp. 90–95.

Gilbert, S. W., & Green, K. C. (1995, March-April). Great expectations: Content, communications, productivity, and the role of information technology in higher education. *Change,* pp. 8–18.
These two articles by Steven W. Gilbert and Kenneth C. Green offer an overview of trends and implications of educational uses of information technology in the late 1980s and early 1990s. Most of their observations continue to apply.

Green, K. C. [http://www.campuscomputing.net/].
The Campus Computing Project, directed by Kenneth C. Green, has been a valuable source of information for years on uses of desktop computing and networking in higher education.

Saltrick, S. (1998). Through a dark wood. [http://www.tltgroup.org/resources/rdarkwood.html]. This classic essay has helped many institutions discuss some of the confusion and fears raised by the turbulent possibilities of new technology.

Early Adopters and Mainstream Faculty

Geoghegan, W. H. (1994). *Whatever happened to instructional technology?* Paper presented at the 22nd annual conference of the International Business Schools Computing Association, Baltimore.

Geoghegan, W. H. (1996). In response. *Change, 28,* 30–37.

Gilbert, S. (1995). An "online" experience: Discussion group debates why faculty use or resist technology. *Change, 27,* 28–45.

Rogers, E. M. (1981). *Diffusion of innovations.* New York: Free Press.
Early adopters of educational uses of information technology differ in many important ways from the mainstream faculty. These four works discuss this issue in various ways. For a rich exploration of some of the more significant differences and their implications, see also some of the messages included in an Internet discussion in the mid-1990s that began with a contribution from William Geoghegan of IBM and concluded with a brief essay by Jane Marcus of Stanford. A selection of these observations and insights was published in the special March-April 1995 issue of *Change*. These ideas are becoming even more important and useful in this new decade as many institutions seek to engage "almost all" the faculty in using information technology to improve teaching and learning. (See also http://www.tltgroup.org/ok/PioneersToMainstream.htm and http://www.tltgroup.org/ok/pioneerstomainstream.htm.)

Changing Demographics

[http://www.tltgroup.org/programs/easi.html].
New legislation, interpretations, and new technology applications all make it more important, cost-effective, and satisfying than ever to provide access to information and instructional resources through information technology for learners, teachers, and others who have disabilities. See this Web site for links to information about EASI, Web AIM, and related resources for enabling those with disabilities to use information technology and information resources.

Ingle, H. T. [http://www.utep.edu/~comm3459/spring97/ingle2.htm].
Henry T. Ingle has done some valuable research and analysis on the changing demographics of the student bodies in the United States and the implications for the ways in which information technology can and should be used for teaching and learning. See this Web site for work by Ingle.

Instructional and Professional Issues

[http://www.gnu.org] and [http://www.tltgroup.org/OpenSource/Base.htm].
The Open Source approach to software development has grown into a significant force and a potentially viable economic option. Some of the principles, practices, and tools that have evolved

to support this movement appear to offer promise for the development of instructional resources and professional development resources. See the works of Richard Stallman and others on these Web sites.

Cleveland, H. (1989, May-June). How can "intellectual property" be "protected?" *Change*.
Harlan Cleveland and others have written about the changing notions of intellectual property. Intellectual works can be captured, represented, and duplicated more quickly, easily, and cheaply than ever before in the rapidly changing digital environment. The foundations on which the current intellectual property system are built are eroding. New perspectives are needed. When almost any kind of information in almost any medium can now be represented and processed with digital electronics, the range of things that can be considered intellectual property is mind-boggling. Perhaps the briefest statement of the need to redefine terms was made by Harlan Cleveland in this 1989 article.

Gilbert, S. W. (1990, Spring). Information technology, intellectual property, and education. Washington, DC: *EDUCOM Review: Computing and Communications in Colleges and Universities, 25*(1), 14–20.
An overview of issues about the changing meaning of ownership and control of intellectual works as a consequence of digitalization of information.

Nardick, D. (2000). An analysis of the teaching, learning, and technology roundtable in higher education. Unpublished doctoral dissertation, American University.
Beginning in 1994, several hundred colleges and universities adapted the guidelines for TLT (teaching, learning, and technology) roundtables. Daryl Nardick analyzed the sustained effort and success of several dozen in applying this approach. In her currently unpublished doctoral dissertation, she developed several recommendations useful to other institutions attempting to integrate information technology into the academic program more efficiently, effectively, and comfortably.

Community and Connectedness

Hallowell, E. M. (1993). Connectedness. In *Finding the heart of the child* (pp. 193–209). Association of Independent Schools in New England. (Available on-line at http://www. tltgroup.org/Share/%HallowellConnectedness+SWGIntro95.htm.)
Edward Hallowell has written many books, leads workshops, and makes presentations to help participants understand their need and capability for many forms of connectedness. He recognizes that new uses of information technology and telecommunications are often overwhelming and confusing, interfering with the need of many for more meaningful connections with each other. But he also advocates using technology to help achieve or rebuild connections. See Hallowell's definition of "connectedness" in this chapter, where he also describes some ways in which different forms of connectedness are possible, important, and at risk: familial, historical, social, institutional-organizational, informational, and religious-transcendent.

Morley, B. Fire at the center. [http://www.bym-rsf.org/pubs.html].

As he shaped the Baltimore Yearly Meeting Camping Program over almost three decades, Barry Morley described some of the principles he developed for building an extraordinary nurturing community.

CHAPTER 21

Diversity Issues

JOSEPH H. SILVER, SR.

O ne of the unique characteristics of higher education is its diversity. The very nature of the academy derives from a diversity of thought shaped by the experiences and environment of the people who work there, the people who receive its services, and the people who are its trustees and supporters. The result of this is that although all institutions have similar functions, each has many things that set it apart from the others and make it distinct. This distinctiveness should be recognized and appreciated.

RECOGNIZING AND APPRECIATING DIVERSITY

This distinctiveness may be manifested in institutional type, target student population and community constituents, program and curricular offerings, and location, size, and mission. Although each of these things is important and makes for very comfortable conversation, discussions of diversity that center on these concepts alone will not adequately prepare institutions to be competitive in this new century. The conversations need to be broadened to include questions of gender, ethnicity, and learning style. On many campuses, faculty members are losing their competitive edge because they seek to clone themselves in the hiring, promotion, and retention (tenure) processes, thus excluding a sector of the population that could make significant contributions to teaching and learning, as well as to the overall educational process. A policy of inclusion celebrates diversity and realizes its positive impact on teaching and learning. Inclusion also recognizes that *different* is not inherently bad or negative. *Different* can be the cornerstone of an institution's uniqueness and quality.

One of the critical leadership issues that you will face as an institutional leader centers on diversity. The absence of leadership in matters of diversity has left many colleges and universities searching for answers to questions posed by concerned students and community leaders. It is common knowledge that colleges and universities marshal their personnel and resources to achieve goals that they think are important. This campus brainpower should be used to develop an action plan to achieve campus diversity, because diversity is as important as any other initiative a university might pursue.

Diversity can be achieved only when it is pursued in the context of the mission and core values of an institution. Whether you are a board member, president, vice president, dean, or department chair, your leadership is needed to help the campus community understand the positive outcomes of being truly diverse. Achieving diversity causes both simple and complex challenges. Only when leaders at all levels work together and embrace diversity as an institutional norm and expectation will the barriers that hinder the establishment of a diverse campus be removed.

TRANSFORMING A CULTURE

As universities move from comfortable to difficult and complex conversations about diversity, many of them stumble because of their institutional history and their members' own personal perceptions. Although the intentions may be the best, the goals will not be reached because the assumptions are faulty. In order to bridge this gap, the conversations you lead about diversity must be mission-driven. You must pursue diversity from an asset model rather than a deficit model. Diversity should be a core value at all levels of the institution, manifesting itself at the macro and the micro levels. Institutions that understand the change agenda and the importance of leadership as one of its central components often use diversity as a transforming agent. The truly transformed campus embraces diversity, and all of those in leadership roles willingly accept their role as transformers. When leaders accept this transformer role, campuses across America will achieve diversity goals in personnel, curriculum, and climate. If you are a college or university president, one of your key roles and challenges is thus to establish this priority among those campus leaders deemed appropriate.

This chapter will discuss diversity as an agent of transformation. It will discuss some common pitfalls you will face in trying to establish a diverse campus but also will provide a blueprint for doing so.

ASSESSING YOUR PRESENT CLIMATE FOR DIVERSITY

Approaching diversity as an asset can transform the campus in many ways. In fact, a strong diversity agenda can actually be a transforming agent for teaching, learning, hiring, promotion and retention, and the entire climate of your institution. Keep in mind that the quality of the teaching and learning experience is affected by who is taught, what is taught, who teaches, and how the teaching is done.

Before undertaking any formal diversity program, determine the present climate for diversity on your campus. Establishing a task force specifically to collect this information and make recommendations for action can be an extremely powerful first step because it can also help build campuswide support for the actions that will follow. Exhibit 21.1 presents a number of questions that such a task force can address.

EXHIBIT 21.1. Climate for Diversity Questionnaire.

- To what extent does the campus accommodate the experiences of diverse groups? Where do such actions or activities take place? Do they reach all students? Do they reach all personnel? Are all areas of diversity addressed (race, gender, ethnicity, and so on)?
- To what extent does the curriculum reflect the experiences of diverse groups?
- Does the makeup of the faculty, staff, and administration reflect the general population or reflect diversity from a race and gender standpoint?
- Does the student body reflect the general population?
- Does the makeup of the student body offer opportunities for students to interact with and learn from students from different groups?
- Does the makeup of the student body offer opportunities for students to interact with different sectors of your community?
- To what extent are "other" voices included in curriculum planning?
- To what extent are "other" voices included in program and budget planning?
- Do teaching styles take into account the different learning styles of students and different life experiences they bring to the campus?
- Does the campus reflect and appreciate the dual consciousness that is evident among many ethnic minorities and women?

CHARACTERISTICS OF A HEALTHY CLIMATE

Diversity must be integral to the campus thinking and feeling. Diversity needs to be viewed in the following ways.

Diversity Should Occur in an Institutional and Organizational Context

In order for any diversity initiative to be successful, it must be achieved in the context of the organization. A diversity initiative must be mission-driven, articulated and supported by the leadership, and readily noticeable in all aspects of the university. Diversity should not be marginalized or on the periphery. Also, diversity should be seen as an asset and it should not be a mystery on the campus. Therefore, diversity should be at the center of what goes on at a university. These ideas must be constantly reinforced not by what you say but through your actions.

Diversity Should Be Mission-Driven

It is common and accepted knowledge that everything that takes place on a university campus should be related to the institutional mission and purpose. This is no different when it comes to diversity. A strong statement about the importance of diversity in the mission statement can quickly dispel arguments against spending time, energy, and resources needed to diversify a campus. If diversity is central to the mission, then every part of the campus will have a front-end conversation about diversity in matters of hiring, curriculum, planning, and budget; this conversation will not occur as an afterthought. A mission-driven diversity agenda will not rely on one individual; rather it will be part of the very fabric of the institution.

Diversity Should Be Evident in the Leadership of the Institution

One of the main contradictions in higher education occurs when presidents or chancellors and other campus leaders give eloquent speeches about the importance of diversity while their own senior leadership team is not diverse. Presidents and chancellors must lead by example. If they are serious about diversity, they must hire minorities and women into senior leadership positions in the university, and they must hold others to the same standard. Once they hire these individuals, they should empower them very publicly. Therefore, no one will be confused about their position, responsibilities, and authority. As they say, "Actions speak louder than words."

Diversity Should Not Be Marginalized

As already noted, diversity should be a shared core value of the institution. It cannot be marginalized by not being a central component of the processes of the university. Issues of diversity should be addressed in the planning and budget processes. Diversity should not be associated with a person rather than the institution. If it is associated with a person, what happens when that person leaves? In contrast, if diversity is institutionalized, then people can come and go but diversity matters will always be central to any campus conversation. This is not an argument for or against hiring a point person for diversity issues and initiatives. However, if a point person is hired, he or she should be given a senior-level position and title and allowed broad scope and interaction rather than being narrowly focused on single-purpose issues. The location of the position on the organizational chart can diffuse many of the negative stereotypes that could taint interactions or it can foster them. The focus should be on diffusing any negative stereotypes so that real progress can be made.

Diversity Should Be Viewed As an Asset

Many times university leaders fail to see diversity as an asset. Instead they choose to view it from a deficit model. Yet viewing diversity from an asset model will help transform people, processes, curricula, and ultimately, the institution. An asset model values the experiences and differences of others, resulting in important conversations and dialogue. These discussions will broaden the range of possibilities for a campus and lead to its transformation. The transformation will have at its foundation the inclusion of people regardless of differences.

Diversity Should Not Be Mystical

On a truly transformed campus, observers will be able to recognize diversity in what they see, hear, learn, taste, and experience. The artwork and textbooks should reflect diversity. The student body should reflect diversity. The people who are brought in as speakers, performers, and faculty, staff, and administration should reflect diversity. The food in the cafeteria should reflect diversity. The policy discussions and curriculum planning should reflect diversity. On a truly transformed campus, the examples of appreciation for diversity are not found merely in a rhetorical monologue or speeches each year at the opening of the fall semester or other convenient times. Rather, they are part of the fabric of the institution and a demonstrated core value embraced by all. We should not need to hunt to find evidence of diversity on a campus. It should be readily seen and identified using any or all of our five senses.

ESTABLISHING A CAMPUS THAT SUPPORTS DIVERSITY

Diversity has to be achieved in the context of a healthy and inclusive campus climate. It follows that a healthy and inclusive climate can transform a campus. Various groups will feel even more welcome at a university if there is a good campus climate. A welcoming climate will affect the productivity of students, faculty, staff, and administrators. An inviting climate can have a positive impact on recruitment, retention, and the overall growth of the university. It will also foster an environment that enhances teaching and learning. Once an institution has a reputation of having a supportive campus climate, new and different things can take place because new and different people will be at the table during crucial conversations. An institution with a positive, welcoming campus climate will also find that it will be sought out by a diverse population of potential employees. What a wonderful boost to recruitment efforts this will be!

The responsibility of achieving diversity on a university campus begins and ends with the person who has the responsibility for every other important initiative: the head of the institution, its president or chancellor. Yet in order for any president to be successful, others up, down, and across the organizational chart must play significant roles too. Some of these key people or "transformers" are chief academic officers, deans, department chairs, faculty, students, board or trustee members, community leaders and supporters, and public officials.

Presidents and Chancellors as Transformers

Presidents and chancellors are the leaders of their institutions. If you are in this role, you must be able to articulate the mission of the university and rally internal and external constituents to work toward achieving it. You must have a clear vision and be able to communicate that vision and how you will use it to achieve the university's mission and goals. Diversity should be a part of the mission and an articulated goal of the institution. You must set the tone for fulfillment of that goal. You cannot be ambivalent or straddle the fence. In this matter, as in any other crucial matter, you should lead by example. Your staff should reflect the diversity agenda, and you should be prepared to use both the carrot and the stick. You should hold everyone who reports to you to the same standard, and they in turn should do the same down the chain. The reward system should support those who meet this objective. However, it should also address those who choose not to meet this objective. Another aspect of your role in the diversity agenda is the influence you can have on appointees to your board or other key roles.

Chief Academic Officers as Transformers

The chief academic officer plays a key role in establishing a diverse institution. If you are in this role, you are pivotal in the hiring, promotion-tenure, and curriculum development processes. The initial charge given to the search, promotion-tenure, and curriculum committees can affect process and outcomes. As chief academic officer, you interact with all facets of the campus community and can use this forum to champion diversity issues. Given your influence on matters of personnel and budgets, you can motivate faculty, staff, and line administrators in a positive manner and encourage them to meet the institution's diversity goals. You should also be able to articulate the education value of diversity in clear and precise terms. As you work with deans, department chairs, and directors, help them shape the strategic initiatives of the various units and align them with the university's diversity concerns. Use the reward system to ensure that the diversity goals of the units are met. If you show little enthusiasm for the diversity agenda, it will be DOA—dead on arrival.

Deans and Chairs as Transformers

Deans and department chairs are also pivotal in developing and maintaining a diversity agenda. In this role, you shape the direction of the academic units of the university. Your attention to personnel and budgets is the key to your success. You should have a keen knowledge of pending vacancies and retirements. You can use this knowledge to be proactive in cultivating relationships with diverse groups among whom candidates for these positions might be found. You can play an important role in shaping the curriculum from a diversity perspective. Your appointment of committees, especially search committees, can also be used to advance this agenda. Appoint only those individuals who have bought into the diversity goals of the university. Once you have succeeded in attracting a diverse group of faculty, you must build a support system around them. You must protect them from becoming the resident "experts" on minority matters—for example, serving as minority representative on search or other committees—which will misdirect their energies and talents. *Belonging to a particular ethnic group does not make an individual a universal authority on that group and its dynamics.* You must help new hires focus on establishing themselves as teachers and getting their research started. You can use your influence to make sure minority faculty are introduced to the campus and the community. Finally, if you detect discrimination of any kind, you must act swiftly and make your actions public. This will send the signal that such behavior will not be tolerated.

Faculty as Transformers

Faculty members are extremely important if a campus is to achieve its diversity goals. In many cases, they are the gatekeepers of either change or the status quo in faculty inclusiveness. After all, it is the faculty who determine who is invited to enter on the front end (hiring) and who is allowed to stay at the back end (tenure). Besides being on the front line of hiring, faculty members are the caretakers of the curriculum. They cannot operate in a vacuum, however. They must operate in the organizational context. If diversity is a component of the mission and goals of the university, faculty should be held accountable for it in the hiring, promotion, and tenure processes. The same should hold true for program and curriculum development. Faculty need to support the success of minorities and women once they are hired, remembering to include them in both formal and informal networks in the department and on campus. It is important to select minorities for campus activities, but do not forget to invite them to lunch or to your house for dinner as well. It is also OK to ask a few personal questions: "How are the children doing?" "Do you need help finding a school, or beautician, or barbershop?" All these things are critical to socializing a diverse faculty. Search committees should be properly charged on the front end and monitored throughout the search process. Promotion and tenure committees, for example, should be made aware of the significance of research and scholarship that may not be mainstream. Committee members should be bold enough to look favorably on people and their work even though they may be different. Remember, "different" does not necessarily mean less important.

Students as Transformers

Next to selecting and being accepted to a college, being able to fit in is probably the most important thing on the minds of students. They wonder about who their roommates will be, who will share living space with them, and who their friends will be. This is true no matter the institution. These are reasonable and accepted questions given the socialization patterns of young people. These questions become even more critical when minority students are placed on a campus that does not have a diverse population or a support system to embrace them. Majority students must reach out and minority students must be receptive to this overture. Student government leaders can use their operational powers to make sure that student committees are representative and inclusive. Leaders on the student union board can make sure that student activity fees are used to increase opportunities for all students. Students must also realize that they can grow as a result of learning about the experiences and culture of others. This kind of transformation can assist them greatly in the workplace after they graduate. The key is to get student leaders involved from the beginning in diversity initiatives. Ask them for help. Involve them in the work of task forces and ensure their participation.

Board Members or Trustees as Transformers

The board member or trustee also plays a role in achieving diversity. If you serve in this capacity, first you must ensure that proper policies and resources are in place to achieve this important goal. Second, you must empower and be supportive of the president or chancellor as he or she executes the diversity agenda, even during the tough times. Third, you must be able to communicate to your peers why achieving diversity is important. Probably the most important thing you can do as a board member or trustee is to support the president publicly and privately when the naysayers start to attack—and attack they will! However, for diversity to be achieved, you and your fellow board members or trustees must first believe in the value of diversity yourselves.

RECRUITMENT, HIRING, AND RETENTION POLICIES

Recruitment, hiring, and retention policies must also reflect the diversity agenda.

Hiring Personnel

There are more excuses than solutions for why diversity cannot be achieved in hiring personnel. Although the excuses are many, they basically fall into two categories: supply and demand. The argument that "we can't find any because they aren't out there" has been heard during the deliberation process of many search committees. In some cases, this might be a legitimate argument. But how do we account for the failure to hire a diverse population when the supply has been identified? The only explanation can be that there has not been an adequate demand made to bring about this needed change. Often, when the search process does find a person who meets all the expressed qualifications, that person is still not hired. The search committee discusses the issues and in many instances never once consults the candidate. We all know the drill. It goes something like this: although that person is qualified, he or she

- Will not come here
- Will not come here for what we are paying
- Will not fit in here
- Will not have a social life here
- Has all the qualities, but there is something that I just cannot put my hands on
- Will not come because he or she will be isolated from "his or her people"

Make sure that committees allow the candidate—not someone on the search committee—to make these decisions. Institutions must hold search committees accountable at all levels of the hiring process. Those making the final decision must also be held accountable.

Individuals and groups in your community can be an important asset in bringing minorities to your campus. Build a solid working relationship with these groups, and everyone will benefit. A diverse workforce can create positive changes that are brought about by differences in perspective, ideas, and experiences. Having more and different people engaged in discussions about policy issues, teaching and learning, and change can truly lead to campus transformation.

Promotion and Retention

An institution achieves very little if it has a revolving door or falls prey to the I-have-one syndrome. In fact, this kind of practice can cause an institution to get a negative reputation in the marketplace. And this reputation can be hard to change. The promotion and retention process (tenure) must reflect the diverse workforce. This does not mean that you have to compromise the quality of research or scholarship or any other standard. In fact, having a diverse faculty, staff, and administration should enhance all of these important matters. Embracing a diverse faculty and staff and the by-products of their labor should transform the teaching, learning, and socialization patterns at all levels of the university. This will mean accepting a different kind of research and scholarship in some cases and rethinking the sanctity of one publication over some others. In some cases it may mean rethinking the reward system. However, if diversity is to be achieved and maintained, then the minorities and women hired must be promoted and retained. For this to happen, the environment must be supportive. The department chair plays a pivotal and critical role in this regard. Support must begin in the academic home. For this reason, the topic of diversity must be placed on the agendas of your deans and in their meetings with their chairs. Exhibit 21.2 lists specific actions you can take to develop a climate for supporting diversity on your campus with a particular focus on faculty and staff recruitment and retention.

Exhibit 21.3 identifies a number of problems you can expect to encounter.

THE CASE FOR DIVERSITY FROM OTHER PERSPECTIVES

I hope that the arguments I have already presented in this chapter were persuasive enough to compel your institution to be inclusive and diverse. Just in case they were not, let us look at what the demographics indicate.

What the Numbers Are Saying

In many areas of our country, minorities are rapidly becoming the majority. Cities in Texas, California, New York, and several other states are experiencing this phenomenon. According to projections, minorities will become the majority in many more cities across the country. This growing population will be seen in the student population in

EXHIBIT 21.2. **Strategies to Create Faculty and Staff Diversity.**

Recruitment
- Make sure search committee members are knowledgeable about diversity goals and are committed to those goals.
- Pay careful attention to search committee appointments.
- Charge search committees with clear expectations.
- Align diversity goals with the mission of the university. Review the mission statement to make sure it has a diversity component.
- Make sure department chairs are active in the search and retention process. They should create a support system for minorities and women in the department and create opportunities for growth and acknowledgment.
- Create opportunities for minority scholars to interact with the campus community (guest lecturers, visiting professors, and so on).
- Develop relationships with minorities and women early in their career to create comfort levels on both sides.
- Recruit with the intent to retain.
- Use the "person-to-person" approach with current faculty and administrators. Also, if you advertise in publications, do not forget those frequently read by minorities (*Black Issues in Higher Education,* minority discipline newsletters, and so on).

universities across this country for years to come. Think about this from a global perspective. Nine out of every ten people in the world are yellow, red, brown, or black. People with ancestral ties to Africa are the second largest racial group in the world. Ethnic and racial minority populations in the United States are growing at a much faster rate than the Euro-American population, with the Hispanic population growing the fastest. In this century, the collective ethnic and racial minority will be larger than the Euro-American population. If universities fail to embrace this reality, they not only show their arrogance but sow the seeds of their own demise.

The Association Point of View

These numbers are revealing and clear. It is against this backdrop that colleges and universities must set their future agendas. It is not in their long-term interest to neglect diver-

EXHIBIT 21.2. Continued

Retention

- Build a multilevel support system (at department, school, and university levels).
- Do not expect the new hire to be the resident expert on minority issues.
- Provide competitive salaries on the front end and be fair in your assessment for merit, promotion, and tenure.
- Do not overburden new minority hires with committee work.
- Do not succumb to the I-have-one theory and practice.
- Be clear about job expectations and what is required for advancement and tenure.
- Provide mentors for each new minority hire.

Climate

- Make recruitment and retention an institutional commitment, with the president or chancellor setting the tone.
- Reward those who meet diversity goals.
- Remove offensive symbols from all campus property.
- Address breaches of civility swiftly and publicly.
- Develop a comprehensive plan to address overall campus climate.
- Make sure that student programs and other campus activities are inclusive when it comes to presenters, entertainment, and frequency.

EXHIBIT 21.3. Common Obstacles to Diversity.

- Failure to have a knowledge base on matters of diversity
- Lack of consequences for failure to meet diversity goals
- Failure to hold leaders and search committees accountable
- Feeling satisfied when one or two minorities are hired in a given unit or the university proper, thus never creating a critical mass
- Failure to address campus climate issues
- Allowing discrimination and acts of racism or sexism to linger without taking appropriate action
- Failure to develop a comprehensive diversity plan

sity. Ideally, colleges and universities will embrace diversity because of the many positive contributions a diverse workforce can make. But if this does not cause them to embrace diversity, then surely the statistics on the recruitment pool will pique their interest.

The American Council on Education (ACE) shared a copy of the higher education community's statement, "On the Importance of Diversity in Higher Education," in a March 10, 1998 letter from the organization's president at that time, Stanley O. Ikenberry. In the letter, Ikenberry noted that the statement was disseminated in the major higher education publications and the *Washington Post.* He reported that at the time of its publication, the statement had been "endorsed by over fifty higher education associations and organizations." The statement offered the following reasons to consider racial and ethnic diversity as one factor among many when considering persons for admissions and hiring: "Diversity enriches the educational experience; it promotes personal growth and a healthy society; it strengthens communities and the workplace; it enhances America's economic competitiveness."

Although it was crafted in 1998, this statement still is valid today. Colleges and universities will do well to adopt, embrace, and implement a diversity agenda for the reasons this statement makes plain. More educational associations should step to the fore and voice their concerns on the matter of diversity. Actually, there should be a call to action to their constituent groups from the leadership of the associations.

A CONCLUDING THOUGHT

An old hymn that has been sung in churches across America says, "Everybody talking about heaven ain't going there." To paraphrase that hymn, I say, "Everybody talking about diversity ain't committed to it." This lack of commitment can be seen in the great deal of talk and very little action going on. Higher education needs leaders who are committed to taking the necessary action to transform their campuses in ways that plan for, pursue, and achieve diversity. Results—not empty rhetoric—will be the crowning jewel.

Resources

Strentny, J. Affirmative action and new demographic realities. (2001, February 16). *Chronicle of Higher Education,* p. B7.
   Affirmative action policy is critiqued. The salient point is that the group the policy was intended to assist is losing ground. This is because of the growing number of nonblack minorities.

The beneficiaries of affirmative action have changed over the years. The article calls for a more coherent policy developed by a bipartisan commission.

American Council on Education. (1986–2000). *Status report on minorities in higher education.* Washington, DC: American Council on Education.
Statistical updates on the number and percentages of minorities at each level of the education ladder. Trend data are presented and analyzed to show cause and affect of access and equity in education.

Healy, B. Berkeley struggles to stay diverse in post-affirmative action era. (1998, May 28). *Chronicle of Higher Education,* p. A31.
The impact of Proposition 209 is addressed as it relates to minority enrollment at University of California-Berkeley. The impact was negative. Dropping affirmative action caused a 52 percent decrease in African American and Hispanic students in the freshman class. Berkeley has always been seen as progressive. This proposition caused the institution to move backward.

Boyer, E. L. (1990). *Scholarship reconsidered: Priorities of the professorate.* Princeton, NJ: Carnegie Foundation for the Advancement of Teaching
This books calls for new ways of looking at scholarship and professional work in the academy. An argument for changing the reward system is made. The parameters for the new reward system are discussed.

Schmidt, P. Federal judge upholds use of race on admissions. (2001, June 5). *Chronicle of Higher Education, p.* A32.
The University of Michigan shows the educational benefits of using race in undergraduate admissions. The university defends its policy by showing that it is narrowly tailored. The decision was upheld in the federal district court.

Price, H. B. Fortifying the case for diversity and affirmative action. (1998, May 22). *Chronicle of Higher Education,* p. B4.
The author provides a framework and a context for viewing diversity that expands the scope. The focus should not be on the institutional good alone but should be broadened to show a compelling societal and state interest. Disputed is the argument that good test scores equal being qualified. Several examples of criteria that can be used to foster diversity are presented.

Pincus, F. I. (1996, November-December). Discrimination comes in many forms: Individual, institutional, and structural. *American Behavioral Scientist, 40,* 186–194.
This article explains that discrimination comes in many forms. The author focuses on three different types of discrimination and demonstrates how each form hinders diversity.

Redeeming the American promise. (1995). Atlanta: Southern Education Foundation.
This is a comprehensive study on the state of education in America. The panel of experts studied and made recommendation on matters of access, attainment, and success. A critical analysis was made of the vestiges of segregation and how best to address them.

Silver, J. H., Sr. (1987). *Minority faculty recruitment in Kennesaw College: 1976–1986*. Athens: University of Georgia.

This article is a case study of how Kennesaw State University addressed its lack of diversity in the faculty ranks. It provides specific information on how this success was realized in the recruitment of minority faculty during the ten-year period 1976 to 1986.

Silver, J. H., Sr. (1994). Assessing perceptions and experiences of African American faculty at traditionally white institutions. In R. Stake, S. Hood, H. Frierson, Sr. (Eds.), Advances in program evaluation beyond the dream: Meaningful program evaluation and assessment to achieve equal opportunities at predominantly white institutions (p. 63). Greenwich, CT: JAI Press.

This book chapter focuses on how to assess the perceptions and experiences of African American faculty once they are hired on a university or college campus. This is a good source to determine the effectiveness of strategies once they have been implemented.

Silver, J. H., Sr., Dennis, R., & Spikes, C. (1988). Black faculty in traditionally white institutions. In *Selected Adams states: Characteristics, experiences, and perceptions*. Atlanta: Southern Education Foundation.

This is a study of 110 universities in ten states and their success in meeting the Adams case mandates to increase diversity in the faculty ranks. The study includes information on the success of these institutions in recruitment, promotion, and tenure of African Americans.

Whitt, E., Edison, M., & Pascarella, E. (2001, March-April). Influences on students' openness to diversity and challenge in the second and third year of college. *Journal of Higher Education, 72*(2), 172–204.

This study investigated influences on second- and third-year college students, focusing on their openness to diversity and its challenges. Approximately 1,054 students took part in the study. The study is part of the National Study on Student Learning at the University of Illinois at Chicago.

Rudenstine, N. Why a diverse student body is so important. (1996, April 19). *Chronicle of Higher Education,* p. B1.

This article cites the benefits of diversity on a college or university campus. Information is provided to show how institutions benefit from diversity from a social, civic, and educational standpoint. A historical context of diversity is provided. The claim is made that society as a whole has benefited from higher education opening its doors to a diverse group of students.

PART SIX

Position-Specific Issues for Academic Leaders

In these constantly changing, always challenging, and frequently threatening times, the race will go to the most creative, innovative, nimble, and flexible institutions that are able to lead their own change, turning challenges into opportunities, while also preserving their core values and sacred traditions. This is to say that the race will go to those institutions that are well-led, not just well-managed.

Jay Morley and Doug Eadie, *The Extraordinary Higher Education Leader*, Washington, DC: National Association of College and University Business Officers, 2001, p. 3.

CHAPTER 22

The Role of Governing Boards

Issues, Recommendations, and Resources

> After ten years of research and dozens of engagements as consultants to nonprofit boards, we have reached a rather stark conclusion: effective governance by a board of trustees is a relatively rare and unnatural act.
>
> —Richard P. Chait, Thomas P. Holland, & Barbara E. Taylor,
> *Improving Performance of Governing Boards*

Serving on the board of a college or university or as a regent in a statewide system is a difficult and challenging job. Although the job brings prestige, doing it successfully requires a great deal more hard work and time than many new members anticipate. Serving in this capacity will provide you with the opportunity to work with a group of dedicated and talented individuals and to have a significant impact on the lives of students, the health of your college or university, and the community your institution serves. Board member is a position for which few are fully prepared. Colleges and universities present unique challenges, and in your position you will require a far greater range of knowledge than you may anticipate. However, the role is one of the most rewarding that a citizen can hold.

The first section of this chapter is an excerpt from *Renewing the Academic Presidency: Stronger Leadership for Tougher Times,* a report of the Association of Governing Boards of Universities and Colleges' Commission on the Academic Presidency (1996). This is an important report for both faculty and administrators because it addresses issues pertaining to a number of challenges now facing higher education and makes specific recommendations. The excerpt is followed by additional observations and a set of recommendations directed to those individuals who serve as members of governing boards. Many of these suggestions grew out of the two Minnowbrook conferences, which were sponsored by the National Academy for Academic Leadership with the support of the W. K. Kellogg, Knight, and Park foundations. The chapter concludes with recommended resources for board members and trustees. Eugene Hotchkiss and Thomas Longin assisted in the development of this chapter.

EXCERPTS FROM REVIEWING THE ACADEMIC PRESIDENCY

At its best, the board of trustees is committed to, and knowledgeable about, its own institution and familiar with the issues affecting higher education more broadly. As engaged and loyal stewards, the best trustees make decisions based on their responsibility to the institution as a whole. The board's fundamental role is to select the president, develop a vision for the institution in conjunction with the president, and provide sufficient oversight to ensure that the vision is realized. To do this, trustees must be ready to ask probing questions, assess different points of view, suggest directions, set expectations, and monitor results.

Problems of Governance: Governing Boards

Unfortunately, too many trustees lack a basic understanding of higher education or a significant commitment to it. In extensive interviewing, the commission found instance after instance in which boards were either inadequately engaged with their institutions, or conversely, inappropriately involved in detail. Understandably, these presidents requested confidentiality. These examples are typical:

- A highly successful private college president reports that his board members are seldom genuinely helpful. They seem insulated, distracted by their own professional pressures, and unwilling to devote sufficient time and energy to a better understanding of the many complex issues facing the institution.
- A public college president describes a small board of trustees burdened with several members who exert undue influence on contract awards and interfere in athletic affairs.

Whether on public or private boards, what this adds up to is a significant problem: Many trustees understand neither the concept of service on a board as a public trust nor their responsibilities to the entire institution. In many cases, these problems arise because the state lacks clear criteria for board appointments, and the institutions provide little orientation or training for new board members. Even where written criteria for appointments do exist, those who appoint—be they governors, legislators, or the board itself—often fail to take the criteria seriously. A president saddled with a board incapable of exercising its trust responsibly and well is a badly weakened leader.

Private Boards

At first blush, private boards enjoy numerous innate advantages. They are self-renewing; they often involve committed alumni leaders in appointing or electing trustees, and they can expect genuine personal interest and commitment from their trustees.

However, private boards sometimes display maladies of their own: an attitude that certain areas of responsibility (for example, buildings and grounds) are their particular fiefdoms, a tendency to value camaraderie over achievement, and an inclination to paper over substantive disagreements and avoid awkward problems. Some private trustees become too enamored of the interests and agendas of particular faculty members, programs, and departments. Some private boards are too large and distracted to cope with accelerating demands for change. Many tend to focus on the short term and on details, rather than long-term fundamental issues facing the institution. Others are wedded to a long-cherished image of the institution as it existed in an earlier day. Still, most college presidents—certainly all that we talked to—would, if given the choice, choose the private-board model every time.

Public Boards

Public boards are far more complex creatures. Basically, there are two kinds. The first is the more familiar—a single board responsible for a single campus. The second—a single, powerful board responsible for multiple campuses in a system—is the norm in the majority of states. In most states, public board members are appointed, generally by the governor with legislative ratification. In a few states they are elected.

Many of the problems that plague public boards are closely related to one overriding characteristic: these boards are highly political. Political considerations are frequently a major factor in appointing board members and often an element in board decisions. Whether the appointment process involves election (at the district or statewide level) or nomination by the governor with confirmation by the state legislature, board selection and appointment are inextricably tied to partisan politics. Although a few governors and legislators carefully seek appointees who have commitment to higher education, others begin and end the search with political considerations uppermost in their minds.

Public trustees tend to be men and women who have achieved some recognition in their fields, especially in business and public affairs, and who have some involvement with politics. There is nothing inherently wrong with that. Governors generally choose trustees on the basis of political connections or loyalty in providing campaign support, and this is not likely to change. The problem arises when they do so without regard to candidates' knowledge of or interest in higher education or trusteeship. For example, two public presidents—again, requesting confidentiality—told the commission about their experiences with political appointees to the board:

> My board doesn't have continuity or perspective. It lacks a consistent level of knowledge about higher education issues, and it often is unable to reach consensus on the basic issues confronting our institution. Board members serve their own purposes and interests, rather than the interests and needs of the institution. Further, the governor's criteria for appointing trustees are merely self-serving: who's interested, who's available, who's an old friend, and who's a political supporter. He's not looking for citizens who are knowledgeable about or committed to higher education. As a result, in my state, public higher education suffers.

> The appointments to my board have been very political. For some, politics was their only agenda. Their thinking and decision making was limited to the expedient, politically popular, short-term course of action. What's more, individual trustees were appointed by different governors who had dissimilar standards for appointing trustees. Some trustees were bought and paid for, answering primarily to the governor. Others were alumni appointed to reverse a decision or action a governor deemed unpopular.

Uninformed appointees tend to focus their energies on single issues or areas of personal interest—a new department, stronger athletic teams, or more money for minority faculty or need-based scholarships. No matter how worthwhile these personal agendas are, a trustee's single-minded support for one program at the expense of others undermines the president's ability to establish institutionwide priorities.

Board Structure

The commission is also concerned that the number of people entrusted with governance responsibility for complex public institutions—institutions with enormous enrollments, huge budgets, and large employment bases—is remarkably small (usually under ten). Can the broad range of institutional interests and needs be adequately reflected or addressed by just a handful of trustees? The evidence suggests it cannot. A small board can be held hostage by the special interests or narrow perspectives of a few members. Moreover, the smaller the board, the more difficult it is for the president to exercise effective leadership. For example, the vice chairman of a public college board in the West reports that two particularly rebellious trustees frequently prevent his entire board from taking significant action.

The situation is even more serious for multicampus boards, whose members make up only 3 percent of all trustees but represent institutions enrolling about half of all students in the United States. Can small statewide, multicampus boards adequately serve these enormous, complex, and sprawling systems?

Many states adopt multicampus systems in hopes of minimizing competition among campuses and costly program duplication. But centralization, cost savings, and efficiency must not suffocate local needs, individual initiative, and innovation. In some states, these systems perform very well and make campus chief executives' lives easier by protecting them from political pressures. In other states, however, campus leaders complain about the remoteness of statewide boards, their centralized bureaucracies, and their tendency to meddle from afar.

Perspective and Focus

Whether a board serves public or private higher education or governs a single or a multicampus system, trustees often lack continuity of perspective—that is, the recognition that they are not simply individuals but part of an ongoing process of institution-building.

Once appointed, such board members neglect the task of educating themselves about the college or university as a whole, content to show up at meetings, contributing when their pet project is under discussion, but otherwise rubber-stamping administration initiatives and decisions. When it comes to their most important job—hiring an outstanding president—many boards fail to define clearly what the institution needs in a president, or to outline clear objectives for that new president. Others join the president in developing new policies, only to back away when opposition develops, leaving the president to face criticism alone. And many boards fail to establish clear criteria and methods for evaluating the president and themselves.

Recommendations to Boards

The ultimate authority for the well-being and effectiveness of the institution is vested in the board of trustees. The trustees exercise this authority, partly by their own understanding and engagement, partly by actively participating in developing the institution's vision, and partly by delegating sufficient authority to both president and faculty to permit the institution to function. As a surrogate for the general public, the board should serve as a knowledgeable and demanding overseer as administrators and faculty members explain institutional performance and make their cases for new undertakings.

To advance that oversight role, the commission recommends that the boards:

Select Presidents Who Are Truly Capable of Leading Their Institutions as Change Agents and Risk Takers

No task is more important for any board than the selection of the campus president. Although many candidates will be found on campuses, a reservoir of talent remains to be tapped in the worlds of business, government, the professions, the nonprofit sector, and the military. Trustees should not shy away from potential presidents from nontraditional backgrounds. The new challenges facing higher education may lead institutions to look beyond the ivy walls to consider leaders whose different kind of experience fits the particular needs of the institution. At the same time, potential leaders who are already on campus should not be overlooked. The essential requirement is experience in the leadership and management of a complex organization. Boards should seek candidates who are consultative yet decisive, respectful of academic traditions yet unafraid to use nontraditional strategies.

Work with the President to Develop a Vision and Clarify Shared Governance

Because both presidents and faculty members exercise academic authority in the board's name, the board must be actively involved in developing goals and objectives that reflect a clear sense of institutional direction and priorities. In particular, the board must take a strong role in identifying, defining, and clarifying the authority it delegates and the governance it shares.

Support and Stand by the Presidents as Long as They Hold the Confidence of the Board

Although ever mindful of the tension between their two roles—one as supporter of the institution, the other as guardian of the public trust—boards must support effective presidents. However selected, individual board members must remember that their primary allegiance and fiduciary responsibility is to the institution and the public interest, in the broadest sense, not to the constituency or party that put them on the board. This will require public boards, from time to time, to buffer the university against undue political pressure.

Presidential leadership requires attention to issues of mission and vision, because the board shares with the president the role of advocate of the essential function and mission of the institution to the outside world. Trustees are expected to ask the tough, probing questions when things are going well, because it may be too late to raise them when things are going badly. Boards also must set policy while avoiding the temptation to micromanage, which can seriously undermine the academic presidency. As long as presidents command board confidence, they are entitled to effective board support in public and reassurance in private, especially when under siege.

Provide Presidents with the Contractual Support They Require

Presidential compensation, always a difficult subject, becomes doubly so in the downsizing environment of the American economy. . . . During the commission's staff interviews, not a single president listed compensation as a major impediment; nevertheless, the commission believes college and university boards should establish a compensation system for presidents that recognizes the risks of leadership. Boards also should ensure that the compensation package is capable of withstanding public scrutiny. [*Editor's note:* For some recent trends in presidential compensation, see "Private Sources," 2001.]

Evaluate Presidential and Board Performance

Presidential evaluation is another major responsibility of all boards. Boards that fail to evaluate presidential performance are not meeting their obligations. For the evaluation to be useful and fair, the president's performance has to be measured against the agreed-upon vision and mission.

The best trustees and boards also evaluate their own performance periodically. This is best carried out with the assistance of external consultants. The commission was intrigued to learn of at least one institution where the board annually evaluates the "president's year" (by contrast with the president's performance) and the president evaluates the "board's year," with both parties sitting down to discuss them informally. Presidential performance depends on board performance. The president and board should be reviewed together for the benefit of the institution they serve.

Organize the Board for Maximum Effectiveness

Like any group that meets intermittently, a board can use its time wisely and well or waste it in busywork. Every board, public and private, can benefit from a comprehensive review of its basic ways of doing business. Terms of office for board members, the role of the chair, and information-sharing practices—all of these and more deserve periodic review to ensure that the time of busy people is used to best advantage for the good of the institution.

The commission also urges boards to see that each new trustee is provided a comprehensive orientation program that fully explains the operations of the institution and the responsibilities of trusteeship. In addition, boards should arrange periodic and substantive in-service education for each member.

ADDITIONAL RECOMMENDATIONS

This section is based on recommendations developed by participants at the two Minnowbrook conferences.

Do Not Generalize Your Own College Experience

Colleges and universities are different today than they were when you were in college. The student body is more diverse, the academic programs are more complex, and the demands of society and governmental and accreditation agencies more stringent. In addition, there have been significant changes in governance procedures and in laws affecting the roles of administrators, faculty, and students.

Make an effort to develop an intimate understanding of higher education, its culture and issues. Understand the implications of "shared governance." Understand your role, the role of the board, and the role of the president, the faculty, staff, and students in institutional governance.

Learn the History, Culture, and Priorities of Your Institution

Each institution has its own culture, strengths, and priorities. Missions should and do differ. Identify your institution's strengths and immediate and long-term goals and vision. When approving new educational programs, make sure they contribute to the institution's strengths and its mission. At all times be aware that goals can only be met and visions realized when faculty and staff are well rewarded for their efforts and when students are excited about their experiences, both in the classroom and as members of a community. Thus, your oversight of the entire community environment, reinforcing as it must its history, culture, and priorities, is an important responsibility that you accept when you become a member of a governing board. Should you serve as a board member of more than one institution, do not expect that the majority of issues you face and the solutions you propose will be identical.

Understand the Financial Structure of Your College or University and How It Operates

Board members hold fiduciary responsibility for their institutions, and those unwilling to accept such responsibility should not accept a board assignment. This responsibility is threefold. First, you must be assured, through reports and audits, that institutional funds are being spent in appropriate ways, supporting the institution's mission. Second, you must be comfortable at all times that institutional investments are prudent, for you serve as a trustee of those funds while serving on the board. Finally, you have a responsibility to ensure the financial strength of the institution not only by contributing generously to it but also by assisting the staff in seeking funding, whether from government agencies, foundations, corporations, or individuals.

The financial base of colleges and universities may be significantly different from what you have encountered in other areas. Unlike business and industry, increasing numbers may not be the solution to fiscal difficulties. A good place to start is by reading Gordon C. Winstone's "Why Can't a College Be More Like a Firm?" (1997). This article does an excellent job of outlining the financial crises facing American higher education.

Be an Advocate for Your Institution

You may, in your career, have gained prominence for your advocacy of a particular point of view, your knowledge of a particular industry or field of business, or your active involvement in one or another political party. Although one or more of these factors may have played a role in your appointment or election to the board, you agreed to serve the institution and use your talents to make it an improved institution. Avoid using your position on the board as a platform for the advocacy of a particular point of view. Your goal should be to support your institution's mission, vision, and financial stability and to serve the community it serves.

Take Time to Learn About Assessment and Learning Outcomes

You should also become knowledgeable about accreditation processes and goals. There is a national movement under way demanding increased institutional accountability, with accreditation agencies focusing on learning outcomes as a primary standard. Institutions tend to resist this movement, but avoidance may no longer be an option.

CONCLUSION

As a number of the recommendations in this chapter stress, learning on your part is a key element to being an effective and supportive board member, regent, or trustee. Although you can expect the president and his or her cabinet to provide you with some resources, you cannot expect that the scope of this material will be as broad and as applicable as you might like.

Be proactive in developing an understanding of higher education, your institution, and the role of the board and the key administrative leaders. If you are assigned to a specific administrative area (budget, academic affairs, financial operations, student affairs and development), ask the institution to provide you with a subscription to one or more of the professional journals serving that area. Although your time will most likely be limited, contact the Association of Governing Boards of Universities and Colleges (Washington, DC; 202/296-8400), and review its list of available materials and its regional and national programs. You will find them direct and practical.

References

Association of Governing Boards of Universities and Colleges. *Renewing the academic presidency: Stronger leadership for tougher times.* (1996). Washington, DC: Association of Governing Boards of Universities and Colleges.

Chait, R., Holland, T., & Taylor, B. (1996). *Improving the performance of governing boards.* Phoenix: Oryx Press–American Council on Education.

Private sources play (more) of a role in paying public university chiefs. (2001, November 30). *Chronicle of Higher Education,* pp. A24–A26.

Winstone, G. C. (1997, September-October). Why can't a college be more like a firm? *Change,* pp. 32–38.

Resources

To assist you in preparing for your role as a board member, we have identified a number of resources that you may find helpful.

Association of Governing Boards of Universities and Colleges. *Renewing the academic presidency: Stronger leadership for tougher times.* (1996). Washington, DC: Association of Governing Boards of Universities and Colleges.

A full report with excellent sections on the challenges facing higher education and the problems of governance. Includes recommendations to presidents, faculty, and to public officials. You will find the information extremely useful.

Association of Governing Boards of Universities and Colleges. (Eds.). *Trusteeship.* [www.agb.org].

This monthly publication specifically for trustees focuses on issues, roles, and resources. One of the publications you should read regularly.

Academic Partners. (Eds.). *University Business: Solutions for Today's Higher Education.*

This monthly is free to academic leaders and board members. It is good reading and it will keep you up on major issues facing higher education and on what other institutions are doing. Scan it and read in depth what you find interesting. (Contact Academic Partners, 135 Madison Avenue, New York 10016; 212/684-9884.)

Board basics: AGB statement on institutional governance and governing in the public trust: External influences on colleges and universities. (2001). Washington, DC: Association of Governing Boards of Universities and Colleges.

The "AGB Statement on Institutional Governance" encourages trustees and presidents to examine their institution's governance structures, policies, and practices. "Governing in the Public

Trust" prompts higher education leaders to consider the perspectives of external voices while resisting political or ideological agendas.

Burlock, T. J., & Chabotar, K. J. (1998). *Board basics: Financial responsibilities.* Washington, DC: Association of Governing Boards of Universities and Colleges.
Trustees have no greater responsibility than to ensure an institution's financial health in support of its mission. In this sixteen-page publication, a Bowdoin College trustee and the vice president for finance and administration discuss the board's role in meeting its financial responsibilities, four fundamental questions trustees must ask when overseeing finances, how to monitor performance, and how to use comparison groups and data sources.

Carver, J., & Carver, M. M. (1996–97). The Carver series on effective board governance. San Francisco: Jossey-Bass.
This series, although based on the authors' experiences with a wide variety of governing boards, includes a number of titles that are relevant to trustees and board members of colleges and universities, such as "Basic Principles of Policy Governance," "Making Diversity Meaningful in the Boardroom," and "Board Assessment of the CEO."

Chait, R. P., Holland, T. P., & Taylor, B. E. (1993). *The effective board of trustees.* Phoenix: Oryx Press–American Council on Education.

Chait, R. P., Holland, T. P., & Taylor, B. E. (1996). *Improving the performance of governing boards.* Phoenix: Oryx Press–American Council on Education.
Based on numerous studies and interviews, these two volumes provide an excellent introduction to the roles of trustees and the function of boards. The 1993 volume identifies and discusses the six skill sets of effective boards. The 1996 volume addresses how boards of colleges and universities can raise their level of competence. These volumes also discuss areas of resistance that can be anticipated when efforts are made to improve a board's effectiveness and how they can be addressed. Loaded with real-world experience and practical advice. If you take your job seriously, read these two volumes. Good resources for presidents, too.

Ingram, R. T. (1997). *Board basics: Trustee responsibilities: A guide for governing boards of public institutions.* Washington, DC: Association of Governing Boards of Universities and Colleges.
This twenty-four-page must-have publication for new and veteran trustees was written by the president of AGB. It sets forth the twelve basic responsibilities of a governing board and distinguishes them from individual trustee functions, and it poses specific questions trustees might consider to guide good practice. The booklet also incorporates "The Commitment to Trusteeship," an excellent guide for those who have been invited to serve on boards.

Ingram, R. T., & Associates. (1993). *Governing independent colleges and universities: A handbook for trustees, chief executives, and other campus leaders.* San Francisco: Jossey-Bass.
This 470-page handbook is the definitive resource for the information, ideas, alternatives, standards, and encouragement necessary to improve board effectiveness and performance. It provides practical information and expert guidance on all significant responsibilities of governing

boards and virtually every issue or topic likely to be addressed in academic boardrooms, including board chair–chief executive relations, board functions and duties, board development and staffing, and performance assessment.

Wilson, E. B. *Board basics: Committee on trustees.* (2001). Washington, DC: Association of Governing Boards of Universities and Colleges.
This twenty-four-page booklet reinforces the thesis that the committee on trustees must perform with excellence if the board is to fulfill its responsibilities with distinction. The author outlines a typical committee mission, structure, responsibilities, and policies and practices. Ten committee responsibilities are described, including designing the board composition and statement of criteria, cultivating a network of trustee candidates, managing orientation programs and keeping former trustees involved, motivating trustees and assessing their performance, analyzing future board talent needs, and ensuring the bylaws accurately reflect current policies and practice of the board. Illustrative bylaw language for the committee on trustees is included.

Wood, R. J. (1996). *Board basics: Academic affairs committee.* Washington, DC: Association of Governing Boards of Universities and Colleges.
The academic affairs committee must ensure that an institution's actions and policies reflect priorities that are consistent with its mission and character. This sixteen-page booklet describes the essential duties of this committee and delivers clear-cut, specific advice on fulfilling this fundamental, yet increasingly complex, responsibility. This title is part of AGB's Board Basics series.

CHAPTER 23

Creating Change
Suggestions for the New President

KENNETH A. SHAW

ongratulations. You are a new president, still in the honeymoon phase of one of the most challenging and rewarding administrative posts in the world. It is tempting to bask in the glow of the warm feelings of the moment, but now is the time to chart the course for a sometimes bumpy but always exciting journey.

It is a safe bet that one of the reasons you have been chosen to lead your institution is your skill as a change maker. No matter how well regarded your predecessor is, your faculty, staff, students, alumni, and trustees will be looking to you at least to reinvigorate the institution if not to carry out a major restructuring. In this chapter I provide suggestions about how you can be a very productive change maker. The steps include knowing yourself, knowing the territory, and knowing how and when to act.

VIVE LA DIFFÉRENCE

My perspective comes from years of experience at large institutions. Yet I believe that the principles I discuss are adaptable to small and midsize colleges and universities as well. There are, of course, significant differences between large and small campuses. Each has its advantages and disadvantages, and individual leaders will find they can be more effective in one type than in another.

Leaders in smaller institutions report that they like cohesiveness and lack of impersonal bureaucracy. They find that consensus can be reached and decisions made with relative ease and speed given the "family" feeling often pervasive at liberal arts and community colleges. Leaders at larger institutions, however, can certainly get things done without becoming mired in arcane rules and regulations. These leaders point out that the personal, more informal atmosphere at smaller institutions can sometimes be a hindrance because faculty, staff, alumni, and even students are loath to change for fear of harming cherished traditions. You have heard, no doubt, the old saw that the reason why arguments in higher education are so intense is that the stakes are so low. Advocates of larger institutions say this is true to a greater degree at smaller colleges.

Size aside, there is greater disparity between public and private institutions. Leaders at private colleges and universities find it is easier to get things done in a market-driven environment where higher tuition translates into greater attention to students' needs. They also say that it is easier to stay focused on the institution's mission. But depending on tuition for a disproportionate share of operating income creates great financial pressure.

Leaders of public institutions must pay more attention to state government concerns and work closely with the governor, the governor's staff, senators, representatives, and their staffs. And when elections change the party in power, public institutions must form new relationships, which often takes a great deal of time. The compensating factor is that tuition is generally so low that enrollment problems are less intense.

Despite all this, the principles I list here are applicable with modifications to public and private institutions and to large and small ones. In fact, the mark of good leaders is their ability to shape guiding principles to the institution and to changing conditions.

One more caveat. I assume that you and your institution have come to a mutually beneficial understanding. They know that yours are the skills and experience they need and have come to consensus on hiring you. If you are not sure that this is the case, it is worth finding out. If not, you could come into a crisis situation that is not of your doing. It is also important to know whether the search committee selected you because you are the opposite of your predecessor. Search groups often forget that the previous president had some very good skills that remain necessary.

KNOW YOURSELF

You do not need to go into deep analysis to take an inventory of your strengths, weaknesses, and leadership style. But you do need to have a good grasp on reality so that you can lead well. In my book *The Successful President* (Shaw, 1999), I describe four approaches that leaders may assume. You will probably recognize yourself as one of these types, or more likely a combination of them.

The Healer

The healer helps her faculty and staff feel good about themselves and their institution. She inspires trust and may effect change by raising morale enough that people are motivated to support her new agenda. Unfortunately, healers often have a hard time keeping the momentum going, especially during difficult times. Once the feel-good atmosphere fades, the change agenda is ignored.

The Caretaker

Caretakers are ideal leaders to take the helm of an institution during the good times when efficient management will suffice. This type of leader makes sure that grades get processed, convocations take place, the budget balances, and things get done right. But in a crisis, caretakers are thrown off their game, finding it difficult to make big changes when they are necessary.

The Innovator

The innovator thrives on change. With great energy and adaptability, these leaders have new ideas, new programs, and new approaches by the dozen. They are certain to move things forward, but often at the expense of good feelings and solid tradition.

The Educational Statesperson   *adaptable, functional, model of behavior*

The educational statesperson combines the best qualities of all the rest. He is able to heal, be a caretaker, and innovate at the appropriate time and place, adapting along the way to the situation and the people involved.

If you have managed to reach the statesperson level, good for you. If not, then work on those areas where you are not as accomplished and surround yourself with people who make up for your deficits. If you are a rapid-fire innovator, fine. But take a step back and learn to appreciate both the people and the institution for what they are. Effective change begins with knowing yourself well.

self-possession + integrity are key.

KNOW THE TERRITORY

You are entering an institution with a history and a culture all its own. Of course, you have studied higher education in general and probably have held other leadership positions, such as dean or department head. Being president, though, requires a panoramic view of the institution.

Things to Do Before You Take Office

It is important to become well acquainted with your context (or the territory) before you move into your new office.

Do a SWOT Analysis

Ask your new senior-level administrators, academic deans, selected staff, and student leaders to tell you in writing what they see as the institution's strengths, weaknesses, opportunities, and threats (SWOT). Limit them to no more than six pages to force them to prioritize. Have this material sent to you long enough ahead of your arrival to allow you to digest and synthesize the information. You will come to some preliminary generalizations about this place you will be calling home—with luck—for ten years or more.

Consult with Key Board Members

Use face-to-face meetings or telephone conversations for this task. Use the same SWOT technique without written responses. They will be flattered that you asked, and you will gain valuable information.

Use a PIP Approach

A more inclusive information-gathering technique is the problem identification process (PIP). Ask your office of institutional research or its equivalent to use the Delphi technique. This involves asking a group of people to list what they believe are the most important issues, and through an iterative process, boiling down those issues to a list of the most critical. By using a stratified sample of faculty, students, and staff you will get helpful and sometimes surprising results. I know a president who did this with good results. Throughout his candidacy and in the early months of his new post, people told him that faculty collective bargaining issues were paramount. Both sides of the issue said the same thing. But a PIP analysis revealed that this was not the primary issue and did not even place among the top five. In fact, the most important issue identified was the need to improve the quality of the student body; the second was to improve the quality of the student experience. Armed with this information, the president was in a far better position to set priorities.

Things to Do in the Early Months on Campus

After you take office, there are other important things to do.

Learn by Walking Around

Take the time to get to know the people who are part of your new environment. Ask questions. People will be delighted by your attentions. Find out if they are satisfied—perhaps too satisfied?—with the status quo. Are they angry because they have had too little leadership? Too much? Are they proud of their institution? Are they eager for it to improve? What do they believe are the institutional values?

Talk with Constituent Leaders

Try a less formal environment where people will be more relaxed. Use the SWOT technique in a less obvious way.

Assess the Campus Climate

Are things in order with minimal dissatisfaction? Are there rumblings of distant storms moving closer? Is chaos reigning and stress rampant? In a public institution, what is the relationship between your university and government officials? Friendly? Neutral? Contentious?

Understand the Governance System

As a change agent, you will be doing things differently, but you will need to know how things happen now in order to be effective. If you ascribe more power to the university senate than the institutional culture requires, for example, you will miss opportunities to lead. If you ignore the system you will find out the hard way that very little happens without its involvement. You will save valuable time when you know just how the governance system is perceived on your campus and how it works.

Find the Seams

Football, soccer, and other team players know that *the seam* is the opening that can lead to a score. In higher education, seams are the areas where change can happen more easily. These are the areas where majority governance or faculty involvement is not as critical. For example, at one institution student services was a seam. There was general dissatisfaction with the level of service, but faculty were more focused on policy issues and left these matters to the administration. The new chancellor was able to make a number of significant changes in student services without extensive consultation. Collaboration, yes, but not approvals. Frequently, another seam is distance education. Generally, the governance system must approve new programs and sometimes new courses, but faculty members are left to determine the method of delivery. It can be argued that distance education is merely a method of delivery. In this way it becomes a seam.

creepy

Take the Reins of the Bureaucracy

Grab hold of the system early and shake it hard. If you focus on your institution's mission and provide leadership, the administrative system will respond. Make sure that everyone understands the mission and the goals to be accomplished, and you will find that staff pride in the institution will propel the necessary changes. Expect superior performance from them and provide meaningful rewards.

Set the Ground Rules

Keep the rules simple. The message to your key administrators might be something like this: "Here at Olde Ivy University, we understand that although we all work in different areas our main job is the betterment of the institution. That means you resolve differences quickly, or bring them to me for a fast and fair decision. Personal differences are to be expected, but they must not interfere with institutional priorities. Your ability to collaborate with others will form the basis of a key part of my evaluation of your work at the end of my first year." Setting the ground rules early helps prevent turf battles that sometimes arise. Your ability to resolve differences for the good of the institution will be a model for your staff to follow.

Know Your Board

Armed with the knowledge you gained during the interviewing and SWOT analysis, you must be certain of the board's expectations of you and the institution. This will not necessarily be what you were told early on. It behooves you to get to know all the board members and learn their individual and collective agendas. This information is critical in planning your change initiatives.

TAKE ACTION

Becoming familiar with the territory takes a good two months of asking questions and absorbing knowledge. If it takes nine months to a year, you will be in trouble. People will expect some visible action long before then. Here are some suggested first-year actions.

Tell the Story

Communicate to the university community, the board, and anyone else who will listen what you believe needs to be done—based on what you have learned. The story, of course, is directly related to your vision for the institution and your plans for reaching that vision. Do not wait until your formal inauguration, which often comes nine months or more after your first day on the job. Much of what you say will be based on the stories you have learned from others and on your new institution's proud history, values, and mission. Only when an institution is in deep crisis should a leader stray from tradition. Tell the story as often as you can and in as many contexts as possible: speeches, articles, Web sites, television interviews, press releases, letters, and so on. You have the advantage of being a novelty, someone in the spotlight virtually every day, all day. With all ears open to you, tell the story with conviction and determination.

Be Open

Share information about the timing and process of change at your university. Remember that people are anxious about you and about the future. There will be fewer surprises and more cooperation if you keep everyone informed. Knowledge is power, so be sure to share yours. It will make you and your institution stronger.

Provide Reassurance

People in the midst of change need to know that things are going according to plan. Provide periodic reports highlighting progress to date. The entire process of change may take five years or more, but there is much to tell about the victories and problems along the way.

Help People Succeed

Resistance to change comes from the fear that one will not be able to meet the challenge. Offer training, skill development, consultants, and other support to build confidence.

Reward, Reward, Reward

Make sure that successes are celebrated with much fanfare. Some rewards may be monetary, but people value many other currencies as well. Some will respond to the vision; others to the resources you give them to get their work done. Some will want to be part of the team and acknowledged as such. Some will seek public acclaim; be sure they get it.

Limit Failures

You will make mistakes, of course. But if your plan is reasonable, feasible, and supported by the community, your successes will outnumber your failures by a hundredfold. Too risky a plan, even though it may bring benefits, is doomed. Chances are you will be gone—and not by your own volition—before any of those benefits are realized.

Involve Others

Make sure the governance system and your key administrators and faculty members are fully involved and have bought into your plan. Their support will help to create a "we're in this together" atmosphere. This will require your knowing who the formal and informal stakeholders are, information you can get by asking around. Your knowledge of the territory will be very helpful in this task because it will make you more sensitive to internal governance issues and the peculiarities of your board.

Cultivate Your Leadership Team

By now you have a sense of who will be very helpful to you and who will be a problem, and of a much larger group of people about whom you have not formed an opinion. Do not press too quickly to place everyone in either the first or second category. Instead, rely on those you are sure of and try to remove, humanely, those you believe will not work out. You cannot afford to have people working at cross-purposes or who have talents that simply do not measure up to the job at hand. There should be only a few of these, but failure to act quickly will diminish your capacity to effect change.

Learn from the Failures

When failures come—and they will—acknowledge them and point out what can be learned from them. Do not waste time blaming others. Instead, praise people for trying hard while encouraging them to move on. Take responsibility for your own mistakes. The most effective way to lead change is to give credit where it is due and accept most of the blame yourself. That way the plan is "our plan, our challenge."

Deal with Change Resisters

Frequently, these are people whom one writer called the *have-mores,* people who have prospered under the old way of doing things. Find out who they are, and if possible, why they feel as they do. Address their concerns if you can, and bring them to your way of thinking. If you cannot, move on, knowing that they will be out there waiting for things to return to normal. Hope that they will be in the minority.

Chronicle Results

The gap between the vision for the future and the achievement of those goals is often a wide one. Keep the information flowing, however, to give people a sense of momentum and the knowledge that it is progress, not perfection, that equals success.

CONCLUSION

Knowing yourself, knowing the territory, and taking action are half the battle in the process of effecting change at a college or university. There is one more thing, though. You must love your new place. Leading a higher education institution is difficult these days, though I cannot recall when it was any easier. You will be taxed physically and emotionally, perhaps more than ever in your life. At times, you will wonder whether you can go on. Do not expect the perks and recognition of the early days to carry you through. Rather, rely on your dedication to improvement, your partnership with your colleagues, and the steady stream of accomplishments, combined with your genuine affection for your university.

I know firsthand that it is worth it. I wish the same for you.

Reference

Shaw, K. A. (1999). *The successful president: "Buzz words" on leadership.* Phoenix: Oryx Press–American Council on Education.

Resources

Association of Governing Boards of Universities and Colleges. (1996). *Renewing the academic presidency: Stronger leadership for tougher times.* Washington, DC: Association of Governing Boards of Universities and Colleges.
A must-read. It will provide you with a governing board's perspective on your role. This report also addresses the responsibilities of governing boards and faculty in the context of shared governance.

Bass, B. M., & Avolio, B. J. (1994). *Improving organizational effectiveness through transformational leadership.* Thousand Oaks, CA: Sage.
Introduces transactional and transformational leadership in the context of major organizational change. Although the book was written primarily for the for-profit sector, the various authors do a nice job of providing specific recommendations for improving your effectiveness as a leader and helping your staff reach their highest potential as individuals and as part of a team. Excellent material on delegating responsibility.

Fisher, J. L., & Koch, J. V. (1996). *Presidential leadership: Making a difference.* Phoenix: Oryx Press–American Council on Education.

Arguing for a transformational presidency, the authors provide insights into the many roles of a college or university president. They offer practical advice on compensation and a number of sample letters and contractual agreements.

Holton, S. A. (Ed.). (1995). *Conflict management in higher education.* New Directions for Higher Education, no. 92. San Francisco: Jossey-Bass.

As the editor states, "Conflict will not disappear from the academy, nor should it. Change will continue to intensify conflict, and the need for people who know how to minimize [it]" (p. 91). This volume includes chapters on handling faculty and faculty conflict, student conflicts, conflicts between administrative and faculty perspectives, collective bargaining, and town-and-gown issues. A helpful volume to have on your shelf when the alarm sounds.

Morely, J., & Eadie. D. (2001). *The extraordinary higher education leader.* Washington, DC: National Association of College and University Business Officers.

Offers practical guidance for aspiring presidents and chief academic officers. Discusses your role in the change process and distinguishes between management and leadership traits and skills. Includes an excellent chapter on leading governing boards.

Nelson, B. *1001 ways to energize employees.* (1997). New York: Workman.

Who says you cannot steal good ideas from business and industry? Focusing on the small things that can inspire personnel initiatives and risk taking, continuous improvement, and empowerment, this books presents many ideas that could easily be implemented at your institution.

Ross, M., & Green, M. *The American college president.* (1998).Washington, DC: American Council of Education.

One of a series of reports on the college presidency published on a somewhat regular basis. Includes data on such diverse topics as career paths, trends in length of service, and differences by gender, race, and institution.

Shaw, K. A. (1999). *The successful president: "Buzz words" on leadership.* Phoenix: Oryx Press–American Council on Education.

With concrete suggestions and practical advice, this volume addresses key leadership issues associated with the college presidency, including interpersonal competence, transforming organizations, and leading change. Includes a section on dealing with the public. The concise nature of the writing and the content make this a book that should be on the bookshelf of every president and everyone else who hopes to become one.

Wildblood, P. (1995). *Leading from within: Creating vision, leading change, getting results.* St. Leonards, Australia: Allen & Unwin.

From the business sector but appropriate for higher education, this volume addresses the need for internal consistency between your own values and those of your institution. Solid suggestions on techniques and processes for leading change and on time management.

Newsletters

Administrator.

Focusing on higher education, this newsletter offers practical suggestions on major issues. Extremely useful resource, including legislative report sections. Published monthly. (Contact Magna Publications, 2718 Dryden Drive, Madison, Wisconsin 53704; 800/443-0499.)

Leadership Strategies.

You would not normally look at this business-focused publication, but every issue tends to include several highly practical suggestions that work in any setting—including higher education. Published monthly. (Contact Briefings Publishing Group, 1101 King Street, Suite 110, Alexandria, Virginia 22314.)

Web-Based Resource

Chronicle of Higher Education.
[http://chronicle.com].

Free to *Chronicle* subscribers. (You receive daily bulletins by e-mail with links to articles on the Web site.) This is an excellent way to keep up with new developments in higher education as well as find resources for additional information.

www.insidehighered.com

CHAPTER 24

Transforming the Small College

A Challenge for Presidential Leadership

EUGENE HOTCHKISS

The opportunity to preside over a college or university, particularly at a time when social forces recommend institutional transformation, can be both daunting and rewarding. Such challenges test both your leadership skills and your energy and commitment, but they can also foster a passion and excitement for the institution's mission and its potential. You will find at a small college that the challenges of leadership are prescribed by a small and often tightly knit community, a community that imposes specific conditions on presidential leadership but also offers generous rewards when that leadership is effective.

THE SMALL COLLEGE DEFINED

It is the nature of its community, and not its size alone, that defines a small college. With the size of their enrollment, not to mention their budget, and their multiple levels of bureaucracies and communities created by schools, divisions, and departments, universities are distinctly different from small colleges. The ethos of the small college community began with a church-relatedness that sometimes continues. The college most often has a liberal arts foundation and is generally represented by a residential campus. Such communities are nurtured by an intimacy of their members—faculty and students and administrators—on a personal as well as an official level, and their values prevail not through indoctrination but because they are transmitted by institutional culture.

The following paragraphs describe certain distinguishing characteristics of small college communities, and how these characteristics in turn shape specific issues that you will confront when you preside over such a college and community. I do not dwell on the obvious need for strong leadership or the imposing tasks of all leaders across the spectrum of higher education. As Daughdrill (1988) so aptly points out in his valuable study, presidents must feel passionate about their institution, its history, and its traditions; have a commitment to stewardship, including fundraising; articulate a clear and far-reaching vision; and demonstrate the courage of their own convictions. Although these qualities are essential for effective presidential leadership of small colleges, they are affected in specific ways by the small college community.

CONSTRAINING CHARACTERISTICS OF THE SMALL COLLEGE COMMUNITY

As you seek institutional change in your college community, even when change is perceived as critical for its survival, you will walk an often-precarious course, a sort of presidential nightmare about boating on the River Styx. On one bank you may accurately observe the considerable opportunities afforded by the absence of a large bureaucracy—most often a lack of direct government control and a relatively simple organization chart. These opportunities are the envy of presidents of larger institutions. Understandably, your trustees will likely believe change under these circumstances should not only be possible but take little time. But from the other bank you will hear the voices of faculty and students, and alumni too, shouting that the institution should remain very much as it is, or "has always been." It is important that you listen to these voices, for what you hear and how you respond may well cast the die of your administration.

The Voice of the Faculty

In your college community, most likely faculty know each other, all but the most junior faculty serve on committees together, and faculty meet around the coffeepot and spend lunch hour together. This contrasts with the anonymity of university faculties, where numbers are large, where campus time is often eroded more severely by research demands in laboratories or libraries, and where, at best, one's colleagues belong to one department or school. The cohesiveness of the small college "family" leads to several specific situations and conditions that presidents of many small colleges confront.

Circling the Wagons

For understandable reasons, the family network of the faculty protects its programs against threats of change suggested or even demanded by finances and enrollments. This silo effect becomes dominant in defending general academic requirements, major programs, and even calendars and schedules. The faculty's defense—often legitimate and not to be quickly dismissed—lies in their desire to protect the current mission of the college and the education provided its students, even though on occasion they are protecting outdated and undervalued programs.

The faculty family also protects the positions of its individual members. All positions receive this protection, whether tenured or not, often regardless of compelling evidence of outdated or underenrolled programs; this stems from the feeling of many that "there but by the grace of God go I." Further, and perhaps of more importance, this protectiveness is deeply rooted in the belief that the family should be self-policed, defended from outside (read administrative) forces.

The "circling of the faculty wagons" in the small college community suggests, and perhaps even requires, that change come from inside and not be imposed from the outside. It is the greatest single issue that the small college defines for a president.

The Common Denominator Effect

There is another reality in a faculty family. As with any family, the family structure can bring out the best in all its members or can lead to smug satisfaction with mediocrity. The group mores in this regard, which are both set by and protected by faculty colleagues serving on committees, can encourage respect and rewards for excellence in teaching and scholarship, or can, out of family loyalty, accept something less and support a complacent faculty. Similarly, the group mores, influenced by key faculty, can support presidential efforts for change or effectively deny them. The common denominator effect can thus either help or hinder a president who seeks quality essential for institutional survival and it can be equally important in encouraging or blocking efforts to change the institution. It too is an important issue, one created by the community of the small college, and it challenges presidential leadership.

Your success in leading your college through a period of transition will rest as much on the faculty you inherit as the faculty you help to recruit. You may find that your faculty have been recruited primarily on the strengths of their academic vitae, with little care given to their commitment to the institution's educational goals—much less their teaching skills. Often one may hear this: "Professor *X* really belongs at a major university rather than a small college." As you consider the faculty appointments to be made under your administration, the matter of faculty fit—in terms of commitment to the college's educational goals as well as interest in excelling as a teacher—is important if the college is to fulfill its mission. And with both the student body and the faculty, a wise president will welcome diversity for the stimulation it provides. But the successful president will also attempt to ensure that the balance lies in favor of a community that is supportive of the institutional mission.

The Voice of the Staff

The small college community, with its dominant faculty, also sets certain conditions on the administrative staff.

Staff Size

It goes without saying that the staff in the small college must necessarily be limited, as much because of its perceived relationship to faculty size and student enrollment as because of budget constraints. Yet the reality is that many accreditation requirements and governmental regulations apply no matter the institutional size. Further, these small staffs must often compete for students and money with the much larger staffs of bigger schools. Most small colleges are understaffed and underbudgeted, and attempts to increase staff budgets are usually difficult to justify in the face of program priorities, not to mention the salary structure of the faculty. Yet when a staff is small and overworked, there is the potential for a negative effect on both morale and productivity. Thus, this becomes another specific issue that college presidents must confront in times of change.

Quality of Staff

Available funds and size also threaten the quality of the staff whose loyalty and shared vision will be so critical in effecting change. Rather than offer higher salaries, small colleges often recruit administrative staff by appealing to their affection for its community values; they perceive, perhaps erroneously, that life will be less intense on the small college campus than at a larger institution. Instead of offering the opportunity for promotion or competitive salaries, leaders of small colleges must encourage professional growth through conference attendance, summer seminars, and the like. Thus, the tasks of both recruiting and retaining a qualified staff, and ensuring good morale, become specific issues for small college presidents. Because of the nature of the community, this is nowhere more important than in the office of the academic leader, whether this person carries the title of vice president, provost, or dean of faculty.

The Academic Leader

Although all administrative officers are key to the transformation of a college, none is as critical for a president seeking change as the individual who holds responsibility for its academic program. More will be said about this later, but it is obvious that such individuals, as the key liaison with their faculties, must support the president's vision and be committed to its implementation. This is true whether these individuals were inherited by the president or recruited with the consent of the faculty. Inherited deans are far more often protectors of the status quo, and one of the early issues confronting all presidents seeking to transform institutions is whether the incumbents' loyalty to the past can be changed or whether the incumbents themselves must be. This is so regardless of whether a dean is the faculty's dean or serves as the president's administrative dean or vice president—an important distinction, albeit not always appreciated, in either perception or reality.

The Students' Voice

The student body is very much a part of the small college community. They are tied to the faculty through respect for their classroom teaching, unsullied by teaching assistants. These feelings are cemented through friendships with the faculty outside the classroom and demonstrated with an informality that makes old-timers shudder. In the twenty-first century, Mr. Chipps has become "my good pal Sam!" Students thus most often echo faculty sentiments on proposed changes to the academic programs, but they contest faculty views on the extracurriculum. Although there are always dissidents (a quality that is often a prerequisite for the editor of the student newspaper!), most students originally chose the college because of the sense of community and values it represents, as well as its curriculum and even its athletics. Change thus becomes a hard sell to this important constituency. One is reminded of the loyal fraternity brother's point of view on hazing: "If I had to go through it, so should they!" This is a reality you must confront as you seek to change the institution. Furthermore, the opinions of today's students are often carried forward as they become tomorrow's alumni.

The Voice of Alumni

"Dear old Siwash" may have been written about Knox College, but it will remain the refrain of vocal small college alumni who have long forgotten the campus protests of a few or the parking tickets for the many in their postdegree glow. Yet these are the very individuals to whom you must appeal for both annual and capital support. In a few institutions, alumni may be represented by an independent organization over which the president has no direct authority, but most of the time the alumni association is a division of the institutional advancement department. The organizational structure, however, does not minimize the very special challenge alumni present for presidents seeking even modest reform of an institution and its culture, its curriculum, and its extracurriculum, including fraternities and sororities, social organizations, and athletics.

LEADERS OF CHANGE

Even if the environment of the small college is distinctive, the pressures on all presidents who seek to transform their institutions are similar. Funds must be raised to support new initiatives, whether from private sources or the government. More importantly, a relationship of trust must be built with the institution's trustees, most notably the chair of the board, particularly if it should become necessary to modify or change the institution's mission. Indeed, as it has often been said, "The board must be onboard if institutional change is to become a reality." Yet it is the college community—its protective faculty with their departmental silos, its students, and its alumni—in whose hands the fate of proposed reform lies. Without the consent of these parties, without the consent of the community they compose, supported by the trustees, it is unlikely that change will take place.

The Presidential Vision

Confronted with the challenge of leadership, wise presidents begin their efforts at reforming their institutions by outlining their vision for their college, based on a thoughtful analysis of the situation that takes into consideration the history of the institution and its strengths as well as its limitations. One of this nation's most distinguished presidents, Father Hesberg, formerly of the University of Notre Dame, confirmed the importance of this step as he reminded us that "there is no leadership without vision" (1988, p. 5). If this vision requires a change in the institution's mission, then that too must be clearly articulated with the obvious support of the trustees. Presidents are understandably eager to move ahead quickly, but to move too quickly, without consulting the community in forming the vision, can sacrifice its eventual acceptance.

Once you have articulated your vision, it is important to implement it with authority and courage; both will be more respected than indecisiveness and weakness. Assuming that the vision will require institutional change, you must set out to sell it to all constituencies, to persuade the community that change is necessary and that the directions your vision suggests should be followed. At the outset, presidents seeking to change a college must determine whether change will take place by replacing programs or adding programs, the latter often requiring significant new funding. Clearly, if funds are available either through the institution's budget or foundation support, the latter is the easiest and quickest way to effect change because the internal community will not be greatly threatened. However, if change is to be by substitution, as is most often the case in the small college because of budget constraints, the community will, by necessity, be changed to some degree, and those specific issues discussed earlier will become even more paramount.

The Role of Deans

The importance of the role of the academic vice president or dean in supporting a president is obvious. That individual must not only favor, and indeed actively endorse, the president's vision but also publicly advocate it. This is most important in institutions where the president delegates much academic authority to the chief academic officer, but it is critical even in those where the president remains a significant player in the academic arena. Without the support of the dean, the odds favoring change decrease dramatically for it will be difficult to win over the most important constituency of the community, its faculty. This position, therefore, deserves an early and careful evaluation.

Similarly, the dean of student life must also support the president's vision and be an advocate of the changes it suggests for student life. Without the support of the dean of student life, the president's vision will fail in the student marketplace and perhaps in the college as a whole. Here, then, lies another key personnel decision you must make early in your administration as you seek to move an institution forward.

Working together with the deans is an important strategy for implementing your new vision for the college. When you are able to work together, a spirit of acceptance for change will grow on campus. And that will allow for terminating both academic and staff appointments, should that be necessary, as uncomfortable as it may be; for raising the quality of the institution's offerings; for substituting new programs for old, or adding newly funded programs; for building morale among an overworked (and underpaid) staff; and for realizing and fully implementing your vision. Then, and perhaps only then, will you feel the joy of being the president of a small college.

PRESIDENTIAL LEADERSHIP

There are as many styles of presidential leaders as there are presidents, and a successful fit with your college depends as much on the circumstances of the college at a given time as on the experiences you bring to the position. (One thing is quite certain, however: there is no fit in these times of change for "do-nothing" presidents, who simply desire to retain their positions until retirement, or for "transitional" presidents, who see each position merely as a temporary stepping-stone to a larger and more prosperous institution.) Presidents seeking to promote change in their colleges usually have one of three backgrounds that cause them to be described as *academic presidents, entrepreneurial presidents,* or *financial presidents.* Along with their different experiences, presidents also bring different styles, or manners, to their positions—at one extreme, the authoritarian and at the other, the collegial. Because the latter is a style familiar to faculty and in the academic tradition, it can safely be said that the odds of your acceptance in leading a small college favor a collegial manner over an authoritarian one.

Regardless of your experience or style, there is one ubiquitous demand on presidents of small colleges: raising money. No president of a college or university, no matter its size, and particularly no president of a private institution, can escape this obligation of office. Institutional size does, however, create a difference in the nature of the task. A president of a large institution usually asks for large funds, whether from individuals, foundations, or in the case of publicly supported institutions, the state government; he or she is often called in to "close the deal" after donors have been cultivated by the advancement team. A president of a small college, in contrast, is expected to ask for gifts of almost any size and often to share responsibility for the early cultivation of donors. All presidents must come to enjoy this official, ubiquitous role, if they are to do well in it. Presidents of small colleges especially, because of relationships formed, often find the wealth of friendship cemented through the contacts they make as rewarding as the monetary wealth they attract.

The Academic President

Several authors suggest that individuals best qualified to preside over small colleges are academic leaders, people with pedigrees similar to those of their faculty, and preferably with administrative experience as deans, who quickly become senior colleagues of faculty (Silbar, 1988; Walker, 1988). The logic is clear: the primary mission of a college is education, and those with direct experience in the field bring both credibility and understanding of the issues involved. Furthermore, such individuals have a head start in persuading the faculty of the power of their visions. Unfortunately, they may not always possess the knowledge and experience necessary to operate the business of the college, including fundraising, nor the art of leadership. Still, most search committees will start their search for a new president by seeking an academic president.

The Entrepreneurial President

For some institutions an entrepreneurial president may be, at a given time, the most effective leader by shaping a creative if somewhat risky vision, and through his or her charisma, persuading others to follow along that path. Such a president may appeal to those new to the community and corporate foundations, but if viewed as an outsider or primarily as an administrator may face resistance on campus from the faculty and even the students.

The Financial President

Increasingly, boards of trustees of small colleges confronting problems both of fiscal management and inadequacy of funds seek individuals who are experienced in finance and have a successful fundraising record. For some institutions, a financial president may be their salvation. Such individuals will lead by providing funding for current programs and even new programs and can thereby implement change in an institution. And if they can raise faculty salaries enough through the magic of their efforts, then it is likely that their community, led by the faculty, will fall into step behind them.

IMPLEMENTING CHANGE

Regardless of the leadership profile that best describes you, the community of your college will demand much from you, for your persona will be felt throughout the small college community and will shape the nature of that community. Duderstadt (2000) reminds us in his recent work that, as the leader of an academic community, a president must protect and honor academic freedom, respect tenure, and defend institutional autonomy. But a president of a small college must also lead by example, illustrating fiscal constraint, civility, and an appreciation for academic integrity in private as well as official ways, and a sense of humor that will be respected and appreciated by all in the community. The small college community demands something more: a visibility not expected or indeed possible at a larger institution; an openness in communication invited by the nature of the community; and a delegation of authority far more cautious than in larger institutions because of the intensity of the president's influence.

Be Visible

Leadership of a small community requires visibility. Whether you live on campus or not is a matter of personal choice, but being seen on campus, walking its paths and attending campus functions, confirms your commitment to leadership. You should make every effort to visit faculty leaders in their offices, meet with students in the dining room on occasion, and attend as many campus lectures as time permits. Institutional travel schedules should be carefully arranged to coincide with vacations, when possible. You must find time, of course, for professional meetings and for a personal life.

Be Open in Your Communications

As a leader of a small community, you must encourage and demonstrate open communication with its members. Writing memoranda behind doors carefully protected by a secretary will destroy the sense of community and raise questions about your leadership. Occasional public speeches, as important as they may be, will not serve to cement your leadership role. A president must have an open door, be willing if not eager to meet informally with staff, faculty, and students and listen to what they have to say.

In these times in particular, presidents must be careful not to substitute e-mail messages, so effective yet remote for immediate communication, for taking the time to listen and talk in personal verbal exchanges.

Delegate Authority

There is perhaps no single area where the difference between large schools and smaller ones has such impact on leadership style as in delegation of authority. In the large institution, given the size of the bureaucracy and the complexity of the organization, delegation is essential. Leaders are judged by how well they delegate. In the smaller institution, excessive or misdirected delegation of authority can impinge on a president's vision and derail change. Although you must rely on deans and vice presidents to implement change, and have their commitment to do so, the process of change starts in the earliest meetings of various college committees. It is here that your participation can do much to steer the direction of change to implement your vision. It is also on such occasions that you can illustrate a willingness to listen and to work toward a shared commitment for change in the community. If committees do not hear the president directly or if they sit with silent deans, the status quo is too often reinforced. Because committee recommendations are difficult to reverse once they arrive on the floor of the faculty, inattention to committee deliberations can often slow momentum for change.

CONCLUSION

Presidents of small colleges have an exceptional opportunity to effect change in their institutions—change that is needed to thrive in the age of knowledge, change that will strengthen their institutions and ensure their continued existence. Presidents meet this opportunity constrained by the very kind of community that defines a small college. There are particular issues in such a community that cause resistance to change, yet they can be overcome if clearly understood at the outset. Most important, to alter the course of a college the president must constantly be a part of its community. To be absent, or to ignore the important position that he or she holds, is to forfeit leadership.

Although the small college community is often constraining, it is just as often rewarding of presidential leadership. In this kind of community, a president can be a colleague with faculty, staff, and students, rewarded not simply by friendships but by an ability to see change take place firsthand. Yes, there is a good bit of ego satisfaction for one who leads well, and more important, there is the knowledge that one really can make a difference. It may take just as much skill to turn around a small boat as a large ship, particularly in the rough seas and high gales of higher education, but it can be done faster and with greater control in the small boat than in the larger vessel. And so it is that presidents of small colleges can turn their boats around, much faster and with greater control, than their colleagues at large institutions. Such is your potential reward for leading a small college and being a part of its community.

A final word to those of you who accept the challenge of leading a small college from one who held such a position for some twenty-three years: because of the nature of the community of such a school, you will find that you will be expected to be both a diplomat and a pastor. If these are your interests and your skills, then you will indeed succeed. My best wishes to all who take on such an assignment.

References

Daughdrill, J. H., Jr. (1988). Essential ingredients for success. In M. Krammer, J. H. Fisher, & M. W. Tack (Eds.), *Leaders on leadership: The college presidency* (pp. 81–85). San Francisco: Jossey-Bass.

Duderstadt, J. J. (2000). *A university for the twenty-first century.* Ann Arbor: University of Michigan.

Hesburg, T. M. (1988). Academic leadership. In M. Krammer, J. H. Fisher, & M. W. Tack (Eds.), *Leaders on leadership: The college presidency* (pp. 5–12). San Francisco: Jossey-Bass.

Silbar, J. (1988). Should college presidents be educators? In M. Krammer, J. R. Fisher, & M. W. Tack (Eds.), *Leaders on leadership: The college presidency* (pp. 13–18). San Francisco: Jossey-Bass.

Walker, J.C. (1988). The independent college and university president as educational leader. In D. H. Dagley (Ed.), *Courage in mission: Presidential leadership in the church-related college* (pp. 65–74). Washington, DC: Council for Advancement and Support of Education.

Resources

Breneman, D. W. (1993). Liberal arts colleges: What price survival? (pp. 86–99). In A. Levine (Ed.), *Higher learning in America, 1980–2000.* Baltimore, MD: Johns Hopkins University.

Fisher, J. L. (1984). *Power of the presidency.* New York: Macmillan–American Council on Education.

Dagley, D. H. (Ed.). (1988). *Courage in mission: Presidential leadership in the church-related college.* Washington, DC: Council for Advancement and Support of Education.

Kerr, C., & Gade, M. L. (1986). *The many lives of academic presidents.* Washington, DC: Association of Governing Boards of Universities and Colleges.

CHAPTER 25

Presidents and Chief Academic Officers of Community Colleges

LOUIS S. ALBERT

A full draft of this chapter was almost finished when the course of our nation's history changed abruptly on September 11, 2001. In its first iteration, the chapter centered on what community college presidents and chief academic officers can do as leaders to support deep, long-lasting, and relevant student learning.

Like so many of us, I found myself reexamining my personal and professional convictions and priorities in the weeks that followed September 11. I thought long and hard about the health and safety of my family, and about the impact of the attack on an already fragile economy. I also reflected on the need for opportunities to make sense of the new reality on the part of our community—our faculty and staff, and most of all, our students. So when I finally got back to the task of completing this chapter, I felt that a set of recommendations for academic administrators written during "good times" just did not seem to fit. Or maybe they did?

Maybe learning is just what is needed now, more than ever before, to move society in the right direction. Despite the uncertainty about the current world situation, I am encouraged by the nearly unanimous comments I hear from educators in all sectors of our profession that our work has never been more important or relevant. This message is particularly strong among community college professionals. Pointing out that more than 50 percent of our nation's college students attend community colleges, one community college president with whom I spoke put it this way: "Our mission, and the priorities that flow from that mission, offer the promise of building a more just, more compassionate, and more effective society. We've been doing the right thing; we just need to approach our work with an even greater sense of urgency and purpose."

COMMUNITY COLLEGES AND THE LARGER
HIGHER EDUCATION ARENA

I agree with that president. Our work as community college educators has never felt more important or relevant—for our communities, for our nation, for the world. Community colleges, and our four-year counterparts, share both a responsibility and an opportunity to help students develop the knowledge, skills, and values needed for effective citizenship in these very challenging times.

Although community colleges indeed provide a unique set of programs and services, it is useful for community college academic leaders to remember that, on issues of undergraduate education, we share considerable common ground with four-year colleges and universities. Like the other sectors of higher education:

- Community colleges play a vital role in community development in their support for pedagogies of engagement, as evidenced by the rapid growth of service learning and other active learning strategies.
- Community colleges make extensive use of learning outcomes assessment and program evaluation in the process of improving student learning and program effectiveness.
- Community college faculty members are engaged in the scholarship of teaching and learning (a line of work advanced by the Carnegie Foundation for the Advancement of Teaching), and pedagogical strategies that encourage faculty to collaborate as teachers (for example, learning communities).

But there are also significant differences between community colleges and other institutions of higher education.

- As open-door institutions, community colleges are committed to working with underprepared learners and providing foundational skills that will enable them to succeed in college.
- Community colleges provide the first two years of baccalaureate degree programs that are closely linked with senior institutions to which our students transfer.
- Community colleges provide vocational, certificate, and contract-learning programs that contribute to local economic and workforce development.
- Community college students tend to be older, more diverse, and often the first members of their families to have a college experience.

Keeping these similarities and differences in mind, the remainder of this chapter first provides a set of guiding principles for consideration by community college presidents and chief academic officers to enhance their personal and institutional effectiveness. After that, the chapter offers a list of priorities that follow from these principles to guide day-to-day work.

ACADEMIC LEADERSHIP AND INSTITUTIONAL EFFECTIVENESS: PRINCIPLES

In order to ensure that their colleges are delivering relevant, high-quality programs and services to the communities they serve, effective presidents and chief academic officers should consider eight principles in their work as leaders: lead with the college's mission in mind, develop and articulate a vision for student learning, recruit and hire strong faculty and staff, identify and develop internal talent, work to build a critical mass of internal leadership for change, create and support partnerships between academic and student affairs, create and support partnerships between the college and the K–12 sector, and support program evaluation and student outcomes assessment.

Principle 1: Lead with Your College Mission in Mind

Although day-to-day responsibilities can cause academic administrators to lose sight of the big picture, effective leaders come back to issues of mission and purpose with intent and consistency.

All higher education institutions share a set of core values and purposes associated with their undergraduate program offerings: contributing to the creation of a just and effective society, providing a knowledgeable and skilled workforce, and developing the next generation of responsible citizens and citizen-leaders for our democratic society. Added to this are the particular responsibilities of the community college to provide foundational skills for underprepared learners, vocational programs for those choosing earlier entry into the workforce, and contract training programs in partnership with local business, industry, and government.

The American Association of Colleges and Universities captures these common purposes in the language of its Greater Expectations project: "Excellence for the twenty-first century implies an education that prepares all students for a diverse society, global interconnectedness, and the rapidly changing work environment. Learning that develops high-level transferable abilities, and uses complex important content matter to do so, is the best preparation for the future world" (Ramaley & Leskes, 2001, p. 6).

Principle 2: Develop and Articulate a Vision for Student Learning

Student learning is both a core value and the most important outcome of our work as community college educators. Putting learning forward as the first priority of our institutions should be more than just rhetoric. Presidents and chief academic officers must be knowledgeable and articulate about the kind of learning they want for their students. They need to understand the difference between surface and deep learning. They need to advocate learning that lasts, learning that is relevant, learning that is developmental and transformative. And they need to "put their money where their mouths are" by deploying human and fiscal resources in support of learning that has these attributes. They also need to measure their use of institutional resources by consistently asking the question: "How does this investment contribute to more effective student learning?"

Principle 3: Recruit and Hire Strong Faculty and Staff

Faculty and staff are our most important investment. No process can shape the quality of institutional programs and services more than the recruitment and hiring process. From an administrator's perspective, paying close and careful attention to recruitment and hiring is critical in creating an effective institution. It is particularly critical when it comes to hiring higher-level academic administrators and managers—deans and division and department chairs. The work of presidents and chief academic officers requires staff who "share the vision," and bring needed insights and skills to the leadership and institutional management process. On this point, the Knight Higher Education Collaborative states in its March 2001 *Policy Perspectives*: "As external changes present colleges and universities with more difficult and unfamiliar challenges, institutions need to attract and retain managers who have both the ability and motivation to be strategic. . . . Not surprisingly, the ability of colleges and universities to fulfill their missions increasingly depends on attracting and retaining effective managers—men and women who are inventive, entrepreneurial, broadly experienced, and trained in the skills that will allow these institutions to be both mission-centered and market-smart" (p. 2).

Principle 4: Identify and Develop Internal Talent

In addition to recruiting and hiring talented professionals from outside the institution, effective leaders also pay attention to developing talent inside their institutions. Community colleges, like other sectors of higher education, tend to attract very bright and capable faculty and staff. Too often, these individuals' talents go undiscovered. Academic leaders need to be more intentional about surfacing and supporting internal talent. The payoff for their institutions can be enormous.

Principle 5: Build a Critical Mass of Internal Leadership for Change

Effectively recruiting and hiring and also identifying and developing internal talent are integral components of a larger organizational change strategy. Over time, this process will create a critical mass of change-oriented leadership that gains its own momentum. The most effective presidents and chief academic officers I know are very patient and deliberate about assembling a staff that becomes a collective force for change and improvement. One position at a time, these future managers and leaders need to be identified, supported, encouraged, and connected with each other until the change process becomes unstoppable.

Principle 6: Create and Support Partnerships Between Academic and Student Affairs

In their joint report *Powerful Partnerships: A Shared Responsibility for Learning* (1998), the American Association for Higher Education, American College Personnel Association, and National Association of Student Personnel Administrators recommend that "administrative leaders rethink the conventional organization of colleges and universities to create more inventive structures and processes that integrate academic and student affairs; align institutional planning, hiring, rewards, and resource allocations with the learning missions; offer professional development opportunities for people to cooperate across institutional boundaries; use evidence of student learning to guide program improvement, planning, and resource allocation; and communicate information on students' life circumstances and culture to all members of the college or university community" (p. 15).

The report advocates support for collaborations between academic affairs professionals (faculty and academic administrators) and student affairs professionals that will contribute to improvements in student learning. Presidents and chief academic officers are in a unique position to broker these kinds of collaborations; the payoff in student learning will be well worth the effort.

Principle 7: Create and Support Partnerships Between Your College and the K–12 Sector

Collaboration with local K–12 institutions, especially the high schools, is essential for the effectiveness of both sectors. Successful partnerships start with committed working relationships between presidents and superintendents, and between college chief academic officers and principals or curriculum specialists in the school district. These partnerships can take many forms: alliances between school and college teachers, curriculum development projects, facilities sharing, and most importantly, direct services to students. Some community colleges offer college credit courses to high school students on the high school site. Others provide college campus facilities for high school students and a variety of options for them to enroll in college-level courses.

Principle 8: Encourage Rigorous Program Evaluation and Student Learning Outcomes Assessment

Institutional and individual effectiveness are enhanced by data analysis and feedback. Presidents and chief academic officers should actively encourage assessment, evaluation, and feedback that lead to improvements in programs and individual performance. A well-developed institutional research office is required to create an environment that values and supports student and programmatic assessment and feedback. But institutional research offices need to go beyond data and analysis aimed at external reporting and compliance; they must also work closely with faculty and staff to shape and provide technical assistance for investigations these individuals initiate.

ACADEMIC LEADERSHIP AND INSTITUTIONAL EFFECTIVENESS: PRIORITIES

Although the preceding list is not intended to be exhaustive, the principles form an important conceptual framework for connecting leadership roles and responsibilities with effective undergraduate education. Working in this framework as they go about their day-to-day lives, community college presidents and their chief academic officers should consider emphasizing the following: trustee relationships and development, enrollment and funding, community support, shared governance–collective bargaining, information technology and resources, and personal development.

Priority 1: Trustee Relationships and Development

Whether they are elected or appointed, community college trustees form the critical governance link between colleges and their local communities. Because most trustees are not professional educators, their effectiveness in setting policy depends on staff efforts to provide them with critical information and analysis as a context for board decision making. CAOs in particular must pay careful attention to developing an informed and effective board of trustees. The board's education should be formal (retreats, study sessions, conference attendance, orientation packets, brief materials) and informal (one-on-one meetings, subcommittees, attendance at college activities and events as well as community activities and events).

Priority 2: Enrollment and Funding

Although the mechanisms vary from state to state, community colleges gain the bulk of their operating support through enrollment-driven funding formulas. It is critical for senior leadership to understand these formulas and their implications for budget development. At the front end, senior leaders must pay attention to issues of student recruitment and retention. Budgets must be created based on realistic forecasts of future enrollments. And there is also the need for effective lobbying efforts, often in collaboration with other community colleges, directed at state and local legislative entities.

Priority 3: Community Support

Trustee and legislative relationships are among the most critical connections between campus and community. But community colleges more than any other sector of higher education engage their local communities in other ways as well. Their students live and work in the vicinity of the colleges and so their relationships with high schools, employers, and community agencies are essential to the student recruitment process. Occupational programs often involve well-defined partnerships with local business, industry, and government. Community members, including employers, serve on college advisory boards.

Cultivating all of these kinds of engagements is a critical task for community college presidents and their senior staff. Campuses that effectively engage their communities reap dividends in the form of taxpayer support for capital funding and annual operating budgets, endorsement of legislative initiatives that affect community college operations, community willingness to partner in program and service development, and community support for student recruitment and enrollment.

Priority 4: Collective Bargaining–Shared Governance

With so many community colleges functioning under collective bargaining contracts, effective senior leadership in today's community college must be well versed in the differences between collective bargaining and shared governance, and in the issues and processes that flow from these two kinds of relationships between administration and staff.

Although many parts of the process of negotiating contracts with employee unions can be delegated, presidents and their senior staffs form the essential link between the trustees and the employee bargaining units. For this reason, senior leaders need to learn all they can about their roles and the limitations of those roles. Presidents and senior staff who have little experience with collective bargaining should consider enrolling in a training program or hiring a consultant to bring them up to speed.

Presidents and senior staff need to be prepared to spend a lot of time with both their administrative negotiating team and their trustees during the negotiation process. They especially need to understand and be sensitive to the impact of difficult negotiations on staff morale and commitment, and do what they can as leaders to maintain morale and move on with the business of the college.

Although collective bargaining as a process focuses on compensation, fringe benefits, and working conditions, shared governance deals with a host of other relationships between administration and faculty as well.

In my home state of California, shared governance is mandated by the legislature. Faculty senates in all of our community colleges have the primary responsibility for developing academic policies, designing courses and programs, evaluating programs, and handling related academic matters. Other employee groups have similarly codified responsibilities.

Whether they are here in California or in other states, effective academic administrators know how to work with employee groups in the exercise of shared governance. In arenas where faculty and staff have primary decision-making responsibilities, effective administrators provide resources and technical assistance for the decision-making process. In arenas where the role of faculty and staff is advisory, they seek consultation and advice. Shared governance that is accompanied by commitment to and respect for the process leads to better decisions and the kind of buy-in needed to make decisions "stick."

Priority 5: Information Resources and Technology

Information resources and technology are essential to the infrastructure and functioning of the modern community college. Presidents and their senior staff need to implement policies and practices that provide faculty and staff with access to information technology, resources, and training that help them be effective in their jobs. Access to information technology and resources should never be viewed as an end in itself but rather as a means to the larger goal of institutional effectiveness.

In addition to providing an infrastructure of equipment, software, and support services, community college presidents and their senior staff also need to pay attention to the educational uses of information technologies. Occupational curricula often focus on training students to work in the information technology field. Senior leaders need to put a high priority on providing up-to-date technology for students, well-trained faculty and support staff, and a process for the ongoing improvement of programs and services as technology itself continues to evolve.

In addition, presidents and senior staff must find ways to support information technologies and resources that improve the learning environment for all students, even those enrolled in traditional courses. And in a growing number of community colleges, being able to reach distant learners means making a commitment to technologies that can support those efforts.

Priority 6: Personal Development

Before coming to the San Jose–Evergreen Community College District in 1998, I spent nearly sixteen years in Washington, D.C., as vice president of the American Association for Higher Education. As an association executive, my job was to search out innovative campus strategies, identify talented researchers, policymakers, and practitioners, and bring all of this work forward in the form of publications, conferences, and meetings. Because it had a membership of nearly ten thousand from all sectors of higher education, I was under the mistaken impression that campus leaders instinctively gravitated to the programs and services of organizations like AAHE.

Then I came to San Jose, where I learned that the day-to-day responsibilities of academic administration left little time to read, attend conferences, reflect on what I had read and heard, and grow as a professional. Frankly, if I did not force myself to continue to learn and grow, it would be very easy to use my daily schedule as an excuse.

Despite the daily press of time, I am convinced that our effectiveness as senior leaders depends on our ability to make the time to learn and grow. It is a wonderful antidote to administrative overload and burnout. In his book *The Courage to Teach,* Parker Palmer (1998) starts Chapter Six with this quote from T. H. White's *The Once and Future King.* Merlyn the magician is talking to the young King Arthur: "You may see the world around you devastated by evil lunatics, or know your honor trampled in the sewers of baser minds. There is only one thing for it then—to learn. Learn why the world wags and what wags it. That is the only thing which the mind can never exhaust, never alienate, never be tortured by, never fear or distrust, and never dream of regretting. Learning is the thing for you" (p. 141).

CONCLUSION

More could be said about relationships with trustees and with state and local government. More could be said about enrollment management, student life, budgeting, and staff development. And so much more could be said about the educational uses of information technologies. Some of these issues are raised in other chapters.

Successful community college presidents and senior administrative staff members operate in a conceptual framework that includes the kinds of issues, principles, and priorities briefly described in this chapter. But the key to successful academic leadership in the community college is to lead with passion—about our mission in relation to the larger profession, about our students, about learning, about the people and cultures of our institutions. Working in the twenty-first-century community college is both a privilege and a high calling. For our colleges to continue to meet the needs of our communities, it is essential to have senior leaders who are willing to acknowledge the call.

References

Knight Higher Education Collaborative. (2001, March). *Policy Perspectives, 10*(1), 2.

Palmer, P. (1998). *The courage to teach: Exploring the inner landscape of a teacher's life.* San Francisco: Jossey-Bass.

Powerful partnerships: A shared responsibility for learning. (1998, June). Washington, DC: American Association for Higher Education, American College Personnel Association, and National Association of Student Personnel Administrators.

Ramaley, J., & Leskes, A. (2001, June). *Greater expectations: Work-in-progress statement.* Washington, DC: American Association of Colleges and Universities.

I read this 2004/2005 as part of Lib. Arts Vision Committee

CHAPTER 26

Chief Academic Officers

LEO M. LAMBERT

Many discussions of leadership in American higher education focus on the presidency or the role of governing boards, but the position of chief academic officer deserves equal scrutiny. The CAO oversees the largest budget in the institution; manages complex personnel processes; plays a critical role in budget, facilities, and technology planning; influences curriculum; participates in strategic planning; and acts in the absence of the chief executive officer. Having an effective CAO in place is a necessary condition for an institution to flourish, whereas an ineffective CAO may cause institutional gridlock.

The desired qualifications for CAO positions listed in the *Chronicle of Higher Education* for a number of institutions include management experience at the level of dean or higher, evidence of scholarly accomplishment and creative teaching, proven leadership ability, experience with academic planning and budgeting, and ability to articulate a vision for academic affairs in a particular institutional context. Many successful people meet and even exceed these and other qualifications and yet still experience difficulty on the job. Why is that? To begin to answer the question, it is useful to examine the CAO network of relationships across the campus.

THE CAO NETWORK OF RELATIONSHIPS

The CAO has several key relationships on the campus.

The CAO Relationship with the President

In order to have a functional, productive relationship, it is imperative for presidents and CAOs to clarify their respective roles. Permit me to share with you my own biases about how such a relationship should work. First, I am an advocate of the "strong provost" model, where the CAO is defined as both provost and vice president for academic affairs (or equivalent title) and is effectively the chief academic and operating officer of the institution. This puts the CAO in a clear number-two position of authority and responsibility. Although other senior leadership will report directly to the president, including the vice presidents for business and finance and institutional advancement, it should be understood that the CAO will play a central role in planning budget and facilities, determining the strategic direction for the campus, and defining annual institutional goals.

Another key advantage of defining the chief academic officer as both provost and chief operating officer is that doing so permits the president to devote a substantial portion of his or her duties to external relations, including fundraising, legislative relations, alumni relations, and national service. Of course, the president is ultimately responsible for the total functioning of the campus and must remain fully engaged with students and faculty. But the demands of the modern presidency require substantial absences from campus, and the president will be well served by a loyal CAO who can attend to the day-to-day management of the institution.

Furthermore, if the relationship between the CAO and president has the following desirable attributes, the CAO will be more effective:

- The president and CAO share a long-term vision for the institution and have clear agreement on annual objectives that are in line with the long-term vision.
- The president and CAO remain in regular communication, including weekly, in-person meetings.
- Although presidents often have served in a provost's position previously, they should assiduously avoid the temptation to "play provost." CAOs are rendered ineffective when deans and faculty can end-run them and take their case directly to the president.
- The president and CAO should think carefully together about an arrangement of reporting relationships and regular channels of communication that make sense for the institution. On my own campus, for example, the vice president for student life reports directly to the provost. This arrangement ensures that the academic affairs–student affairs connections are as seamless as possible, because this coordination is essential to improving student retention and fostering an environment that educationally engages students both in and out of the classroom. And yet, the vice president for student life attends

the president's weekly senior staff meeting, ensuring that his critical perspective is offered directly at the table.
- If the CAO aspires to be a college or university president, the president should provide him or her with insights into the presidential role and professional experiences that are preparatory.

The CAO Relationship with Deans

CAOs chair the academic affairs leadership team, and their skill in doing so goes a long way in determining whether the campus academic culture is cohesive or fractious. The leadership team usually includes the deans of the schools and colleges, the chief library officer, chief technology officer, director of general studies, and senior staff in academic affairs, such as an associate provost.

One quality of successful CAOs that is especially important to healthy institutional functioning is their ability to select and develop academic deans who can be *both* strong advocates for their respective colleges or schools *and* champion all-institutional goals at the same time. This is no easy task, especially at institutions that have adopted a budget model where each school and college is financially a "tub on its own bottom" and every institutional dollar is viewed as a resource won or lost for a given dean's academic unit. I once knew a provost who described his academic affairs staff as "organized like the former Yugoslavia: a loose confederation of potentially hostile ancient cultures." This is not the model for your college or university! Here are indicators, in my judgment, of an effectively led academic affairs council, where the CAO, the deans, and the academic affairs staff work toward a common agenda:

- Ensuring that the liberal arts and sciences are a central part of each undergraduate student's education is not just the purview of the dean of arts and sciences; deans of professional schools support and embrace the idea fully.
- The team works actively against a silo mentality—in other words, you should seldom hear statements like "Only education classes may be taught in the education building" or "My department's faculty will not teach that required interdisciplinary freshman course."
- Members of the academic affairs team understand and appreciate the special circumstances that affect specific schools and colleges—for example, accreditation requirements for business or teacher education.

- There are general agreement and support for institutionwide academic priorities, including library acquisitions, the technology plan and associated staffing, and centralized functions, such as counseling or general advising offices.

It is critical, therefore, for the CAO to define and defend the common ground of academic affairs and to help each member of the academic affairs team become an advocate for the all-institution academic affairs agenda.

The CAO Relationship with the Chief Financial Officer

A productive working relationship between the CAO and the CFO is essential for institutional health, but this relationship has a built-in natural tension. The CFO is charged with keeping the institution in the black, preserving resources such as reserves and endowment, budgeting revenues realistically but with a measure of conservatism, and helping the CAO understand the competing needs of support areas such as physical plant, staffing and safety, and security. At the same time, the CAO is continually seeking new resources for smaller classes, new faculty positions, faculty development, new media, and escalating library costs.

Here are some suggestions for forging a strong relationship between the CAO and the CFO:

- The CAO and CFO should be partners in creating an institutional budget for presentation to the president and the board. Together, they can develop a list of issues that require presidential advice or direction if competing priorities come to an impasse.
- In order for the institution to be led effectively, the CFO and CAO need to spend time educating each other about their respective priorities and goals. Over time, they will become advocates for each other's goals—for example, the provost will understand the need for more maintenance staff in order to keep facilities for teaching clean and in good repair, and the CFO will better understand class-size issues.
- As president, I meet separately with my CAO and CFO each week, but in addition schedule a weekly conference for the three of us. This helps ensure we are on the same page with regard to important problems and issues.

The CAO Relationship with Faculty and Faculty Governance

The CAO's relationship with faculty governance is also critical. A regular, ongoing dialogue between the president, the CAO, and the leaders of faculty governance is essential to institutional harmony. Lack of communication leads to distrust and fear among the faculty that their needs and desires are not being attended to. Here is a checklist for CAOs to consider in developing good relationships with faculty leaders:

- Consult informally with senior faculty about important matters that affect the institution. Effective CAOs will have diverse networks of faculty colleagues to whom they can turn for advice and candid feedback about institutional issues of interest to the faculty. Using this network appropriately may help avoid unnecessary stumbles.
- Invite the chair of faculty governance to institutional planning retreats.
- Consider thoughtfully when to appoint ad hoc task forces and committees as opposed to using standing committees of faculty governance. Ad hoc or special groups have their place, such as to rewrite the institutional mission statement or to reconsider the balance of teaching, scholarship, and service in the institutional rewards process. Special committees have the advantage of a clear focus, no competing work on the agenda, and ideally, carefully selected and interested membership. But take care to avoid overusing special committees and employ the regular channels of faculty governance whenever practical.
- Attend faculty governance meetings regularly, and sit with the executive committee or agenda committee to clarify issues and problems before they come before the larger faculty body for debate.
- Invite the faculty governing body to provide the administration with its planning and budgeting priorities on an annual basis. (*Hint:* Faculty salaries will *always* be at the top of the list!)
- Provide governance groups with data and enlist their aid in adopting multiyear, incremental solutions for expensive or complicated problems. For example, an institution may find itself lagging in faculty salaries compared with a chosen set of peer institutions. It may not be possible to agree on a target for all faculty ranks in a single budget year, but adopting a slightly longer time frame (two or three years) may allow for the goal to be reached eventually. This requires patience and cooperation on everyone's part.

The CAO Relationship with the Board of Trustees

The CAO should be a visible spokesperson for the academic and educational affairs agenda for the institution's board of trustees or board of regents. Although the president is naturally the board's principal agent, the CAO's voice is also crucial in providing the board with information about needs for new programs, broad measures of student progress, educational program effectiveness, and faculty issues. Here are some ideas to keep the CAO prominent in the board's mind as a key institutional leader:

- The CAO should have an opportunity to work with trustees directly in important institutionwide processes, such as long-term strategic planning.
- The CAO should have regular opportunities to report to the board on matters of curriculum and the educational program.
- The CAO should keep the board apprised of progress on important educational benchmarks, such as retention rates, faculty productivity in research, grants received, and honors bestowed on faculty and students.
- The CAO should regularly bring before the board examples of faculty and student work that board members will find illuminating and inspiring.

Many boards conduct a substantial portion of their business with many members of the senior staff present, which gives them a firsthand view of the president's leadership team in action. This is healthy both for the board and for the institution.

CRITICAL CAO ROLES

This section of the chapter considers essential roles of CAOs. Many of their basic functions are vital to institutional functioning and are relatively similar from institution to institution, such as developing and approving academic budgets, evaluating faculty candidates for promotion and tenure, and providing leadership for curriculum. Much has been written about these basic functions, but there are other critical roles that the CAO may play to increase leadership effectiveness as well.

Articulator of Vision and Mission for the Institution and Programs

The CAO should play a central role in articulating a clear and compelling vision and mission for the institution and its component programs. A successful institution takes responsibility for controlling its own destiny, and clarity of vision and direction provided by both the president and the CAO are vital to defining distinctive and excellent institutions.

Strategic Planner and Change Manager

Modern institutions face continual change, but change does not come easily to the academy. One of the best ways for the CAO to help campus constituencies face change is to develop a well-defined strategic vision for the institution that all constituencies understand and can easily articulate. Planned change that is directly related to the strategic vision is easier to understand and accept. On many campuses, commonly understood, broad overarching goals are absent, and this leads to frustration among campus constituents.

Champion for All-University Academic Affairs Priorities

Many of the most important academic priorities of the institution cross departmental, divisional, or school and college lines. Included among these are all-university programs in general education, international education, undergraduate research, and programs that promote civic engagement, such as Campus Compact. With guidance, resources, and the backing of the CAO, these programs can become campus hallmarks and points of institutional distinctiveness. When the CAO is keenly invested in and supportive of these priorities, they have greater stature on the campus. Without the CAO's investment, a general education curriculum, for example, can become the purview of a faculty committee that lacks resources and administrative leadership, and discussions can quickly degenerate into predictable battles over academic turf. Selecting which all-university priorities to champion is a critically important consideration for the CAO.

Faculty Developer

The CAO must make a serious effort to support faculty in their work by providing opportunities for professional challenge. This might include helping to incorporate new technologies in the classroom, providing incentive grants for curriculum renewal, instituting various forms of research support, or supporting a center for excellence in teaching. Although others on the CAO's staff may have day-to-day responsibility for these support structures, an effective CAO leader should be constantly seeking means to support faculty professional growth.

Data-Based Decision Maker

The CAO can model rational decision making on campus by using good data to benchmark the institution's performance on a given measure against peer institutions. The *National Survey of Student Engagement* (Improving the College Experience, 2001) is an excellent source of data about student engagement with the academic program, faculty, and co-curricular experience. Many institutions are members of consortia, such as the Associated New American Colleges, that share key financial data. Faculty salaries are often benchmarked against a carefully selected list of peer institutions. Each of these data sets, and many others, can provide useful guides for measuring progress in student, academic, and fiscal performance, and can elevate the level of campus discourse on strategies for improvement.

Reward Systems Architect

The reward systems for an institution must be correlated closely with its mission. Although this seems obvious, there are often disconnects. In the faculty reward system, for example, an institution may tout a commitment to undergraduate teaching but reward principally scholarship, or use a shallow, unidimensional approach to evaluate teaching. Another campus that makes claims of "excellent teaching supported by scholarship" may provide little support for faculty scholarship in summer support, grants, or other tangible aid. But there can be disconnects in other campus reward systems as well: fundraising goals that are not matched with academic priorities or facilities plans that do not take into account needed improvements in central arts and sciences disciplines. CAO leadership needs to ensure that these disconnects are minimized.

The individual faculty or staff member is usually the unit of analysis in constructing the reward systems on most campuses, but this does not always have to be the case. Reward systems can be constructed so that goals and performance of a department, program, or other academic unit are evaluated as well as the individual faculty member. For example, a department may set goals related to undergraduate teaching and advisement, graduate teaching and advisement, campus service, service to the discipline or profession, and scholarship, assuming that not every faculty member will concentrate equally on every goal each year. This takes into account the naturally occurring phases of faculty careers—for example, for a given faculty member, research may be a concentration during one phase, whereas another time period may be characterized by intense teaching innovation and curricular experimentation.

PERSONAL CHARACTERISTICS OF EFFECTIVE CAOS

Every CAO whom I have observed has had the basic tools for the job: intelligence, academic credentials, management experience, and high energy. Some have been success stories, whereas others have failed miserably. Circumstances certainly are determining factors; CAOs facing a string of budgetary crises, difficult tenure and promotion cases, and battles over curriculum may have shorter terms. But there are personal characteristics that I believe can help CAOs weather the demands of the job in both good and bad times:

- *Be a faculty advocate.* Faculty perform the most important work of the institution. Do not forget this. CAOs who approach issues with the faculty on an "us versus them" basis will likely fail.
- *Be a staff advocate.* The goodwill and hard work of the staff (and I mean *all* the staff, including research technicians, counselors, secretaries, custodians, carpenters, and so on) are essential to the smooth functioning of the institution. Take care to reward and praise excellent staff performance.
- *Be a student advocate.* Effective institutions do not forget that the institution exists to serve students and look out for their welfare. Asking the simple and important question, "What is best for students and their learning?" on a regular basis can help the CAO cut through muddled and convoluted rationales to avoid doing the right thing.
- *Demonstrate integrity.* Follow through on your commitments. Sometimes you will alter your course unexpectedly because of changing circumstances; explain your reasons for doing so. Acknowledge errors appropriately—you will likely make more than a few. Above all, act in the long-term good of the institution, not for short-term gain.
- *Toughen up.* CAOs are sometimes faced with tough decisions—no matter which way they go, 50 percent of the affected constituency will be alienated. This goes with the territory, so this is not a job for someone with a thin skin.

- *Bear no grudges and try not to settle old scores.* I admire CAOs who may have strong differences with others over matters of importance but then can move on without allowing these differences to spill over into all future deliberations and decisions.
- *Give credit to others.* And do not worry about taking credit for yourself. Hopefully, you have already figured this out.
- *Have a sense of humor.* If you do not have a few really good laughs every day, you are in big, big trouble!

CONCLUSION

The chief academic officer's role is vital to effective institutional functioning. The CAO is an interpreter and shaper of campus culture, a leader who challenges the status quo by nudging seemingly intractable problems toward resolution, a champion of academic life and the campus intellectual environment, and a solver of dozens of nonroutine problems in academic life, which, if left unresolved, would lead to chaos. It is one of the most difficult, demanding leadership positions in academe, but one that has strong potential to guide an institution toward a clearer mission, an improved environment for teaching and learning, and a healthy climate for positive change.

Reference

Improving the College Experience: National Benchmarks of Effective Educational Practice. (2001). *National survey of student engagement.* Bloomington: Indiana University, Center for Postsecondary Research and Planning.

Resources

Bensimon, E. M., Neumann, A., & Birnbaum, R. (1989). *Making sense of administrative leadership: The "L" word in higher education.* (ASHE-ERIC Higher Education Report No 1). Washington, DC: The George Washington University.
This helpful text includes chapters devoted to higher education and leadership theory and conceptual explanations of leadership.

Diamond, R. M. (1999). *Aligning faculty rewards with institutional mission: Statements, policies, and guidelines.* Bolton, MA: Anker.
This book is a helpful and practical guide to linking the faculty reward system with institutional priorities. It contains sample documents from numerous institutions.

Hecht, L., Higgerson, M., Gmelch, W. H., & Tucker, A. (1999). *The department chair as academic leader.* Phoenix: Oryx Press–American Council on Education.
This is a useful study of one of the most difficult jobs in the university: department chair. This book will provide chief academic officers with helpful insights into academic leadership at this grassroots level.

McLaughlin, J. B. (Ed.). (1996). *Leadership transitions: The new college president.* San Francisco: Jossey-Bass.
McLaughlin coordinates the Harvard Seminar for New Presidents, and this book would be a guide for anyone making the transition to a senior leadership position. Many topics, such as administrative reorganization, dealing with controversy, and keeping your professional life in perspective, would be helpful to chief academic officers.

Rosovsky, H. (1990). *The university: An owner's manual.* New York: W. W. Norton.
Henry Rosovsky was dean of the faculty of arts and sciences at Harvard University for eleven years. His book is full of wisdom and real-world examples. The section on governance will be especially helpful to chief academic officers.

Shaw, K. A. (1999). *The successful president: "Buzz words" on leadership.* Phoenix: Oryx Press–American Council on Education.
Although this practical guide is intended for college and university presidents, many insights are valuable and appropriate for the chief academic officer and other senior administrators, especially the chapters titled "Leadership Defined" and "Interpersonal Competence."

CHAPTER 27

Academic Deans

DERYL R. LEAMING

This summer in nearby Nashville, the metropolitan board of education was in the process of replacing its director, and school board members faced the dilemma of selecting from a field of talented applicants who had varying strengths. Their challenge in many ways resembles that of the people who must select academic deans: Does the college need a strong leader with a solid grasp on how educational change occurs? Would a bold reformer be better? What about someone who is outgoing, passionate, and honest? Or should the college choose someone who pushes change but prefers building careful relationships?

Just as those selecting an academic dean face challenges, so too do the aspiring leaders. In this chapter, we will examine what are believed to be a dean's most critical duties and responsibilities. We will then review some advice about avoiding pitfalls. Finally, we will look at strategies to help leaders better understand themselves, including a behavior audit survey that is designed to help people begin the process of learning how to be strong academic leaders.

THE ROLE OF DEANS: SOME UNIQUE RESPONSIBILITIES

Are there position-specific issues for deans? If so, what are they? Most deans have access to the help they need to keep their offices functioning somewhat smoothly; they usually have support for tracking expenditures and budget matters. They can get help planning buildings and raising funds. Where they must be on their own and do for themselves, it seems, is in interacting with faculty and staff members, students, vice presidents, presidents, other deans, and any number of individuals who have no direct relationship to academics. There are parents, alumni, and advisory boards to deal with, and the dean is the person to contact when individuals disagree with decisions at lower levels.

Solving personnel problems is a time-consuming and demanding undertaking for any dean. Deans must possess special leadership skills when they deal with disgruntled faculty members, find help for those with substance-abuse problems, settle disputes between faculty members—or even between departments—or help department chairpersons handle morale issues. These, and other people-problems, require finesse, patience, knowledge, and a variety of other leadership skills. Deans need special communication skills to persuade faculty members in their units to accept and feel ownership in their vision and the shared vision of the college, and they must make time for strategic planning—just to name some other tasks that call for their attention and time.

Deans, and all leaders, must have a basic set of leadership skills, and they must find ways to create leaders, not followers. A dean needs to have special problem-solving skills, though these skills generally are acquired through experience, provided that the individual has leadership talent to begin with. Deans also need to lead with their hearts as well as their heads, which some of us find confounding and perhaps even contradictory at times. This is another challenge.

First Know and Accept Yourself

Above all else, academic deans—and all leaders—must come to terms with themselves. They must understand their own inclinations and motivations and be comfortable with who they are. Think for a moment about leaders you have known, both those you admired and those you considered inadequate. Did anyone on your list of admired leaders seem uncomfortable with himself or herself? Did anyone seem lacking in self-knowledge or self-assurance? Now, what about those who did not seem up to the task? Chances are the leaders you admire and see as successful are confident and comfortable with themselves, whereas those who seem to be less than adequate are probably insecure, still attempting to appreciate and understand who they are.

The simple truth is that we cannot be leaders unless others look up to and want to follow us, and the likelihood of that happening when we are insecure in who we are is remote. Everything about us—our words, actions, body language, very demeanor—is exposed to others whenever we are out in front of them. Thus, when we feel insecure and unhappy with ourselves, others sense it. We lack confidence in ourselves when we are insecure, and it soon becomes obvious that others do too. Insecure people tend to be defensive and overly sensitive and do not respond well to criticism. Yet, as we know, all those who make decisions will sooner or later be criticized.

Deans who dare to do something are prepared for opposition, especially when there are risks. They often take a courageous stand, suggesting that even if something is not "broke," it should be fixed nonetheless. Deans who have the courage of their convictions and are ready to be ridiculed and opposed should be open and forthcoming with faculty and staff members and not back down in the face of inevitable resistance. Deans must have the confidence that comes from being at ease with themselves. Competence never compensates for insecurity.

Bennis (1989) reminds us that by "the time we reach puberty, the world has reached us and shaped us to a greater extent than we realize. Our family, friends, school, and society in general have told us—by word and example—how to be," and he points out something especially important when he adds that "people begin to become leaders at that moment when they decide for themselves how to be" (p. 53).

Let us accept for a moment Bennis's premise that leadership really begins at that moment when *people decide for themselves how to be.* Have you decided how to be? Do you know how to go about deciding how to be? Even though we accept the premise, we must realize that believing it and acting on it are vastly different concepts, with the latter being complex, and for many, seemingly impossible. Even after we have mastered for ourselves "how to be," there is much to learn about what it takes to become a successful dean. Let us assume, for the purpose of this chapter, that you are a secure person and have a good sense of self, which means you have a relatively good understanding of your strengths and weaknesses. Also, let us assume that you work hard to correct your weaknesses and play to your strengths and that others value your strengths and are, for the most part, willing to overlook your weaknesses.

The Next Step: Understand and Interact with Others

Now we are ready to address the question, *What next?* In addition to understanding yourself, you must understand and interact with others. Leaders need to be honest, forthright, fearless, and able to think big. They must learn to plan, develop, and communicate their vision, and must not be afraid to make tough decisions or take risks. They must be able to build and maintain consensus and work collaboratively. As Hesselbein, Goldsmith, and Somerville (1999) suggest, we as leaders need to "mobilize our people and lead them and the organization beyond the walls where the community calls for a new kind of collaborative leadership" (p. 4). This is just one of many clarion calls that leadership scholars and thinkers have made for a new kind of leadership that involves collaboration. As Chapter Six noted, you need to have a good sense of your own leadership and interaction styles, as well as the styles of those who report to you and to whom you report. The more sensitive you are to differences in style and the conditions in which individuals are most comfortable, the more effective you will be in developing a positive working relationship.

Collaborate

Collaboration demands that leaders build consensus. In *Leadership Reconsidered* (Astin & Astin, 2000), the authors rightly point out that "practically all of the modern authorities on leadership, regardless of whether they focus on the corporate world or the nonprofit sector, now advocate a collaborative approach to leadership" (p. 4). This is critical in higher education. A dean must always be mindful of the need to engage chairs and faculty and to share plans with them in an effort to achieve consensus.

The authors of *Leadership Reconsidered* also make note of the fact that most institutions of higher learning in the United States are organized and governed according to two seemingly contradictory sets of practices: hierarchical and individualistic models. "When we get to the 'bottom' of the rung in the professional hierarchy, we find something very different: individual faculty members, who on paper appear to fall 'under' chairs, actually enjoy a great deal of autonomy in their work and seldom 'take orders' from anyone (especially chairs!)" (Astin & Astin, p. 5). We know this is true, and any dean who fails to recognize or believe it is in for a rough time. We have all known deans and other leaders who have tried to operate or lead from a position of authority, and we have watched their failures—every one of them! Often it is a painful thing to witness, and it is not difficult to feel sorry for the individual who seems to know no other way of trying to get something accomplished.

Develop Consensus

So how do we best work with faculty members to get their support for accomplishing goals that we believe are in the best interests of students in our colleges? What is a dean to do?

Creating consensus calls for preparing chairs and faculty for change and encouraging them to embrace it—or at least not to fear it. In most enterprises in these times, change is demanded. As many have said, the only thing constant in today's society is change.

Know Your Unit

When it becomes obvious that change is needed, any dean would be foolish to approach it without first learning a lot about those in his charge.

This means studying its history and examining why the unit is what it is today. Who are the people, and what can the dean do to recognize their value and worth? In his excellent book *Managing People Is Like Herding Cats,* Bennis (1997) reminds us what Alfred North Whitehead once said: "Every leader, to be effective, must simultaneously adhere to the symbols of change and revision and the symbols of tradition and stability" (p. 12). We should not ignore the advice to take the time to learn about an organization and the people who work in it. Leaders who make the mistake of coming in and announcing change without first acknowledging the value and worth of the organization and its people are doomed to fail. They will succeed in accomplishing their goals only by running roughshod over those who believe—rightfully—that they have a big stake in the organization. Many will do all they can to sabotage the leader's efforts.

Take Your Time

The essential principle is to take your time. Talk to everyone in the college to begin planting the seeds of change. You must, of course, come to understand the college's culture and history, and you must have good listening skills—all leaders must. In the process of talking and listening to others, we can learn a lot about our colleagues' dreams. Deans must learn that one of their critical tasks is enlisting others to identify their constituents' common aspirations. No matter how grand a dean's dream, if faculty and staff members do not see in it the possibility of realizing their own hopes and desires, they will not follow. To be a successful leader, deans must make it clear to faculty and staff members how they, too, will be served by the long-term vision. Faculty and staff members must see how their specific needs can be satisfied.

Become the Voice of Your Unit

Deans must possess the ability to sense the purpose in others. By knowing their faculty and staff members, by listening to them, and by being sensitive to their needs and desires, deans will be in a position to give voice to their feelings. This last point seems to me to be particularly important: that we as leaders be able to give *voice* to the feelings of those in our academic units. We take on the role that some writers say is important for a leader to take on: the role of follower.

We know that most successful deans do the same things when they take charge of their colleges. They pay attention to what is going on, they determine which of the events and initiatives at hand are important for the future, they establish a new direction, and they focus everyone's attention on that vision.

Formulate a Vision

You learn all you can about the academic unit and its people so that you can begin formulating a vision of what the unit *can* be. I used the word *people* rather than *faculty* because it is important to know how staff members feel as well. They, too, must feel valued if you are to succeed in changing the college. Try to determine how those in the organization define the common purpose. My guess is that you will get many different views. To some faculty it will be research, to others it will be teaching, whereas some—particularly staff—are likely to have a vision of the organization running smoothly and of deadlines being met.

Be a Leader and a Manager

One important distinction made in today's literature between the meaning of *leader* and *manager* is that managers protect the status quo, whereas leaders seek change. Leadership is viewed as a process that is ultimately concerned with fostering change. Management, in contrast, deals with an organization's day-to-day business in a somewhat bureaucratic fashion. Successful deans have a larger-than-life view of what can be. They dream of a better place for their college, and they have a passion about it that is contagious.

Build Trust

Leaders must cultivate change, and as we know, many of our colleagues find any kind of change distasteful. To work effectively with faculty and staff, we need to have their trust.

Trust is something earned; it cannot be bestowed. Trust and acceptance come in part when we make others feel important.

There is no greater motivator of human behavior than making people feel they are important. It is more powerful than money, promotion, working conditions, or almost anything else. As deans we do not pay enough attention to this important aspect of leadership. There are so many little things we can do to make each faculty and staff member feel important, and most of it costs little or no money. One thing we can do is to ask others what they think. Showing that we value the opinion of faculty and staff makes them feel important. Caring enough to know something about their families and other things that are important to them shows that we value them. Business leaders who have been particularly successful understand this. One example is the late Mary Kay, founder and CEO of Mary Kay Cosmetics, who built a $300 million company starting with a $5,000 investment. One of her secrets, she said, was that she imagined that every person she saw wore a sign on his head that read: "Make me feel important." And she did everything she could to obey the sign's request. Faculty and staff will follow you when you make them feel important, not when you make yourself feel important.

ADVICE FOR THE NEWLY APPOINTED DEAN

The need for the dean's leadership skills will never be more evident than when he or she first accepts a deanship, especially at a new university. The newly appointed dean may avoid some pitfalls by following the advice outlined in the following paragraphs.

Do Not Establish New Policies Before Understanding the College's Culture and History

If there is anything that can unsettle faculty and staff and give you headaches that you would just as soon be without, this is it. You must move cautiously—take your time, be patient. In time you will be able to work with leaders of the college to establish policies that correspond to your goals and objectives.

Forget Vision

For the time being, establish tone. Listen constantly. Talk less. You will avoid lots of trouble this way.

Watch What You Say and How You Act

Others are going to try to "size up" the new dean—see if they can get a fix on your agenda, what pleases or displeases you, what your character is like, how you express yourself—and learn whatever else they can about you, including personal and private matters. You can be open and friendly, do your work, and still present yourself professionally while guarding private and personal information, which you may not be ready to share. Your actions must be ethical and beyond reproach; breaching ethics or giving the appearance of being unethical can cost you your job. It really is that simple!

Be Wary of Those Who Gossip About Others

If you listen to it—or worse yet, engage in it or form opinions about others from gossip—you may give the impression that you condone such behavior. The spreading of rumors is insidious, and it is a practice that should not be condoned or practiced by anyone in a leadership position. Engage in it and you will live to regret it.

Be Cautious About Forming On-Campus Friendships

If this sounds a bit paranoid, let me explain. Deans, chairs, and faculty who have been at an institution for any amount of time carry some baggage, and in due time you will have your own. Unfortunately, there are those who will form opinions of you based on the "baggage" of the people you befriend. In a sense, that is a sad commentary on the human condition, but it happens. You should, of course, be friendly and pleasant to others, but chumming around with certain people may hurt you. Give it some time; be selective in forming friendships.

Be Fiscally Conservative

This is good advice—not only in how you spend money but also in what you ask for or even estimate. Let me give you a personal example. I took a new position more than a dozen years ago, and one day I got a call from the provost who asked me to put together the cost of creating a new laboratory. When I tried to get a sense of how much he would be willing to spend, he indicated that I should be generous because he wanted a first-rate lab. I worked hard to get good estimates on what it would cost to equip the lab that he and I had discussed. Although I did not get carried away by including any frills, I did recommend good equipment that I thought would not become obsolete too quickly and would stand up to a lot of student use. A couple of days after giving him the information, I was told by one of his close friends that he had lost confidence in me because I obviously was extravagant and did not appear to be a good steward of public funds. His only example was my lab estimate. It took some hard work to convince him otherwise, and our relationship was damaged for a long time.

Be Careful Not to Rock the Boat

Well, it is OK to rock the boat *some,* but do not get carried away. You are likely to capsize. I have seen new administrators—and even faculty, for that matter—who shortly after they arrive begin telling most everyone on campus how to do their jobs. They call loudly for change and can even be insulting to those who resist. Not a good strategy.

Avoid the Temptation to Tell How You Did It at Your Last School

Doing this can be deadly. Faculty members and other administrators will soon be making fun of you and talking behind your back if you insist on saying, "At My Old State University this is how we did it"—implying, of course, that those at your new institution just are smart enough to have figured out how to do something as well as others.

Be Careful Not to Say Negative Things

Do not talk negatively about the state, the university, or the town. Chances are many of your new colleagues are natives of the state where your new institution is located, and others will have developed loyalties even if they are transplants. Nothing grates on us more than someone who constantly bad-mouths something we like. We should remember that no one is forcing us to relocate or accept the new job, and even after we move to a new university, we are not chained to the place.

Quickly Learn University and College Policies and Procedures

Even if you are an experienced dean who is new to the university, you would be well advised to study carefully the policies and procedures. Do not overlook local custom, history, and the institutional culture, either. Here is a hard-learned lesson: When I took a dean's position at a new university, I approved a requisition for payment to a vendor that was in line with what I believed to be policy, based on my many years of experience. I even ran it by a colleague who had been at the university for several years. I made a mistake. It was one of those situations that fell into a gray area in which I should have asked for competitive bidding. Ignorance, of course, is no defense, and in this instance I fell prey to it.

Remain Nimble

Deans must be flexible and prepared for things they may have never before faced. Indeed, in the changing environment in which we find ourselves, new challenges are bound to arise, and we may not have ready answers. This means we must stay on top of issues that higher education faces now and in the future. Deans must be ever alert.

Communicate! Communicate! Communicate!

This cannot be overemphasized. You must from the beginning of your tenure as a college dean be open and forthright, and keep the lines of communication open. Do not forget that communication is not a one-way process. Listening carefully for any kind of feedback is critical and will enhance your communication.

Practice Two Strategies

For a fast start as new dean, first, always tell the same version of the truth to everybody, and second, never promise what you cannot deliver. (At the same time, "Maybe" and "Let's see" usually are better answers, than "No!")

Follow Emerson's Advice

Finally, I recommend that deans and all other leaders—whether new on the job or not—follow the sage advice of Ralph Waldo Emerson: "To laugh often and much; to win the respect of intelligent people and the affection of children; to earn the appreciation of honest critics and endure the betrayal of false friends; to appreciate beauty, to find the best in others; to leave the world a bit better, whether by healthy child, a garden patch, or a redeemed social condition; to know even one life has breathed easier because you have lived. This is to have succeeded." Good advice.

STRATEGIES FOR SELF-UNDERSTANDING

Now that we have examined some of the most important challenges faced by academic deans and reviewed the most critical and essential elements of their specific duties and responsibilities, it is time to turn our attention to ourselves. Understanding ourselves is essential if we are to be leaders of distinction. What might we do to gain insights into who we are and how to work toward feeling comfortable with that person so that we will be in a position to provide enlightened leadership?

If you are anything like me, you have struggled over the years with the elusive and perplexing problem of trying to understand yourself. More than likely you have been to conference after conference where you have been subjected to discussions and tests of one kind or another that purport to help you understand yourself better. Yet, if you are anything like me, you are still searching for better self-understanding.

Does this mean that these sessions and exercises have been useless? Of course not. Indeed, what we soon discover is that coming to terms with ourselves, and understanding who we are, never ends; it is a lifetime pursuit. We need more than self-improvement sessions. We need a useful way to understand who we are and develop the wherewithal to accept ourselves—knowing, of course, that even if we come to terms with who we are, we still can find room for improvement.

The Behavior Audit

My solution for all of us who are leaders or aspire to leadership positions is to begin by conducting regular behavior audits. The information you will collect by completing this behavior audit can provide you with an excellent idea of how well you are doing.

We must begin by asking ourselves tough, direct questions and answering them as honestly as we know how. Exhibit 27.1 presents behavior audit questions. It is a good idea to ask them on a weekly basis, though other periods are acceptable and can be equally useful. Arm yourself with a short journal during the week so that you can provide more helpful answers. At first you may find keeping a journal awkward, but soon you will see that the time you spend doing it is most worthwhile.

Other Strategies

At times it also is a good idea to have a friend who can be honest with you look at your behavior and answer some of these same questions. The 360-degree instruments described in Chapter Six are also designed to collect quality information from those with whom you work.

What else? The behavior audit can be done in an hour or so, and to me it is well worth the time. But we cannot stop there if we are seriously interested in understanding ourselves and coming to terms with who we are. If we want to be confident leaders, much more is demanded. Post your weekly self-improvement goals in a spot where you must look at them several times each day, and assess your progress daily. For example, and for the purpose of illustration, let us assume that you have a confrontation with a colleague. Afterwards, ask yourself how well you handled your differences. Were you honest? Did you become defensive? Did you keep your dispute on a professional level? Were you able to resolve the problem? If you had to do it all over, what changes would you make in how you handled yourself and the situation? What can you learn about yourself from this experience?

If we are willing to give this kind of time and effort to self-understanding, we will surely become better leaders. We will soon see that we have confidence in ourselves, that we make tough decisions more easily and comfortably, and that others respect us and trust our leadership.

CONCLUSION

This chapter opened with an examination of what others look for when searching for a leader. We asked whether it might be of value to have a strong leader with solid academic knowledge about how educational change occurs or whether they might look to someone who is a bold reformer. And we posed questions about whether they might want someone who is outgoing and passionate and stresses honesty, or a person who pushes change but carefully builds relationships. Frankly, leaders should have all these qualities and more. Successful deans are human and will make their share of mistakes,

EXHIBIT 27.1. **Behavior Audit Questions.**

1. What action(s) did you take during the week that you are proud of?

2. What did you do during the week that you are not especially proud of?

3. For those things you did that made you proud, what did you do right and how can you duplicate this behavior in the future?

4. Did you accomplish during the week what you set out to?

5. How did your accomplishments come about? Did *you* make them happen? If so, how?

6. How did your failures occur? How did you let these responsibilities fall through the cracks? Was it your fault or the fault of others?

7. Were you honest and forthright with all those with whom you interacted? (You must not pull any punches here; this is an especially important question for all leaders to ask themselves.)

8. What did you do this week to fulfill your vision, and how well did you communicate this vision to others?

9. How would you rate your decision-making ability if you scored it on a scale of 1 to 10, with 10 being high?

10. Are there things you could do or change next week so that you could honestly give yourself a higher decision-making score?

11. How effectively did you communicate with all those who report to you and those to whom you report? If you used the same scoring system as in 10 (preceding), what score would you give yourself?

12. Did you do any strategic planning this week?

13. What can you list as evidence of building consensus and fostering teamwork?

14. Are you willing to look at how your college should change, and are you honestly prepared to advocate change? Or is it your tendency to favor the status quo?

15. How well did you interact with others? Did you consult others when decisions had to be made? How well did you involve others in the college's business?

16. Are you empowering others and giving them a sense of ownership of the college?

17. Have you been fair to others, giving them the benefit of the doubt?

18. Have you successfully put yourself in the shoes of those who disagree with you? Could these persons have been right?

19. Have you been upbeat and cheerful? Do others enjoy your company?

20. What part of who you are needs to be changed immediately, and what goals should you have for the coming week to make these changes happen?

but they will know what to do in most instances. This chapter's discussion, if studied and acted on, may help you avoid getting the reaction once illustrated in the comic strip *Calvin and Hobbes*. Calvin says, "I'm the decisive take-charge type. I'm a natural leader." He adds, "See? We'll go this way." Hobbes, however, immediately heads in the opposite direction, shouting, "Have fun!" Calvin then concludes sadly, "The problem is that nobody wants to go where I want to lead them."

If you come to know yourself, have the other leadership qualities outlined here, and follow the advice about how to foster change and build consensus, you will be on your way to becoming the kind of leader whom others will want to follow.

References

Astin, A. W., & Astin, H. S. (2000). *Leadership reconsidered: Engaging higher education in social change*. Battle Creek, MI: W. K. Kellogg Foundation.

Bennis, W. (1989). *On becoming a leader*. Cambridge, MA: Perseus Books.

Bennis, W. (1997). *Managing people is like herding cats*. Provo, UT: Executive Excellence Publishing.

Hesselbein, F., Goldsmith, M., & Somerville, I. (1999). *Leading beyond the walls*. San Francisco: Jossey-Bass.

Ralph Waldo Emerson's quotes. (2002). [http://www.cp-tel.net/miller/BillLee/quotes/emerson.html].

CHAPTER 28

Chairs as Institutional Leaders

DANIEL W. WHEELER

An institution's department chairs or heads work to translate its vision and mission statements into the actual programs, services, and products that make a difference in the lives of the clientele both inside and outside the institution. Some have described the department and its chair as "where the rubber meets the road." The department chair has the opportunity to orchestrate this important effort, and through the efforts of others in the department, meet critical needs of society and the institution's clientele.

Since Tucker's seminal 1984 work, the department chair has been a creature of intense study. Some of these writings and resources are outlined at the end of this chapter and will also be mentioned in the text, as appropriate. These resources are carefully selected and annotated for your further reference.

THE EFFECTIVE CHAIR

A number of issues are paramount to success in the chair role: knowing the focus of your institution (its vision, mission, aspirations, history, and politics); understanding the uniqueness of your department (its history and politics); knowing how things get done in the institution and in your department (history, politics, leadership networks); performing four crucial roles—manager, leader, developer, scholar; modeling integrity; being knowledgeable about the institutional operation; working effectively with deans and higher-level administrators; developing an effective shared governance system consistent with the departmental mission and culture; examining the use of technology to help you do what you want to do; considering the importance of succession planning; and building your own support structure.

Know the Focus of the Institution

It is no accident that the top-of-the-list requisite for change is a mission-vision statement that is consistent with the institutional values to guide the work of faculty and staff. When we face multiple demands, the mission and vision statement keeps everything in perspective. The following institutional profiles will help you think about your institution's mission:

- Research institutions are multifaceted institutions (even more complex in land-grant universities) with a heavy emphasis on research.
- Doctoral institutions often emphasize teaching and service but develop a more expansive doctoral and research emphasis.
- Comprehensive institutions have a strong emphasis on teaching and often service; research is also emphasized.
- Liberal arts colleges put the emphasis on teaching, often with strong service and some research.
- Community colleges focus on teaching, often on service, and job-related training, but usually little research.

Some of these institutions are dedicated just to doing better at being who and what they are. In this case, the messages about what is valued and rewarded are usually straightforward and consistent. If the institution is attempting to become something different—moving from a comprehensive to a doctoral institution, for example—then the messages will be more complex and conflictual. How would you describe your institution in these terms?

Get to know the history and politics that have led to the current situation. Which people can help you fill in the gaps in your knowledge? Is there a clear statement of where the institution is going? Is it shared? How do you know? Be careful about staking your future on an up-and-coming president or chancellor. What will happen if he or she leaves within three or four years, a common occurrence today?

Understand the Uniqueness of Your Department

In the institutional context, your department exists, thrives, or may be thwarted. You and your department members have much to say about whether it will thrive if you align with the mission and goals of the institution. Choices and initiatives need to take into account the department's history, disciplinary orientation, previous experience (including past departmental leadership), size, and capacity as well as its alignment with the institutional vision and mission.

If there are inconsistencies between the departmental and institutional vision and mission or if they are unclear (see Exhibit 28.1), you need to face these issues squarely and be sure that you are making intentional decisions that move the department forward in line with institutional priorities. This means you may have to craft new statements, present them internally and externally, and keep them in front of faculty as criteria for decisions. An important question to ask is this: How does this choice move us in the direction of our vision for the future?

Understand How Things Get Done

Some believe that if a good idea emerges, it will sell itself. However, in each institution, no matter what the idea, there are ways to get it implemented—or not. Even when institutions are similar, things may not happen in the same way or in a similar time frame. Obviously, the people involved are different. Do not make assumptions about the process. Success requires careful analysis of the major players and campus culture and careful cultivation of information and political networks. The patterns and players may not be apparent, so talk with others to understand how to accomplish your goals. You may see opportunities for programs and services by identifying the gaps between institutional mission and societal needs. If you are a new department leader, keep in mind that your predecessor's legacy will affect your relationship with your enabling network. Make sure you define or redefine your vision and goals with those who can help you get things done. If problematic relationships in areas crucial to your success existed before you assumed leadership, take the time to put a new face on them.

Perform Four Crucial Roles

Over the years, as many as 180 roles and responsibilities for chairs have been identified (Seagren, Creswell, & Wheeler, 1993). We suggest that you examine four key roles: manager, leader, developer, and scholar.

Manager

In the past, management has often been the focus for chairpersons, particularly when departmental leadership is short-term. Even though management will not make a difference when it comes to decisions that affect the future, it still must be addressed. If

EXHIBIT 28.1. Checklist for Clarifying Goals and Objectives.

	Present	Well Done	Needs Revision	Remarks
1. Have you examined institutional documents?				
• Vision	___	___	___	_____
• Mission	___	___	___	_____
• Goals	___	___	___	_____
2. Have you examined departmental documents?				
• Vision	___	___	___	_____
• Mission	___	___	___	_____
• Goals	___	___	___	_____

Do you need to revise the statements?

3. Have you identified the main players who make things happen?

4. Have you assessed how the chair and department will address the roles of manager, leader, developer, and scholar?

management of the everyday operations is not addressed, you will not only be consumed by trying to catch up but will gain a reputation for being disorganized—something you do not want. To succeed you need to have good systems in place, excellent support staff, and a procedure that ensures that exceptions are brought to your attention.

Your first year in any position is difficult because you have not yet gotten a picture of all the tasks and issues that have to be addressed. A mentor or experienced person (perhaps someone on your office staff) can list for you when key events and activities normally happen (budget, class scheduling, faculty evaluation). Be sure you document when these events happen so you can plan ahead for them next year. Of course, there will be other tasks that you cannot anticipate, but at least put as much in place as possible and delegate tasks to others when possible and appropriate.

Leader

Chairs are increasingly expected to be leaders because of the importance of change to remaining relevant or even on the cutting edge. Unless the chair pushes the agenda forward, departments often maintain the status quo through rationalizations such as maintaining traditions, concern about compromising quality standards, and a belief that change efforts are "fads" and that things will return to normal (the way they were).

A crucial challenge is to make sure that the department's talent is used appropriately. Departments have a range of research, teaching, service, and administrative functions to perform. These functions should be divided among the faculty in a way that makes the best matches; this can create a synergy greater than the individuals' talents might suggest. A good resource on this is *Aligning Faculty Rewards with Institutional Mission: Statements, Policies, and Guidelines* (Diamond, 1999).

Another important leadership role is to empower faculty and staff. The chair cannot do everything because of the sheer magnitude of the enterprise. Furthermore, such empowerment will develop more commitment. Some changes will require second-order, fundamental change, whereas others will require first-order or incremental change (see Chapter Two, "Requisites for Sustainable Institutional Change"). In either case, the more involvement and commitment you have from faculty and staff, the better.

A key responsibility for you as both leader and manager is to maintain institutional standards—promotion and tenure, classroom professionalism, and collegiality. These are the building blocks for developing and maintaining integrity and commitment to excellence. Another important aspect of leadership is to provide a clear picture of where the department is going. Without this vision, the department can become too focused on the past or present. If there is no focus on the future, decisions will be shortsighted.

Finally, leadership requires taking time to think and reflect. Build this into your schedule by not overscheduling (coach your support people) and by making appointments with yourself—they are important.

Developer

Development is a crucial role that requires individual attention and a commitment of time. To move into the future you will need to have informal conversations and make plans to help departmental members develop the skills, knowledge, and expertise they need to be successful. Some of these activities may be formalized, such as going on sabbatical, taking courses, or redefining roles, whereas others are more informal, such as department discussions, conferencing, and individual reflection.

One aspect of the developer role is to relate to everyone. Previously, especially if you were a faculty member or in a specialized function, you may have had the luxury of choosing the people with whom you would relate. As chair you have to emphasize fairness, talking with people in informal settings and encouraging others even if you did not hire them or do not like them.

Scholar

Even though many of you achieved your career success through scholarly activities, much of the work you will now be doing is not particularly scholarly. Not only for your own intellectual stimulation but also as a way to continue your professional career, you will have to come to terms with how you handle your scholarship. Some institutions, especially those with many chairs of large departments, do not expect chairs to continue their scholarship. Others, especially research institutions, expect them to model scholarship, particularly through research and grant writing. Some chairs also believe that being a scholar is a part of their identity, so they will find time to carry on these activities.

Make sure you understand the expectations for your scholarly role. Also keep in mind that if you focus on your administrative career but then decide to return to a teacher-scholar role, your scholarly portfolio may be inadequate. Research on chairs suggests that about 35 percent of them will ascend the administrative ladder, so the largest proportion will return to full-time professorial roles, often after three to five years of service (Carroll, 1990).

Model Integrity

You must model integrity in all you do and expect it from others in your department. As someone once said, "You will have opportunities to sell your soul and, if you do, it's all over." Certainly you have to negotiate and compromise, but be sure you do not compromise your integrity. Here are some things you can do to encourage integrity in departmental relations:

- Make the operations of the department as transparent as possible. Open the budget, do not make private deals that will not stand inspection, and talk openly (at least as much as you can) about difficult issues.
- Let others know that dishonesty will be dealt with swiftly. The first level of commitment is letting others know your expectations and having them make adjustments. If departmental colleagues continue to disregard policies, expectations, and priorities, let them know there will be repercussions and then do what you say you will. Be sure to get legal advice and inform the next administrative level of your intentions, but do not let threats from others deter you.
- Integrity carries over to the classroom; instructors should be on time, prepared, and available to students. If they are not, correct the situation or it will affect the department's reputation. Department members must understand that your primary interest is the integrity of the department, not your own power trip! Professional commitment demonstrates integrity.

If you model integrity, department members will give you the benefit of the doubt if you have to make a quick decision or move forward without the ideal amount of consultation and input. Keep in mind that if you lose your integrity, you may as well resign. There will be lingering doubts in peoples' minds, and they will be on the lookout for other situations where you have shown a lack of integrity. Be careful.

Be Knowledgeable About the Institutional Operations

As department chair you will be required to be more knowledgeable than most other administrators about not only the details of your operation but how to work with the rest of the institution to make things happen. This also means that you may have to know more than others about content areas, such as learning and assessment. For example, if you are meeting an expectation of institutional assessment, you will have to determine the parameters for the department, the actual content to be assessed, and how this fits with the bigger institutional picture, as well as how the assessment will be accomplished. Others will help you pull this together, but you will need to articulate and orchestrate the process inside and outside the department. Often these institutional initiatives come with little advance notice and may have a short turnaround period, so you will be required to learn quickly.

Work Effectively with Deans and High-Level Administrators

Do not think that you can do anything just because you have your department members onboard. You need to inform deans and other higher-level administrators about your goals and about how they can help you. Above all else, make sure they are not surprised. If you know that something is coming up (a potential staff grievance, financial shortfall, problem with an outside client, or anything else that might blindside them), let them know about the situation, what your goals and intended actions are, and how they can help.

Also realize that these situations are often quid pro quo. If you provide what they want, they will provide what you want. For example, if you are asked to provide some departmental information for a report, make sure you provide it in a timely, accurate, and complete fashion. If you are sloppy or delinquent, you may find a less than enthusiastic response to your next request.

Another common issue is a difference in management or personality styles. Explore with the dean or supervising higher-level administrator how that person prefers to be informed and what he or she wants to be informed about. If you have different styles, it will be important to acknowledge that and make sure you agree on goals even if you have different ways of getting there.

Develop an Effective Shared Governance System

Shared governance is a term that is used frequently but has multiple meanings. As a department chair, you need to clarify what it means, how it fits with the campus culture, and how it works in your department. A few factors to consider are the following:

- *Present culture.* Especially if you are new, it is important to consider the departmental culture and how it works. Certain things can be changed. If current structures, policies, and communication channels work well, you may want to maintain them. If not, you can propose, or have a respected group—such as an advisory committee or senior faculty leaders—propose something different.

- *Size of the department.* Because of their numbers and complexity, large departments usually have multiple levels of influence and decision making. Often there is an elected advisory group and coordinators to streamline the decision-making process. In small departments, decisions are often made by a committee of the whole. A danger here is that much time and energy can be put in—some would say wasted! Of course, it depends on how skillful the group is at the decision-making process. At any rate, these processes too can be streamlined.

- *Commitment and buy-in.* No matter what the governance structure, it is important to have commitment to the departmental efforts. Without this buy-in, life for the chair will be difficult, even if a few victories are won.

Examine the Use of Technology

Consider the appropriate use of technology to achieve learning and management goals. As chair, you will need to make many decisions about the use of technology, not only for learning but also for attempting to develop more effective and efficient departmental processes. Some aspects to consider are these:

- Is the technology appropriate to promote the learning desired? Just because it is available or "glitzy" does not mean it is appropriate.
- What are the trade-offs in using the technology? What are the expected gains? Losses? What are the initial costs? Ongoing costs?
- How will you assess whether you are getting the payoffs you expected? Provide the questions you want answered, and then expect answers before committing more resources.

Consider the Importance of Succession Planning

Even though you presently occupy the department chair position, consider developing a plan that will allow you some freedom in deciding whether to continue in the position or encourage others to move into it. One bad scenario is for you to be kept in the position because no one else will do it or because the situation is so idiosyncratic that no one else can do it. Just because you became chair does not mean you have given up your options. If the department is a transparent place, other people will be able to step forward into the chair position.

Inviting outside candidates to apply for the chair position can complicate the situation. If you groom others internally to take leadership roles, however, and they understand what the department is all about, they will be competitive candidates.

Build Your Own Support System

Many chairs report a sense of isolation in the position. Often they indicate that people treat them differently, particularly if they were an internal choice for the spot. Can you remain friends with departmental members without being seen as playing favorites now that your view of the world has changed to a broader institutional perspective? This is something each chair has to answer. Given this scenario, how do chairs build a support system? They rely on the following individuals:

- *Higher-level administrators.* Higher-level administrators often become mentors. Do not be afraid to seek out good mentors.
- *Other chairs.* Even though on one level they may be competitors, particularly for resources, they can also offer counsel and support. Chairs from other institutions, often met through professional meetings, can also be helpful.
- *Senior faculty in the department.* The cleanest procedure is not to continue or develop these friendships (it is like putting your stocks in trust when taking a government position). But some chairs seem to be successful in maintaining friendships with departmental colleagues without undue interference in the departmental workings. Of course, one possibility that haunts many chairs is that they may have to make decisions that may jeopardize their friendships.
- *Spouse or significant other.* A number of chairs say that they can discuss everything with their spouse. They value their advice and the conversation remains confidential. Of course, some spouses do not want to take on this role.
- *Service and resource offices.* Many campus offices (teaching and learning centers, employee assistance programs, and others) play both formal and informal roles in the chair's life. For example, the relationship may begin with a formal request for help. If things go well, these personnel may become sound-

ing boards or confidants. Staff in these offices understand the importance of confidentiality and are not usually seen as competitors.

CONCLUSION

This chapter emphasized the importance of understanding the history, vision, and mission of both the institution and department. Everything occurs in this context. We have also emphasized the importance of modeling integrity, being knowledgeable about how to get things done, and being versatile enough to carry out the four roles of manager, leader, developer and scholar.

Your role as department chair is crucial to the success of your department and your institution. Jack Pelterson, former president of the American Council of Education, contends that "an institution can run a long time with an inept president, but not with inept chairs" (Tucker, 1984, p. xi). You have an opportunity to make a difference in the lives of people by developing and implementing successful programs and services and addressing societal problems. Sometimes you will need to make second-order changes in order to accomplish your goals; other plans may require first-order (incremental) changes. You and the approximately eighty-five thousand other department chairs can put your stamp on higher education by being bold and forward-looking within the framework of your institutional vision and mission.

References

Carroll, J. B. (1990). Career paths of department chairs. *Research in Higher Education, 32,* 669–688.

Diamond, R. M. (1999). *Aligning faculty roles and rewards with institutional mission: Statements, policies, and guidelines.* Bolton, MA: Anker.

Seagren, A. T., Creswell, J. W., & Wheeler, D. W. (1993). *The department chair: New roles, responsibilities, and challenges* (ASHE-ERIC Higher Education Report No. 1). Washington, DC: George Washington University.

Tucker, A. (1984). *Chairing the academic department: Leadership among peers* (2nd ed.). New York: American Council on Education-Macmillan.

Resources

Roles and Responsibilities

Bennis, W. (1989). *On becoming a leader.* Cambridge, MA: Perseus Books.

Bennis identified some outstanding leaders from a wide range of fields and then spent considerable time observing and interviewing them to identify what made them outstanding. He focuses on four aspects: mastering the context, understanding the basics (the difference between leadership and management), knowing yourself, and knowing the world. The book is full of examples and incorporates a wide range of leadership and management literature.

Gmelch, W. H., & Miskin, V. C. (1993). *Leadership skills for departmental chairs.* Bolton, MA: Anker.
Emphasizes the four broad roles of chairs—leader, manager, developer, and scholar—as well as a range of strategies to measure and develop goal setting and faculty productivity. Also offers a number of ideas about time, stress, and conflict management.

Seagren, A. T., Creswell, J. W., & Wheeler, D. W. (1993). *The department chair: New roles, responsibilities, and challenges* (ASHE-ERIC Higher Education Report No. 1). Washington, DC: George Washington University.
Provides a research base of roles and responsibilities. A unique aspect is a chapter addressing power and politics of the chair's position. Also addresses future issues for the chair.

Strategies to Develop the Department and Its Faculty

Creswell, J. W., Wheeler, D. W., Seagren, A. T., Egly, N. J., & Beyer, K. D. (1990). *The academic chairperson's handbook.* Lincoln: University of Nebraska Press.
This book, based on extensive interviews with department chairs, focuses on what effective chairs do to facilitate faculty and departmental growth and development. Pertinent chapters address helping newly hired faculty, improving teaching performance and scholarship, refocusing faculty efforts, and addressing personal faculty issues. A multitude of strategies are provided to address these issues.

Tucker, A. (1984). *Chairing the academic department: Leadership among peers.* New York: American Council on Education-Macmillan.
A classic that addresses the many roles and responsibilities of department chairs. Provides checklists, activities, and strategies in a number of areas crucial to chair success.

Walvoord, B. E., Carey, A. K., Smith, H. L., Soled, S. W., Way, P. K., & Zorn, D. (2000). *Academic departments: How they work, how they change* (ASHE-ERIC Higher Education Report, *27*[8]). San Francisco: Jossey-Bass.
A recent review of the literature on department chairs. A unique feature is providing five lenses to view and leverage change in the department. Numerous examples and strategies are provided.

Departmental Processes

Collins, J., & Porras, J. (1994). *Built to last: Successful habits of visionary companies.* New York: HarperCollins.
Although they focus on business, the authors provide examples and insightful narrative on the power of these successful organizations. Chapter Five, "Big Hairy Audacious Goals" and Chap-

ter Eleven, "Building the Vision" are particularly useful to thinking about vision, mission, and goals. The essentials from the book have also been reproduced in the *Harvard Business Review on Change* series as "Building Your Company's Vision" (Harvard Business School Press, Boston, 1991).

Diamond, R. M. (1999). *Aligning faculty roles and rewards with institutional mission: Statements, policies, and guidelines.* Bolton, MA: Anker.
Provides a framework for examining institutional expectations and mission with alignment of activities and rewards. Presents numerous examples from a range of institutions as well as suggestions for developing congruence among role, mission, expectations, and rewards.

Leaming, D. R. (1998). *Academic leadership: A practical guide to chairing the department.* Bolton, MA: Anker.
A practical, wide-ranging book that provides examples and strategies to address many departmental processes (budgeting, recruiting students and faculty, fundraising, assessment, promotion and tenure, and so on). Also contains a number of tips for addressing the chairs' effectiveness and efficiency.

Nanus, B. (1992). *Visionary leadership: Creating a compelling sense of direction for your organization.* San Francisco: Jossey-Bass.
A vision captures the imagination and encourages people to see beyond their self-interest. Nanus presents a solid foundation for thinking through visioning and a framework for developing a vision. Nanus also has designed a guide for participants and facilitators that provides a sequence of activities for developing a vision (*The Vision Retreat: A Participant's Workbook,* published by Jossey-Bass in 1995). The book and companion workbook provide a framework and process for leaders to develop a vision—a crucial component of leadership. The workbook provides a step-by-step process to develop a vision.

Change

Bensimon, E. M., Ward, K., & Sanders, K. (2000). *The department chair's role in developing new faculty into teachers and scholars.* Bolton, MA: Anker.
A comprehensive guide to hiring and developing new faculty. Uses critical questions and checklists to aid in developing strategies to encourage success. The emphasis is on demystifying the promotion and tenure process and identifying structures and strategies that new faculty can use.

Eckel, P., Hill, B., Green, M., & Mallon, B. (1999). *On change: Reports from the road: Insights on institutional change* (Occasional paper series of the ACE Projects on Institutional Transformation, No. 2). Washington, DC: American Council on Education.
The second in a series of twenty-six wide-ranging institutional transformational initiatives supported by the Kellogg Foundation. A fundamental emphasis is that change is not an event but an "ongoing process in which one change triggers another, often in unexpected places, and through which an interrelationship of the component parts leads to an unending cycle of reassessment and renewal" (p. 1). The report offers a number of principles to follow.

Kouzes, J., & Posner, B. (1995). *The leadership challenge: How to keep getting extraordinary things done in organizations* (2nd ed.). San Francisco: Jossey-Bass.

Helpful ideas, strategies, and examples for inspiring a shared vision, enabling others to act, modeling the way, and encouraging the heart. The authors suggest that the most important role of visions in organizational life is to give focus to human energy. The last chapter, "Become a Positive Force: The Leader Who Makes a Difference," provides some useful ideas for continuing self-development.

Lucas, A. F. (1989). *The department chairperson's role in enhancing college teaching.* San Francisco: Jossey-Bass.

The basic premise is that the chair is a role model who can set the teaching agenda. This book provides many good ideas and strategies to help the chair encourage good teaching and learning.

Lucas, A. F. (Ed.). (2000). *Leading academic change: Essential roles for department chairs.* San Francisco: Jossey Bass.

Provides tools and strategies for making changes in the department. Numerous contributors address a range of issues germane to the department (teaming, assessment, curricular design, organizational learning).

Senge, P. (1990). *The fifth discipline: The art and practice of the learning organization.* New York: Doubleday.

Senge provides a framework and five basic skill sets for leaders to use in order to create a learning organization. One of the five is personal visioning: providing background and ways to encourage individual visions within a collective vision. Senge provides practical examples and activities to develop the learning organization in *The Fifth Discipline Fieldbook: Strategies and Tools for Building a Learning Organization* (written by Peter Senge, Art Kleiner, Charlotte Roberts, Richard Ross, and Bryan Smith, also published by Doubleday, in 1994).

Tierney, W. (1999). *Building the responsive campus: Creating high performance colleges and universities.* Thousand Oaks, CA: Sage.

Written with a focus on higher education, the author integrates the concepts of organizational redesign, leadership, performance, and culture. Offers a helpful analysis of vision and mission. Through a series of examples and questions, readers are challenged to examine these aspects of their institutions and are provided with strategies to shape their institutions in the twenty-first century.

Newsletters

Harvard Management Update.

Short pieces from various business practitioners, researchers, and consultants address leadership, management, change, and finance. Many are appropriate to higher education issues. (Contact Harvard Business School Publishing Corp., 60 Harvard Way, Boston, MA 02163.)

The Department Chair.

Focused articles written by practicing chairs and deans as well as consultants on a range of higher education administrative, professional development, and institutional issues. Also highlights resources useful to chairpersons. (Contact Anker Publishing, P.O. Box 249, Bolton, MA 01740-0249.)

Web-Based Resources

University of Las Vegas. Handbook for department chairs. [http://www.unlv.edu/Provost/HBMain.htm]. August 1999.

Written specifically for individuals in the department chair role, this handbook is well-written and provides great insight into the challenges associated with being "the first and most visible representative of both your discipline and your department." Three sections prove to be particularly helpful. Section I, "Defining the Departmental Chairperson," succinctly offers action steps required for effective advocacy in the college, the department, department faculty development, and for students in the department. Section II, "The Departmental Chairperson as Manager," provides specific guidance for dealing with diversity issues, international programs, ADA awareness, and conflict management issues. Section III, "University Standards," provides guidance on professional and ethical standards. Although written specifically as a handbook for UNLV chairs, the main themes are certainly relevant for any individual in this role, regardless of location.

University of Minnesota, Office of Human Resources. Administrative development program. [http://www.umn.edu/ohr/adp/]. March 2000.

This site showcases a wide range of development opportunities presented to academic leaders, managers, and supervisors to enable them to perform their roles more effectively. The University of Minnesota's Center for Human Resource Development, a division of the Office of Human Resources, offers other management education, training, and support services, examples of which follow.

University of Minnesota, Office of Human Resources. A competency model for the position of chair/head of an academic unit at the University of Minnesota. [http://www1.umn.edu/ohr/adp/heads]. July 1997.

A very useful resource, this model includes key function definitions (main activities carried out in the unit that subsequently influence the roles and responsibilities of the chair-head), a checklist of roles and responsibilities (representing the work agenda of chairs-heads), a checklist of competencies (the KSAAs needed to carry out the position roles and responsibilities effectively), and much more. Multiple links and references are also provided.

University of Minnesota, Office of Human Resources. Academic department enrichment program. [http://www.umn.edu/ohr/ADP/ADEP.html]. July 1997.

Short project summaries of this ADEP program, a two-year pilot program funded by the Bush Foundation, are included on this Web site, as well as links to various development opportunities sponsored by ADEP in the past. Its goal is to assist selected academic units in solving complex academic issues. Units involved in this project address curriculum development, developing departmental leadership, curricular and administrative restructuring, reinventing departmental outreach, improving the culture of teaching and learning, building bridges to the community, and designing the future of basic plant science, among others.

University of Minnesota, Office of Human Resources. Orientation seminar series for new chairs, heads, and directors of academic departments and programs. [http://www1.umn.edu/ohr/adp/orientation.html]. June 2001.

New academic administrators will find that this orientation seminar series was designed to help them understand the roles and responsibilities of their positions. Issues addressed in the 2001–02 program include roles, responsibilities, and priorities for department administrators; financial resources; planning, acquisition, and management; developing and supervising staff; maintaining and developing faculty; legal issues and external relations; and fostering a positive culture and productive atmosphere in academic units. Designed primarily for University of Minnesota employees. (For information on program content, contact program coordinator Shirley Nelson Garner, professor and former chair, English Language and Literature at sngarner@umn.edu.)

University of Minnesota, Office of Human Resources. Deans' conversation series. [http://www1.umn.edu/ohr/adp/conversations.html]. June 2001.

The University of Minnesota also offers an opportunity for the deans to meet informally with chairs, heads, and directors of academic units to network and discuss topics of concern to the university. Past topics have included how not to do faculty promotion and tenure, how to deal with an impossible dean or impossible chair, and hiring strategies for departmental renewal.

University of Minnesota, Office of Human Resources. A summary of national higher education leadership and management development programs for academic administrators. [http://www1.umn.edu/ohr/adp/summary/extended.html] and [http://www1.umn.edu/ohr/adp/summary/brief.html]. August 1997.

Describes programs ranging from one day to one year in length offered through such sponsors as the American Council on Education, H. John Heinz III School of Public Policy and Management, Committee on Institutional Cooperation, Wellesley College and Higher Education Resource Services, Bryn Mawr College and Higher Education Resource Services, and the Harvard University Graduate Schools of Business Administration and Education. These sites are an excellent source on administrator development programs offered throughout the United States, listing schedules, fees, and contacts.

University of Minnesota, Office of Human Resources. Directory of employee development programs: Twin Cities campus. [http://www1.umn.edu/ohr/adp/empdev/]. July 1999.

This directory offers a description of the wide array of employee development programs offered at the Twin Cities campus. Links to the homepages for providers of career, professional, and academic skills development sessions are included as well as resources for diversity awareness training and resources.

Kansas State University, Division of Continuing Education. Academic chairpersons conference. [http://dce.ksu.edu/dce/cl/academicchair/2001/agenda2.html] and [http://dce.ksu.edu/dce/cl/academicchair/2001/workshops.htm]. August 2001.

Conference content is provided for the 2001–02 Academic Chairpersons Conference hosted by the IDEA Center and Continuing Learning Division of Continuing Education, Kansas State University. These sites may be most helpful in that they provide speaker contact names and associated university affiliations for the wide range of topics presented at the most recent conference.

Colorado State University, Training and Development. Challenge ropes courses and team building. [http://www.hrs.colostate.edu/training/workshops/group.html]. August 2000.

One of four programs and workshops highlighted at this site, this workshop is simply one of the many innovative team-building activities designed to encourage collaboration, teamwork, mutual support, and personal goal setting.

Florida State University, Office for Academic Affairs. Institute for Academic Leadership. [http://www.fsu.edu/~acaffair/ial/ial.html] and [http://www.fsu.edu/~acaffair/ial/ial_presentations.html]. August 2001.

The history of the Institute for Academic Leadership as well as its purpose is highlighted at this site. A link to IAL presentations provides a series of printable Microsoft PowerPoint and Word format presentations available on-line, including "Multiple Roles of the Department Chair," "Building and Maintaining a Positive Work Environment," "Authority and Responsibility of Academic Administrators," "An Approach to Departmental Assessment and Faculty Assignments," "Enuff Is Enuff! Dealing with a Nonproductive or Disruptive Employee," "Academic Medication," "Rights and Responsibilities of Academic Administrators," and "What Else Should Be Included in the Evaluation Letter?"

Lucas, A. (1999, November). Myths that make chairs feel they are powerless. *AAHE Bulletin.* [http://www.aahe.org/Bulletin/nov99fl.htm].

Subtitled "Six Fallacies That Stifle Change—and How to Overcome Them," this article available on the Web presents a realistic view of the external demands on higher education and their subsequent effects on faculty, particularly department chairs. Feeling powerless to initiate change, chairs have often stated they do not know how to be change agents and do not believe they have the power to bring about change. Dr. Lucas presents the "six most frequent fixed beliefs, or myths, that are dysfunctional for the chairs who hold them, accompanied each time by my rebuttal."

Center for Institutional & International Initiatives. [http://www.acenet.edu/programs/ciii.cfm]. June 2001.

Composed of multiple links to leadership programs, this site serves as an excellent resource for those seeking to promote institutional improvement and change. The center's goals are to identify new leaders, improve administrative skills, encourage dialogue and debate on the challenges leaders face in promoting institutional change. Specific programs of significance that are linked include "Chairing the Academic Department" and "The Project on Leadership and Institutional Transformation."

American Association for Higher Education. Search AAHE. [http://www.aahe.org/aahesearch.cfm]. August 2001.

A multitude of Web site links are provided at this address, including sites for book reviews, articles, bulletins, and conference highlights.

American Council on Education. On Change occasional paper series. [http://www.acenet.edu/bookstore/index.cfm?pubID=231]. August 2001.

This ACE bookstore site primarily addresses organizational change; multiple sites are linked to occasional papers I through IV as well as other titles on change and change management. Specific titles are as follows: "On Change I: En Route to Transformation" (1998), "On Change II: Reports from the Road: Insights on Institutional Change" (1999), "On Change III: Taking Charge of Change: A Primer for Colleges and Universities" (2000), "On Change IV: What Governing Boards Need to Know and Do About Institutional Change" (2000), "On Change V: Riding the Waves of Change: Insights for Transforming Institutions" (2001). Papers I through IV can be purchased or downloaded from this Web site; paper V is not available for downloading at this time.

Academic Leadership. The Online Journal. [http://www.academicleadership.org/]. August 2001.

This on-line journal is updated on a quarterly basis and provides research papers, essays, and bibliographic information. In addition, the journal provides a growing list of links that will prove helpful to those in academic leadership.

Academic Leadership. Resources. [http://www.academicleadership.org/resources.html] and [http://www.academicleadership.org/links.html]. August 2001.

These sites provide a reference-bibliography listing of a multitude of books, journal articles, journals, and other publications and links to other Web sites associated with academic leadership.

PART SEVEN

Conclusion

The challenges we face as a society demand not incremental but quantum improvements in the outcomes of higher learning. These will only be achieved by serious changes in the "deep architecture" of our colleges and universities requiring fundamental redesign of systems, habits, and culture in which the learning enterprise is pursued. I think one of the great questions we face is whether leaders will emerge who are willing to undertake such a narrow, unknown, and demanding path rather than the broad and already well-traveled road to comfortable mediocrity.

Sanford C. Shugart, president, Valencia Community College, Orlando, Florida

CHAPTER 29

Some Final Observations

ROBERT M. DIAMOND

The *Field Guide for Academic Leadership* is a resource about change and institutional improvement. It addresses the crucial relationship between research and practice, with author after author emphasizing the importance of having a clear and agreed-upon institutional mission and vision and reminding us that learning must be at the heart of the academic enterprise. The *Field Guide* is also a book about courage—the willingness to make tough decisions, accept risk, and maintain a vision of your institution's best future along with a sense of how it might best get there.

Individual chapters have discussed the skills and knowledge needed to lead significant and sustainable change, qualities of leadership, academic issues, technology, and assessment and have offered guidance that is position-specific. Some additional topics still need to be considered here: learning from the experience of other institutions, how to initiate change and overcome barriers to change, fundraising and institutional development in the context of mission, and the phenomenon of "mission creep." In addition, we will take the always-risky opportunity to look into the future. Finally, we offer a list of resources that have not been highlighted earlier.

LEARNING FROM OTHERS

As you move ahead, always remember that the problems you face are not unique. Other academic leaders at institutions much like yours have found themselves dealing with the same pressures, the same constraints, and much the same cast of characters. In some instances they have been successful, in others not. You can benefit from their experience. In far too many instances we make the same mistakes time and again because we have little knowledge of what others have learned and have done little to find out about it.

As an effective institutional leader it is important for you to develop a campus climate that investigates what others are doing, keeps up with the literature, and before any initiative begins, makes sure you are aware of what exists elsewhere that might be useful. Most institutions are more than willing to share information and materials. We often hesitate to ask for assistance or advice for one of two reasons:

- *We have an exaggerated sense of our own uniqueness.* The fact is that colleges and universities face many of the same challenges, and human nature and our cultural influences ensure that folks react in similar ways to challenges across institutional contexts.
- *We want to protect an image of our institutions or ourselves as leaders beyond or above such difficulties.* We misconstrue our competitive advantage as dependent on an image of superiority. In fact we exist in an era of greater interdependence—not less.

So look to see if there are published reports or articles, have representatives from your campus attend workshops and conferences, and if certain projects appear to be particularly on target, have a team visit the institution. Often through such visits you will learn about successful implementation strategies or what did not work. This information can prove to be invaluable. Although this kind of inquiry will take time and cost you money, the return on the investment can be substantial.

Keep in mind that you can learn from experiences at institutions different from your own. For example, although Alverno College is certainly not a typical institution (small, church-related, single-gender), the work that has been done on that campus over the past decade to develop a student-centered curriculum that addresses lifelong learning issues offers much that can be tailored to your institutional type and culture. In fact, as a service to other institutions Alverno has fully documented both the process and the results of its efforts. See *Learning That Lasts: Integrating Learning, Development, and Performance in College and Beyond* (Mentkowski & Associates, 2000).

Described as "finding and adopting best practices," *benchmarking* is the formal process of identifying and implementing good practices and processes from organizations anywhere in the world to help your own organization improve its performance (Grayson, 1998, p. 106). Benchmarking is a systematic process for yielding the greatest amount of information and then using it. There are a number of reasons why higher education has not embraced this approach and most have to do with misunderstanding or mistrust: "There's nothing we can learn." "It's only useful in the for-profit sector." "We'll be punished if we find that others are doing a better job." A good starting point for understanding how benchmarking can assist you in making the changes you envision is the chapter "Benchmarking in Higher Education" by C. Jackson Grayson, Jr., in *New Thinking on Higher Education: Creating a Context for Change* (1998).

Putting in place a process for seeking out information and learning from others will save money and energy, and over time, improve your institution. One final comment: Do not just look at the most prestigious institutions. Many of the most exciting innovations are taking place in midsize public institutions, community colleges, and smaller, nontraditional programs. They have to innovate, others do not.

INITIATING CHANGE

All too often one of the most important steps in any initiative is the one that is given the least attention—selecting the individuals who will serve on the leadership team. Whether the focus is developing a new approach to budgeting for the institution, designing a new curriculum, improving the working relationship between the development office and academic affairs, or revising the faculty reward system, the combination of individuals chosen to lead the initiative will quite often determine the effort's success. Leaving certain individuals out of the early discussions can lead to big problems later on, while at the same time giving key responsibility to the wrong individuals can lead to unnecessary conflict and compromise.

Task Force Versus Standing Committee

Although in some cases you may prefer to use a standing committee to lead an initiative, there are a number of advantages to establishing a task force.

First, you can choose its membership. Because a task force is focused on a single task, it is designed to disband once the task is completed. Consequently, you may find individuals willing to participate who would not otherwise—you can get the best people. Second, because a task force is oriented to a single task, it tends to be far more efficient than committees with a number of items on their agenda. Finally, establishing a task force signals that the initiative is important and that the institution is committed to its success.

Choosing the Right People for the Job

Deciding who should serve on your task force is one of your most important decisions. Before you make your final choices, get advice from others. Be sure to get feedback from a range of constituencies. Their insights can prove extremely helpful as you put your team together. Appointing a task force is one of those things that you should never do without consulting others.

- *Key campus leaders.* Every unit or area that will be affected by the effort should be included from the beginning with representation on the leadership team. Based on the potential impact of the initiative, it may be advisable to select the head of each area. Group size will always be a concern, and there will be situations in which you may choose a strong representative group. For example, on a large campus, if the project involves all your schools and colleges, four or five of the stronger deans might be appropriate.
- *Key resource people.* If the project is going to rely on professional expertise, such individuals should be included. Although important, their membership should be limited to two or three individuals at most.
- *Senate committee chairs, union representatives, faculty leaders,* and others who could prove to be extremely helpful or create obstacles to implementation. Here, take care, for these individuals may not be readily apparent. In some cases an individual may be selected solely because she may stop or slow down the initiative if she is not onboard. A warning: Do not put more than one or two potentially critical individuals on the task force. Although getting their "ownership" of the project is extremely important, you do not want to place them in a position to kill or delay the process.

Although you never want the leadership group to be too large, it is important that it be perceived as appropriate by the institutional community. A lack of participation at this level, by any key group, can be disastrous. If, however, your task force is becoming larger than you would like—above fifteen members or so—consider having a leadership team that establishes goals and procedures, coordinates publicity, and then appoints a number of implementation-action teams once specific activities have been identified.

Selecting a Chair

Presidents and provosts rarely want to be in the position of chairing an initiative of this magnitude. Chairing such a task force is extremely time consuming, and if a member of the cabinet is placed in such a position, the administration may be accused of manipulation and heavy-handedness.

The person you choose to chair the group should be someone you trust and can work closely with. The person should be respected by the entire community as bright, fair, and open; have a high level of facilitative skills (the ability to lead a group is far more important than expertise in the subject area); and not be perceived as an advocate for a particular solution if there will be a number of different viewpoints in the group. At times, a chair who is seen as neutral is particularly important. For example, the chair of a curriculum committee should *not* be seen as having a vested interest in a particular course or program or as an advocate for the status quo. Make sure this individual buys into the need you are addressing and understands where you hope to go with the project.

Giving the Charge and Providing the Resources

After you have selected a chair and the individual has agreed to serve, you have a number of responsibilities.

- Meet with the chair to develop the charge and time line for the task force and to discuss committee membership.
- Appoint all task force members, and do this personally. There is no better way to get their commitment and to show evidence of the importance of the initiative.
- Communicate your vision (including the importance or rationale for the initiative) to the task force members and to your entire community.
- Provide the needed resources. Do not shortchange the task force. Provide funds for meetings and phone calls, the purchasing of resources, and in some cases, travel expenses for task force members to attend national meetings or visit other institutions. You may also want to set aside some funds for possible consultants and clerical support for the task force chair. Plan for an intensive meeting or retreat early on and for a more public activity when the task force has completed its work. Involving the chair in establishing a budget for the task force can be a very good move on your part. The more significant the initiative, the more resources should be made available.

OVERCOMING BARRIERS TO CHANGE

Authors in the *Field Guide* have addressed the complexity of dealing with change in colleges and universities. Some have focused on the process of change; others have addressed cultural issues or concerns related to your role and specific responsibilities. In general, you can expect to encounter five distinct types of barriers in your role as an academic leader.

- *Process barriers,* where the problems are directly related to the steps you take.
- *Cultural barriers,* where tradition and different experiences and needs stand in the way of change.
- *Knowledge barriers,* where those involved are simply not prepared for the roles they need to play—both in skills and knowledge.
- *Personal barriers,* where individuals, for any number of reasons, are simply not comfortable with change.
- *Economic barriers,* where needed resources for implementation are not available.

There are two important factors to keep in mind before you undertake any initiative. First, most barriers can be identified even before you begin. Second, by recognizing and dealing with them as part of your planning process, you can significantly reduce their impact. Understanding some of the factors that influence reactions to change can be very helpful.

Several years ago we had the opportunity to conduct a number of workshops focused on institutional change at national meetings attended by presidents, provosts, deans, department chairs, and faculty. As part of the workshop, participants were asked to identify what they believed to be the main barriers to change at their institutions. We then compared responses from faculty with those of administrators. The results were interesting. There were some areas of agreement on existing obstacles to change:

- Too much change already
- Lack of community; territoriality among units
- Lack of trust, respect, and openness
- Lack of will, inertia, fear of the unknown
- Less risk in maintaining the status quo
- Vested interest in maintaining the status quo
- Lack of money, time, equipment

There were, however, a number of obstacles that appeared different to faculty than they did to administrators. Administrators described faculty responses to change as follows:

- They have knee-jerk reaction to change.
- They have a siege mentality.
- They fear losing job, tenure, control.

- They are skeptical (things are always changing, but nothing really changes).
- They are suspicious of administration or trustees.
- They lack concern about external constituencies.
- Senior faculty are simply not interested in getting involved, period.

In contrast, faculty identified the administration as an impediment to change in the following ways:

- They lack courage or vision.
- They believe that change initiatives are the responsibility of faculty.
- They fear losing control.
- They are suspicious or skeptical about faculty.
- They lack knowledge about change models or processes.
- They are poor communicators.

In short, although there was some agreement on the main barriers to change, each group also perceived that the other group presented the main obstacle to institutional reform.

Environmental and Cultural Barriers

Compounding these different perceptions are other barriers more directly related to the change process and the culture of an institution.

- Individuals may believe that there is simply no problem or need to change.
- Developing consensus on a campus is time consuming and difficult.
- External review procedures (accreditation agencies, state departments) may be resistant to change.
- Faculty may fear that working with the administration will alienate them from peers.
- Faculty do not see themselves as employees, and their priorities are often more focused on their discipline than their institution.
- Departments are often isolated.
- Faculty tend to rotate through management and nonmanagement positions, making major change at the department level difficult with "rotating" chairs.

For an excellent discussion of the faculty-administrative relationship, read C. Berryman-Fink, "Can We Agree to Disagree? Administration-Faculty Conflict" in *Mending Cracks in the Ivory Tower* (1998).

Stonewallers

Keep in mind that those who resist change will rarely do so in a direct manner. That is simply not the way things are done in colleges and universities. Instead they will miss meetings and deadlines, and the stated reasons for not supporting an initiative will often have little to do with the reality. Faculty may have learned that if they do nothing when initiatives are proposed, the status quo will be maintained and their behavior will never have consequences.

Edgar Dale, a senior faculty member at Ohio State University in the 1960s, observing the behavior of his colleagues, listed the most common reasons for resisting change (Dale, 1960). You can expect to hear the same good reasons for doing nothing today:

- The proposal would set a precedent.
- There is no precedent to guide us.
- We have not yet conclusively proved that the old method cannot be made to work or that the proposed new one can.
- It is just another fad. (Wait long enough and it will go away.)
- The time is not ripe.
- The situation is hopeless.
- We cannot afford it.
- It is a controversial issue.

Immovable Objects

Because resistance is to be expected when almost any new idea is proposed, how can you best deal with it? The most effective way to address these barriers is, obviously, not to let them arise in the first place. All change models address this point when they stress involvement and ownership. The more your campus community members accept the urgency for change, the more they feel part of the process. The more care you take in selecting your leadership team, the fewer hurdles you will have to overcome as the initiative evolves. Every change model stresses the importance of building momentum from the very beginning. How you get your project under way is a vital first step. Use every public forum available to help build support for the initiative and keep the campus informed.

As much as you may try and as hard as you may work at getting involvement from the beginning, you can anticipate not always being 100 percent successful. Some faculty and staff will always perceive any change as a threat to their present comfort level.

Others will worry that your proposal may diminish their power or advantage or reduce their resources. They may be right.

If, after trying everything, you fail to win such people over, ask yourself, "How important is this individual or group to the success of the initiative?" If your answer is "Not very," then your best option is just to proceed without them. Continually try to address their concerns but understand that you may never win them over, and at some point the effort simply will not be worth it. Do not let a small group of negative individuals stop progress. Endorse consensus and the will of the majority.

In contrast, if a program or individual is essential to your success, you must deal with that resistance immediately and directly. Your first step should be to try to get the individuals to buy into the initiative by reinforcing the importance of the effort to the health and vitality of the institution and to their program. Communicate also the risk they take by not being active participants. With leadership comes power, and this is one place where you may need to use yours.

If a department or unit is involved, try to identify those in the group who may be willing to work with you and move ahead and do your best to keep the others informed, hoping their attitudes will change over time as they see the benefits of what is being accomplished. If, however, you are finding resistance from a key individual, you need to take action. Your options (depending on how important the initiative is) are as follows: You can move the individual to a less powerful position—the "diagonal arabesque." On one campus the registrar, who was all for change "having tried it once," was reassigned as institutional historian. You can place the individual on administrative leave. You can enthusiastically encourage the individual to seek new employment.

Although these actions are certainly drastic, you may have no option. Your move sends a message that resistance and lack of cooperation will not be tolerated, whereas your unwillingness to act will be seen as a lack of commitment and a weakness in your ability to lead. Keep in mind that negativism is not the same as having different viewpoints. There is much to be learned from an honest critique. The key is this: Is the individual open to discussion and compromise? Not dealing directly with these individuals will only lead to more contentious problems in the future.

Resource Barriers

Resource constraints are real and more stringent in certain environments and at certain times; however, hard choices can usually make resources available. Consider dropping underenrolled courses or programs, merging or eliminating small or weak departments or programs, reassigning faculty, and using less sophisticated or more cost-effective technology.

Review Resources Regularly

To avoid such drastic measures, develop an ongoing program of resource review. There are a number of other actions that you should be taking on a regular basis to ensure that resources are being used as effectively as possible. Course enrollments should be reviewed regularly to ensure that demand is there, curriculum committees should be charged with reviewing programs to reduce duplication, and the faculty reward systems must support activities that are crucial to the future of your institution. Another important challenge is to ensure that faculty workload is balanced across departments and colleges. It is not uncommon to find that faculty in one department are totally overloaded with teaching, advising, and other important assignments whereas in another unit, the workload is less rigorous. In the final analysis, the old adage "Where there's a will, there's a way" applies with respect to resources. The key is to maintain your vision and commitment in the face of unpopular decisions.

Explore Partnerships

You should also explore the possibility of forming partnerships with other institutions, public school systems in your area, business and industry, and governmental agencies. Colleges and universities are finding that these cooperative ventures can not only save money but also, in many instances, result in improved programs and services.

Institutions across the country are reaping the benefits of joint purchasing agreements and shared technological systems and library resources. There is also the possibility of sharing assessment and faculty development expertise and faculty positions if neither institution has enough funding to support a full position yet each requires the specific area of specialization for its academic program. This type of arrangement also makes sense when an individual you would like to hire wants to retain a professional role in government, a public agency, or the for-profit sector. Split appointments between a school of education and the public schools may also be worth exploring. Although agreements of this type require care and sometimes difficult negotiations, the long-term results of these collaborations can be substantial.

Improve Productivity Through Clerical and Technical Support

There are also times when a modest investment can significantly increase productivity among your most talented faculty and staff. Do not shortchange your institution in clerical and technical support. Make sure you have a proper balance between faculty, administrative staff, and clerical support and that there is adequate technical support for faculty and staff. Training and retraining and hardware troubleshooting and maintenance are part of the cost of doing business in a technological age. In some public systems one of the biggest challenges faced by campus leaders is getting legislators, board members, and central office staff to recognize the importance of providing sufficient resources for support personnel. The bang for the buck is certainly there when efficiency and productivity can be improved or enhanced.

FUNDRAISING AND INSTITUTIONAL DEVELOPMENT

Other chapters have discussed the need for good relationships between academic affairs and student affairs and coordination between academic priorities and the budgeting and fiscal operations. Although the subject of fundraising has been mentioned, the supportive relationship between the development office and deans, department chairs, and faculty is significant. It is certainly an area in which a real disconnect is often felt by faculty and staff.

Keep in mind that when we discuss fundraising activities we need to consider these distinct, but sometimes overlapping, areas: grants from corporations and foundations obtained directly by the institution's development office; grants and research projects where the main initiative comes from a faculty member whose interest is directly related to her own scholarly pursuits or the goals of her academic unit; general fundraising through alumni, parents, and others formally associated with the institution; and project-related fundraising activities to support specific existing or new programs with the efforts initiated by the unit involved.

It is important that all four fundraising activities focus their energies on supporting the mission and priorities of the institution. This requires coordination, clear criteria, and cooperation in an area where competition among units tends to be the norm. The leadership of the president and chief academic officer are needed to communicate that this coordination is clearly a priority.

We are not suggesting a complex central control system, but we are recommending that priorities for each funding area be clearly articulated and communicated and structured to support the stated mission and vision of the institution. If problem areas are identified—such as growth in a particular new academic area, the improvement of the advising system, new facilities for specific high-priority programs, or funds to support academic innovation—then that is where the funding priorities need to be. The system also needs to be flexible so that when a new opportunity arises no formal decision or action is made until both its positive and negative potentials are explored. Although some grants or donations may be somewhat tangential to meeting the higher priorities that have been established, they can still have a benefit that makes them worthwhile. There will, however, be other instances where this is not the case. As a result of saying no, you can expect some unhappy people both inside and outside the institution, but these problems will be significantly lessened if the rationale for supporting projects is clearly stated and the process is perceived to be a fair one.

Before an initiative goes too far or dollars are accepted, several important questions need to be asked:

- Does the project support the mission and vision of the institution and the priorities of the academic units involved?
- Are all associated costs covered (space, staff, equipment, operating, and maintenance)? If not, are the necessary funds available from other sources?
- Might the project have other, indirect benefits (improved retention and recruitment of students, prestige, and so on)?
- Will the proposed project have a short- or long-term negative impact on other programs or options (moving key faculty away from teaching and students, taking space and resources away from other important programs, and so on)?
- Does the project have the potential of improving high-priority initiatives and programs, reducing costs, or raising discretionary income?
- Does the project have strings attached that could be detrimental to the institution?

In short, does the project make long-term institutional sense? Is the timing right and does it fit in with your vision of the future?

Coordinating fundraising initiatives is an important institutional function. A lack of communication and coordination here can have negative effects, both long-term and short-term, on the institution and its faculty, staff, and students. Sometimes the best decision is to say, "Thanks, but no thanks." It is important to reward departments and recognize individuals not for how much money they raise or how many grants they receive but by how much their efforts directly support the mission, vision, and priorities of your institution.

MISSION CREEP

On a regular basis there will be a published report that a college president has announced that his institution is committed to moving up to the next "tier of excellence" or Carnegie classification. Although this may be an appropriate move, it is more often the result of desires of key campus leaders to move up professionally. Most initiatives of this type require a significant shift of resources, changing roles for individuals, and new priorities for academic units. In some instances, the move can be a disservice to the institution, its students, and the community it serves.

When the pressure for such a shift starts to grow, a number of questions should be asked by the trustees or the board and by the president, assuming the president is not the main proponent of the action.

- From whom is the pressure coming? In some instances the pressure may be coming from faculty or administration who would prefer to be at an institution more like the one from which they graduated. In other instances the move may be more ego-based or politically motivated than anything else. However, the move could have a positive long-term impact on the health of the institution.
- Is the move appropriate for the institution, for the community, and for its students?
- How much support is there for the move by faculty and staff?
- What would be the long-term benefits of such a move?
- What negative impact can be anticipated?
- What would the move cost, in dollars, in facilities?
- Is it doable? In many cases when an institution's goal is to move into the top twenty of a given category, little thought is given to its capability to compete with the institutions already on the list. In most cases those on the list have far more resources than the wannabes.

Finally, keep in mind that most of these classification systems are based on criteria or academic reputations that have little to do with how well an institution is serving its public or educating its students.

LOOKING INTO THE FUTURE

There is little question that changing demographics, more students with greater diversity among them, an increased number of individuals going on for advanced degrees and certification, rapidly changing technology, increased competition from the private sector, the establishment of new coalitions and international universities, decreasing financial support for students in the public sector, and the continuing demand for greater accountability are all going to have a significant impact on higher education. Of course, it is always risky to attempt to see into the future, but a number of changes can be anticipated as a result of all the forces that are now at work. Some of these will seem obvious, others will be far more subtle.

- As state and federal aid per student diminishes and the number of students being served increases, large state institutions will behave more and more like the private schools, with greater selectivity and an increased emphasis on fundraising.
- There will be growth in the number of global universities and increased competition from the for-profit sector as well. The competition from the for-profit sector will be solely in the teaching function. Revenue-poor research and service functions will be left to traditional institutions.
- The character of a number of institutions will change. Arthur Levine (2000) has envisioned the emergence of three distinct types: traditional residential institutions (brick universities), new commercial virtual universities (click universities) and a combination of the two (brick-and-click universities). However, some observers, such as Frank Rhodes (1999), believe that although change will occur, the university will still depend on an established campus base as an essential platform for both its specialized facilities and its scholarly community.
- Institutions will become more sensitive to student needs and demands, with administrations becoming more proactive in determining departmental programs and institutional agendas.
- On a growing number of campuses, the traditional power base of the arts and sciences will shift to the professional schools, with increased pressure on the arts and sciences to focus energies on the core program for all students and less on programs for majors, many of which (particularly the humanities) will continue to experience an enrollment decline.
- Faculty will have less control over what they do and how they spend their time. Although research will continue to be supported at research and doc-

toral institutions, there will be increased efforts to align this research with the mission and vision of the institution.

- Relying heavily on technology, state institutions will expand their efforts to establish satellite units to serve students in remote locations.

- The focus of higher education will continue to shift from teaching to learning, with increased attention paid to learning outcomes and program accountability. The pressures for accountability and assessment from accreditation agencies and state offices will continue to increase.

- Degrees will become less important to a growing sector of students as emphasis shifts to applied programs and certification. As Daniel Pink (2001) has observed, "As the shelf life of a degree shortens, more students will go to college to acquire particular skills than to bring home a sheepskin" (p. 9).

- Certificate and other nondegree programs will increase in number. If you are interested in developing a certification program on your campus, see "Certificates: Credentials of Choice" (2001).

- The home base of faculty at many campuses will shift from traditional disciplinary-based departments to programs. This will have significant impact on assignments, the faculty reward system, and on the nature of faculty leadership.

- Greater emphasis will be placed on improved learning and the use of more interactive teaching methods and technologies, and the role of many faculty will shift to mentoring and program development. A greater proportion of student-faculty interaction will take place outside of the traditional classroom, and through creative uses of technology, at nontraditional hours and in nontraditional places (Duderstadt, 2000).

- Individual accountability, including faculty and unit rewards and recognition, will be more closely aligned with priorities and missions.

- Multiyear faculty appointments and the number of part-time positions will continue to increase with the benefit and support given to the individuals in these positions also increasing.

- Academic affairs and student affairs programs will increasingly work together and blend their efforts.

Finally, it is important to note that faculty demographics will certainly change, the result of three factors: the elimination of mandatory retirement in 1994, the increasing reliance on temporary and part-time faculty to reduce costs and provide more flexibility, increasing numbers of women faculty (43.8 percent of all new hires in 1998), more international appointments, resulting in more diversity in new hires.

The implications of these faculty trends may be subtle now but over time they may become quite pronounced. More senior faculty means fewer young people in the pipeline being prepared to take over the leadership roles when older faculty retire—and a large number of retirements are anticipated over the next few years. With each tenure track position that is eliminated, you lose a potential committee member, adviser, and campus citizen with a long-term commitment to your institution.

A 1999 report from the National Center for Educational Statistics showed that faculty on term contracts spent significantly less time in informal contact with students than do their colleagues with tenure line appointments. The shift to more women faculty, more international appointments, and more ethnic diversity means a shift in style, in personal priorities, and in perspective.

It will be crucial to your success as a leader and administrator that you recognize the implications of these demographic changes, and the unique opportunities they present, and explore ways in which your institution and programs can benefit. For a quick update on the subject and its potential implications see the October 2001 issue of the *AAHE Bulletin*. Two articles in that issue—by Arden and by Finkelstein and Schuster—on changing faculty demographics and the impact of the elimination of mandatory retirement are excellent.

In sum, although some colleges and universities, particularly the highly prestigious and wealthy ones, will remain much as they are, most will change. For some institutions, it will be a matter of survival, for others, the challenge will be to meet the demands of constituents. There is little doubt, however, that we are living in a period of transition in American higher education. The more sensitive you are to the forces for change, and to their potential consequences, the more effective you will be as a leader and administrator.

SOME FINAL THOUGHTS ON LEADERSHIP

Not everyone in a leadership position leads. In contrast, there are others who, regardless of their position, assume informal leadership roles, and thanks to their talents, dedication, and the respect of their colleagues, make a major and lasting impact on their institutions. One key to being an effective leader is the willingness to accept responsibility along with the challenges.

A leader cannot be effective working alone. Leadership requires the active support of those in key roles throughout the institution, working together toward common goals. There will be times when people other than yourself should lead an effort and when you will need to take a more supportive role. Leadership requires on each individual's part a wide range of skills and competencies. In *The Successful President* Kenneth Shaw (1999) identifies sixteen leadership attributes that are as appropriate for deans and chairs as for presidents or provosts:

- *Competencies:* ability to deal collectively with reality, capacity to adapt to change, relative freedom from excessive anxiety or tension, capacity to find satisfaction in both giving and receiving, ability to form and maintain close relationships with others, ability to differentiate between the impossible and the possible, ability to redirect hostile energy into constructive outlets, capacity to love oneself and to love others, willingness to self-evaluate
- *Skills:* ability to deal creatively and effectively with conflict, ability to deal effectively with groups, ability to listen, ability to be assertive with people at all levels, ability to move others to "yes," ability to use power effectively, ability to motivate others

To this list we would add a willingness to take risks, to say no, and to make unpopular decisions. If major change were easy and if everyone agreed with both the goals and the process being used to reach them, it would not be so difficult to find effective leaders. The key is believing that what you are doing is right for your institution or program. Leadership is never easy. Do not expect it to be.

In the *Field Guide for Academic Leadership* we have tried to provide you with knowledge to help you be a more effective leader of lasting institutional change. In the long run, however, it will be your decision whether or not to become an active force for change. No one else can make this decision for you. Accepting the challenge will mean hard work, facing a number of complex issues, and taking some risks. However, if you are successful you will know that you have played a significant role in improving the quality of your institution and the lives of students, faculty, and staff. You may also have a great deal of fun along the way.

The image others have of you and the vision for the future that you communicate to others are not the result of a single action. They are the sum total of your professional career and of who and what you are. As the following story suggests, it is important to know where you are going. We may have excellent management and interpersonal skills, but if we fail to articulate a vision for the future, we may find ourselves tilting at windmills.

The Reverend Billy Graham tells of a time early in his career when he arrived in a small town to preach a sermon. Wanting to mail a letter, he asked a young boy where the post office was. When the boy had told him, Graham thanked him and said, "If you'll come to the Baptist church this evening, you can hear me telling everyone how to get to heaven."

"I don't think I'll be there," the boy said. "You don't even know your way to the post office."

On behalf of all the authors, we wish you well in setting a course for the future.

References

Arden, E. (2001, October). When it's time to leave—leave: Mandatory retirement is good for higher education. *AAHE Bulletin, 54*(2).

Berryman-Fink, C. (1998). Can we agree to disagree? Administration-faculty conflict. In S. A. Holton (Ed.), *Mending cracks in the ivory tower* (pp. 141–163). Bolton, MA: Anker.

Certificates: Credentials of choice. (2001, November). *University Business, 6*(9), 48–54.

Dale, E. (1960). *Good reasons for doing nothing.* Columbus: The Ohio State University.

Duderstadt, J. J. (2000). *A university for the twenty-first century.* Ann Arbor: University of Michigan Press.

Finkelstein, M. J., & Schuster, J. H. (2001, October). Assessing the silent revolution: How changing demographics are reshaping the academic profession. *AAHE Bulletin, 54*(2).

Grayson, C. J., Jr. (1998). Benchmarking in higher education. In J. W. Meyerson (Ed.), *New thinking on higher education: Creating a context for change* (pp. 105–119). Bolton, MA: Anker.

Levine, A. (2000, October 27). Nine inevitable changes. *Chronicle of Higher Education.*

Mentkowski, M., & Associates. (2000). *Learning that lasts: Integrating learning, development, and performance in college and beyond.* San Francisco: Jossey-Bass.

Pink, D. (2001). School's out: Get ready for the new age of individualized education. *Reason Magazine OnLine,* p. 9.

Rhodes, F. (1999). Characteristics of the new American university. In W. Z. Hirsch & L. F. Weber (Eds.), *Challenges facing higher education at the millennium.* Phoenix: Oryx Press.

Shaw, K. A. (1999). *The successful president: "Buzz words" on leadership.* Phoenix: Oryx Press–American Council on Education.

Resources

Print

Astin, A. W., & Astin, H. S. (2000). *Leadership reconsidered: Engaging higher education in social change.* Battle Creek, MI: W. K. Kellogg Foundation.

The product of the foundation's initiative to develop leadership abilities in college undergraduates at thirty-one institutions, this report describes the need for colleges and universities to develop curricula that will produce graduates who can be effective leaders. The authors address the role of students, faculty, student affairs professionals, and presidents in developing a climate where leadership development is a critical and integral part of the college experience. Along the way they highlight ways you can improve your effectiveness as an institutional leader of change. Well worth reading.

Duderstadt, J. J. (2000). *A university for the twenty-first century.* Ann Arbor: University of Michigan Press.
Challenging. As the title implies, this book focuses on change at large institutions, building on the author's experiences at the University of Michigan. Includes chapters on a wide range of topics, including research and scholarship, service, diversity, technology, and governance. The final section focuses on institutional transformation with a look to the future.

DeZure, D. (Ed.). (2000). *Learning from change: Landmarks in teaching and learning.* Sterling, VA: Stylus Publishing.
Copublished with the American Association for Higher Education, this excellent source book identifies the over two dozen important developments that have changed teaching and learning in higher education over the past thirty years. Includes 160 excerpts from articles in *Change* magazine and introductory comments from experts that place the materials in context. In the Introduction, Theodore Marchese provides an interesting review of the trends and main agendas of the twenty-first century.

Dickeson, R. C. (1999). *Prioritizing academic programs and services: Reallocating resources to achieve strategic balance.* San Francisco: Jossey-Bass.
Every administrator faces the challenge of having more requests for funding than dollars to support them. Here you will find a description of how to develop a prioritizing system that is fair and appropriate for evaluating programs. Extremely useful.

Fullan, M. (2001). *Leading in a culture of change.* San Francisco: Jossey-Bass.
Focusing on the key aspects of leadership in a period of change, the author provides a strong rationale for change and details your role in the process. The importance of having a moral purpose is highlighted, the advice is sound, and the book is an excellent read.

Hanna, D. E. (2000). *Higher education in an era of digital competition: Choices and challenges.* Madison, WI: Atwood Publishing.
For a quality, in-depth discussion of ethics and equity of access, as they apply to technology and leadership decisions, see Chapter Eleven by David Olcott, Jr. Good material.

Meyerson, J. W. (Ed.). (1998). *New thinking on higher education: Creating a context for change.* Boston, MA: Anker.
Covers a wide variety of topics from systems planning, evaluating administrative performance, benchmarking, the market for private education, and budgeting to the impact of technology on libraries. The book contains some useful information for almost everyone. The writing is clear and to the point.

Seldin, P., & Higgersons, M. L. (2001). *The administrative portfolio.* Bolton, MA: Anker.
A quality resource to assist in the evaluation of deans, chairs, and other midlevel administrators. Focuses on leadership development and documenting personal growth.

The Administrator: Practical Wisdom for Higher Education Executives.
Offered by Magna Publications, Inc., this newsletter provides interviews, reviews, and updates. Useful and up-to-date information. Twelve issues per year; $159.

Electronic

Academy Today. [daily@chronicle.com]
This daily Web-based newsletter from the *Chronicle of Higher Education* is free to subscribers. Excellent for a quick review on what is going on in higher education. Includes brief updates on important happenings with special sections on technology, education. Highlights the most recent issue of the *Chronicle* and offers selected excerpts from another publication. The full story being highlighted can usually be obtained for a fee. Easy to use. Well worth the time.

Online Journal of Academic Leadership. [http://www.academicleadership.org].
You will find the topics in this journal, which is published quarterly, to be varied but interesting and often useful. In one recent issue there was an article on accreditation and assessment of distance learning, several on leadership, and a report on how chairs rate the importance of their various tasks. Take a look.

The Futures Project: Policy for Higher Education in a Changing World. [http://futuresproject.org].
Located at Brown University and directed by Frank Newman, this new initiative will be producing reports that address key issues in higher education on a regular basis. The first, "A New Challenge for Higher Education Policy: Channeling the Power of Market Forces to Achieve a New Vision for Higher Education" is now available. You should keep abreast of this work.

Tomorrow's Professor. [http://s11.stanford.edu].
One of the best listservs and the price is right—it is free. Produced in cooperation with the American Association for Higher Education and the National Teaching and Learning Forum, this on-line publication will provide you with carefully selected excerpts from a wide range of sources. An excellent way to keep abreast of the latest publications. (Subscribe by sending the e-mail message "subscribe Tomorrow's Professor" to majordomo@lists.Stanford.edu.)

University Business.
University Business will provide you with updates on key national issues and trends in higher education in the area of financial issues. Because many of these have direct bearing on academic affairs and how we operate, do not let the title discourage you from taking a look. The writing is excellent, the material is clearly presented, and you will be pleased to know, the publication is free to administrators. (Contact University Media, 488 Main Avenue, Norwalk, Connecticut 06851.)

Participants at Minnowbrook Conferences

Note: Professional affiliation shown from time of meeting: *1998, **1999.

Bronwyn Adam* **
Associate Director, Institutional
    Priorities & Faculty Rewards
Syracuse University

Louis Albert**
Vice Chancellor
Educational Services
San Jose/Evergreen Community College
    District

Clayton Alderfer*
Director, Organizational Psychology
Doctoral Program
Rutgers Graduate School of Applied and
    Professional Psychology

Howard Altman*
Director, Linguistics Program
University of Louisville
Modern Languages & Linguistics

Ann Austin-Beck**
Associate Professor
Higher, Adult & Lifelong Education
    Program
Michigan State University

Trudy Banta**
Vice Chancellor
Indiana University-Purdue University

Nora Kizer Bell*
President
Wesleyan College

Milton Blood*
AACSB—The International Association
    for Management Education

Judith Boettcher*
Executive Director
Corporation for Research and
    Educational Networking

Sharon Bradwish-Miller**
Dean, Continuing Education
College of DuPage

Paula Brownlee* **
President Emerita
Association of American Colleges
    and Universities

Thomas Brownlee**
Private Consultant

491

Mary Burgan*
General Secretary
American Association of University
  Professors

William Cashin*
Professor Emeritus
Kansas State University

Richard Chait*
Professor of Higher Education
Harvard University

Nancy Chism**
Associate Vice Chancellor–Associate
  Dean of the Faculties
Indiana University-Purdue University
  at Indianapolis

Susan Clarke**
Principal
Unconventional Wisdom

James Deegan**
Dean, Special Programs Division
Eckerd College

Robert M. Diamond * **
Research Professor and Director
Syracuse University

Gerald S. Edmonds**
Associate Director, Project Advance
Syracuse University

Paul Eickmann*
Provost and Operating Officer for
  Academic Affairs
Cleveland Institute of Art

Donald Ely* **
Professor Emeritus
Syracuse University

Ann Ferren*
Vice President for Academic Affairs
Radford University

Jonathan Fife*
ERIC Clearinghouse on Higher
  Education
The George Washington University

Joanne Florino* **
Cornell University Council

Sylvia Galloway*
Director, Private Sector Programs
Association of Governing Boards
  of Universities and Colleges

Lion Gardiner* **
Associate Professor, Zoology
Rutgers University

Charles Glassick* **
Interim President
Converse College

Russel (Rusty) Garth*
Vice President
The Council of Independent Colleges

Susan Gilmore*
President
New Economy Management Mastery,
  Inc.

Adelaide Gomer*
Board of Trustees
Ithaca College

Kenneth (Casey) Green*
Director, Campus Computing Survey
   & Technology
Claremont Graduate School

Alan Guskin*
University President Emeritus
Antioch University

Diane Halpern* **
Professor of Psychology
California State University-
   San Bernardino

Wallace Hannum* **
Associate Professor of Education
University of North Carolina
   at Chapel Hill

Gary Hanson*
Coordinator, Research & Student Affairs
University of Texas

Ben Hayes**
Director of Faculty and Staff
   Development
Kansas City-Kansas Community
   College

Barbara Holland*
Associate Provost for Strategic Planning
   and Outreach
Northern Kentucky University

Carla Howery* **
Deputy Executive Director
American Sociological Association

Christine Johnson*
Director, Urban Initiatives
Education Commission of the States

George Kuh*
Professor of Educational Leadership
   and Policy
Indiana University-Bloomington

Deryl Leaming*
Dean, College of Mass Communications
Middle Tennessee State University

Catherine LeBlanc*
Executive Director
Initiative on Historically Black Colleges
   and Universities
U.S. Department of Education

Cheryl Leonard-Perkins**
National Academy Staff

Thomas Longin**
Vice President for Programs & Research
Association of Governing Boards of
   Colleges and Universities

Ann Lucas*
Professor of Organizational
   Development
Fairleigh Dickinson University

Christine Maitland**
Higher Educational Coordinator
National Education Association

James Morley**
President, National Association
   of College and University
   Business Officers

James Morrison* **
Professor of Education
University of North Carolina

Margaret Neal**
National Academy Staff

Joan North* **
Dean, College of Professional Studies
University of Wisconsin-Stevens Point

Reverend Mary Newbern Williams
Associate Racial, Ethnic Schools
   and Colleges
Presbyterian Church (USA)

Judith Ramaley*
President
The University of Vermont

James Ratcliff*
Professor
Pennsylvania State University
Center for the Study
   of Higher Education

Michael Reardon**
Provost
Portland State University

Margaret Rivera*
American Association of
   Community Colleges

Kay Schallenkamp*
President
Emporia State University

Jack Schuster*
Professor, Center for Educational
   Studies
Claremont Graduate University

Joyce Scott
Deputy Commissioner
   for Academic and Student Affairs
Montana University System

C. Clinton Sidle**
Cornell University
Johnson Graduate School of
   Management

Joseph H. Silver, Sr.**
Vice President for Academic Affairs
Savannah State University

David Smith**
Director, Center for Professional
   Development
University of Pennsylvania

Mary Deane Sorcinelli**
Associate Provost for Faculty
   Development
University of Massachusetts at Amherst

Allen Splete* **
President
The Council of Independent Colleges

Charles Spuches* **
Associate Dean, Academic Affairs
College of Environmental Science
    and Forestry, State University
    of New York

Joan Stark*
Professor of Education
University of Michigan

Marilla Svinicki*
Director, Center for Teaching Excellence
University of Texas at Austin

William Tierney*
Director of the Center for Higher
    Education Policy Analysis
University of Southern California

Jon Wergin**
Professor of Education
Virginia Commonwealth University

Daniel Wheeler* **
Professional & Organization
    Development
University of Nebraska-Lincoln

Thomas Wickenden* **
Associate Director of Academic
    & Student Affairs
Arizona Board of Regents

Kenneth Zahorski* **
Director, Faculty Development
St. Norbert College

360-degree instruments: Survey-type instruments used to determine how you are perceived by others around you.

Advising: The process of helping students to explore their educational environment, make informed choices in planning their course of study, take responsibility for their own learning, and prepare to become effective lifelong learners.

Advising, centralized: Advising provided by full-time professional advisers.

Advising, decentralized: Advising provided by faculty and staff at the departmental level.

Alignment: When a group of people function effectively as a whole and resources are allocated consistent with the institution's educational mission and values.

Appropriation: An expenditure authorization with specific limitations on amount, purpose, and time; formal advance approval of an expenditure from designated resources available or estimated to be available.

Assessment: Any process primarily intended to gather and use information for purposes of improvement or change, without necessarily having the attending goal of making final decisions about merit or worth. An external review designed to provide other perspectives to the activity, not to pronounce judgment.

Auxiliary enterprise: An entity (for example, food services, bookstore, student housing) that provides a service to campus constituents and charges a fee for those services. In addition to self-support, some auxiliaries may contribute to the general revenues of the institution.

Capital asset: An asset that has a life of more than one year and is not purchased or sold as part of the institution's normal business.

Capital budget: Budget that is composed of expected costs for new construction, major renovation or repairs, and major equipment items. The period can be from one to five years, depending on the institution's practices.

Change, universal principle of: Learning must precede change.

Change advocate: Person or group who supports a change but has no authority to sanction the change effort.

Change agent: Person or group who is responsible for implementing the desired change.

Change sponsor: Person or group who has the authority to legitimate a change.

Chargeback system: Method of assessing the cost of support activities to campus departments by charges for services based on specific requests and established rates. One example is a campus print shop that charges departments based on the type of printing and number of copies made.

Collaborative learning: When individuals work to understand the perspectives of coparticipants and to share with them a mutual responsibility for learning.

Computer-mediated instruction: Using the World Wide Web to facilitate communication between instructors and students or among students.

Consequential evaluation: Evaluation concentrating on the outcomes of teaching or educational experiences (for example, learning or other changes in students).

Consequential validity: The effect of a measure on behavior—that is, the act of measuring an activity or outcome enhances its importance.

Constructively aligned teaching: When relevant higher-order learning or skills are addressed both by the teaching and the assessment methods chosen.

Continuous improvement: Promoting change for the purpose of increasing productivity.

Cost center: Unit of activity or area of responsibility into which a department or other organizational unit is divided for control and accountability and to which costs are allocated.

Criteria: Evidence collected as measure of quality.

Critical thinking: Higher-order thinking that attempts to understand the world in an accurate, fair, and unbiased fashion.

Cross-functional: A team, group, or language that includes and has meaning for various groups within the academy.

Culture of evidence: A spirit of reflection and continuous improvement based on data.

Curriculum: A planned set and sequence of learning experiences that is designed to ensure that each student's development occurs in an orderly, balanced, and thorough fashion.

Data management: The description, organization, handling, control, analysis and reporting of information for any purpose.

Debt financing: Obtaining an asset by borrowing money through an instrument such as a loan or a mortgage.

Debt service: Payments made to pay back borrowed funds. Debt service includes principal payments and interest. Depending on the indebtedness agreement, it can also include legal expenses, payment to reserves to ensure proper upkeep and maintenance of the facilities, and other items related to indebtedness.

Depreciation: A charge to current operations in the income statement that distributes the cost of assets over their estimated service life.

Designated funds: Funds that can be expended only for specified purposes.

Developmental advising: A form of teaching that can directly address all of a student's needs for guidance.

Direct costs: Expenses that are readily identified with specific programs or cost centers.

Distributed general education curricula: Students select their courses from menus of options.

Effective education practices: Programs, policies, and practices that the research literature shows are highly correlated with desired outcomes of college.

Endowment funds: Institutional funds that are generally not spent beyond their earnings or yield.

Epistemological development: The gradual modification of assumptions a person makes about the source of knowledge and value.

Evaluation: A process whose goal is always to provide information about an activity, program, individual, or group for the purpose of making decisions about merit or worth.

Faculty development: A support program that focuses primarily on the faculty member and his or her professional development.

Fixed costs: An element of cost that remains constant over a period of time regardless of the volume of service provided.

Formative evaluation-assessment: Evaluation or assessment with the role of providing information for ongoing revision and improvement; based on evidence of quality, collected during an educational process and used for program improvement.

Indirect costs: Costs that are not readily identified with a specific program or cost center. Generally they reflect the cost of support services provided to campus units but are not readily related in a direct way to any single one. Examples are the operations of human resources, accounting, and contracts and grants.

Instructional development: A support program that tends to focus on the course or curriculum and the interplay between faculty and students.

Instrumental evaluation: Evaluation concentrating on the processes used (for example, teaching methods or characteristics of effective instruction).

Integrated change: Where leaders and units of an institution work together toward an agreed-upon goal. Includes a planned process for change.

Learning (verb): Gaining capacity (willingness and ability) for effective action; *(noun)* capacity (willingness and ability) for effective action.

Learning communities: An intentionally structured student cohort, the members of which co-enroll in two or more common courses, an experience that often results in greater coherence in learning as well as interaction with faculty and peers. Some learning communities have a residential component.

Learning culture: Where learning is valued and designed to bring all members of the society to the fullest development of their powers.

Learning organization: An organization skilled at creating, acquiring, integrating, and transferring knowledge and at changing policies and practices to reflect new knowledge.

Learning outcome (see *Outcome*)

Mental models: A set of tacit beliefs and assumptions about "how things work" that guide behavior of different groups in the academy.

Merit: Judgment of work by external standards.

Mission: Describes what is unique about the institution. Expresses the core values of the college or university. Focuses on the clients and stakeholders who are being served.

Myers-Briggs Type Indicator (MBTI): A personality (style) instrument named after its authors. Uses four pairs of self-reported preferences to identify a matrix of sixteen type categories, based on four processes.

Operating budget: A plan for current operations that includes both estimated revenues and estimated expenditures for a year or other specified period.

Outcome: A result of a process; learning-desired goals are stated as intended outcomes. A statement of all intended learning goals that includes a verb that describes an observable action, a description of the conditions under which the action takes place, and the acceptable performance level.

Outcome goal: Describes a relatively broad result that is more fully described by two or more outcome objectives associated with it.

Process assessment: Compares the behavior of specific programs with the characteristics shown in the professional literature to be important for success-learning.

Relational database: A database structure that allows efficient, nonlinear searches of information on the basis of topical relationships, as opposed to linear searching of each item until the desired one is found.

Reliable (in assessment): The process functions similarly from one use to the next; its behavior is stable.

Restricted current funds: Funds limited by donors or other external sources to specific purposes, programs, departments, or schools.

Seamless learning paradigm: Systematic efforts to arrange and connect students' in-class and out-of-class experiences so that they are complementary, mutually supporting, and result in higher levels of learning and personal development.

Seven principles for good practice in undergraduate education: The list developed by Chickering and Gamson describing characteristics of effective higher education institutions.

Sponsored projects: Projects that are funded by external entities and that are performed in accordance with agreements with those agencies, generally government agencies or foundations.

Stakeholders: Individuals or groups with a degree of interest or involvement in an activity.

Standards: Benchmarks against which evidence is compared.

Student development: A concept that broadly defined includes cognitive and intellectual development as well as affective and social-emotional development induced through various transactions between students and their environments, both in and out of the classroom.

Student ratings of instruction: A common term for any process that involves gathering student opinions about courses, teachers, instruction, and related matters, such process is also called student evaluations of teaching (SETs), student rating forms (SRFs), or teacher-course evaluations (TCEs).

Summative evaluation-assessment: Evaluation or assessment with the role of providing information for making terminal decisions about the merit or worth of individuals, groups, programs or units; occurs at the completion of a process to determine success or impact.

Systems or systematic approach: A method of planning and organizing teaching or other activities that takes into account a variety of factors that can affect outcomes.

Tenure: An institutional policy designed to protect academic freedom, provide employment security through a conditional employment contract, and facilitate the employment of highly qualified people in a highly competitive market.

Transformation: A fundamental change in condition, nature, or function.

Transformational activity: When the results of the work alter the culture, are intentional, occur over time, and affect the whole institution.

Ubiquitous learning: Learning for everyone, every place, at all times (continuous learning).

Unrestricted current funds: Funds received for which the donor or other entity made no stipulations about the purpose for which they should be used.

Valid (in assessment): Assessment measures what it intends to measure.

Variable costs: Costs that change in direct proportion to the volume of units of service provided or goods produced.

Virtual classroom: An on-line classroom that attempts to duplicate what is possible when instructors and learners are physically in the same room.

Vision: The preamble to, and shorter than, the mission statement. Speaks in generalities about the hopes and aspirations of the institution.

Worth: Judgment made about work by standards developed with the unit itself or by those involved.

NAME INDEX

Credits:

p. 1
quote from Levine, A. E. *Chronicle of Higher Education*, October 27, 2000. Used by permission.

p. 5:
quote from Benjamin, R. W. *Breaking the Social Contract: The Fiscal Crisis in California Higher Education* (RAND/CAE-01-IP). Santa Monica, CA: RAND. Copyright © RAND 1998. Reprinted by permission.

p. 25
quote from Findlay, R. "Develop a Passion for Leadership." *The Institute, 25*(9), p. 11. © 2001 IEEE. Used by permission.

p. 87
quote from The Futures Project: Vision for Higher Education, 2001 (www.futuresproject.org). Used by permission.

p. 223
quote from Eckel, P., Hill, B., Green, M., and Mallon, B. *On Change—Reports from the Road: Insights on Institutional Change*. American Council on Education, 1999, pp. 1–2.

p. 293
quote from Astin, A. W. and Astin, H. S. *Leadership Reconsidered: Engaging Higher Education in Social Change*. Battle Creek, MI: W.K. Kellogg Foundation, 2000, p. 2. Used by permission.

pp. 373
quote from Morley, J. and Eadie, D. *The Extraordinary Higher Education Leader*. Washington, DC: National Association of College and University Business Officers, 2001, p. 3. Used by permission.

Chapter 22:
portion of chapter from Association of Governing Boards of Universities and Colleges. *Renewing the Academic Presidency: Stronger Leadership for Tougher Times*. Washington, DC: Association of Governing Boards of Universities and Colleges, 1996. Used by permission.

p. 375
epigraph from Chait, R., Holland, T., and Taylor, B. *Improving the Performance of Governing Boards*. Phoenix: Oryx Press-American Council on Education, 1996. Used by permission.